the ULTiMATE SURViVAL GUiDE to the NEW MUSiC iNDUSTRY

Handbook for Hell

JUSTiN GOLDBERG

 lone eagle™

The Ultimate Survival Guide to the New Music Industry
Handbook for Hell
Copyright © 2004 Justin Goldberg

LONE EAGLE PUBLISHING COMPANY
1024 N. Orange Dr.
Hollywood, CA 90038
Phone 323.308.3400 or 800.815.0503
A division of IFILM® Corporation, www.hcdonline.com

Printed in the United States of America
10 9 8 7 6 5 4 3 2 1

Cover artwork by Justin Goldberg
Interior artwork created by Justin Goldberg
Photographs courtesy of Lindsay Brice
Cover and book design by Carla Green

Library of Congress Cataloging-in-Publication Data

Goldberg, Justin
        The ultimate survival guide to the new music industry : a handbook for
hell / by Justin Goldberg
                p.   cm.
        1. Music trade. I. Title.

        ML3790.G65 2003
        780'.23'73—dc22   2003054673

Books may be purchased in bulk at special discounts for promotional or educational purposes. Special editions can be created to specifications. Inquiries for
sales and distribution, textbook adoption, foreign language translation, editorial,
and rights and permissions inquiries should be addressed to: Jeff Black, Lone
Eagle Publishing, 1024 N. Orange Drive, Hollywood, CA 90038 or send e-mail to
info@ifilm.com.

Distributed to the trade by National Book Network, 800-462-6420.
IFILM® and Lone Eagle Publishing Company™ are registered trademarks.

"A wise friend of my father's had said to me: 'You should not go into music unless it is a compulsion. In the end, all you really have as a center is the music itself. Make sure that you have to be with it every day. If that's true, then you should become a musician.'"

—*Michael Tilson Thomas*

"And be what?! A Jewish Willie Nelson?"

—*My father, on my wanting to become a professional musician*

CONTENTS

ACKNOWLEDGEMENTS

It's hard for me to imagine choosing a more difficult time in my life to assemble a book: two daughters in diapers screeched, cried, giggled or otherwise demanded my attention with each and every line of text in this volume; somewhere in the schedule there was a new company to helm, a new house to move into and new paintings to finish in time for a few art exhibits. It is no small miracle that everyone is still breathing, let alone that this book ever got finished!

Because I am only truly skilled at one art—the art of procrastination—I have many people to thank for their support, inspiration and encouragement:

I am indebted to Jeff Black for his limitless faith and patience, my brave editor Lauren Rossini who survived far too many broken deadlines (and several extra hundred pages of material), Carla Green for deciphering my notes and making everything look terrific, Mitch Davis for coming up with the idea in the first place; Adam Kaller, Ken Hertz and Fred Goldring for their legal insights, friendship and support; my fearless creative designers and developers Lorenzo "Lono" Ciacci and Kevin "Ludicrous" Painchaud, Jennifer Bransford for her early, invaluable insights, Joe Maggini and Mary Thiessen for their tireless and inspired research, Stephanie Figura and Jill Zitnik for their patience throughout the long transcription process, Jaime d'Almeida at LiveWire Contacts and Andrea Powell for database organization skills above and beyond the call of duty, Julie and Greg Maniha for their sharp expertise with pop music history facts, Ed Shapiro for always coming through with contract templates and detailed explanations, Anthony Marinaccio for his stories of early rock 'n' roll with the Four Dons, Jules Thornton for her boundless energy and support—without which this book would certainly not exist, Lindsay Brice for her fantastic photographs (and for introducing me to the late great Timothy Leary), and my family—my wonderful parents Jay and Rema Goldberg, my wife Toni-Ann Marinaccio and my daughters Grace Lilly and Charlotte Rose—all whom put up with me throughout the writing this book.

I am also very grateful to the following people and organizations whose contributions of time and energy in one way or another made this project possible. Thank You:

Adam Frank, Alain Johannes & Natasha Shneider, Albert Hoffman, Alisse Kingsley, Amie Donegan, Amy Fruit, Andy Olyphant, Ann Marinaccio, Barret Jones, Bill and Mandy Robinson, Bob Weir, Bonnie Nelson, Bradley White, Bret Reilly, Brian Landau, Brian Seymour, Brian Alper, Bruce Haring, Bruce Kolbrenner, Brett and Cassandra Berns, Charlie Feldman, Chris Castle, Chris Standring, Christopher and Jo Gartin, Christina Ambrose, Cindy Alexander, Clyde Lieberman, Damon Evans, Dani Lacey-Baker, Danny Hayes, Danny Strick, David Andersen, David Bendeth David Landau, David Leach, Dayle Gloria, Dean Serwin, Deborah Radel, Dennis McNally, Deirdre O'hara, Diane Warren, Donald Trump, Doug Hirsch, Ellen Moraskie, Elizabeth Brooks, Emily Wachtel, Fred Davis, Fred Disipio, Frederik Nilson, Gary Savelson, Gates, Gaylinn Kiser, George Gottlieb, Greg Lauren, Greg Maniha, Greg Sarfaty, Gretchen Friese, Guy Garvey, Guy Oseary, Gus, Hal B. Selzer, Hameed Shaukat, Harry Poloner, James Dowdall, Jason Markey, Jane Applegate, Jay Faires, Jeff Aber, Jeff Conley, Jeff Rabhan, Jeff Zukerman, Jennifer Bransford, Jim Jacobsen, Jim Lacey-Baker Jim Vellutato, John Lenac, John Zinman, Jordan Berliant, Josh Sarubin, Josh Zandman, Jude, Justin Arcangel, Julie Horton, Keith Holzman, Kerry McCarthy, Kevin Edelman, Kevin Martin, Kevin Weaver, Kris Sarfaty, Kurt Deutsch, Lana Nelson, Larry Dvoskin, Lysa Nalin, Marisa at Bowhaus, Mark Rothbaum, Marshall Altman, Martin Sexton, Matt Reasor, Maureen Crowe, Melisa Morgan, Melody Silverman, Mickey Hart, Michael Badami, Mike Gormley, Mike Jones, *Music Connection* Magazine, Niki Rowling, Nikki Wheeler, Norma Foerderer, Ota House, Pamela Klein, Panos Panay, Penny Guyon, Phil Roy, Rachel Diersk, Randy Gerston, Richard Rowe, Richard Gottehrer, Rich Jacobellis, Robert D. Summer, Rodel Delfin, Roger Stein, Ron Broitman, Ron Fair, Ron Handler, Ron Kuzon, Roy Forbes, Sam Plotkin, Sat Bisla, Scott Francis, Sera and Liquid Gallery, Sharon Lieberman, Shawn Smith, Sherry Maitland, Shooter Jennings, Staci Slater, Starbucks, Steffo Mitakides, Steve

Hayes, Stephen J. Finfer, Steve Zuckerman, Sue Devine, Sue Landolfi, Susan Kasen-Summer, Susan Koc, The Painkillers, The Viper Room, Twain's Restaurant, The Mejia Family, Timothy Leary, Victoria Hochberg, Willie Nelson and Yasmin Kidwai.

A special thanks to artists and songwriters everywhere who manage to overcome whatever stands in their way so they can write and create music. Let us not forget that, without them, there is no music business.

A final thank you to the late (and great) Waylon Jennings, my first music industry guide.

—J.G.

ABOUT A&RT

Throughout these pages you will see black and white versions of watercolor and acrylic paintings I created based on my experiences in the music business. Both an homage and an indictment of the business itself, all of the pieces focus on and document the mercurial faction of those in and around the business of acquiring new talent, known as A&R, thus it being dubbed "A&Rt". (For a more colorful view, visit www.TheOnlineMusicChannel.com.)

**Justin Goldberg, *Talent Scout, Excellent Benefits*,
watercolor and acrylic on canvas, 54"x48"**

I based this painting on what a want ad in a newspaper might look like if a record label were to truthfully describe available A&R positions, which are the most coveted and least understood job in the music industry. All A&R departments have a golden boy, and I was once one of them. Golden boys get more and the best of everything—more smiles in the office, better tickets to cool shows and their expenses approved without scrutiny. My ride through this business isn't over yet, but I've got plenty to tell if you're bent on doing music. In fact, if you're short on time, you can just read this ad and imagine what the rest of the book is like. It reads: Major record label seeks dynamic, creative, self-starting professional for A&R management position. Will be responsible for identifying, evaluating, and signing musical talent to label. Must have, or appear to have, vast knowledge of the entire contemporary musical spectrum, with an emphasis on all genres of alternative media and culture. Must be extremely organized, available 24 hours a day, 7 days per week, and will be expected to travel weekly, go out nightly, work office hours daily, represent company at daily showcases, nightly gigs, all trade shows and conferences in the U.S. and abroad. Must have no scruples in courting artists and must not become too attached to talent. Must be young. Must respect and revere the corporate paycheck. Must be prepared to get another job when this one abruptly ends. Must be able to appear to be supportive of artists while resisting the temptation to speak your mind and stand up for music in the face of corporate greed and the big bottom line that killed rock and roll. Qualified applicants only.

A BRIEF EDITORIAL NOTE

All Access Passport

CD-ROM

Throughout this book you'll see the icon on your left again and again. Whenever you see it, it's marking a place in the text that specifically relates to the enclosed CD-ROM (we don't want you to miss anything!). The enclosed CD-ROM contains a wealth of information. Not just forms and templates that will save you innumerable headaches, your sanity and possibly your bank account, but also the unexpurgated interviews and a database that will make you head spin. Check it out.

Included in the database:
- Contracts
- Marketing Plans and Budgets
- Press Lists
- A&R Lists
- And over 25,000 listings in 27 categories of and for music professionals worldwide!

1

WELCOME TO THE MACHINE
reality bites

Subj: **Re: TERMINATION NOTICE**
Date: 10/24/2002 12:00:55 AM Pacific Daylight Time
From: Blackbeat248@■■■■■■■■■
To: Peter@■■■■■■■■■■■
Cc: RonnieC@■■■■■■■■■■■■■

peter —

we just got your voicemail. We drove all night to get to the show so I only just now played your message for the rest of the band. We don't get it—they sent a termination notice before contacting either of us? As in, that's it, they're dropping us? What's going on?

I'm sure you can appreciate that this is hard for us to swallow, and almost impossible to believe that after almost two years of sweating this out from the rehearsals to having to record practically the whole album twice—not to mention what must be almost 500 grand of their money—that they've decided to not even release the record.

What does this even mean, that we own it, or do they? We also just heard that the single just got a ton of other adds yesterday, so we're just really stunned.

Did this come from Green or from business affairs or…?? Should we call Green and ask him w'sup, or is that a bad idea now, legally speaking? If the album goes on another label, do we re-do the tunes that he's got the co-writing credits on?

How bad do you think this will hurt us in getting a new deal? Sorry for all the questions, but we're just freaking out a little bit.

DC

Welcome to music and its business—two opposing words that have struggled to function together for the better part of a century. Through countless cultural changes and spectacular technical leaps, the worldwide musical community has grown into an intimidating economic beast; composed of billion dollar corporate conglomerates, start-up independents and thousands of examples of everything in between. What drives all this business? Songs.

They reach us through speakers large enough to soak the air of sports arenas and tiny enough for two small eardrums on a headset. We have them placed into cars, malls and supermarkets. They mark our every significant human experience and are arguably our most durable and personal items; with a strange ability to often lift our spirits, guide our innermost thoughts, and even govern our moods, music is for most people a critical and timeless resource of solace and celebration; yet what and who is it that safeguards and exploits this intangible commodity, this precious domain of magic we occasionally pay to hear and experience but cannot really own or touch? Who are the musical gatekeepers controlling the public's access to music and who gets past the gate? What forces control the projection of expression in sound—and in terms of new music and the new music industry, who is behind them and what is their mandate?

The Internet's early anarchists and Utopians predicted with certainty that the electronic delivery of music over the Web would put corporate music—and perhaps all traditional recording companies—out of business. Like a great flood from heaven aiming to drown the wicked and end an extended reign of corruption, they envisioned the dawning of a new era for great music long ignored; one where righteous independent music companies and unsigned artists would at last see justice done and have an equal artistic voice.

Ever since records were made of shellac, music's middlemen have been involved in shaping artists' images and creativity. As these middlemen evolved into modern record executives, the goal of getting signed and locating A&R people has become the chief objective for thousands of new artists seeking to create a livelihood in music—many of whom for decades felt they were unjustly denied the blessing of getting "discovered." But by the end of the nineties, any singer, songwriter or performer, anywhere in the world, could own and control their very own radio and television broadcast via the Internet, 24 hours a day.

Yet as tens of millions of both new and familiar songs freely entered cyberspace and played on computers and stereos all over the globe, via Napster and dozens of Web sites just like it, a strange thing happened to this promising frontier of artistic integrity and musical freedom as the millennium came and went: record companies not only maintained their influence and power over popular music, they swallowed up or litigated away much of what the Internet had to offer to unsigned, independent artists in the name of artists' rights protection, progress or market share.

So what exactly must occur for new music to reach a significant audience in today's music industry? And for those who choose, or would like to choose, their vocation as part of the process, where does one begin? How do those with a predisposition toward music find their way through the business and the people who control it?

As the email before this introduction will attest, those who embark on a professional musical journey often find a twisted road at odds with their initial expectations about how the music industry really works. Internal and external record label politics and behind-the-scenes affiliations delicately interact on a daily basis with the personalities (and egos) that fuel the machinery of the record business.

The notion of the record business behaving like a big machine is a common one: in fact, I had early on planned on titling this volume *Stokin' the Star Makin' Machinery*—a line from Joni Mitchell's early classic "Free Man in Paris" which first graced the airwaves more than twenty years ago and is widely believed to have been written for and/or about then-aspiring music mogul David Geffen. I can assure the reader that its analogy of the music industry as a machine stands as accurate and as poignant as ever in today's industry.

On the first page of this book, we have supposedly half a million label dollars invested in a band's career: the artists apparently have a completed album only a month away from its scheduled release to retail, a single on national radio, and a team behind them that—in addition to a seasoned label staff—likely also includes a national booking agency, a professional music manager and a competent music attorney. Somehow, despite all this unusual fortitude and luck, the band is quite unceremoniously informed while on tour and many miles from home, that they are being "dropped" from the record company's roster. And just like that, thanks to some behind the scenes maneuvering that very likely has nothing to do at all with the band's performances, songs, or the quality of their recordings, the music business framework of their world is shattered; their creative and economic future probably damaged beyond repair.

How do such things happen? In the highly competitive field of pop music, which is still coming to terms with its uncertain future in the age of rampant online piracy, massive debt from corporate consolidation and an unstable employment landscape, it's probably easier to ask why a new artist *wouldn't* be dropped: there is much to go wrong, and it often does.

It is possible that the particular case here, let's call them The Starflowers, could weather the storm of being dropped, find a new label and move on simply because they are "stars" destined to "make it." Possible, but not likely. Once an artist is dropped, little is guaranteed other than there is plenty to rebuild. A dropped artist is perceived as damaged goods in an industry endlessly obsessed with the introduction and acquisition of the new. Talent acquisition is a lot like shopping for new furniture: the price and perceived value usually peaks in the original showroom, not at a thrift shop or on eBay after someone else has had it in their house.

Better still, often the reluctance to sign such acts is based on the belief that if the act is successful on another label, it would only validate the creative vision of the original executive who signed or was most publicly associated with the artist in the beginning, which can make for a bittersweet victory if they are lucky enough to find success even with the rare second shot at the game.

Yet at the start of their odyssey, only two years earlier, The Starflowers could hardly believe their good fortune. Out of the tens of thousands of bands across the country formed with the hope of one day getting signed to a deal with a major record label, they had managed to defy the odds and taste the early joy of being part of what many have always considered an esteemed elite—recording artists signed to a major label.

How exactly they got there is worth examining, as it helps to lay the blueprint for how this machine can operate, and how early decisions play a critical role in determining artists' future success, or their lack of it. We will review their story in some detail in the chapter that follows.

It is a great paradox of our industry that if The Starflowers had in fact not been dropped, the outlook for their career could be equally dismal, if not worse. They could have recorded an excellent album completed on schedule and under budget—just in time to compete with five other great albums delivered during the same quarter. And with label resources limited to support and release four of them, that means that one great record would not be released at all. Worse than being dropped, an amazing album from The Starflowers (or anyone else, for that matter) could be shelved until a better release date is determined; during which time the public's taste and band's momentum could easily shift, rendering their sound dated and unpopular. Imagine a hot boy band being released a full year or two after the boy band craze at the turn of the millennium, or a rock band from the Pacific Northwest after all things related to the word grunge became passé. Sometimes labels refuse to let artists even leave their rosters because of public embarrassment; it is often easier for labels to deliberately keep such executive decisions in limbo, waiting for factors affecting a release to change, in theory, for the better. Sometimes companies are simply too overwhelmed with reorganizing the structure of their own operations to generate what surely can seem like a deliberate plan to thwart artists' careers and screw them out of money and opportunities.

AN EVIL PLAN FROM HELL

Are record companies inherently heartless or evil? Hardly. But it can certainly seem that way. Having functioned for many years as an A&R executive at one of the world's largest music corporations, I can tell you that the question is worth asking for a few reasons: when you interact with artists and writers as a representative of a major music company, you quickly learn there is a deep and widespread suspicion about record labels and those who work for them. It's hardly paranoid thinking; it's based on nearly a century of very real and well-documented deceptive business practices overwhelmingly skewed against creative music people. There are few legal businesses that operate on such a tilted scale. Consider that record labels put up the financing for musicians to record albums and handle their manufacture, promotion and distribution. In exchange, fledgling artists with little or no sales history (and thus, no leverage) make enormous concessions with career-long implications. They sign long term-agreements, usually when they are very young and inexperienced, that typically guarantee at least 85 percent of their profits from selling records will never reach them.

They sign away most of the rights to their own recordings, transferring the actual copyright ownership to the record company. As if this were not extreme enough, they then contractually agree to pay back any money received when they signed their deal (the "advance") including a practically all-encompassing list of promotional costs—all out of the 15 or so percent designated for them. The money they finally do receive is then subject to sizable reductions, from deductions based on "breakage" of record shipments (still in effect but merely an outdated contractual relic from the days when records were actually made of shellac and were often broken during transportation), to packaging deductions, promotional "free goods" deductions, independent radio promotion related deductions, video cost deductions—all items that, if they do sneak their way into your royalty statement, will generally not require your approval to be billed against your account.

Which brings us then to a fascinating hypothetical equation: what if The Starflowers were not dropped or shelved, but actually sold what would appear to be a lot of records? Let's imagine their album is released, gets on the radio, receives great reviews, makes a cool video that appears on MTV or VH1, opens for a known band on a well-publicized tour and goes "gold," reaching the fairly unlikely sales mark of five hundred thousand copies. Incredibly, this quite lucky scenario would hardly put the band in a position to spend any time shopping for Ferraris and mansions. In fact, they might be better off staying at home rent-free with their parents, because they won't be receiving any royalties just yet. In fact, they are likely to be still several hundred thousands of dollars in debt to their record label and possibly even be in danger of being dropped if sales slide on their current or next album.

Hard to believe? In today's hyped-up industry cost structure, it shouldn't be—it happens all the time. The Starflowers probably felt that receiving a quarter million dollars as an advance from their label was a generous and even enormous amount of money. But divided amongst four members after commissions were paid to their lawyer and manager (which totaled 5 and 15 percent, respectively, thus removing $50,000 from the band's revenue "pot"), their take really amounts to just over $40,000 per member after taxes are accounted for. $40,000 stretched over a period that in their case apparently lasted almost two years before they were able to see any other income (if they were able to see other earnings, possibly from touring or music publishing advances). Not exactly big rock and roll money.

Let's do the math:

- If their album was priced in stores at around twelve dollars per unit (which is probably a bit low industry wide but certainly common for newer, developing artists) and...
- their contractual royalty rate was around 15 percent (which is relatively high for a new artist) and...
- the company spent $500,000 between promotional and recording costs (which is actually quite low based on industry standards) then:
- The Starflowers need to sell almost platinum (1 million units) just to break even!

They would essentially be earning a mere 80 cents for each album sold—although this would more likely be closer to the "industry standard" figure of a $1.50 if their album was sold at five or six dollars more than indicated above. This would also not include any music publishing revenue, which we will discuss in detail in Chapter 4. For artists to receive royalty income from major record label sales with today's promotional cost structure on their first album, they would need to sell over a million copies—something that approximately less than 1 percent of all major label releases manage to do.

> For artists to receive royalty income from major record label sales with today's promotional cost structure on their first album, they would need to sell over a million copies—something that approximately less than 1 percent of all major label releases manage to do.

Being lucky enough to go gold would hardly resign The Starflowers to obscurity; in truth, the label would likely take a number of factors into consideration before letting any artist off the roster without serious evaluation of their growth potential. On the other hand, it is not unusual for major record labels to routinely drop artists whose debut albums sell less than 100,000 units.

DIY OR DIE

By dramatic contrast, artists releasing their own material selling a fraction of those units can reap impressive profits without giving up their copyrights or anything else. Even sales as low as 5,000 units on an independent release can generate substantial income, when you consider that as much as 100 percent of a CD sold at $10 per unit might be received directly by the artist.

Starting to sound appealing? It should. There are a great many reasons to release your music to the public by your own means, without aiming for getting signed to a major label—especially if that is exactly your end goal.

GETTING WHAT YOU WANT BY NOT WANTING IT

Major labels have evolved into precisely the kind of talent-absorbing machinery that tends to help artists the most when there is an existing foundation of activity and awareness already being generated by the artist on his or her own—long before the idea of attracting a label is in the picture. A fan base and awareness within the right music scenes on an independent level is not only a helpful extra if you are good enough to develop major label industry momentum, it's practically become a prerequisite for even entering the game.

Before they were bought out or merged into beverage companies, telecom conglomerates and Internet concerns, record companies were run on instinct and driven by entrepreneurial personalities connected with the process of breaking artists and selling records. But as the companies grew larger via mergers and consolidation, those instincts were replaced with bottom lines and balance sheets; the era of slow and steady artist development quickly evaporated. Now labels expect and need artists to explode on impact.

ARTIST DEVELOPMENT IS DEAD.
LONG LIVE ARTIST DEVELOPMENT

Throughout the process of conducting interviews for this book, I encountered a familiar theme in my conversations with industry executives of every size and style. At some point in the conversation, virtually all of them said, "Artist development is dead." What does artist development even mean? I'm still not sure frankly, but probably most would agree that it has something to do with having faith in an artist to create profits over time, rather than perform specifically well within a finite period, as opposed to now when an artist must sell a massive number of records immediately or simply disappear. It was not that long ago when new artists signing with labels would be expected to release four or more albums, allowing the public to become familiar with their material gradually. Artists who signed with major labels were also less likely to be as polished as they are today. Raw talent itself probably went a lot further.

AMERICAN IDOL?

Although music-related so called "reality" TV programming captivates audiences and takes them on a wild ride of an insider's experience in new musical talent discovery, such shows belie the truth of how the industry really functions with respect to talent acquisition. Such contest-oriented programming often misleads the public into believing that the music industry is set up like one big gameshow—some kind of grand network of industry star makers evaluating a never-ending line up of would be diva-waifs and rock stars parading their wares—their voices, looks and dancing ability. As if once they locate an ideal candidate, all that remains is to simply plug the winner into a dream team of producers, songwriters and promoters working in concert to pump out a complete star package ready for public consumption, complete with a Pepsi commercial tie-in and a tour in support of the album.

TV aside, nothing could be further from the truth. Granted, some stars are "manufactured" in the sense that they were discovered or signed without having written their own material or developed their own sound or dance routines. But by and large, this kind of star makin' machinery has been a shrinking phenomenon ever since the Beatles and Bob Dylan made it clear that singing your own material with your own message and image was the definition of cool. It is far more likely that an artist with a proven independent track record of sales and/or some kind of interesting awareness on the music scene will be taken seriously by the industry than a great vocalist with no material or sound sending in examples of their vocal talent into the abyss of an A&R mailing list, or worse, a TV show promising stardom.

The moral of these first pages? With the enormous financial pressure placed on artists (and music executives) today to succeed from the outset of their careers, there is little time or financial patience to wait for an artist to develop in today's market. So know how the rules have changed and what this new market expects. Be deliberate with your choices and plan steps toward doing what you can to get your music out there. It's cheaper and easier than ever to create broad exposure for, and legitimate sources of income from, your own music.

HOW THE STARFLOWERS GOT DROPPED

The Starflowers began their career as many American rock legends have: with two fourteen-year-olds making noise in a garage with drums and an amp. Still in high school but writing songs on school nights and dreaming of being in a signed, touring rock band, their hopes for an actual career took a substantial leap forward when their ad for a new vocalist and bass player produced two guys they felt were an instant musical fit; the personalities mixed, the songs came together and enough of a certain sound came together to be born as their own.

They were also particularly impressed with their new singer's cool industry credentials. A slightly older teen already a year out of high school, his previous band had received some industry attention and he had a relationship with a music attorney who represented other signed artists. The newly formed group quickly began regular rehearsals and wrote new songs. Energized by their rapid progress, a band name was chosen and their first show booked. Some weeks later, a small audience was impressed, as was the club's owner, and soon The Starflowers had a weekly gig that drew increasingly large crowds.

In only a matter of months, the band grew into a local phenomenon; packing kids into local "all ages" venues and selling merchandise: a simple demo of six songs recorded at a friend's studio was duplicated onto a few hundred CDs as an "EP" and quickly sold out. They designed a logo, made up a few dozen hats, t-shirts, stickers and a Web site, while a friend attended shows armed with a clipboard to collect names for their growing mailing list.

The music attorney eventually surfaced, and became a presence at rehearsals and gigs. A friend he brought with him on one fateful evening turned out to be an A&R rep: the rep had heard The Starflowers EP and wanted to talk. Excitement about the possibilities soon grew, a buzz circulated at school, and the kids parents joked that maybe something would come out of the noise from their garages after all.

The Starflowers soon found themselves in a slick record label conference room. Framed gold and platinum, intimidating and promising, lined the walls. It would be the perfect setting to hear the magic words they had all been waiting to hear since their very first show: that their songs and sound added up to a artistic vision distinctive enough to warrant high hopes and a great album that this particular label was particularly equipped to produce and market—all while meshing credibility with commercial appeal, of course. They left the building walking on air, hardly able to conceal their excitement. It was all they could have hoped for.

Paul Green, their newfound number one fan and A&R rep, turned out to be quite the executive on a roll, too—they now learned he was no ordinary A&R guy: although he had only signed two artists to the label, one was white hot and still climbing the charts, having reached the treasured platinum mark of selling a million copies, and his other signing was almost half way there. A label rep with that kind of track record was like finding the goose to lay the golden deal in the rehearsal space. Surely, they imagined, Green's signings would be highly regarded at the company where his other creative and business choices were generating such success.

To aid with the courtship of his new acquisition target, lead singers from both the other groups made trips down to The Starflowers' rehearsals and gigs, and all were suitably impressed. Green was also now so taken with their music, he professed, he was not only planning on urging his employers to generate an imminent offer to sign them, he was interested in producing the first album himself, something that to The Starflowers sounded almost like a plus and hardly unusual. It *did* seem unusual to their attorney, despite the fact that he was the one to broker the fruitful introduction between Green and the band—but he was reluctant to dampen any enthusiasm; after all, his payment would only be derived from the completed deal.

Despite a brief period of wondering how, where and when The Starflowers might go about showcasing for other labels now that the group was perhaps about to receive a real label offer, the group soon found themselves enthusiastically signing their names to a 100 plus page recording agreement as directed by dozens of small red arrows. Champagne was uncorked, and the future, as the Tom Petty tune goes, was wide open.

After some more trips to that conference room, and more free meals where excited discussions about production styles, recording techniques, touring and marketing took place, Green officially requested the band's blessing in naming him as the producer. He was so passionate about the group's material, he told them, he just didn't feel comfortable not being directly involved at every stage of making their first record. Not wanting to offend their most critical musical champion or somehow jeopardize their deal, The Starflowers agreed. Soon they were in a studio recording their first album—just like they had always dreamed.

Early buzz about their soon-to-be completed debut was tremendous. Green had boasted to most of his peers and in a front page *Billboard* article that The Starflowers were the most important artists of his career.

Sensing blood in the water, music publishing companies and booking agents also began calling and courting the band.

But it wasn't long before Green appeared to become oddly concerned about the songs themselves: although The Starflowers' demo recording had him declaring it contained some sure-fire hits before their deal was signed, as their new producer he suddenly felt an urgent need to rearrange or rewrite their material. The Starflowers grew increasingly uncomfortable. When the record was complete, he further astonished his band by presenting his own contract designating himself as a co-writer on three of the best songs on their album—and the band couldn't understand how the songs had even been changed. In fact, all of the songs were written many months before they had even met Green and were still played the same way. The band members, angry and confused, called their lawyer.

But his advice was hardly what they were looking for, "Don't rock the boat," he warned, "If keeping your A&R guy and link to the label happy means giving up some songwriting royalties, get over it and consider it the price of doing business." The band decided to turn to a different lawyer.

The new lawyer, Peter, agreed: it was outrageous enough, he thought, that a salaried employee—already making perhaps as much as $450,000 annually—would also be paid as a producer after choosing himself for the job. Then, to have the audacity to demand songwriting credit and thus a percentage of music publishing royalties was just unconscionable. He said as much in a fax to the label, and the very next day, everything was about to change.

With the complaint came some internal meetings with Green, who flew into a rage. Furious at the band for what he said was a betrayal of trust and respect, he threatened to not release the record at all, and proceeded to launch his own personal campaign to separate the band from their new lawyer, calling on other attorneys to contact The Starflowers directly to have Peter replaced.

It had become an increasingly difficult time for Green, and not just because of The Starflowers' songwriting dispute. The president of his label, who had hired Green, had recently "resigned" as part of a political shake up, following a big merger designed to cut costs. The new president, who would be Green's new boss, disliked him and was more focused on the urban music scene. His vision of the label included an increased focus on rap and hip hop, not on rock. Also, Green had a reputation for being arrogant and his loyalty would continue to belong to the ousted president.

To make matters worse, the band's radio outlook had evolved from dramatically promising to doom-and-gloom before the album was even released. The song ultimately used as the group's first single was the band's least favorite track; it was chosen because its production was more of a fit for the radio format where the label had their best relationships. The song had little impact, other than giving the label cold feet; a new plan quickly formed to hold off on the release only after taking another shot at radio with a second single—but before that had a chance to happen, the band would be dropped and their story would freeze in time. The Starflowers would join the immense tapestry of promising "once signed to a major label" acts dropped and then relegated to virtual obscurity.

Exactly why they were dropped, we may not ever know. It could have been the lack of good response from the radio promotion department. It could have been Green's threatened ego. It could have come directly from Green's new boss. Or the new attorney and the threat of litigation may have been too unnerving for the label to live with. Perhaps The Starflowers should have never let their A&R rep be their producer, or perhaps they should have fought harder for their songwriting vision, or perhaps they should have avoided confrontation completely—or at least picked a battle later on in their career that they had a better chance of winning, when they might have more leverage.

Ultimately, being a great artist is one thing and being successful in the music business is another, which even the biggest names in the industry will tell you is in no small measure a matter of luck. But there are basics—there are some things that every musical aspirant can do to create the best odds, habits and attitude which can at least help you put your best foot forward.

> Ultimately, being a great artist is one thing and being successful in the music business is another, which even the biggest names in the industry will tell you is in no small measure a matter of luck.

Justin Goldberg, *Last Day at Sony Music*, watercolor on canvas, 45"x28"

Frustrated by the creative confines of corporate life, I often plotted a fantasy escape. It went something like this: Purchase a motorcycle. Cash in the 401K to start an indie label, get a rock star involved to help launch it, sell my car to finance recording a first album, tell off the abusive boss, hop on the bike and drive a thousand miles north on Pacific Coast Highway to leave Los Angeles behind.

Which is exactly what I did in August of 1996. The above painting reveals my final call sheet, complete with my assistant's dutiful play by play rendition of the drama that ensued shortly after my departure.

Unfortunately, life after corporate happy days was hardly a picnic. I started Seattle-based indie label Laundry Room Records with Producer Barrett Jones on the limited funds referenced above, combined with what he was probably receiving from royalties on the first Foo Fighters record—an amazing debut he had produced with Dave Grohl a few months before. Dave was generous enough to give us a boost with our first release as well—an old group of master recordings from an early project he made with Jones before he was in Foo Fighters or Nirvana. Called Harlingtox, Angel Divine, it was recorded in the spring and summer of 1990 with two other musicians—Tos Nieuwenhuizen and Bruce Merkle.

The mantra of our newly minted label was to split all revenues 50/50, an artist-friendly haven for talent and a great and generous idea—assuming there were revenues to split. What I would quickly learn over the course of the next four years of indie label life is that running a label can be hell—especially without a handbook like this.

Not long into my new venture I realized that most of the friends and relentlessly phoning colleagues I had accumulated during the period when I was able to write fat company checks for talent were pretty much around me because, well, I could write fat company checks for talent! And so the reality of my newfound freedom started to set in. This was going to be a lot more work with a steeper learning curve than I had anticipated. Without assistants to help coordinate, without an expense account to ease the pain, without a business affairs department to dispense advice, without, without, without! With no car and a soggy, rusting motorcycle, I went about the business of launching the label, signing, producing and releasing over a dozen releases over the course of the next few years. From various helpful musicians, attorneys and other music professionals, I would learn a great deal about running an organization on fumes, squeezing money out of thin air, obtaining national and international distribution deals for our little known roster and manage to have the label survive.

2

THE ENCLOSED CD-ROM:
your weapon for war

All Access Passport

CD-ROM

From my collection of contracts, marketing plans, press lists, A&R lists and dozens of other database resources, directories, programs and forms I began to assemble the ultimate indie label file from hell. From all the horrible lessons I had to learn the hard way about both sides of the business—both indie and major—I was determined to create a collection of files on my computer that would equip anyone with virtually any document they would need to survive doing what I was doing. And I was trying to do it all—from pursuing international distribution to major label talent shopping, press, pursuing joint ventures—name it, I was out on the street, hyping new talent, acquiring publishing rights, meeting with anyone in music I could do deals with because I was hungry to make it happen.

My hunger is now your meal. Behold, I give you a very unique weapon for war in the music industry: information. Data. Knowledge. And video too. The LSN DBP All Access Passport™ (CD-ROM Silver LE version) is enclosed with this book. Simply insert the disc into your computer's CD-ROM drive. If you have a PC, the program should launch itself; if you are using a Macintosh, just click on the CD icon and the program will launch.

(Note: If you are running Windows Professional 2000, your browser default may not launch automatically, so double-click "My Computer", then double-click "All Access Passport" and then choose "Terms", which you will need to drag onto your browser. The program will open to the "terms of use" page and then simply click into the program with the bottom right button.)

The LSN DBP All Access Passport™ (CD-ROM Silver LE version) is the music industry's best and only all digital contact and contract template solution. You now hold in your hands a powerful tool; the ability to manage your music business as well as reach thousands of music professionals throughout the globe who may need what you have—great music, skills, or a great service.

UNSOLICITED ADVICE ON UNSOLICITED MATERIALS—
Our Genre Chart + Your Ambition

The LSN DBP All Access Passport series contains comprehensive listings of music industry professionals. I know it's tempting to send out unsolicited music. But there isn't any reason for you to send out unsolicited music—for one, it's virtually guaranteed to wind up in the trash; and two, it's too easy to access so many of the representatives that A&R departments already have their doors open to. If you are an artist or an artist's representative and you're looking to forward your music, follow the steps in the A&R section of this book and resist (at least for now) the temptation to send out unsolicited music.

Because of the effective reach of this tool, we ask that you respect it and the legal rights and professional wishes of those listed in our database. A&R personnel listed herein usually do not accept unsolicited material unless they indicate otherwise on our genre chart indicator. If they do, send away. This is for many logical reasons, including legal necessity, as many record companies are advised to limit their liability for copyright infringement suits. LSN and Measurement Arts, LLC request that you respect such policies and be forewarned: most record labels prefer to hear music from managers, attorneys and other industry professionals with whom they have personal relationships and deal with on a regular basis. For this reason, if you are looking to reach out to A&R executives, you might consider approaching music attorneys and artist managers first.

The LSN Virtual Attorney section, and the resource section of this book, contains templates for legally binding agreements. Please remember: music business attorneys are trained professionals and are familiar with critical information that can easily elude the layperson. *Always* consult with a reputable legal representative before signing a contract! The contract templates are provided for assistance with drafting and reference purposes only—nothing herein should be construed as legal advice.

SO WHAT'S IN THE DISC?

Some extra marketing muscle and industry expertise. Invaluable interactive resources and tools for the real music business shopping music, licensing, publishing, music supervision, budgets, contracts—every document and piece of information necessary to professionally exist in today's music business. The LSN DBP All Access Passport has over 25,000 listings in twenty seven categories of and for music professionals worldwide and includes such functions such as the Virtual Booking Agent, the Virtual Music Supervisor and the Virtual Attorney, all of which provide important contacts, contracts and other tools to help make your life easier online and offline.

3

DO NOT PASS GO:
WHAT YOU NEED TO KNOW TO BEGIN
what the industry looks like now:
a brief history of time

File Sharing! Corporate mega merger disasters! Copyright law panic! Downsizing!

For the music business, it's been a hell of a few years and judging by the headlines, you'd think the sky was falling. For some industry players unable to adapt to new challenges, it has already fallen. To others, it's business as usual; it just depends where your business stands in the food chain. The trickle-down effect from such large shifts in the business has touched both consumers and industry executives at every level, and the changes—from the online music revolution to corporate consolidation—seem to have taken effect in a quick and successive blur of confusing, negative headlines and bleak economic predictions.

If you have picked up this volume because you better want to understand or participate in the music industry, it's important to refresh yourself on some recent industry history to give some context to today's marketplace. Let's rewind the tape back to the days before the word Vivendi was on everyone's lips and retrace the more relevant corporate tactical blunders and achievements so we have a better sense of where the business might be headed.

UNIGRAM: THE BIGGEST MUSIC COMPANY IN THE WORLD

Towards the close of the millennium, rumors began to circulate about the possible formation of "Unigram"—a reference to two of the largest and most prominent music corporations—Universal and PolyGram, combining their music groups.

What was the big deal? Perhaps nothing more than a plan to elevate stock prices on paper. But in the hearts and minds of those who have worked within the music industry for any portion of the last four decades, it threatened to extinguish the last few spiritual flames of what was once the American music industry—an industry born of creativity and fueled by entrepreneurial vision instead of a balance sheet. Record companies that had defined what a record company was for decades were rumored to potentially disappear into a Power Point presentation on some MBA's computer screen in a board meeting populated by people unconnected to music. Companies woven into the very fabric of America and its deep musical traditions such as Motown, Geffen, A&M and Mercury, could shrink into mere imprints or worse, vanish entirely.

Sure enough, 10 billion dollars later, PolyGram was sold and Universal bought out Interscope; New Year's Day of 1999 probably began with somebody somewhere in Vivendi's corporate office sitting down to plot out the integration and complete corporate overhaul of what would now be the largest music company in the world. It would involve massive employee reorganization all over the globe, represent thousands of layoffs and the dropping of dozens of great recording artists unable to meet a new revenue criteria. The very concept referred to in thousands of record deals for decades as the "Big Six"—EMI, Warners, Sony, Bertlesmann, Universal and PolyGram—was suddenly down to five.

The idea of creating this monolith, the more brilliant on Wall Street suggested, was that a newly revamped Universal Music Group could then leverage its enormous power and reach to create new "paradigms of synergies" and untold new revenue streams. But as the initiated well know, merging companies of any size is easier said than done—and culture clashes can imitate the worst quarreling in-laws. Not to mention that today, even the least tech savvy among us roll our eyes at "paradigms" and "synergies."

As it turned out, the initial aftermath of Vivendi's acquisition binge would prove that housing water, utilities, telecom, beverages and entertainment under a single roof can be extremely difficult. And expensive: with a steep 18 billion dollar debt from acquisitions, the company made many changes, from firing its CEO to selling off under-performing and non-core assets.

And then there's the online music revolution, which continues to eat up profits and cast a dark spell on a once-thriving industry.

YOU DON'T NEED A WEATHERMAN TO TELL WHICH WAY THE WIND BLOWS: WHAT IT MEANS FOR NEW MUSIC

Throughout the interviews I conducted for this narrative, while many disagreed on such issues as file sharing on the Internet and the quality of today's music, all agree that it is generally tougher and tighter economically all around—for producers, for executives, for established attorneys shopping deals, and (of course) for new artists both signed and not. Anyone in today's music business who must interface with a label and their shrinking budgets for talent has likely been affected by the enormous downsizing trend. This does, however, present a welcome opportunity in the independent music marketplace: with fewer dollars being spent by the majors during this uncertain period, smaller companies are filling the void with great music that the majors are missing, and informed, motivated independent artists are using new tools and information to thrive.

DEFINING GOALS: YOUR PLACE IN THE GIG REPORT:

"If you want to get paid for making music, you are going to start compromising immediately. It doesn't matter if you are standing on the street corner singing 'The Times They Are a Changin'' for quarters—somebody's going to come along and say, 'Can't you play "Maggie's Farm"?' It depends how bad you want that quarter."

—*Clyde Lieberman, Sr. Vice President A&R, MCA Records*

Indeed. If you don't want any negative feedback for what you create, may I suggest painting; it's a lot less noisy, there are no cables or contracts, and no one tells you that the chorus needs to come in earlier. Like it or not, most musicians and music business people are driven by the dynamic illustrated in Mr. Lieberman's poignant remark above. Decisions about music have to be based in commercial concerns because there is and always will be business surrounding music makers. They don't call it music fun, they call it music business. What people do in it largely depends how badly they want or need that quarter. And people in the music business like a lot of quarters.

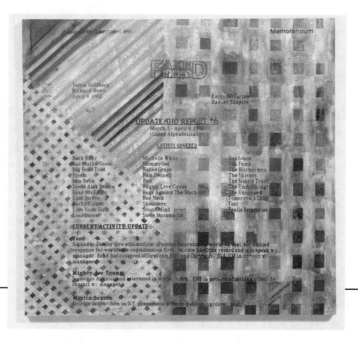

Justin Goldberg, *Gig Report #6*, watercolor on canvas, 49"x47"

1992 began an exciting time for new music in Los Angeles, especially if you were just starting to do A&R: new bands like Tool, Rage Against the Machine, Eleven and Mighty Joe Young (who would later change their name to Stone Temple Pilots because of a blues musician of the same name) played on the same bill at small venues for a few dozen early believers who started to feel a resurgence of compelling sounds and personalities at the club level. My new boss at the time, the president of Sony Music's publishing company, had asked me to create monthly gig reports such as the one here as a guideline for tracking new artists at our A&R meetings. It was a task I am grateful to have been given as it now provides a rare snapshot of new music going on at the time in almost every genre.

But it's not really a financial equation that lures us away from pure and creative instincts and towards uncomfortable career compromise: dilemmas related to the battle between art and commerce are rarely presented in such unambiguous terms. In fact, I would argue that the spirit of Mr. Lieberman's remark is that one of the key issues in music is not how badly one needs money in order to reach a threshold for compromising their art, it's a matter of philosophy and consciousness, and understanding that once your creativity is captured on CD, it enters a maze of personalities and documents that will either beg or demand that you compromise.

WHAT WAS IT YOU WANTED

If you study the gig report painting in some detail, you will perhaps recognize some other names alongside the rock stars. Others you will not recognize—I guess some might say they didn't "make it." They will have stories for their children and grandchildren, perhaps, about the big concert they once played opening for a big name, and perhaps some old scratched CDs or vinyl to pass on, but that's it. No big royalty checks. No special table at the restaurant, no annual Grammy tickets from Clive, no bad hair and drug problem referenced in an edgy episode of *Behind the Music*.

While I hardly claim to be a Nostradamus of A&R, there are many patterns, tendencies, beliefs and identifiable factors that can be traced to increasing and decreasing odds for success in today's business. Of course there are certain names on this gig report that simply represented more compelling live shows and better songs that others; a single great song written in a dingy rehearsal hall with the potential to be a number one hit can change the financial destiny of an entire corporation. But it is never simply a matter of talent. If I had to choose one single factor for success, it would be the ability to define your goals. It is critical that you define what you want so you can understand what you're going to do to have to get it.

You would be amazed by some of the statements that artists and others have made to me in creative meetings over the years, because everyone has their own definition of success and their own notion of how they are going to achieve it. Most aspiring musicians learn about the music business from the media, which is often manipulated to sell product by corporations. This isn't conspiracy theory time, it's just pointing out that success isn't usually what it seems, and the stories about the lack of success are rarely heard.

TWO DIAMONDS IN THE ROUGH, BUT ONLY ONE JEWEL:
Imagination Required

Some might say that Jewel was destined to be discovered. There was just something too unnervingly genuine; a sweetness, a strength, an irresistibly compelling and intangible "it" that she had.

Justin Goldberg, *Offer Jewel Kilcher,* **watercolor and acrylic on canvas, 38"x48"**

Jewel's explosion onto the national stage was at first, at least to me, only in the form of an angelic vocal carried over an acoustic breath of fresh air in early 1995. It came from behind the hiss of the overworked espresso machine at a small coffee house called the Innerchange Café somewhere near San Diego, California. Despite seeing her on a makeshift "stage" in a tiny venue where she struggled to strum guitar chords, performing new songs for maybe twenty people, it was clear that she could very well someday be playing before large audiences and become a bona fide star.

At least, it sure is easy to think that now, because she did become a star.

The trick, when you are on the business side of the talent equation, is in choosing the right talent amidst a confusing lineup without the benefit of hindsight. That is the challenge of doing A&R: you are hired to gamble on new talent and despite the number of powerful and confusing influences pushing you to favor certain artists, you are left to depend on what only your gut will tell you. In fact, the best wizards of A&R fortune telling (if there are any) will claim they rely on nothing more.

Perhaps Jewel's tremendous talent and success seem obvious or even inevitable now, but it was hardly such a certain bet only a short decade ago. True, she was heavily courted during a lengthy and competitive sign-ing derby by some of the bigger industry names of the day and eventual-ly was signed by the venerable Danny Goldberg. But by the time her album was remixed to better suit targeted radio formats, he was no longer employed by Atlantic Records—the very company he had signed her to. For what seemed like an endlessly nascent initial period of introduction at radio and retail, Jewel's debut album, *Pieces of You*, did not sell copies and did not get on the radio. It was hardly an overnight success. After Goldberg's departure, many felt that unless she did well relatively quick-ly, Jewel was not likely to last on the label for long.

It was around that time that I attended one of her performances and she mentioned to me she would soon be driving herself on a tour playing small venues as part of an acoustic solo tour around the Chicago area. Anxious to win her over so that she might sign a music publishing deal with the company I worked for (and I confess I had a bit of a crush on her too), I booked a flight and called an old friend in the area whom I invited to join me for her gig. It was a classic winter's evening in Chicago—bitter cold air, snow and ice on the sidewalks, and then suddenly, even more snow began to fall. As it continued to pound and pile on the streets, we debated the wisdom in leaving the apartment, and wondered if the show would still go on as scheduled. Upon hearing that the venue was actually a coffee house (with no alcohol) and on the outskirts of town, we began to question going at all.

When we arrived, we discovered a small but dedicated audience of mostly preteen children and a few parents. Apparently, Jewel had per-formed at a local school and the kids and teachers were so taken with her that they had arranged to attend her show. Jewel soon arrived, bouncing into the venue in high spirits, loaded down with clothing and radiating a perpetual cheer. Walking toward the stage set up, she seemed to somehow greet each of us warmly, then tuned up her instrument and walked up to the mic, where she stood performing songs and telling stories without a break for over three hours. For that very small audience it was a very spe-cial evening. Her mainstream success would still be many months ahead of her, but the seeds of that success were sown, in my view, by the hard work and dedication she brought to the occasion and her determination to pull her music through, as I experienced on that snowy night in Chicago.

The company I worked for wasn't exactly expecting her "meandering little folk songs" (as they once were described in an A&R meeting) to even get on the radio, let alone have a series of hits. So after missing the Jewel deal and watching her debut soar through the sales charts, I decided that the next Jewel would not slip so easily through my fingers. It would not be long before I was to be put to the test: a beautiful, young, female singer-guitar player who wrote complex, soul searching material with hit potential was knocking at my office door. Would this be my opportunity for a big hit and promotion? My permanent slot at the cool insider golf tournaments? It certainly started off in the right area—in the first five minutes of our meeting, she compared herself to Jewel's music and her label's marketing plan in almost every sentence.

This artist, let's call her Emily, a stunning beauty in her mid-twenties, was already having some fairly impressive professional activity with her songs—one was being recorded by a mid-level artist on a major label, and two others had impressed a music supervisor who had licensed to them to a television show and an important moment in a feature film, all of which she likely used to gain the attention of a major music attorney, who was now shopping her for a record deal. She had already recorded practically an album's worth of material with a major record producer, who was himself enjoying some success with another pop artist who was beginning to break at commercial radio. Certainly these were impressive talking points for a submission letter from her lawyer and in A&R meetings, which she was taking at labels all over town.

But there were two unsettling details she mentioned in our first meeting that I knew would completely kill or plague her career: first, when I asked her what her goals were, she said, "I just want a record deal."

Okay, fair enough. But then I asked her when her next show would be, and promised to bring some people from the office with me down to see her. That's when she told me that she didn't "play out." In fact, she claimed a fairly serious aversion to most things related to playing live or touring at the unsigned artist level. She loved singing in the studio, and didn't mind the idea of singing on live radio shows or opening up for a known act at larger venue, but she felt that the notion of organizing and dealing with actual band members and routinely rehearsing and playing local clubs was beneath her somehow. She felt her energy was best spent taking meetings about her deal and playing her songs from her CD at labels; after all, she already had songs covered and placed, and had already found a great sounding producer and attorney to represent her— so why would she need to subject herself to the often demeaning rigors of playing at local clubs? What was the point? Her goal was to get signed and to be in the studio making a record as her next step—and she didn't see the point in performing at small venues where presumably, few labels would be seeing her. Maybe, she suggested, if labels needed to see her and would pay for it, she would perform at a private showcase. Maybe, I suggested, she should be a painter; they don't perform live either.

Now don't get me wrong—not everyone needs to perform live to get signed or have a career. In fact, for many composers and artists in every genre, from hip hop to country, there can be less or zero need to play live while still earning fortunes and being famous. But for an artist planning on having live shows be a substantial component of a future career, it certainly helps to prove you can be compelling live. As we've learned, labels are looking at steep, high risk investments in signing new artists—and while the music should speak for itself in terms of radio playability, it is only natural for labels and publishing companies to want to examine all foreseeable strengths and weaknesses in their prospective new investment.

In Emily's case in particular, the irony was that her music was very much like Jewel's—and her material did actually have a similarly intimate storytelling dynamic. It was the kind of music that would benefit from being delivered live to incorporate and show off the intangibles that propel interest in a new artist—intangibles like charming smiles when certain lyrics are delivered, or knowing glances at just the right guitar riff. Emily's material and imaging probably should have been developed and marketed in a similar orbit as Jewel. The trouble, of course, is that she had no real idea what it might take to launch into that orbit—to play countless coffee houses, grimy acoustic festivals and be exposed on her own to the rigors of a solo acoustic tour with minimal funding. She wanted the MTV version—the one where she's greeted in the greenroom by her make-up artist and casually waltzes onstage to pick up a pre-tuned guitar in front of the camera as the audience coos when they hear the intro bar of her big radio hit. Ugh.

The words "music business" can mean different things to different people. Even the words "world tour" mean different things; there's the world tour opening for Bon Jovi and fifty thousand screaming Japanese fans that your major label tour support fund just paid for, and then there's the word tour of the United Kingdom on your own indie label that you financed by selling you mom's mini-van when she went to Hawaii for vacation. Both visions are valid—either scenario could easily lead to enormous financial reward, or ruin—there are no rules. It's rock and roll, man, anything can and does happen.

There are as many directions and benchmarks to this industry as there are personalities in and around the business. There are artists and writers who consider it their primary function to feed the commercial radio machine at almost any price, and there are those who prefer the folk festival circuit and would never want a major label recording contract. Reaching success is a different story for everyone; it depends only on your own expectations. Think them through and define *for yourself* what your goals are.

RESEARCH!

Do your homework on labels and artists. Find out what labels and artists release music you connect with or admire. Research current models of artists in your genre and take a closer look at how they got there. If and when you wind up having meetings with music attorneys, managers, label, or publishing people, they will ask these questions or at least want a sense of your level of awareness about the market. Be prepared to impress them with your ideas about your own career. The music industry is always hyper-aware of all things current—be focused on current artists and the ways that labels try to break them. This will help you to know when to move onto the next stage.

I AM A ROCK STAR. I MEAN RECORD PRODUCER.
(Did I Mention I Was Actually a Budding Label Mogul, Who Is Currently a Music Magazine Editor and Session Player While Studying for My MBA?)

Don't forget to allow yourself to be reinvented—many a failed rock star has become a far more wealthy and powerful musical force as a record producer. If you love music, there are many ways to ruin or better your life by staying connected to it. There can be many lives for creative people willing to reincarnate themselves into different roles. Success is not a thing; it is the name we sometimes give to evolution.

YOUR PROFESSIONAL POSSE:
AN OVERVIEW OF INDUSTRY PLAYERS
(And Why and When You May Need Them)

Choosing an attorney and a manager, for an emerging artist, can be a critical decision. It's not necessarily a permanent decision, but if you choose poorly it could be—especially if you don't correct any bad choices until it's too late. When an artist's career is in full swing, there are four main players (outside of any record or publishing company personnel) typically tending to the key areas requiring routine business attention. They include:

1. The attorney, whose role is to represent an artist's legal interests, which may including leading or participating in all activities related to deal making and contract negotiation (including shopping artists for record deals);
2. The manager, who usually is the chief advisor charged with counseling, directing and overseeing all aspects of an artist's career;
3. The booking agent, whose role is typically limited to arranging for all aspects of an artist's live appearances and;
4. The business manager, who is responsible for organizing and attending to an artist's financial affairs.

The latter two players on your team, agents and business managers, don't usually come into play until an artist's career is substantially on track in connection with a signed or impending record deal. Booking agents often have their ear to the ground for new talent (the same way that attorneys, managers, labels and publishers need to) so they do occasionally take on emerging unsigned talent, but it's not typical at the earlier stages. Business managers essentially process, structure and maintain an artist's financial affairs, so if money is in your picture, or looks like it will be soon, then it's time for a business manager.

Managers and lawyers, however, can play important roles in the early stages of an artist's career. There are many reasons for needing lawyers and managers, and there are few set rules; it should depend on your particular focus, goals and needs. But if you are a new artist, label or even a budding manager or attorney yourself, you are going to eventually find yourself in a position where you may want to connect with other management companies or law firms in order to elevate your project to the next stage.

As you will learn from some of the professionals interviewed here, many lawyers and managers are transforming their roles in response to changes in the business. With the decrease in new artist signings and most promotional budgets at the labels, some management companies and law firms have taken more pro-active positioning in career development, creating in house press and radio departments to compensate for the lack of that support at record labels. Law firms have now so evolved into paradigms for shopping new talent that some firms even have hired A&R scouts to find new artists to represent as early as is commercially viable. It has become a very competitive business.

For many new artists, finding and garnering interest from a good manager and attorney may also be a kind of catch-22, because people who are good at what they do are generally already busy. This is even more true for music managers and attorneys whose client roster may have them working days, nights and weekends—and those are just for the artists who are known or on their way to being known and therefore likely to be generating income. This usually presents a situation where the managers and lawyers who are most available or interested in representing you, may be the least qualified to do so if their availability stems from having no viable clients. For that reason, try to identify management companies and law firms that represent artists you feel are in the same general category musically as yourself; if the biggest name in hip hop wants to manage you, but you are a rock band, think twice—(unless someone like P. Diddy is about to sample your album on his).

Nevertheless, if you believe in yourself and in your career, then there is no shame in trying to get successful people to pay attention to you (but Thou Shall Not Stalk) because busy managers and attorneys can very quickly be un-busy if their current client list dries up or their current star band suddenly finds itself dropped by their label. In other words, new emerging talent is the lifeblood of the music industry: all artists have limited career runs and most industry professionals must to some degree stay in tune with the ever changing new artist landscape—and that might include you!

ATTORNEYS

Attorneys are a first step for many artists because they do not require exclusivity agreements, and the commitment on both sides is less than that of a manager, who may commission from 15-20 percent of income in contrast to a law firm's typical 5 percent. Attorneys in the music industry have been likened to agents in the film industry in that they can be effective catalysts for an artist's career by making label introductions and "shopping" music to labels. The flip side to this is that attorneys typically work on a long list of projects and thus need to budget their time carefully in order to maximize revenue for themselves and the firms they work for. Emerging artists without record deals don't offer the opportunity to charge for work, as there isn't much work to do prior to an artist signing a record deal, at least in terms of billable legal representation.

TALKING ABOUT MUSIC AND DANCING ABOUT ARCHITECTURE: A WORD ABOUT THE INTERVIEWS APPEARING IN THIS BOOK

I once heard the phrase "talking about music is like dancing about architecture," which may be true; music is something that you experience emotionally and it transcends words. But alas, we will attempt it here as it relates to how the business around music works. For this book, I spoke with some of the more intelligent and interesting minds at work in music today about a broad range of topics in an effort to piece together an accurate tapestry of the various and often invisible energies driving the business. It is a vast business, comprising many different personalities.

ATTORNEY

FRED DAVIS
Partner
Davis, Shapiro, Lewit, Montone & Hayes

First concert attended: Poco at the Fillmore East

Best concert attended: Billy Joel at the Bottom Line in 1972

Top five album recommendations:
1. Allman Brothers *Fillmore East*
2. Billy Joel *Piano Man*
3. Carole King *Tapestry*
4. Coldplay *Parachutes*
5. Elton John *Goodbye Yellow Brick Road*

Little known resume entry: I once worked at the admissions office of Bellvue Hospital.

Best project you were involved with that never made it big: Chris Whitley

---

TODAY'S SHIFTING INDUSTRY LANDSCAPE: BUSINESS AS UNUSUAL

AN INTERVIEW WITH ATTORNEY FRED DAVIS, FOUNDING PARTNER OF DAVIS, SHAPIRO, LEWIT, MONTONE & HAYES

Justin Goldberg: As a prominent representative of new and emerging artists in music, how have the dramatic changes in technology and corporate structure over the past few years changed the industry? Has it changed?

Fred Davis: The boring answer is it hasn't changed at all. The music changes in the business, the types of bands that may get signed changes. But the process of getting bands signed has not changed. There are clearly fewer buyers than there used to be in the sense that there are fewer labels than there once were, but the basic elements of getting a deal signed and doing a deal haven't changed at all. There are still very expensive deals that are very competitive situations and are about a lot of money, but most of the artists signed are under the radar and nobody has ever heard of them; [those deals] are done for reasonable amounts of money. On the urban side it's the same process, on the rock side it's the same process.

The dramatic change that our business has seen is two-fold from my perspective: the consolidation has affected the business in that the buyers are maybe placing greater emphasis on immediate gratification from the artists they're signing. Again, the types of artists being signed might be different, but the process of signing them hasn't changed. With the artists who are being signed, they're emphasizing more immediate responses because the corporations that own the labels are requiring quarterly, annual and semi-annual results, creating much greater pressure than the old-school entrepreneurs ever had. So that's one degree of change. But the big issue is that, from a technological point of view, we are as an industry, trying to sell black and white televisions to an audience that wants color TV. And, we haven't figured out yet that the new generation of consumer doesn't want to buy CDs, and we're trying to set them up and make CDs more attractive—when a twelve-year-old doesn't even want to own a CD player. He wants his music downloaded on his computer and he wants it on his iPod. As an industry, we're incredibly adept at selling CDs to the cassette/LP audience, but we haven't realized that the new generation wants a new format, and we haven't fed them yet. We haven't figured out how to sell to the new generation; an embarrassment for our industry which has always been the most progressive of cutting-edge industry. We're the old establishment and we are not cutting-edge anymore.

> As an industry, we're incredibly adept at selling CDs to the cassette/LP audience, but we haven't realized that the new generation wants a new format, and we haven't fed them yet.

Justin Goldberg, *The Law Firm of Fred Davis,* **watercolor on canvas, 18"x24"**

JG: A lot of people are talking about new paradigms for revenue at record labels. Do you think there will be a fundamental shift in approach to new artist deals? Has that already started to happen?

FD: I think that the audience is still buying music. I believe that the reason the consumer isn't paying for music right now, in my theory, is not because they wouldn't, but because they just can't. You cannot buy the new Eminem record on the Internet. You cannot legally download the album right now. It's impossible. So again, you're a twelve-year-old kid and you want to buy Eminem and you don't have a CD player, how do you think you're going to get it? You don't want to wait for Mom to drive you to the mall on Saturday between her hair appointment and her yoga class, you want it now. You can't buy it on the Internet so what are you going to do? If you can download tracks for free, why not? But if we continue the defensive measures that we have—a lot of the fake files and a lot of the CD-burning technological blockings, we do a little of that, and we simultaneously make music available for purchase on the Internet, then we'll solve a lot of our problems.

JG: That seems like a reasonable approach. Do you think that there will be aggressive penalties and initiatives to crack down on the everyday people who download, for example, some Dave Matthews songs from an unofficial fan site or a file sharing service like LimeWire or KaZaA?

FD: Absolutely. I think we're going to find a three-pronged approach, and it's our industry that is just waking up belatedly years later, where you'll see an aggressive campaign, public-service campaign, to explain to people that it's illegal. When you put in a DVD, what's the first thing that you see? The FBI warning. If you put in a CD, nobody says it's illegal to burn it. You don't even know, so it's an educational process that we have to go through. Then, there'll have to be an aggressive legal campaign, a lot of the fake files, and again, we have to make the music available to be purchased.

But the sense of entitlement has to change. The sense of the younger generation is that they are entitled to music for free. We can't allow that to continue. Should we be more sensitive as an industry to consumer desires? Sell singular tracks, sell compilation records? Sure, it's supply and demand. Clearly we should be more sensitive to the consumer. I think a lot of the conglomerates have not been sensitive to the consumer. "You can only buy 14-track CDs for $17.98 at Tower Records, period." That's wrong. We've been wrong in that, actually wrong as an industry.

JG: Is the culture and spirit of the entrepreneur being forced to disappear amidst all of the industry's consolidation and downsizing? Are we evolving into such a dire collection of balance sheets and artists-as-investment that we're evolving into an overly antiseptic, corporate business?

FD: I think you're going to find two things. I think, as an industry, we're going through our adolescence. The essence of the industry's first stage was rebellion, and whether it was the rebellion of the artists' message or rebellion of the industry as a whole, we were always on the outskirts. We are no longer left of center. We are mainstream as an industry right now, and how do you grow up as an industry and how do you mature as an industry without being rebellious? A lot of that entrepreneurial spirit initially wasn't about making money. It was about the message and the rebellion. Now, we have to find our voice as an industry. We clearly went through a period in the early nineties where it was wrong to make money. The indie rock scene was antithetical to making money. The next generation was the dot com era where all the entrepreneurs got pulled into some sort of bubble fantasy that had nothing to do with the music. Are we now going to evolve into an era where those will be merged? Can I see somebody starting up a record company in Minneapolis with the only way they sell music is on the Internet? Absolutely. Periods of industry downturn bring opportunities, and it will, I think, bring back the entrepreneurial spirit. The one thing that I tell everybody to keep in mind is that the music industry is very healthy—it's the traditional record industry that's not. The analogy is that the television industry is very healthy. More people watch television now than ever. But the traditional network business is suffering. They missed cable the same way the traditional record business is missing the Internet. And it'll evolve because kids still want music more than ever. That you have five billion downloads happening, that's the good news. It'd be a shame if nobody wanted to download the music. We, as an industry, have to figure out how to monetize that interest, but thank God the interest is there. And we'll figure that out, and through that, there'll be entrepreneurial opportunities and a lot of activity. We don't know how it's going to evolve. The phone company may be the record company. Pepsi might become the new type of record company, Microsoft might be....We don't know how it's going to evolve, but somebody somewhere in this landscape understands the power of music and how it connects to kids. That's why things haven't changed—because the same connection still works. It's the economics, the technology, those are what's changing. The basic relationship between kid and music, or adult and music, is still there.

> It's probably a poor reflection of our industry as a whole that the man or woman who has gone to law school is now the most qualified person to be a conduit between the musical community and the record companies.

JG: Lawyers transforming into a primary talent discovery source is another major change in the business, wouldn't you agree? It was not long ago that artists often seemed puzzled as to why they would even need an attorney if they were just starting out.

FD: When I started practicing in the late eighties, my biggest fight with my bosses at the time was trying to explain to them why we needed to take an A&R executive out to lunch. "Why? Are you going to get business from that lunch?" No, but it was establishing a network and the access. Why the lawyer has become the "agent" of unsigned bands in our industry is beyond me. It's probably a poor reflection of our industry as a whole that the man or woman who has gone to law school is now the most qualified person to be a conduit between the musical community and the record companies. It's wrong, but it just happened. It's happened because the lawyer became entrepreneurial and it was a way to create a business. Nothing in our training or background allowed us to do that, but it's a bad reflection of our industry that is exactly what has happened. Absolutely. But I'm damn well going to take advantage of it. And what has happened is, the muscles of the record company executives atrophied and they became more reliant on us and we became more incentivized to play the role; and it becomes a cycle, and became part of the fabric.

. . . .

ATTORNEY

PAMELA L. KLEIN
Serling, Rooks, & Ferrara, LLP

First concert attended: Alice Cooper (at age seven)

Best concert(s) attended:
1. Art Blakey & The Jazz Messengers (six months before Blakey passed)
2. Springsteen (Born in the USA tour)
3. Stones (Voodoo Lounge tour)
4. Eric Clapton (1990)

Top five album recommendations: What is this, *Sophie's Choice*? I can't choose…!

Recommended film: *This is Spinal Tap* (Embassy Pictures, 1984)

Recommended reading: *Miles* by Miles Davis

Instrument played: Piano

WHAT'S THE DEAL?: THE MANY HATS OF TODAY'S MUSIC ATTORNEY
SOME BASICS WITH ATTORNEY PAM KLEIN
OF SERLING, ROOKS, & FERRERA

Justin Goldberg: When do you get an attorney if you're a new artist?

Pamela Klein: The best time to get an attorney is before you sign any paper at all, or after you've got some good demos that you think are worth shopping and people are starting to make noise about. Or the first time an A&R person contacts you and says, "Hey, I really like your stuff."

JG: The roles managers, lawyers and booking agents play is sometimes confusing for people just starting out. Exactly whose job is it to shop an artist?

PK: Well, theoretically, it could be any of the above. It could be the manager, it could be the lawyer, and it could be somebody's friend. Your band may know somebody, who knows somebody, who knows somebody. But, in the big scheme of things, when you have both a lawyer and a manager on the team, the things that would fall into the manager's lap would be anything having to do with the more day-to-day activities of the artist, such as booking gigs or finding the booking agent to book the gigs, making those connections, talking to other managers and maybe swapping gigs for bands in different cities if they've got connections that way; whereas the lawyer's job is to really look over those agreements to the extent that there is even documentation related to them. The lawyer's job can certainly be to shop talent, but a manager also shops, and it ideally becomes very much a team effort, with both parties working together, and everyone keeping each other informed in terms of who they are talking to and what the status of the conversations are. Maybe one person knows a certain A&R person at a label and somebody else knows somebody else on the West Coast versus the East Coast, and you hit both ends. Then you coordinate and talk about who has the greater interest and who has more power to make something happen for your artist. But when you've got both players involved, the day-to-day stuff falls to the manager and the technical details fall to the lawyer, because, at the end of the day, it's the manager who's going to be commissioning all these activities, and the lawyer will typically make a much smaller percentage.

JG: Well, let's talk about that for a minute: what are some common arrangements made between new artists, who may be on a budget, and lawyers for the purpose of shopping a deal? Is it typically a set percentage, and is it ever on a cash basis?

PK: Sure, we all want cash up front. Small bills, preferably! But seriously, the numbers vary. I've seen agreements where the lawyer says, "Give me X number of dollars, flat-fee," and what the X stands for depends greatly on how big the deal is. If an artist is getting an in-pocket advance of twenty-five thousand dollars, the lawyer can't take fifteen. I mean, that's just not what's typically done. I suppose there are some lawyers who do that but most lawyers will not. You take a smaller percentage of it. And on that deal, which might be a small deal, you're going to want to look at how much paperwork is actually involved. How early on was the lawyer involved in the project? There are many things that I do that, hey, I don't get paid for along the way. Then some little small deal comes along and I'm going to have to make up for the twenty hours that I put into the band from this small pool of cash that's coming in, without raping the band and while still making sure they've got money to eat throughout the process.

JG: And that could be a delicate balance.

PK: Absolutely. You have to have some general idea of where the fairness lies at the beginning of the relationship, before you're even talking about any deal. There are other situations where a lawyer for shopping and for doing the paperwork for the recording agreement will get 10 percent of the first album funds, sometimes the first period fund. In other words, if they are able to get two albums firm in a deal, then you might get 10 percent of both the first and the second album. But certainly for shopping you'll get about 10 percent of that first album fund. And again, it depends on what the fund is. For example, if the fund is five hundred thousand dollars including all recording costs and the equipment funds and anything else, you might say, "Well, I don't need the full fifty thousand if all those numbers add up to five hundred thousand; I don't need the full fifty, but give me thirty."

JG: What if a band hears from an attorney who wants to charge a few thousand dollars to shop a tape?

PK: In my experience, it means that the lawyer doesn't have a lot of faith in the band. I know that there are a lot of lawyers who do that, and the reason they do it is because shopping takes a lot of time. It takes a lot of time, and the only things that I'll shop or that anyone in my office will shop are things that we really believe in and that we love, because you're looking at a year worth of free work, minimum.

JG: How difficult has it become to get new artists signed?

PK: The deals are smaller and harder to get. I also think that record labels are more afraid than they ever have been—in really the last ten years now—about what kind of music is going to be the next big thing. I don't think that anybody really knows. It was very much like the mid-nineties when grunge was sort of fading out and you didn't really know what was coming next. So, there's a lot of that going on. And I think the biggest thing is consolidation in radio. To me at least, because it's become outrageously expensive for even major labels to get new music played on the radio and have any sort of success, that it makes doing many deals cost-prohibitive. The smaller deals where you would just sort of test it out and give an artist time to develop, you can't do anymore because it's a million dollars just to give it a shot.

. . . .

MANAGERS

There's a saying in the industry that you don't need a manager until there's something to manage. This is only partially true. Choosing a personal manger who will be effective for your career depends on what you need a manager for. Some artists really need an objective voice of reason and a guiding hand with a long list of creative issues ranging from production, song selection and visual presentation to detailed coordination of live appearances. Some artists may not have a record deal on the horizon but may be a touring act or busy local live performers generating substantial revenue and need constant attention and assistance on the road or at clubs.

Both managers and attorneys should be at least somewhat passionate about your talent. Passionate believers make for great artist mouthpieces: you want your professional representatives to be behind your music. They don't have to be fanatic fans or musicians themselves, but they should be enthusiastic about what you do. How else will they convey their belief in you in the course of representing you to others, if it's not reflected in exchanges with you personally? Your manager is your head cheerleader and interim parent; he or she is responsible for cheering on the team and being the heavy when things don't go right.

It is important to learn about the other artists a manager or an attorney represents simply because if your music is in the same genre as those artists, it is likely that their existing personal relationships may be again utilized on your behalf. This could apply in connection to a live touring situation that might benefit you, or a record company that could be predisposed to signing you because they like working with that representative—who for them is a known quantity. Do not however, make this your only criteria. Managers with huge and impressive clients making a ton of money tend to focus mostly (or only) on those clients, and managers with clients who were "huge" many years ago may no longer be operating in the current mix of A&R executives responsible for new signings. So don't get star struck because a manger represents one of your old favorites and promises to introduce you or have you work together. The music industry is unfortunately focused on all things new—so stay focused when you present your music in meetings.

Also remember that the majority (not all—but the majority) of reputable managers and attorneys truly operating in the American music industry are typically located where the industry is—Los Angeles, New York City, Atlanta and Nashville. Of course, there are exceptions to this everywhere, but if you are being courted by a management or law firm based outside of one of these cities, do your homework and find out how and why they exist outside of the mainstream.

GOT INCENTIVE? 15 PERCENT VS. 20 PERCENT— WHAT'S THE RIGHT PERCENTAGE TO GET CHARGED?

Let's first answer this question by doing some math: 10 percent of a 100,000 advance equals 10,000, which leaves 90,000 left (of course this is hypothetical—lawyers, recording funds, business managers and Uncle Sam are all laughing at these figures) for the artists. Twenty percent of a 200,000 advance equals 40,000, which leaves 160,000.

Most managers charge between 15–20 percent. This varies depending on the manager, on the amount of work required by the manager or by the artist, or by the amount of money likely to be commissioned by the manager within a certain time frame. It is based upon the gross earnings of an artist. If you are an artist with an existing revenue stream, then you are in position to negotiate for a lower percentage. If you are a manager about to take on a band with a record deal without high record sales, it can be a catch-22—in many cases the first big monies an artist sees from their publishing and record deal are already gone—into the pocket of the first manager. It's nice to waltz into a management situation with artists when they have deals, but if a band has already received record deal and publishing deal advances, then there's probably no money coming in for a year or longer—or never. Secondly, if you are an artist thinking you want to push for a better arrangement—here's why I recommend you at least think twice: having someone as your partner who's in for more money if you're in for more money can be a good thing, and not necessarily bad. Often it's a question of incentive; if you are a manager working with different artists and an opportunity comes up that could be applicable for several artists on your roster—perhaps a licensing opportunity, or a live show where the manager's discretion is the only guide for business, savvy managers will do business on behalf of the artists they have the best deals with. So don't just think of the percentage as something you want to limit, think big, think incentive.

MANAGER

JORDAN BERLIANT
General Manager
10th Street Entertainment

First concert attended: Joni Mitchell, 1974

Best concert attended: Pink Floyd at Soldier's Field in Chicago, 1979

Top five album recommendations:
1. Radiohead *OK Computer* & *Kid A*
2. Neil Young *Tonight's the Night*
3. Jeff Buckley *Grace*
4. David Bowie *Scary Monsters*
5. Led Zeppelin *Physical Graffiti*

Little known resume entry: I have recorded on other peoples' albums under several aliases.

Best project you were involved with that never made it big: Coal Chamber

Recommended reading: *The Dirt: Confessions of the World's Most Notorious Rock Band*, by Motley Crüe and Neil Strauss

Instrument played: Guitar

Notable clients: Meat Loaf, Motley Crüe, Hanson, Motor Ace, Clint Black

TODAY'S SHIFTING INDUSTRY LANDSCAPE: MANAGING THE FUTURE
AN INTERVIEW WITH JORDAN BERLIANT, GENERAL MANAGER OF 10th STREET ENTERTAINMENT (FORMERLY THE LEFT BANK ORGANIZATION)

Justin Goldberg: When is it time for an artist to get a manager?

Jordan Berliant: I think if you look at the economics of it, it's when a manager can bring more value to your career. Managers typically commission anywhere between 15–20 percent of an act's earnings, so you have to determine—as an artist—at what stage do you need management to add value to your career.

JG: People coming into this business often have misunderstandings about what a manager's job actually is, as compared to say the artist's business manager, road manager, or attorney. What are the responsibilities of an artist's manager?

JB: Well, in terms of management, there are very few things that aren't ultimately our responsibility. A good manager will be able to organize the resources on behalf of an artist to take care of some of those things. For example, we always hire a tour manager to go out with our artists on the road. There are some managers who also act as the tour manager. That's not a terrific use of a manager's time, and if you're an artist paying the manager, then you're not really getting a return on your investment. We tend to make it pretty clear to the artist before we take them on exactly what we do and what we don't do. We don't act as valets here. Certainly, there are some artists who need personal assistants who we help hire— and I gave you the example of tour management—but in terms of the professional aspect of the job, I think a good manager has to take responsibility for making sure that the artist's needs are met in every professional area, whether that's touring, or marketing and promotion on the record side, the exploitation of their songs and their publishing, the way an artist is imaged through media and publicity, or even the exploitation of their brand through licensing and merchandising. And while it's not the manager's job to sell the T-shirts per se, it *is* the manager's job to make sure that the artist enters into a merchandising agreement that will be lucrative and successful. So managers have to take responsibility for the partners they bring in to an artist whether that's a merchandiser, a publisher, an agent, or a record company.

JG: How have changes in the industry affected you and your company as managers?

JB: When I got into this business, touring was very localized. The promoters who had been around for years and years were guys you had relationships with and whom you'd book a tour through. And now what's happened is that SFX, which was subsequently bought up by Clear Channel, bought up a large number of the concert promoters and then House of Blues bought up a lot of concert promoters—so now you've got some pretty big gatekeepers if you want to get a band out there.

Especially in the case of Clear Channel—which also owns over twelve hundred radio stations in the market—with the importance of radio to drive awareness of a record or a tour and drive demand for those things. It's a pretty big vertical that you have to navigate through.

JG: Is Clear Channel really so organized that they have the ability to actively work against you as a cohesive force?

JB: It has as much ability to work for you as against you. Leverage becomes the name of the game. Similarly, in the arena of the recording industry, you have media trying to buy up record companies. For instance, you have AOL, which bought up all the Time-Warner labels. They were a media giant to begin with, now they're a new media and traditional media giant and in everything from ISPs to cable television distribution—and now they own entertainment content as part of this new media strategy. You've got Vivendi, which bought up Universal and PolyGram. And you've got BMG, a media giant out of Germany, which has bought up what used to be RCA and Arista.

You've never had to really look at records fitting into a corporate strategy before, but it's important that you understand as an artist with a manager who records for a corporation, that from a corporate sense what you do is viewed as content and leveraged to make other plays happen from a corporate perspective—which never used to be the case. You used to have these entrepreneurs like Clive Davis, Jack Holtzman, or Lenny Waronker, who started record companies because of their passion for the music and their passion for the artists, and that tended to guide their business thinking and their principles. Today, basically what you have is the record industry and touring industry as part of a corporate vertical strategy to elevate stock prices.

It used to be that people took pride in breaking an artist, even if that took until their eighth or ninth record; artists were always supported by their record companies if their art and craft was appreciated. Nowadays, with the pressure on record companies to satisfy their numbers and quarterly billing obligations in order to make their shareholders happy, you essentially get one single and then you're in or out; and because of the amount of competition out there, a very, very high percentage of records and artists fail. There's only so much water you can put through a one-inch pipe, and the record industry tends to overflow the pipe and inevitably there are good artists, talented artists who no longer get the time to develop and to reach an audience.

JG: Is this going to force labels to reach for compensation in areas traditionally reserved for managers?

JB: That's something we here at 10th Street have been telling people is going to happen, because of the amount of money that it now takes to work a record; because of the consolidation of radio and retail and the expense of putting a band out on the road now. The breakeven point for a record company is now north of half a million units, which is gold.

There were only 185 records in all of last year that sold 500,000 copies according to SoundScan, and there were over 30,000 released. So what that tells you is that the record companies either have to limit themselves to projects that they think will be home-runs instantly—which traditionally they are never really good at predicting—or they have to find other revenue streams. They are looking at having to invest a huge amount of money, and it's not uncommon for a record company to invest a couple of million dollars in a new artist who they believe they can break, because that's what it takes to work multiple singles at radio at multiple formats these days. Looking at it from an ROI perspective, they're looking for a bigger return on their dollar. So if they believe, that through the spending of *their* money in marketing and promotion, and the investment of *their* resources and to make and sell records, that through those things they enable artists to make money in publishing, in touring and through their merchandising...what [the record companies] are trying to do is get a piece of that revenue.

> There were only 185 records in all of last year that sold 500,000 copies according to SoundScan, and there were over 30,000 released.

JG: Does that make you less likely to pick up new artists?

JB: Yes, but only from the standpoint of, well, a couple of things. Number one: you have to spend just as much time and energy to fail as you do to succeed as a manager. And given the accounting practices of record companies, very few artists, even artists who sell platinum, end up making much money through a record royalty because so much of the marketing and promotion ends up getting charged back against them. But even the failure rate of the record companies, again 185 records last year out of the 30,000 released sold half a million units...with the failure rate, you have to be very selective about what you put your energy into as a manager. The second thing, which may be something more specific to 10th Street, is we actually invest in our own infrastructure here to help service our clients in the areas that are important to their careers. We have people here who do publicity, who do international, who do radio marketing and visual imaging. We made an investment in order to help make the outcome a little more favorable for the artists that we do manage. The scarce resources of record companies, given the number of releases they have—it's not only their money but it's their time and attention. Again, our artists don't make much money out from their record royalties. Their money is made through touring and publishing and the exploitation of their brand. At 10th Street, we think of ourselves as partners, marketing partners, for the artists we market, promote and sell the content they make and brand their image. So, developing the image of an artist and the brand of an artist is really, from the artist's perspective, what can be monetized. Getting records to sell and getting records played on the radio is a tool to achieve the goal, but it's not the goal in and of itself.

JG: So management companies like 10th Street are recreating resources traditionally provided by the labels?

JB: Right. The sad thing is that within the record companies they have things called priorities. Which means, by definition, that there are releases that are *not* priorities for them. In management, everything we do is a priority. Every artist that we have is a priority or else we don't take them on. We have to succeed 90 percent of the time in an industry that fails more than 90 percent of the time.

JG: What is a "priority"? Is that just a word that everyone's A&R guy makes up to make them feel better?

JB: A priority within a record company is the record that they're going to go out and kill for at radio and allocate resources to from a marketing and sales perspective. When I worked at a record company, the priorities were laid out as those records that you wanted your partners in the value chain to focus on, whether that was radio or retail, and those were the records that you were willing to throw down on in terms of dollars. That's really what it's about. It's very uncommon for a record company to get more than one of its records added to a radio station's play-list in any given week. So, some things have to be given priority.

· · · · · · ·

BOOKING AGENTS

The word agent is often misused when it comes to the music business, as it implies someone who functions as a mediator, negotiator and representative for the artist. Certainly music agents do function in this way, but their role is limited only to live performances. In terms of a new artist's career, managers and attorneys, as we have seen in the preceding pages, are usually on the scene earlier and take on broader responsibilities. When a booking agent joins an artist's team is usually an economic consideration; unsigned artists without large audiences do not usually generate much income and are thus of limited interest to booking agencies unless a record deal or some other incentive is clearly on the career horizon.

There are also many different kinds of booking agencies that handle different kinds of artists for different venues, ranging from cruise ships to the college circuit, from hotels and casinos to vacation resorts and amusement parks. Within major booking agencies, there are different departments devoted to handling specific areas for different artists; these may be focused on international markets, arena work, or regional domestic bookings. Once a band is at the level of promoting a nationally distributed album, or managing to draw sizable crowds routinely enough to warrant regular, revenue generating shows, a booking agent can be an essential piece of an artist's puzzle. Established booking agencies typically have long-term relationships with the more reputable venues and thus usually have methods for saving money that might elude an artist with either limited or no agency representation. Due to consolidation in the touring industry, there are also fewer promoters in the market, which leaves a smaller pool of dealmakers to negotiate with. Once a competitive market open to entrepreneurs and truly independent promoters, the U.S. market is now dominated by three main companies: Clear Channel, Concerts West (which houses Goldenvoice) and House of Blues.

All Access Passport

CD-ROM

FYI

AGENT PERCENTAGES & REGULATIONS

It varies from state to state, but agents in California are franchised by the state and recognized by the unions (AFM, AFTRA & SAG). The maximum that the unions allow agents to charge is *not more than* 10 percent! Check with the unions if you have any questions—they're all listed on your CD-ROM disc.

AGENT

NIKKI WHEELER
United Talent Agency

First concert attended: Hall & Oates

Best concert attended: Madonna's Blond Ambition tour

Top five album recommendations:
1. Don Henley *Building the Perfect Beast*
2. Bruce Springsteen *The Rising*
3. Madonna *Like a Virgin*
4. Anything by Tom Petty
5. Anything by Shawn Colvin

Best project you were involved with that never made it big: Push Down and Turn

Recommended reading: *USA Today*

Instruments played: Guitar and piano

Notable clients: Lizzie West on Warner Bros., Joe Firstman on Atlantic

---

TODAY'S SHIFTING INDUSTRY LANDSCAPE: PAY FOR PLAY
A CONVERSATION WITH AGENT NIKKI WHEELER
OF UNITED TALENT AGENCY

Justin Goldberg: When do you think is the best time to take on a new artist?

Nikki Wheeler: You can talk to so many people in the industry and do research; you can sign something and you *still* never know if it's going to hit. Speaking for myself, I like to sign artists that I'm extremely passionate about because there is no money in it at the very beginning.

JG: How can unsigned artists best position themselves to open up for established artists?

NW: That's pretty much from a band knowing some other guys in a band or girls in a band, and that's up to them. It's hard to get an artist on a tour when they have no product. The trend that I'm seeing, and I'm sort of shocked by it—I have a couple of bands that wanted to get on a tour recently and I was told that if I wanted to be on that tour, great, but I needed to pay twenty grand to be on that tour. And a lot of bands are doing that now. It's like, "Listen, you want to tour with me, give me twenty grand up front towards marketing."

JG: So in contrast to the old days, where touring was perhaps one of the dependable areas for generating an income while you sat in debt to your record company, it's now being looked upon as a marketing cost that goes up with the size of the tour?

NW: Correct. And some labels like to package their bands together because they'll get more bang for their buck in terms of marketing. Other tours come together because managers and other managers are friends, or the agents are friends and they think it'll be a cool package idea. Basically, you submit your band for other tours that are going out there and you've got to surround it. It's a big thing right now trying to package the right artists. You've got to have labels call the other labels. You've got to have the managers call the managers. You've got to have the agents talking to all the agents. It's really a team effort to try to come up with packaging ideas, making them become a reality in terms of packaging a tour.

JG: So who usually is the final decision maker? Is it the promoter, because they ultimately pay the artists and the venues directly?

NW: A promoter would pay for the headlining act and then it depends on what the headlining act wants to do; maybe they want to go out and they just want a strong local band. So they could just pay a top local band a hundred or two hundred and fifty bucks. Or everybody submits material to that band and then the band decides. Maybe all the members of the band decide, maybe just the lead singer decides, maybe the manager decides. Some bands take out friends, and friends don't generate any ticket sales; other bands need a band on the road with them that can bring in some ticket sales.

JG: Let's talk about how some deals are structured in terms of guarantees and percentages.

NW: If you're just starting out, I seldom do door deals. All of my bands get a guarantee, and some have percentage deals. For example, five hundred plus 85 percent of the gross box-office receipts after taxes and 15 percent promoter profit, because that's how the promoter makes their money. So after all the expenses and taxes are, then we would definitely get the overages for that 85 percent, and then to make it 100, there's 15 percent in there for promoter profit.

JG: Is it difficult to monitor the transactions and ensure accuracy? Are disputes common?

NW: Yeah, sort of...but not really. I mean, you have to have receipts for everything. If you want to claim it as an expense, you've got a sound company, or you've got catering, or you have had to bring in the production—whatever, there are always receipts.

JG: Do those items get charged back to the artist?

NW: No, it doesn't get charged...nothing gets charged back to the artist. Basically, your tour manager will sit down with whomever is settling the show, they'll go through what the expenses were for the evening and say, "Okay, great. Here's the amount of money that we made. Here's our gross box office receipts. That's how much you've grossed for that show. Then you take out the guarantee and you take out all of the expenses for the room—like stage-hands, I could go through a whole list for you—and then after that [the artist] could take home that money. Eighty-five percent of what's left over. That is what's called your overages.

JG: What advice would you give to new artists just entering the business who are considering getting an agent?

NW: They could think about getting agents, but first I would say find an attorney, talk to some other bands locally that are maybe represented by a law firm. Submit some music to them. It's really all about relationships. It's funny, people talk about being in this business and you can say, "Well, I went to college, I went to this school," and none of that means anything. It's truly all about networking. It's about your friends and your associates and fellow colleagues that really make things happen for you in this business. I have friends of friends who call me and say, "Okay, there's this band;" I have singer-songwriters whom I've met with and I've tried to set them up with an attorney, get representation, and then try to shop for a record deal. It's really all about networking. There are several people who call me and want representation but if they don't have anything going on and it's like they're cold calling me—with that, I won't be able to do anything. But if it's somebody I know and somebody who has been referred to me, something like that, I'll try to help out—because I think research, development, finding bands and being involved in the beginning stages is the best part.

· · · · · · ·

BUSINESS MANAGER

BRUCE KOLBRENNER
Kolbrenner, Pagano, & Schroder Inc.

First concert attended: The Tokens

Best concert attended: Jimi Hendrix at Fillmore East

Top five album recommendations:
1. Billy Joel *Piano Man*
2 Fleetwood Mac *Tusk*
3. The Eagles *Hotel California*
4. *Saturday Night Fever* soundtrack
5. *Grease* Soundtrack

Little known resume entry: Was the CFO for the Moscow Music Peace Festival, 1989, Lenin Stadium, Moscow (featuring Motley Crüe, Bon Jovi, Ozzy Ozbourne, The Scorpions, Skid Row).

Best project you were involved with that never made it big: Sons of Angels (from Sweden)

Recommended reading: *It Doesn't Take A Hero: The Autobiography of General H. Norman Schwartzkopf*

Instrument played: Accordion

Notable clients: Bon Jovi, Terence Trent D'Arby, Anthrax, Vanessa Williams, LL Cool J

....

THE CFO OF YOUR ENTERPRISE: THE BUSINESS MANAGER
AN INTERVIEW WITH BRUCE KOLBRENNER OF
KOLBRENNER, PAGANO & SCHRODER
....

Justin Goldberg: First of all, when is the right time for somebody to even get a business manager in the music business?

Bruce Kolbrenner: I would say the right time is when they sign their first deal, or are contemplating signing their first deal.

JG: So let's say you are an artist signing your first deal with Warner Bros. What is the pitch that's generally given from a business manager? What are the kinds of things that they manage and do?

BK: The pitch is various levels. It starts with the business concept of being an artist in the music business and what type of an agreement and how should they enter into it—whether it be as a sole proprietor, as a corporation, what type of corporation, and what the filing requirements would be for the different types of entities. If it's a touring band, then the business manager's job is to manage the business of the band while they're on the road and to create a set of books, financial records, utilizing the bank accounts that would be maintained by the business manager, and at the end of the year creating partnership returns, corporate returns, etc. What we do is, if we have a band that goes out, we do all the payroll tax returns for the band, we do all the salaries, we make the deposits for the band, we work in concert with managers to create the budget, and we do budget to actual for touring. We also review any and all of the expenses that are incurred by the road manager/tour manager while they're out on the road. We collect money from the agencies if they go out and we're required to get the deposits from the agents and record the income. That's one level of an artist's deal, especially if it's a touring artist.

Another situation that we get involved with is in the publishing and writers area. There we would be responsible for receiving the monies, and if we are reviewing the royalties statements, whether or not the royalties have been reported based on the licenses that have been issued—making sure the financial statements match. We also make sure that we receive the checks from ASCAP and BMI. On the artist royalties side, or when the artist gets into a recoup position, we would be reviewing the royalties statements to determine whether or not royalties had been paid correctly or incorrectly, or if European/foreign sales have been reported; we would do a desk audit to make that determination. In addition, if a band is touring and merchandise is involved, we're the ones who receive the advance monies on merchandising and review the records from the merchandiser when they're out there on the road, as far as creating the sales. And we'll review the inventory and then the other reports that they had while they're out there.

FYI

ALL YOUR MONEY COULD BE GONE

Your money could be gone if don't choose your business manager carefully. While you sing, dance, play, write and travel, your business manager is the individual charged with maintaining your bank account statements and your debts in a timely manner. Business managers also file your tax returns and sometimes manage investments. In some states, they are not regulated like other financial advisors are, and have no minimum requirements for training or expertise. Find the ones with the letters CPA next to their names. A CPA, or certified public accountant, requires a great deal of training and expertise and is almost always going to be a worthwhile expense. Watch out!

JG: So you are basically the engine room, in some ways, for an artist's career. I mean, everything and everyone that gets paid, and all of the elements of basically keeping the machine rolling with payments, and monitoring where the payments are going...

BK: Yes, we're the CFO.

· · · · · · ·

DOT BOMB DOT COM:
The End of the World As We Know It

Sometime in late 1998, a colleague came by my office and abruptly announced to me that the music industry was over. He asked if I knew about a Web site called Napster yet; when I confessed my ignorance, he asked me to log onto the Internet so he could be the first to show me how anyone with a computer—anywhere—could obtain a high-quality digital version of almost any song they could think of, for free. This, he boldly predicted, was the end of the world as we knew it: leading me through the search function on Napster he asked me to pick a song title and appropriately enough I named "Estimated Prophet" by the Grateful Dead, a title which instantly generated a list of dozens of versions available for free download. Even on a dialup connection we were able to hear the version we chose spring clearly from my speakers within minutes. It took only that long to see he was absolutely right. Big trouble lay ahead.

It would take the music industry a lot longer to come to this conclusion. So long, in fact, that it's arguable that they will never recover the lost time, opportunity and revenue—worst of all is the almost universal perception that the industry was collectively asleep at the wheel, unable to see their Titanic-like ship hitting the iceberg of the Internet's distribution threat until it was too late. And like the very passengers on that ill-fated ship, too confident to believe it could sink so quickly or at all, arrogance and miscalculation cost the industry dearly.

SDMI AND OTHER UFOS

It is hard to imagine it now, but it was only a few short years ago that the music world desperately held its breath for the imminent arrival of something called SDMI—an acronym for the Secure Digital Music Initiative. Few seemed to know exactly what it was or how it would work, but as the Internet swelled into a massive and free digital music bonanza, SDMI was

I feel this obscene gold rush greedgreedgreed vibe that bothers me a lot when I talk to dot-com people about all this. You guys can't hustle artists that well. At least slick A&R guys know the buzzwards. Don't try to compete with them. I just laugh at you when you do! Maybe you could a year ago when anything dot-com sounded smarter than the rest of us, but the scam has been uncovered.

Gersh, Silva are >en fathers

By Marc Pollack

Former Capitol Records CEO Gary Gersh and Gold Mountain Management chief John Silva, principals of the newly formed G.A.S. Entertainment Co., have joined Digital Entertainment Network Inc. to launch a new music group.

As part of the acquisition and

Silva will be co-presidents of the new DEN subsidiary and are on the board of directors of the Digital Entertainment Network.

The >en music group (pronounced den) will forge a 21st century multimedia music concern and unveil a number of new

Justin Goldberg, *Dot Bomb Dot Com*, watercolor on canvas, 27"x34"

Music and the Internet—a marriage made in hell if you were on the wrong side of the equation. Long before Napster was shut down and MP3 sued, many notable names in music were handed buckets of money for a broad variety of initiatives, not all of them completely clear. This painting features some of the companies and personalities given plenty of play in the media during Internet music's heyday: the aptly barbed quote at the top of the piece deriding "dot com people" is from Courtney Love, the circular blue logo is of Al Teller's failed online label Atomic Pop, and the dominating article by Marc Pollack announces the launch of >EN, the infamous new media and music venture which closed its doors in 2000. (A profit and loss statement from Tonos.com, which finally shut down in 2003, lies beneath the article.) The painting now hangs in Mr. Pollack's office at *Hits* magazine.

consistently touted as the answer to corporate concerns that the MP3 phenomenon was getting out of control and likely to seriously threaten profits. SDMI's purpose was to create a cross-platform scheme for copy protecting digital music files and prevent illegal music sharing, thus sending corporate music companies back along their way to their typical comforts and profits. Companies were hoping to create files that could be sold online, but not copied.

As a gaggle of geniuses sat sequestered away somewhere in front of a bank of overpriced flat screen monitors, programming this impenetrable code that would stabilize the industry, the newly sprouted, highly funded "new media industry" found itself in its own race against time; this one a rush to the finish line for a digital download standard. Some people suggested that songs would ultimately not even be encrypted as MP3 files. Others suggested MP4 files would be faster, smaller and more versatile. Some looked toward the innovative minds behind Apple's QuickTime technology. Windows media and RealNetworks also promised smaller file sizes with increased versatility. Companies such as Red dot net, Real networks, Liquid Audio, a2b music and hundreds of others rushed into the music and media conference circuit to launch their players, platforms, interfaces, subscriptions and services to vie for dominance in this new world. Similarly, the majors were engaged in their own contest to achieve dominance with a new format that they would create, own and control. Research companies like Jupiter Communications announced with confidence that Sony's Magicgate system would dominate the market, eventually stepping into the relam of the MP3 file as the defacto standard. BMG announced Pressplay and revved up their own plans. The new technology landscape was fast becoming a school yard with a lot of balls in every sense. Each company wanted their own, controllable, ownable, licensable system; they did not want to give up their precious content rights to something unsecured. It was a world where online music-related content companies pitched their investors on long term skyrocketing revenue streams from an industry gone digital, and found a goldmine of available cash. Suddenly there were new media music themed conferences everywhere, with impassioned keynote addresses from rock stars and rappers, well-known techies, legitimate politicians and snake oil salesmen who sprung forth everywhere like a fungus after a long warm rain. They would all proclaim more or less the same thing: the commencement of a new and holy alliance—technology and music, serving each other in a more pure, more fair and more accessible way than had ever been imagined.

Each group would see the other as their savior: new media companies would quickly learn what those in the A&R community have always known—that there are enormous numbers of people in the world recording music they feel passionately enough about that they will demand your ear...and a record deal. Some of them deserve record deals; most do not. The affordability and simplicity of high quality recording devices like ADATs and ProTools increased the overall output of fairly well-produced recordings, but the industry has always had only so much room for new music to squeeze through its channels, which inevitably leaves a large number of passionate music makers out of luck and desperate for listeners. For labels, publishers and anyone interested in finding a handful, or even one, single great artist that will rise above the dreck and masses, wading through the constant barrage of mediocrity from artists and available material had always been "homework" responsible for eating up time rather than being enjoyable.

Enter the world of hosting and posting MP3s. Enter MP3.com. Finally, a company with an equation of success for turning sheer quantity into a quality in itself. The mission for companies like MP3.com was essentially the opposite of the record labels in terms of their quantity to quality ratio; suddenly it was the more artists the merrier. And better still for them to use the site's own automated tools for editing their profiles, and having time on their hands to add sound and image files; with dozens of new submissions hourly, the perceived value of the site grew exponentially.

Companies like MP3.com truly defined the business school mantra of servicing an unmet need—and the word amongst musicians worldwide seemed to spread like wildfire worldwide: post your music on MP3. Maybe it was the name, maybe it was the timing, but this was definitely the place. By the end of 1999, musicians would speak of MP3.com as if they had joined the Moonies or the Gen X version of EST—it was beyond a place for the unsigned to post and sell their music, it was a religion. The tiny percentage of artists generating sizable revenue from the site were touted by the company and its members as living proof that a valid and new paradigm for independent musicians to thrive economically—outside of the mainstream of the industry—had indeed arrived. Wall Street agreed. Other players jumped into the fray, each with their own vision, or worse—multiple visions—nearly to the point of corporate schizophrenia.

There were online labels and distributors like Emagine and Atomic Pop who were formed and funded with the idea of distributing music online; there were the new music "discovery" sites like Farm Club, I am, Riffage and Garageband. Video streaming of concerts would be the next holy grail; no longer dependent on networks like HBO to charge high pay-per-view fees, companies like Pixelon, Icast and Ibeam would pay substantial licensing fees for video broadcast rights to superstar level acts such as the Backstreet Boys and Paul McCartney, all for a broadband pay-per-view audience that didn't yet exist.

Talent discovery itself, it was argued, would be in for a major over-haul. A&R people were becoming perceived as outdated gatekeepers of new music and talent—posting music and letting the people decide on the merits of the music business would be the way of this new and democratic world order. "Brick and mortar," or physical distribution, would cease to exist and so would the ways of the old world.

It would be a time of reckoning for music executives—many an A&R and marketing staffer who had put in the years to rise slowly through the ranks and attain prized (and relatively stable) executive appointments, would leap at the chance to trade spacious corner offices and lucrative employment agreements for risky positions at start-ups with potentially lucky stock options and cheap IKEA desks. Executives making a quarter of a million dollars a year at major labels would routinely be stunned with envy to hear their dot com colleagues talk of cashing in stock options worth millions. The difference in potential earnings was astronomical, the lure of quick and easy riches never more visible.

But, like a Greek tragedy written to warn against the evils of greed, this music "space" as it had come to be known was in for some reality checks that were coming in fast.

E-PILOGUE

Many of the companies listed above are long gone, having blown through millions of dollars in overhead costs, dubious acquisitions, hirings and firings. Hundreds of millions of shares, once representing pie in the sky riches and retirement funds, aren't worth anything—or in some cases, even less if cashed out options still require cash payments.

And SDMI never happened. Perhaps the amateur programmer from Sweden who cracked the DVD copy encryption code that the video industry spent 12 million developing was a discouraging sign. MP3.com seemed to take on the characteristics and career trajectory of an artist itself—the kind who starts out grateful, earnest and independent...and ends up hard, glossy and demanding better vodka backstage. After artist-friendly headlines and soaring stock prices, the company would go on to betray much of its original membership by selling out to Universal and pushing their artists, but not before launching their controversial "my MP3 locker" service, which would eventually invite lawsuits from dozens of record labels and artists like Bob Dylan, Billy Joel and James Taylor over copyright infringement. Sony's Super Magicgate technology never even launched.

The story is far from over, but many music and tech folks continue to look to Apple computers for the future—my own guess is that they are poised to finally get it right, and very, very soon.. The impact of technology on the business is a complex issue, and is worth exploring with some of the professionals who are likely to both affect and be affected by, the way the business responds to the changes we've discussed. Let's dive in a bit deeper and hear directly from those on the front lines of these issues...

NEW TECHNOLOGY ALLOWS FREE TRADING OF MUSIC, CIRCA 1968
MICKEY HART AND BOB WEIR WEIGH IN ON FILE-SHARING

What happens when new technology allows music fans to bypass record companies' traditional distribution channels and make copies of new music to be freely traded without paying the artists? Ask the Grateful Dead—it's a topic they practically invented. Some thirty years ago, the band decided to allow their fans to bring recording devices to their concerts and create their own recordings free of charge to trade amongst themselves without having to go through a record company or ever visit a Tower Records or a Best Buy. To this day, some of the band's best recorded material isn't offered for sale anywhere, it's on a bootleg cassette, DAT, or CD somewhere, made by a fan while attending the concert. How does that affect their careers and financial lives? Difficult to measure, especially given their unique audience, but it probably had a substantial impact—for the better. The Grateful Dead (and its subsequent post-Jerry Garcia incarnations) enjoyed perhaps the longest running and most successful professional operation in the touring industry, consistently out-grossing artists with much higher record sales figures. I caught up with Mickey Hart and Bob Weir on their summer leg of the Further Festival just before Napster was shut down. It only made sense to solicit their thoughts on the more modern version of the phenomenon they themselves boldly put forth more than three decades ago:

Justin Goldberg: There is much talk right now about MP3 file-sharing and its impact on the music industry. I would imagine there are some familiar elements to this debate, as the Grateful Dead has created such a legacy of free trading of music. How is this different?

Mickey Hart: We gave it away. It was our prerogative to give it away. It wasn't taken from us.

JG: And that would be the key?

MH: That's the difference. In Napster, it's being taken without our permission. It's our intellectual property, we have ownership to some part of it—

not all of it, some of the things that come in the moment, we don't know who owns that. I mean, it took years for us to learn our skill and it is a business and that's how we pay our rent. What Napster really points to is that a new model has to be formed. You know, we started it years ago by letting people take. So this will spawn a new series of initiatives for how to distribute and make music. But music costs money to make. You have to have instruments, recording studios, machines, engineers; you have to travel; you have to pay the rent in order to live; you have to eat; you have to support your family. So if the music is taken from you and you can't get any kind of payment for it, it's unrealistic. Cyberspace is still an Earthbound technology, it doesn't live up there on Mars, you know, cyberspace doesn't mean it lives in an ether. It's still governed by some the laws, and it's attached to Earth. And there have to be laws, fair laws, that govern this new frontier. We're seeing the growing pains now. And of course it's freaking out the majors because they've been making a tremendous profit from their CDs and music, and the residuals and so forth. I appreciate that, but music being taken for free and traded without the permission of the artist, well, that's just not moral and that's just really wrong. And what it will do is it won't promote good music. All the good music will not be made, because it takes a lot of time and energy and money to make music.

Bob Weir: This is different and it's new. If an artist spends, oh, a couple hundred thousand bucks to make a record and then tries to put it on the market and everybody just pirates his record, he's not going to do that again. The fact is, he may be tempted to go out and get a day job. So that bird don't sing. On the other hand, it'd be nice to think that all intellectual property belonged to everybody. That's a Utopian sort of ideal, and it has obvious benefits for everyone. Somewhere in the middle is where this matter is going to be resolved, but I don't think anybody has enough of a grasp of it to really have a qualified opinion yet. People will maintain they do, that they're absolutely right that this is the way it should be, but the facts aren't all in and they won't be for a while. One thing we know is that technology will be here, it doesn't quite exist yet, but it will be here to deliver really high quality music over the Internet. By that time, hopefully, we'll have to have sorted out how it is that people are going to make a living making music, if there is no means of getting paid for it. It's going to be a real interesting question and music—music's really the canary in the coal mine here, and what happens with music is going to happen with all intellectual property in short order. People are going to need to have a reason to do something, or they won't do it, they won't do anything. How many people are just going to go and make music for fun? I used to, but I don't know if everybody can afford to do that. I can afford to do that now because I've done well enough in my days in music, but if I were young and starting out, I'd have to wonder how I was going to make a living if I wanted to make music but couldn't get paid for it. Are we going to lose the best and the brightest of the crop of musicians? Are they going to be bagging groceries or working in dot com firms in order to put food on the table? What are we going to do?

MH: Unless they just want to hear music live, which is another alternative. If it goes on like this, then people will only play music live. Or you'll just hear garage bands that want to give it away. They're journeymen. They're not necessarily the master musicians that you know and love: the Eric Claptons, the Bob Dylans, even the Lauryn Hills and the Santanas. It costs over a million dollars to make those records; [they're] very skillful and they take a lot of technology.

JG: Do you think it might drive people to do maybe what the Grateful Dead has done for years: alternative revenue streams, more performance-oriented acts?

MH: Sure, absolutely. But not everybody is a performance artist, and they shouldn't be driven there because of this situation. Some people, like Carly Simon or many other artists, they *can't* get up in front of people to perform because they have stage fright. Robbie Robertson, he gets physically ill, and he's a marvelous musician. So he should have the right to be able to record and to make his living in the studio. This is not for everybody, going out in front of thousands of people every night and baring your soul. It's a scary, scary thing, if you don't really love it and have a passion for it.

BW: And not all good writers are performers. Robert Fripp has a point; for him, and he's very visceral about this, he says that watching people record his live shows is like watching somebody rape his wife. You know, he doesn't particularly care for that, and he has reasons, solid reasons that he can state to support that. We have been on the other end of that scale; as soon as we're done playing it's off into the cosmos, it belongs to whatever ears it falls upon. We've got to sort all this stuff out, but it's going to take time. The people who want everything to be free right now are going to see in short order that the quality of music is going to suffer.

· · · · · · ·

THE HOTTEST CD ON THE SALES CHART: THE BLANKS

ATTORNEY

CHRISTIAN CASTLE
Akin, Gump, Strauss, Hauer, & Feld LLP

Justin Goldberg: Let's talk about file-sharing and how that has impacted the music business.

Chris Castle: One of the problems that you have with file-sharing is that there is a push and a pull to it, and while it's undoubtedly contributing to some of the decline, it's also something that allows people to discover new music. On the one hand, you have managers who, trying to promote new acts, want to have their band on the current file-sharing bazaar, and at the same time they know that it's a dangerous path because ultimately it's gonna cut into their income.

I recently came back from Austin and was talking with some artists who are trying to break out and sell CDs at their shows; they appreciate all the promotional value from file-sharing services, but they know that if people can burn their recordings into CDs, they won't buy the CD at the show. Nowhere does it come home more directly and more pointedly then when someone who is only selling CDs at shows—they notice the decline immediately. So, the artist isn't making money, and the listener is not really exposed to anything else the artist wants him to hear.

No artist that I know of ever sat down and said, "Okay, let me record one good song and 12-13 bad ones," that's just not the way it works. But if you listen to the kids who are doing the file-sharing, that's a very common opinion. The reason you should have to buy the whole record is because that's the artist's conception and their creative contribution to the music industry. To me, it's the ultimate commodization of music that people are justified in getting their hands on one or two recordings by a particular artist as opposed to experiencing what the artist wanted them to experience by listening to an entire record.

MANAGER

JORDAN BERLIANT
General Manager
10th Street Entertainment

Jordan Berliant: There has been this trend, especially in developing artists, to sell their CDs through retail at very, very low prices compared to where frontline superstar artists sell. They may have a $18 or $19.98 list price on a superstar artist, but you might be able to find a Vines record in the store for $7.99. There does seem to be a little price elasticity there, especially given the demographics in the buyers of new artists these days, which are kids with a limited disposable income. Does that [lower price] discourage Internet piracy? I think that in some degree it does, but to some degree Internet piracy is also a reflection of the perceived value of an entire album to a consumer. I believe that very few albums are released that are complete entertainment experiences anymore, and I think consumers are tired of shelling out fifteen or twenty dollars to get one or two songs they like. And I think that has more to do with decline in sales and adds more fuel to the piracy than the economics.

JG: Are you suggesting that Internet piracy has more to do with the decline of great albums than people think?

JB: Y'know, when I was growing up, you could go buy a Pink Floyd album and you would enjoy listening to the album in its entirety. How many albums can you go out an buy and want to sit down for forty or fifty minutes and listen to from beginning to end anymore? That doesn't seem to be the way that consumers behave anymore, and I have to attribute a lot of that, from my own personal experience, to not really looking at albums as complete entertainment experiences anymore, but rather as vehicles or carriers for one or two hit songs and with the remaining songs there to justify an album price. If you look at where the hardware manufacturers have been moving toward—whether it's the three hundred CD jukeboxes that will play a song randomly and then go to the next one, or MP3 players that allow similar functionality—almost all of it serves the song-by-song jukebox mentality as opposed to a long-playing mentality. And I think the industry needs to get back to being able to market CDs as complete entertainment experiences. Think about it: people are spending a lot of money on DVDs, but they're getting a complete entertainment experience when they watch a movie from beginning to end. It would be ludicrous to have a three hundred DVD player that skipped from scene to scene of famous movies. And that's the big difference between the way the consumer behaves with respect to audio entertainment as opposed to audio-visual entertainment.

ARTISTS & REPERTOIRE, PRODUCER, MUSICIAN
RON FAIR
President
A&M Records

Ron Fair: The connection point between the kid and the music itself has changed. The very nature of it has changed. Whereas growing up in the Summer of Love, being thirteen years old in 1968 and experiencing while it was happening and in real-time—The Beatles, The Stones, The Doors, Jefferson Airplane, Cat Stevens, Harry Chapin, Jackson Browne, The Eagles, The Who, The Fugs, Iron Butterfly, Joni Mitchell, Dylan, The Archies—when you bought a record in my generation, it was like a subscription. You became a fan. You signed up for the subscription, and when you bought that Beatles record, you bought the next Beatles record. You bought the next Who record. You bought the next Stones record. You loved the music and you became a part of that vibe. Maybe you liked this album better than that album. But everybody had every Simon and Garfunkel album. Everybody had every Cat Stevens record. Everybody had every Who record. We had them all and we would debate. When you buy a record today, you are not signing a subscription to an artist, you are just buying a record—if you even buy it. You're buying a record because you like a song, or because you like a video, or because it reminds you of something, or because you got laid to it; but there is nothing more to it than that. So, it's like the blouse in the window of Wet Seal. A little girl is walking down the mall and she says, "Mom! Look at that blouse with the little Indian collar and that necklace. I want to see that." "No, no, we have to get home, you have to do your homework." "No, please, Mom, please, let me see it." "Okay." They walk in, look at the mannequin. "How much is that?" "Mom, it's only twenty-two bucks. Please, please. I could wear that with my brown skirt, I could wear it with my blue jeans, I could wear it with my white shorts, please buy me that blouse." "Okay." Mom buys the blouse, kid goes home, wears the blouse once, twice, three times, ends up at the bottom of the drawer. She wore it. She liked it. It was cool. It still ends up at the bottom of the drawer. That's music. That's where we are today. It ends up at the bottom of the drawer.

ARTISTS & REPERTOIRE

JASON MARKEY
Immortal Records

Jason Markey: I think kids know what music they want, they know how much they want to spend on it, they know what the value of it is in their own heads. Whether that's the value the artist or the label thinks it's worth, it's the value of what the kid is willing to spend for it. I think in the film industry they're in the same place with DVDs that the music industry was in when CDs came out. It's really the first time quality movies have been available to own. Videotapes always broke, or had lines in them, or had static or whatnot. And the sound quality wasn't that great. Now you're getting amazing audiophiles who want great movies in their homes with great sound. And the experience of being involved in a movie is much greater than being involved with an album because when you're getting a movie on DVD, more than not, you're also getting great music in the movie, which is making DVDs sell for what retail thinks they're worth, which is around twenty bucks. I don't know if they're going to have a backlash or not, but people are buying them. They feel like a movie is worth more than music.

Justin Goldberg: And right near that shelf with the $20 DVD is the $17 soundtrack to the same film.

JM: People feel a movie is worth $20 and a CD is only worth $5. Who's to say which art is worth more? Which are you going to use more?

JG: The CD.

JM: Right, so why is that worth only $5? Let's say a guy goes to the movie theater. He went and saw the next sequel to *Star Wars* or something. He paid $10 for his ticket to see it, he paid $4 for his tub of popcorn, he bought a $4 Coke and a $3 bag of candy. This guy's already $20 in the hole for the movie. And then maybe parking in a big complex where he brings his girlfriend and has dinner or whatever. So for the two tickets, he's $50 to the wind on this movie already. Right? Then at the same time, we build this excitement up for him in the movie industry that it's coming out on DVD, there's a commercial, he gets all excited, he goes to the store, he pays $24.99 for the DVD. Now he owns the movie. Now he's $75 in the hole to this movie. Maybe it's *A Bug's Life* and his kids flipped out over it; now he owns all these stuffed animals, he's got a blanket, he's got t-shirts. Now he's maybe $300 of a fan of this movie: That used to be music. What happened to that? Where is that excitement? Where did it go?

JG: And if there is still excitement, record companies aren't banking on it.

JM: Record companies aren't banking on it because record companies aren't sharing in where the bands are making their profits. The bands are making the profits on their concert tickets, which aren't $5 anymore like they were in 1971. Tickets are now, for an average band, $40 plus a $10 service charge. It's fifty bucks for one ticket. To take someone to a show on a date is $100 plus food and drinks. Is it that exciting? The movie is ten bucks, the concert's a hundred. Which one do I go to do on a Saturday night? To buy the t-shirt, it's not $10 for a t-shirt anymore. It's thirty-five bucks, and then you don't want the t-shirt, you want the hoodie, which is $75. Because that's the cooler piece of merch to have. And there's no program. The program used to be five bucks at the door. Now you go in, you stand in line for twenty minutes to get this $30 book and it's a piece of shit. There's nothing in it. I don't know anything about this band. Why am I spending $30 on a book? It's so expensive to enjoy music now. We've priced it out of the range for the kid. When I was a kid, I went to Corvette's in South Field, Michigan; I bought the Ted Nugent record for $2.50, which was probably a lot of money back then. I spun that record so many times. I got into it. I'd go to the concert for $5 or $10; I'd be way into it. I'd get the t-shirt for five or six bucks. And they gave you something because you had a 12" album—and the artwork was such a big part of the thing, you'd open it up and you'd pull it out and there'd be a big 24x16 poster. You could hang it on your wall. You felt like you were a part of that artist. In today's world, you get a little 5x5 CD, you get a little booklet with a little bit of information in it that means nothing. There's no ownership of the band anymore. And if there is ownership, it's so expensive: you're looking at $50 for a ticket, you want to have a drink at the show, you've got parking for $15. Your girlfriend is another $50 for the ticket. Then you stand in front of the band you came to see for just twenty minutes. You don't feel like you sat in front of an epic movie for two hours, then went online with that movie and you played the games they're putting online leading you up to the sequel or whatever.

JG: So we've basically priced music out of reach of the consumer?

JM: And the consumer is saying, "Price it back down where I can afford it and I'll be a fan. If not, fuck you." There will be someone else willing to give it to me, or I'll listen to the local band. I'll go to the pub and drink a beer and listen to a local band. And they'll give me their CD for free.

ATTORNEY

FRED DAVIS
Partner
Davis, Shapiro, Lewit, Montone & Hayes

Justin Goldberg: As we both know, entrepreneurs involved with Internet record labels flooded our world for a relentless few years there. Here we are four years and a few hundred million dollars wiser, and you can't point to even one single artist that was broken by an Internet venture or online label. Why do you think the entire Internet-as-a-record-company concept failed?

Fred Davis: Because nobody appreciated the music. Nobody stopped to listen to the music. They thought that through volume and quantity they'd break records. Nobody understood the process of breaking records. We've had two major frontiers in our industry over the last forty years: one is the rock explosion in the late sixties, and one is the hip-hop explosion in say, the eighties. And those merged by entrepreneurs who were getting in for the music. They were great A&R people: Chris Blackwell, Jerry Moss, David Geffen, Russell Simmons. They listened to the music. It's about the music. It's about the music and the message, and they figured out how to market and promote it to the audience. The Internet explosion that you just referred to was the antithesis of that. It was saying, we don't have to listen, let's just put it up on the Web site and somebody else will discover it. No. You need to select the best. If you make the right selection and you hone in on the best, it will sell.

4

THE ZEN OF A&R

the process and psychology of getting signed

THE HIDDEN FACTORS OF TALENT ACQUISITION: THE LEMMING PRINCIPLE

Whether you are an A&R mogul, or just an assistant with a vibrating Rolodex in the A&R department, you will eventually notice your own opinions sounding vague and ephemeral as you perfect what has evolved into a music industry art form in itself: the art of saying something without ever voicing a real opinion (because you are never sure).

COMMITING TO ANYTHING BUT AN OPINION

If you are puzzled by this, don't be, it's meant as a lighthearted rip on the strange and occasionally uncomfortable tendency that talent acquisition professionals have toward committing to an actual opinion. But let's look at this tendency from the A&R perspective for a moment: why take the risk of publicizing your musical opinion about any artist being shopped when you don't know if that artist will wind up on your roster or somehow associated with other business that you're doing? It can be downright dangerous for your career to commit to an opinion about new music if you work for a big company where big money is at stake on creative decisions. After all, it's possible that someone you report to creatively may actually like an artist you dislike. If you've already professed your opinion, you could have myriad problems. Consider this: imagine that you find out later that a

Justin Goldberg, *Wheels & Deals*, watercolor and acrylic on canvas, 48"x48"

Music insiders will likely recognize many familiar industry faces in this piece, titled after *Hits* magazine's widely read A&R column, which has chronicled talent signing activity in its own inimitable fashion for decades. The repeating text appearing amidst and beneath the "players" is taken from a *Los Angeles Times* article criticizing the industry's tendency to sign copycat artists and then compete for expensive deals in what has become known as a "bidding war." It reads—"Millions of dollars are routinely thrown at mediocre acts in a prime example of the lemming principle. Insecure executives see others going after an act so they think it must be valuable." I couldn't resist including an article like that in a painting like this! Industry insiders will also likely recognize the logo for Dominick's, a Beverly Hills restaurant owned by music industry executives.

label president has a relationship with the artist-in-question's attorney or manager, and signs that artist and you wind up having to work with them.

Artists, managers and lawyers often complain when A&R people show interest in an artist and maybe even meet with the artist, but then avoid pulling the trigger, or—sometimes even more frustrating—avoid passing on the artist. Try not to imagine this as a negative commentary on the music—it's just business. From an A&R perspective, it's important to be involved and get to know who's active in the market. Sometimes A&R people are just sniffing around, waiting to see if someone else jumps. If someone else is interested, that can help them justify trying to bring you in to their company. It's a frustrating game with some inherent guile but that's just how the process goes. Don't take it personally, play the game with them instead and accept it the way you would accept an alien custom in a foreign country (think escargots, shark fin soup, deep fried Twinkies).

BLAME CANADA

Being a songwriter and a loudmouth, I have made the mistake of stating my opinion over and over throughout my career. I suppose it all started in 1992, with a new French Canadian singer who had been flown, along with the rest of my department, to a private showcase in Switzerland. Having only recently been hired, I wasn't originally supposed to be there and my flight was arranged at the last minute without much planning—or sleep, as I had been to a very late gig the night before. Arriving at my hotel in Switzerland exhausted and confused, the concierge presented me with a schedule of the night's events, which would begin with a long company dinner and toasts and end with a showcase of the company's priority acts from all over the world. Wonderful, I thought. The schedule I had in mind was a little bit different and slightly more focused on sleeping. Wanting to prove that I was a trouper, however, I showed up at the venue and sat through the first few presentations. Hoping to stage a low-key disappearance, I asked which band was up next. No band, I was told—up next was a pop singer, singing in French and English. My thoughts pretty much exactly were, "Oh great, I'm the rock A&R person and I haven't slept in three days and now I need to hear an unknown diva wannabe sing in French. Get me out of here."

"Hello, my name is Celine, it's so nice to meet you!" said a slender and energetic, albeit odd-looking, young woman as I was halfway out the door. I replied in kind. I then whispered to a colleague—is she any good? He didn't know, and I was too tired to find out. After waiting long enough to see her take the stage and sing a few notes, I decided it was probably going to be a great era for rock 'n' roll and she'd be worth skipping. No one would notice, right?

I caught hell the next morning for missing young Miss Dion's set, and realized that sometimes, sleep is overrated.

Justin Goldberg, *Jeff Buckley Ticket,* **watercolor on canvas, 15½"x25"**

Justin Goldberg, *Last Goodbye to*
Eternal Life (Buckley #2),
watercolor on canvas, 20"x14"

I made an even worse call with Jeff Buckley. When his management company sent some early demos, the office was abuzz about this artist, who had cultivated a following of die-hard believers in New York. With the tragic history of his late father's career as backdrop, most things about Jeff Buckley had an aura of mystery and a grasp of the religious. I fell in love his debut EP, *Live at Siné*, which was recorded at the now-long-closed Café Siné in the East Village; it was a haunting and personal recording. But when he showed up in Los Angeles for an office meeting, a private show-case and a subsequent gig at the El Rey Theatre, he struck me as a talented guy starting to believe too much of his own press. In between songs at both performances, he made unwarranted and snide comments deriding Los Angeles in favor of New York. It was an odd and ill fit with his talent and image and I said as much to the head of the company when she asked my opinion. That didn't go over well, as she went on to explain to me that breaking Jeff Buckley was to be the number one priority at the label. The next time I had an opinion, I kept my big mouth shut.

CODE CRACKIN' FUNDAMENTALS

A&R people are the matchmakers in the strange marriage of business and expression who decide the fate of musicians everywhere—at every level, from the garage to the amphitheater. But what is their mindset? Do most see themselves as guards at the gates of coolness, or are they merely the litmus test for the acidity of the people? The answer is probably both.

The important lesson to absorb first is to accept and believe that A&R people do not even have musical opinions per se, and as such they cannot determine whether or not you are talented or determine your future (only you can do that). So, if you've recently been turned down by a record label, publisher or other music professional, cheer up! Assume they know nothing. *But* if you gave them material without cultivating your

FYI

THE 6 COMMANDMENTS OF A&R WHEN SHOPPING TALENT

Repeat after me: I, talented artist/talent shopper/songwriter/producer/ mogul and possible genius, hereby recognize the following:

1. That A&R people at record companies are not hired to listen and imagine the potential in the material I give them, and that

2. Instead, they exist to preserve their own employment by identifying artists most likely to sell the most records in the shortest amount of time, and that

3. Usually this means that artists who have proven they can sell records and/or draw and/or dramatically impact live audiences are more likely to be signed, and

4. I will not expect any A&R person to have a positive opinion of my material or project until and unless there is a competing offer on the table,

5. I acknowledge that physical attractiveness is not always part of the equation, but usually helps.

6. Genius knows no boundaries.

**Justin Goldberg, *Will the Wolf Survive (From Waylon to Shooter)*,
watercolor on canvas, 24"x17½"**

Being the son of a prominent New York criminal attorney occasionally had some unusual perks for a kid about to hit fourteen: the first person I ever met in the music business was Miles Davis, and the second was Waylon Jennings. Surprisingly, it was Waylon who would make the strongest lasting impression on me. I eventually worked up the courage to send him demos of my own music only years later when I started thinking about leaving college to be a musician. Contrary to his tough exterior and outlaw image, he was surprisingly encouraging about my songs and available to talk music. My first dose of advice about the business would come from him, and I pass it on to you: when I asked him what I should do first, he said, "Always remember this: let them come to you. Don't go to them."

It would be years before I would realize just what this meant. This painting, titled after one of Waylon's albums in the early '80s, incorporates imagery from Waylon and his son Shooter's excellent Los Angeles based rock band, Stargunn. Check the Viper Room schedule and go down to catch them live.

story and offering valid reasons for them to find your project compelling, well, then you should assume that you know nothing.

After reading that, a lot of A&R people—many of them my friends—are probably ready to kick my ass; there are many A&R people who are extremely skilled and knowledgeable about music, making records and signing new talent. My point is that you should try not to be critical of their role, which is tough. Artists need to understand that they are responsible for creating the factors necessary to motivate A&R people and keep them interested. A&R reps are not employed by record companies to imagine what a rough demo might sound like if it only had great production, better songs, better players and a few hundred grand to record it, in a great studio with a $25,000 Neumann microphone.

THE CODE CRACKIN' FUNDAMENTAL PLAYERS

All representation is not created equal. You must realize, in the music industry food chain, great attention is paid to the positioning of the players. The career arc for A&R positions can be very short and often is as brutal as it is for artists themselves; lawyers, managers and A&R people must constantly survey the changing climate to see how they should be positioning their musical tastes and relationships in order to survive. In fact, some of the most successful A&R people are successful not because they signed anything of particularly massive sales/critical acclaim, but because they are skilled at the political process of remaining employed. Often this means preserving the status quo and not going out on a line to try to sign expensive talent who might put the company at risk. This is called moving up by standing still.

Many a mediocre band has been signed because of top-notch legal representation and/or management, and the reverse is of course even more true—many a genius or potential pop phenom has been overlooked because his or her music was presented by someone who didn't carry enough clout in the political picture. The music industry is all about relationships and how these relationships really work can often be difficult to identify. To make things even more confusing, sometimes big representatives don't have the time to focus on you, and it doesn't matter who you're linked to if they're not willing to lend their influence and relationships to helping move your career forward.

**Justin Goldberg, *Goldenears at Goldeneye: Guy, Ron, Naomi & Adam in Ocho*,
watercolor on canvas, 48"x43½"**

There are some people who just seem born to find talent: Maverick Records'
Guy Oseary is pictured here with Dreamworks' Ron Handler. As the title hints,
this painting was modeled on a photograph I took in our jeep during a romp
through Ocho Rios in Jamaica. We had the privilege of spending some time
at Chris Blackwell's [the founder of Island Records] home, named after the
James Bond film *Goldeneye*, which was written there. Adam Clayton [of U2]
was staying there with then girlfriend model Naomi Campbell. (Their faces
float above the clouds in the painting if you look closely...)

LABELS: WE ARE DYING FOR HOT NEW TALENT!!
WE HAVE NO GREAT NEW ARTISTS!!
BUT PLEASE!! DO NOT SEND US MUSIC!!
(Or, the Catch-22 of Unsolicited Materials)

People often wonder why record companies will not accept unsolicited materials. If they are so interested in finding new great records to release, what gives? Well: Lawyers. And money. If you monitor the trades, you'll always read about some songwriter claiming that he helped Mick Jagger (or someone like him) write some multiplatinum hit and is now suing for a chunk of the fortune. Defending such claims, even when they are ludicrous, is a time-consuming and expensive task for copyright holders, so companies generally like to limit their liability by not accepting materials that they don't request. It's also the least that A&R people can do to all but stop new music submissions from piling so high they can't find their telephones.

TALENT SHOPPING 101:
YOUR ONLINE PACKAGE

All Access Passport

CD-ROM

You *could* use your All Access Passport program to send out your music or your promotional puffery to a long list of A&R people. But you would be wasting your time and postage. Consider this: A&R people are under tremendous pressure to find the "right" talent to sign for their labels and as such they are routinely flooded with material to review. Throwing out a pile of unsolicited music is an easy and every day affair in an A&R office—just check out the dumpster in any label's mailroom. While it would certainly be nice to imagine that all music is treated equally and given equal airtime, by a fair and orderly A&R listening panel in the sky, the truth is that the kind and amount of attention given to new music is almost entirely dependent on how and who presents your music. It will also rely heavily on the action you've got going for your music, in terms of either radio play, press, live performances, or impressive online activity. And as closed as those doors may be on the record and publishing side to "unsolicited" music, the doors to many other music professionals who do have direct or indirect channels into A&R are actually often quite open. It's an equation of knowing who to approach in the right order and then locating them.

PIECING TOGETHER YOUR STORY:
The First Approach

The first step towards generating awareness, your buzz or "story"—all the elements you will need to eventually approach A&R—begins with getting copies of your music out to people who have those open channels, and (of course) first asking them if it's okay to send it. This is not only something you should do out of common courtesy, it also helps to plant a seed about the project in the minds of those you send materials to; they are more likely to pay attention to something they have been told about prior to its arrival. If your interaction with the person you are sending material to is positive, whether via email or on the phone, it can also help to establish the beginnings of a desirable professional relationship. When you send material without any personal connection, it's a lot like receiving one of those junk mail offers from some company pushing a new vacuum cleaner or a way to clean up your Visa bill; it is just too east to toss everything into the garbage—don't let that happen to your music.

A BRAVE NEW EMAIL WORLD:
Today's Music Business Office

In the old days (say, prior to 1996), the music industry was eternally ruled by the telephone—making plans for recordings, showcases, finding artists, gossiping and doing deals. Fed Ex, UPS and U.S. Mail were there to send the materials of music around, and messenger services were there to hand-deliver items like DAT tapes of freshly recorded material. Today's music industry office largely looks the same (at least the ones still occupied with actual people) but for one dramatic paradigm altering detail—email.

Emails. We all get way too many of them, but there is no denying their worldwide impact on almost every industry. In the music business, email has taken over almost completely—replacing human conversation in a way few could have anticipated, occasionally replacing complete lines of communication between some. With its ability to transmit audio and video media, it has also evolved into an entirely new method for finding and promoting new music. Email essentially begins and ends most music professionals' days at the office. The workday now revolves almost entirely around email: meetings are scheduled by email, documents are circulated by email, directives are given via email, major company announcements are delivered via email, the day's to do lists are circulated by email, and most work is done in email. People get hired—and fired—all via email. That's a lot of email.

Email is an odd media as well—it's at once both intimate and remote. It seeks immediate response and allows direct access, but not everyone is email savvy or on the same schedule of checking or returning emails. In fact, a great number of "people at the top" dislike using email for that very reason; in some ways it disrupts the traditional chain of command that defined the corporate hierarchies for decades. It used to be that no one knew exactly what the CEO thought, and that distance defined the sensibilities of how companies were run. Now the mailroom clerk can zap the CEO with some of his own thoughts about the company's budget or new signing. Then there's "Instant Messaging," which allows for multiple and simultaneous (yet silent) conversations. Add to the mix everyone's cell phones with text messaging, PDAs, Apple's iSight video chats and other mobile messaging gadgets and you have a brave but confused new world that is highly connected at all times.

There are some fantastic benefits—and drawbacks—to today's easy access to just about everything, online. The benefits for musicians are obvious—you can transmit music via MP3 files, either posted on a Web site or transmitted as an attachment to your emails, at almost no cost. If you are trying to reach a large number of professionals and turn them on to your music, only a few years ago this could have meant hours or days of preparing a "mailing" which usually included printing and assembling mailing labels and affixing them to padded envelopes with notes, letters, photos and once it was all in place, a small fortune was required for postage. You may still want or need to send physical copies of your music or promotional materials for a variety of reasons we will examine later in this chapter, but there is no denying that the overall reach and degree of effective communication provided by the Internet is remarkable. The very idea that your music can make its way from your computer into the speaker system of an A&R person's office halfway around the globe in the time it takes to read this sentence is nothing short of revolutionary; this chapter is devoted in part to examining how you can best take advantage of

FYI

A&R EMAIL RULES
1. Do not instant message people you do not know personally.
2. Do not attach large files (such as MP3s) to emails unless requested to.
3. Do not write unsolicited novels (unless you are a novelist)—keep your emails short.

this technological feat, because with new paradigms come new rules and acceptable ways of behavior, even online.

EMAIL ETIQUETTE:
Some Rules and Some Even More Common Mistakes

This section should not be about realizing that the enclosed CD-ROM can be used to spam unsuspecting A&R email accounts. Quite to the contrary: it's about building your enterprise step by step and finding the right ears for what you do in the right order. Some basic no-no's include instant messaging people in the industry whom you don't know personally; I can't tell you how disruptive it is to receive bizarre requests to "chat" on instant message programs with people I do not know when I'm in the middle of an important call or other instant message communication with someone relevant to my business day. It is rude and almost always seems to come from someone seeking an easy industry "in," which simply doesn't exist. If you have a question for an industry professional, present it like a professional, in a normal email. If you are an instant messaging fiend (and I know you're out there), save the urge for when you have a relationship with that professional. Many companies who offer instant messaging services, such as AOL and Yahoo, offer features for blocking unwanted "IMs," but even being presented with a request can be off-putting.

MUSIC INDUSTRY ADDD
(Attention Demo Deficit Disorder)

I strongly suggest that you do not send actual MP3 audio files as "attachments" unless they have been specifically requested. For all the talk of easy MP3 file sharing because of their relatively small size, they are actually fairly large files to be transferring them back and forth for everyday listening. (I hope this book will last on the shelf long enough to have someone laugh at the previous sentence, as it's almost certain the standard will shrink in size and be called something new—but as of this writing MP3 is still the standard.) Many email accounts cannot accept large files, and most MP3 files of a single song are typically between 1.5 and 3 megabytes. For people who cringe at reading the very word "megabyte," this means that most music industry professionals, who typically have high speed connections, will spend around 2-4 minutes downloading your music. That's a short amount of time if the recipient requested the MP3 and is compiling material to burn music, but it can seem an eternity to someone with a short attention span and no idea what they are receiving.

If you are sending MP3 files to someone who will receive them on a dial-up connection, forget it!—the MP3 could take anywhere from 12-25 minutes to download—clearly not an effective way to introduce your music to first time listeners.

STREAMING VS. DOWNLOADING

The answer to this dilemma is choosing instead to "stream" your MP3 file/song so that a listener's MP3 "player" launches almost immediately and begins playing music. Streaming refers to having multimedia files (such as music) hosted on a server, so that the file itself does not actually need to be transferred to the listener's hard drive as a separate file, it can simply be accessed and played from another Web site. The music industry is always running late and out of time—don't give people an opportunity to tune you out because your technology choices slow people down. Trust me, this is an industry where Attention Deficit Disorder is practically a job requirement. Nobody waits.

ONLINE SOLUTIONS FOR STREAMING MUSIC AND INTRODUCING YOUR PROJECT

CD-ROM

There are hundreds of online music Web sites designed to aggregate MP3 files from every level of musician out there. Some are free, some are fee-based; several of the more popular locations are listed and linked to from the "get music" function in your All Access Passport disc. But there are some important elements to consider in this posting and hosting game when it comes to the venerable MP3 file:

ARTIST WEB SITE STREAMING

There are some decisions to make about presenting your music via MP3 files: most new artists today realize that a well-organized and professional looking Web site is a key first step in assembling the tools necessary to spread their music. Having an original Web site allows a full range of options, where artists can offer listeners the choice of either downloading MP3s or streaming their material at different speeds—one set of files encoded for slower online users who use a dial-up Internet connection, and another set for broadband users who can launch a higher quality audio file immediately. (We'll get into some additional detail on creating artist Web sites in the DIY chapter, so hang on if you're curious about what can help make your Web site rock.)

MP3.COM (AND THE LIKE)

One potential drawback of offering your music streamed or downloaded only from your Web site is that if you do wind up creating a phenomenal online buzz resulting in massive downloads and/or streams, there is no official claim you can make that it has actually happened. Often bands claim that they've had a few hundred thousand online visitors or downloads—a very meaningful statistic to a record label (if it's true). But proving it happened from your own Web site can be tough. Companies like MP3.com, however, track this kind of progress in detail—and artists who do show high numbers indeed can reap serious industry-wide attention. Often artists choose a combination of both solutions and have their own Web site's music section linked directly to their own designated artists area on sites such as MP3.com—this way artists maintain control over the appearance of the content on their own Web site but allow a company such as MP3.com to handle the music end, which is both cost effective and allows the artist to enjoy the other benefits of being a member of MP3.com (check their site and others like it for details; I'm not singularly promoting MP3.com in particular here, just noting that as of this writing their site is the most common choice for artists incorporating music streamed from a third party accessed from their own personal Web sites).

COOL TRICKS

SAVING EMAIL UPLOAD TIME: One good tip to keep in mind when emailing large files to groups of people is that if you are going to be sending actual MP3 files over the Internet, you should save yourself time by simply emailing the file to your own email address and then forward the entire email with the attachment, to your intended recipient. This way, if you need to again send the email to another recipient, you will no longer need to "upload" the file again and again to have it reach new recipients. The file will already be on the server of your ISP, and in your email out and in box. It will take you far less time to simply hit the forward button with the email already floating out there as an existing attachment.

SAVING EMAIL UPLOAD TIME: Another great angle on playing music within emails is to simply copy the html text where a file is located on a Web site where it's being streamed. That way, instead of emailing a URL location (e.g., www.theonlinemusicchannel.com/mgmt) you can copy the entire song title and section of the site where song can be found. If the html code is copied correctly (which won't be visible to the recipient) it will appear as if the song is playing directly from the text message area of the received email. This allows for a clean musical experience—unsophisticated online music listeners can hear a song quickly and without having to launch a browser and visit another Web site.

PLEASE REGISTER! TAKE A MOMENT TO MAKE SURE YOU NEVER HAVE A FREE MOMENT

Keep in mind, however, that many such companies are in the business of gathering data and members every musical step of the way. This means that if an A&R person or other talent evaluator finds their way to your Web site and attempts to listen to your music as it is being streamed via MP3.com and their servers, the A&R person is more than likely going to have to stop for a moment to first fill out a membership form with some personal details so he or she can "join" the membership in order to listen to music. Even though it's free and only takes a moment, it can slow down the momentum; even if a potential listener is already a member on such a site, the site may not recognize the "cookies" from a particular machine and will annoyingly require a new registration.

WAIT, I DON'T EVEN KNOW HOW TO MAKE AN MP3!

CD-ROM

You are not alone. Making MP3s is easy and the basic software needed to do it is available for free. There are many software options that will allow your computer to generate MP3 files from CDs and other digital music sources. Some of the most popular at this particular time include Music Match (which can be linked to from the All Access Passport disc or via www.musicmatch.com—although it's currently only available for PCs), iTunes (which is built into most new Macintosh computer systems), Win Amp, Windows Media, Real Player and Adaptec EZ CD Creator—all offer good platforms, value and other related products and services you may find useful. Most of the interfaces are fairly easy to navigate, and usually involve simply placing a prerecorded CD into a disc drive and compressing and converting the large ".wav" files on the CD into the smaller "MP3" files, which are relatively easier to have floating around the Internet.

OF COURSE I KNOW HOW TO MAKE AN MP3—BUT WHAT'S AN MP3i?

Welcome to the world of the interactive MP3 file. What is it? MP3is are simply MP3 files that are loaded with multimedia files to go along with the audio. MP3is can be played by standard MP3 players, but if they are played in a Win Amp player (version 2.81 or higher, to be exact) with a free plug-in, they will automatically launch into a multimedia audio visual presentation, complete with whatever promotional jazz you already have—animations, artist photos and lyrics all synched with audio. Depending on how you are presenting your music, taking the time to create a MP3i can be a dynamic way of introducing the sound, look and lyric of a new artist project. Although there isn't anything about an MP3i in particular that you couldn't create on your own Web site, for those users who do have the plug-in (something you can offer on your own artist Web site for free download) it's a dynamic single file that can launch on it's own without Internet access (once it's downloaded). Cool, huh?

THE NEW VERSION OF THE ELECTRONIC PRESS KIT OR "EPK"
Press kits are simply informational packages presenting pictures, lyrics, bios, reviews and other materials, which are typically sent to garner additional press or achieve other promotional goals. Electronic press kits have the same mission but go a step further in terms of presentation—they usually incorporate those very items into a video production. The idea behind an EPK is to break beyond the clutter with an inspired and cohesive presentation that requires and invites a certain focus—not usually something gained from a busy package composed of randomly assembled printed material.

Further to this concept is the online version of the EPK, which as specifically offered by a unique company called Sonicbids, has fast become the new standard for what you might refer to as the online EPK. They've even trademarked the very word EPK (why didn't I think of that!). What is Sonicbids? They are an online music company with an excellent, easy to use interface that allows musicians to create a standardized informational package, or EPK, containing all of the information and media that would normally be sent in a bulky padded envelope or box. While an EPK from Sonicbids in itself is arguably no different in content from most well-organized artists' Web sites, a compelling reason to set up an EPK there is that their interface is quickly evolving as a new standard for both sides of the talent equation: for musicians, the standard professional look combines easy to navigate categories of photos, bios, music, video, reviews and a live appearance calendar, even including a section for set lists and onstage technical requirements; for live music buyers, labels and perhaps most importantly, music festival and convention producers and organizers, the highly functional interface they see during the submission process allows for more accurate listening, more detailed review and faster processing when they receive applications and do their reviewing. Reviewers can leave comments for other reviewers which also helps streamline the process.

For musicians, the Sonicbids EPK also allows for instant access to over a thousand music events worldwide. Once your EPK is created on the site, top music festivals, conventions and contests can be applied for on the spot with no extra hassle or paperwork—major music convention events such as NXNE, Atlantis, NEMO, BillboardSong Contest, Locabazooka and the Newport Jazz festival represent just a small list of the companies who look exclusively to Sonicbids for their artist submissions. If you hate filling out applications as much as I do, do it once there and send that around forever. Another pretty cool feature with their EPK system is that even if you have already sent out a great number of EPKs as emails, your data is updated everywhere automatically as soon as you edit your own EPK data. So if your touring schedule changes a few days after you've alerted your fans or industry people with a mass email, the moment you make the changes to your own schedule, all of the previously sent emails automatically update when they are reopened by the recipients.

Occasionally, EPKs can really hit their mark: when Fiona Apple first started recording her debut album, *Tidal,* I happened to be working on another project in the same studio. I had heard some great things about her material, and there was an early expectation that she could truly become the "next big thing." Snooping around after the sessions, I heard some of the early mixes and was impressed enough to try to make an offer for her music publishing rights. But for some of the other executives at the company, who observed her timid demeanor and frail frame—darting from the studio courtyard to the label's cafeteria week after week—it was a stretch to imagine that this young singer-songwriter could hold an audience captive or endure the physical rigors of real life stardom and touring. But shortly after *Tidal's* completion, someone at the (now defunct) Work Group label had the idea to film her singing and create an EPK around the song "Shadowboxer." The intimacy of the performance was overwhelming; something was captured on video that made her talent simply undeniable. The EPK created such an immense buzz that even other labels wanted copies for themselves. Someone stole my copy from my office and I haven't seen it since. The point? If you've got the goods that come off well on video, an EPK is a great and immediate intimate introduction to an artist.

CD-ROM

The Industry Contacts category, which is the first category "box" on the All Access Passport, has twenty-seven juicy categories for you to dive in and start networking. But not so fast! You should not be sailing into those waters unarmed. You should at least make sure that a few of the tools we've described thus far are easily accessible to you on your computer. Let's review again what they could include:

1. You should have 2–4 of your best songs encoded as MP3 files (or MP3is) and have them sitting on your desktop for easy email attachment access, and/or
2. You should have the same number of songs posted online for easy streaming access, and available from either your own Web site or have your material set up within the artist section of an MP3-oriented site like MP3.com and/or
3. You should consider creating an online EPK that will allow you to enter festivals and generally submit materials to anyone with an email address so they have a complete idea of your project from sound to photos without ever having to visit your Web site, make the effort to see you play live, or even reach for scissors to open your package.

If you have these digital tools literally at your fingertips, you are already way ahead of the game. Most people will be weeks behind you, as they call to request permission to send in big packages and CDs that get lost in big piles. So now we're ready to examine the pecking order of submitting materials out in the real world. Some of the categories above are easier to approach earlier than others, and certain categories should only be approached when you have reached a certain level of awareness, representation, radio play or sales as your career progresses. What are the easy targets?

CD-ROM

RADIO: In terms of your actual music on CD (or MP3 versions of your CD) getting airplay, the college radio category, the indie and underground radio category, and the worldwide online radio category may be considered "low hanging fruit" from the proverbial music opportunity tree. Although many of these stations will have completely varying tastes and be associated with various genres, the entry barrier is much lower than other radio venues. These types of radio stations all represent a much different financial equation than most commercial radio, which has evolved into an extremely competitive and complex mega system of advertisers and paid airplay that we'll review later, in Chapter 6: Radio Rules. Radio at this level is also filled with music lovers who actually want to find promising new music and play it on their station. Below is a letter I recently received from a college station after sending them a CD of a Los Angeles based band I worked with called ZÜ:

Subj: ZÜ
Date: 3/24/2003 1:25:34 PM Pacific Standard Time
From: music@███████████
To: Measarts@███████████

Justin,
Hey this is Adrian from WXAC. I just got the Zü album in the mail today. In fact, I'm listening to it right now. You definitely made a good comparison to Smashing Pumpkins and Radiohead. I'll add it to our formats next week and see if I can get some of my DJs to play it. It definitely will fit in well with the other stuff getting played right now. If you have any questions or need anything, feel free to write. Thanks for the music!
Adrian Chesh
WXAC Music Director

_____

And this was the letter that I had sent him with the CD:

Adrian Chesh
91.3 WXAC
Albright College

RE: ZÜ CD

DearAdrian:

I wanted to turn you onto a great new band I am working with called ZÜ.

They are based in L.A., and I would describe them creatively as eclectic pop with a commercial feel, say somewhere between the Smashing Pumpkins and Radiohead. The band consists of Omar, Erik Eldenius (drums), Steve Luxenberg (bass) and Mike Fonte (guitar).

There is a video of the song "Abedeen" on the band's Web site, which is located at www.zumusic.net. Please visit our management page as well for updates, which is at www.TheOnlineMusicChannel.com

Please give me a call after you have reviewed the disc.

Best regards,
Justin Goldberg

CD-ROM

PRESS: Similarly, there are all kinds of publications in the world that are hungry to review music. Some are online, some are very independent fanzines specializing in your specific genre—again, use the LSN genre gauge to locate exactly those companies that deal with your area of music. Obviously, the higher the circulation and reputation of the publication, the more difficult it usually is to obtain coverage. But this is a numbers game, and if you wind up with even one or two impressive legitimate written reviews of your release, you will have something to show those you need to impress on your campaign trail. The smaller publications listed in the Worldwide Indie Music publication directory and the American Music Publication Directory will be easier first targets for response. Remember to be polite, professional and follow up if you want results.

CD-ROM

MUSIC INDUSTRY TRADE CONFERENCES: Music conferences and festivals are also good first step activities for new artists. They occur all over the country and often a great early step for artists trying to connect with those who can help move their careers forward. With the Sonicbids EPK format, applying for industry trade conferences, festivals and conventions is a breeze. Create your EPK once and use the same template to apply for dozens of conferences you feel can be of benefit to your project.

CD-ROM

MUSIC SUPERVISORS: As we'll learn in greater detail in a later chapter, music supervisors play an active role in how music is used in TV programs and films. They are also often under budgetary and time constraints that compel them to turn to unsigned or independent artists in order to achieve a high production value at a low cost. While it's probably not right for me to label them "low hanging fruit," they are at least an option worth considering as this is an area of the music industry that is healthy and growing. Getting your music placed in a film or a TV show can often be a random affair because it is dependent on so many factors related to a show's needs and context, but if you're lucky enough to have some "synch" use, it's a great career booster. Exposure via film and TV has helped to launch and boost many careers.

A&R AND POKER: AN INSEPARABLE PAIR OF ACES

My good friend Jenny is an experienced poker player (actually, she's a fiend) and she kindly offered to help me put some of the early chapters of this book together in some kind of sensible order (thanks, Jenny!). As we sat in my office sorting through my randomly disorganized notes, I described to her how I wanted the book to have a focus on the psychology of A&R and how its peculiar dance is something that should be analyzed and mastered by aspiring artists just as much as they analyze and master a new recording technique. As I described some of my own experiences in A&R, the inevitable analogy sprung from her lips, "You know," she said, "this is really poker." And Jenny really knows poker.

Poker Jenny Says:
Lesson 1—Know How To Bluff

In poker, it often doesn't depend on what hand you have, it depends on what hand the people you're playing *think* you have. In the music industry perception is everything and people generally want things they can't have. It's a lot like dating someone in high school: if you play your crushes cool, you are more likely to wind up with who and what you want. Rushing out and proclaiming your devotion from the rooftops is usually the best way to ensure that who or what you want runs away from you as fast as possible. And thus it is with all things A&R. For either side of the equation, it is a delicate dance of bluff and intentions. Cultivating a sense of mystique and self-sufficiency creates interest. Asking people to confirm your musical direction and ability only puts you at another's mercy and almost invites criticism. Desperation is the ultimate turn off and the ultimate fear. Bluffing is all about playing it cool and pretending that you don't want what you want.

How does this relate to shopping talent? In other words, project an image of success. Don't talk about what it will be like one day if your this or that, make that day today. Be successful now in your own mind, at whatever level is truthful and reasonable, and project an image of self-assuredness and self-sufficiency. If you need money to best do what you do, don't make it an obstacle and an excuse for not doing anything at all. If you want or need to put together a band, fine, put it together as best as you can afford in terms of time and money. But don't let it keep you from writing new material and meeting other people who can be helpful to your career. Whatever it is that you *can* do with the resources you *do* have, use those resources and move your project forward.

Almost every day for the past fifteen years, I have received music-related packages from various sources at various stages of development. Some packages have lyric sheets, photographs, liner notes, extensive press kits, EPK videos and extensive CD inserts. Sometimes the most interesting packages are nothing but a CD burned off the board from a studio session. But so often deals result from packages that don't even exist at all—they're phone calls, they're tips at lunch meetings, they're rumors, an instinct or a vibe on the street through contacts you have come to trust.

How hard is it to get to A&R attention when some truly amazing musical uprising is happening? I'm sure there are great artists who go completely unnoticed all the time. But if there is a scene around a project or an artist in any way, I can assure you that it will be pounced on immediately no matter where in the world it is. Not too long ago I heard about a new band that was creating quite a stir in their hometown. I had a friend from college who had moved there who told me about the music and sent me articles from the local paper. The band didn't have a package together: there was no band photo, demo, or even a lawyer to hype it up on the telephone, and yet, somehow—after hopping on a plane for several hours, renting a car and navigating confusing local directions—I arrived at a small venue, in a small town, in the middle of nowhere...only to look around and see the same group of A&R weasels and lawyers I see every week on the Sunset Strip. There are millions of bands, but when something is just white hot everyone knows it immediately. It's amazing how quickly word spreads when something legitimately great is happening. If you are that great, and/or you can sell tickets or records at a local level that's substantial, A&R people—believe me—will find you. SoundScan systems are also set up nowadays at labels to locate artists unaffiliated with majors who sell above a certain level. Regional A&R scouts employed by majors labels are paid to scour every nook and cranny of the national english muffin. There are few places left to hide if you are the next Jimi Hendrix or Joni Mitchell (although, why would you?). And there have never been more venues for independent artists to play and have their music heard.

> If you are that great, and/or you can sell tickets or records at a local level that's substantial, A&R people—believe me—will find you.

The most important element in even getting to this point however, is in convincing others that you are on to something. Being onto something and creating a sense that you have a momentum all your own is key to knowing how to bluff. In my experience, this often directly relates to recording and releasing music on your own that generates positive response somewhere, anywhere—just enough to make a great impression and raise awareness about your music so that others will start to see that they might be left out of something you're onto.

> Be honest but be smart, be driven but not desperate.

That is the key to the psychology of the A&R mindset: they are interested in competing, they want to know what others are after. You must remind yourself the role of A&R is to identify promising uprisings in the music world, and most legitimate ones invite competition. Music companies, as we reviewed in the first chapter, have become less talent discovery or development machines as they are talent absorbing machines. The labels want less risky investments that will be more likely to be successful because they are proven; labels tend to actually do better with those artists because indie success sets up the systems, channels and relationships that make for higher sales when a indie project is ready to switch to a higher gear of reach and operation. Be honest but be smart, be driven but not desperate.

Poker Jenny Says:
Lesson 2—Know What A Good Hand Is

The best talent doesn't sit around waiting for their Kinko's copies to dry and coming up the with perfect font for their perfect record cover. Hot things are hot; they move fast; they connect quickly; they find a way. There are different kinds of A&R people, but most have to maintain a connection to what's going on in the clubs everywhere should something ignite. Even when record labels downsize and refuse to commit signing funds, they're still interested in having an awareness to what's hot because they can't afford to miss a chance at a huge moneymaker.

Not that there couldn't very well be genius hiding at the bottom of the demo submission pile, but the nature of A&R is the nature of the hunter: you can't give a pet snake a dead mouse to eat, it's got feel like it's chasing down dinner in order to survive. And thus it is with A&R, there has to be a compelling story, and compelling stories are the mouse. Many A&R departments are structured differently, but most have at least a few layers between the "scout," who first looks to sign talent, and the director level/VP level/president level/CEO who eventually pulls the trigger to get a deal done. So what does that make your job as the artist? When the A&R

scout/underling goes to bat for you at an A&R meeting, make sure you have a compelling story. This is where you need to know what a good hand is, and what makes a compelling story.

A compelling story can be almost anything. It really depends on your genre of music and what your angle is. A compelling story could be major film or TV usage of one of your wholly owned songs that you license with a music supervisor. It could be an extraordinary radio situation, where a major station takes a liking to your material and gives you a substantial number of spins, which creates a reaction with the public. It could be an unbelievably compelling live show. It could be a famous artist or producer being involved with your recordings. If you're a writer it could be a great cut by a big artist. It could be an opening slot for a major artist that garners terrific reaction. It could be indie sales that Soundscan reports in the realm of 5–10,000 units. It could be just that you are extremely attractive. But it has got to be something that rises beyond the everyday banter and reaches the point of relevant news.

FYI

RADIO OP KNOCKS, BAND WON'T LET IT IN

A great band I know with a great indie record came to my office recently to make a case to have me manage their career and help to get them signed with a major. Their frustration was immense. For over two hours they described the highlights of their past twenty-four months of career highs, ranging from opening for platinum-level artists to playing live on major radio stations. And yet, their A&R packages went unnoticed, their calls to labels unreturned.

As I am a fan of the band, I took the time to walk through the band's past year of activity and discovered what may have been their huge mistake: when a top five major market station decided to spin the band's single incessantly and featured them live on the radio, it hadn't occurred to them to make a big A&R push *then*, and they didn't have a lawyer who was really familiar with a lot of A&R people to help spread the word. Their amazingly fortunate moment came and went without having the relevant industry apparatus to capitalize on their luck. With a good following that probably already had peaked in number and was now starting to trail off a bit, and only a vague awareness within the A&R community, the band could be at a crossroads— around too long to be of interest to label people, but with nothing current in their story to make them a compelling pick for pitching in an A&R meeting.

Poker Jenny Says:
Lesson 3—Know How Long to Stay in the Game

Jenny also says, once you have a good hand, it's important to use it. Don't stay in the game past the point of your best leverage. Here are some true stories to help illustrate the point.

MANAGING YOUR EXPECTATIONS

Most artists dream big. The idea of having a radio hit and living large enough to have the *MTV Cribs* camera crew come over to your pad is at least within the realm of every musician's imagination. While it's important to maintain a level of confidence and project an image of self-sufficiency and existing success, it's still a good idea to live in reality in terms of reviewing potential offers that may ultimately save your career—even if they fall short of what you initially anticipate might come your way.

It's also important to understand the context of your music as a potential piece of product sold by a corporation, with motives that are driven by profit-hungry shareholders interested in cash, not the long-term artist development that might create the next Neil Young or help change socie-

Justin Goldberg, *Flicker Shtick*, watercolor on canvas, 23½"x8"

Dallas based rock act Flickerstick was chosen by VH1 for their *Bands on the Run* program, a reality-based TV program which documented the band's antics on the road as they performed in venues across the country as part of a competition between other artists. Although the group won the contest and was later signed by Epic Records, the band was dropped before the album was released. This painting depicts my own efforts to sign the band with then label partners Randy Spelling and Eric Hochstein.

ty for the better. So if you do manage to align yourself with appropriately connected managers or lawyers, follow your own conscience, but heed the advice and information they give you.

Of course great songs, great talent, following up properly, having good contacts and being nice stand for a lot and always will, but it's also true that you get a very short window to tell the world what your doing and why you are so great. If you hum along for too long without musically making it clear that you should rise above the background, you will be relegated to a lower rung in the ladder of the industry. That's okay for plen-

FYI

REGIONAL HYPE A LA MODE

Boiling Point was a hard rock band from Virginia. With a hometown following that managed to purchase over 4,000 of the band's debut indie release, and local radio support that initially garnered regional A&R attention for a few hundred miles in every direction, the band played sold-out shows in all the surrounding states and quickly found legal and management representation that was convinced they could convert the band's regional rise into competitive major label level attention and big signing advances. Showcases were arranged, A&R folks were flown in, label and publishing meetings were scheduled, meals were arranged and the derby of high expectations began. As it turned out, the 9/11 tragedy happened shortly after the band's showcases, and most activity in the industry ceased for many weeks. Suddenly, the band's momentum was dead. There was, however, one single indie label offer. It was low money, and an okay royalty, but enough for the band to get themselves out on the road and begin touring and building a national fan base that could lead to a long-term career. Stunned that their major label signing advance was no longer imminent, and still convinced that bigger attention lay just beyond the dark cloud hanging over the nation after the 9/11 tragedy, the band decided to turn down the indie offer and look elsewhere. A huge mistake! With dashed hopes and dampened interest even from their own representatives, the band would break up before another offer would ever arrive. It is easy to always imagine that the golden moment lies just around the corner; when you are creative person, you almost have to live your life hoping that it will all pay off in the end. But one must recognize opportunity when it knocks—not look back in hindsight and realize that a realistic expectation might have created a career instead of regret. Manage your expectations, and run your career like a business and not from an emotional point of view.

ty of people, and there are entire music industries around this level. It's nothing to be embarrassed about, but it's not the mainstream, major label rock star/pop star/big time that this volume is primarily focused on trying to dissect. Grading for Rock Star 101 is not cumulative and it's not based on a curve. It's a one-shot deal and it's based what's going on *now*. So when you reach a certain career point, it's time to go for broke at the height of your momentum.

MYTHS VS. REALITY:
Or, Why Development Deals Don't Usually Develop

Development deals are the kind of recording contracts that can often wind up offering not much recording and even less in the way of contract satisfaction. Artists are usually offered development deals at the start of their careers when there is not much competitive interest from other labels. These contacts represent a situation where an artist has a limited amount of leverage and is given a chance by a label to record some material; if the label likes what it hears, they can enter into a prenegotaited set of terms as set forth in the agreement. Over the years, I have often heard artists complain or proclaim that all they needed was just such a chance. If only they could get the ear of a record label president or some other A&R decision-maker, someone who could just provide them with the opportunity to make some professional-sounding recordings, they would meet the challenge and prove they could be the next Big Star. So do you want a development deal? You do? *No, you don't.*

FYI

YOU WANT ME TO FLY IN FOR A SHOWCASE!?
CAN'T DO IT, NEED TO WASH MY HAIR

Another artist I know was recently asked by a label head to fly cross country at the label's expense to do a private showcase. The artist had recently added a keyboardist, a new drummer and a guitar player to the existing lineup, but the label was only willing to pay for his expenses with the initial two other players. Short on cash to pay for his other players, he declined the invitation and decided to wait.

The timing for consideration is very short—things happen at lightning speed at label A&R departments, and if there's heat, you have to follow up on it because it can very short-lived.

There have been some great artists to have come out of development deal situations (as we'll hear from Ron Fair in the case of Christina Aguilera) but they are few and far between. Most development deal artists vanish without a trace. Why? Well, have you ever noticed how easy it is to lose cheap sunglasesses? It's like that: somehow it's harder to lose expensive sunglasses, but the cheap onces are easily lost and replaced. Artists often think they want to be given a chance, but that's not the strategy for creating a balance of power in a label/artist relationship. Development deals are one-sided and *heavily* weighted in the label's favor. Because the label is tossing the prospective artist a bone, the ball remains in the court of the label, and *if* an artist manages to get to the point of being interesting enough for someone at a label to spend a little bit of money on a development deal, then common sense suggests it can't take too much more effort to have that interest stoked a bit more—to the point where others might be interested and the balance of power could shift toward the artist and a deal that is not entirely one-sided. There are reasons for wanting to create a competitive situation with labels that are very real and concrete: competitive situations force labels to create more fair terms for artists. It's like that commercial for online mortgages: "When banks compete for your business—you win"; it's the same principle—you want labels to be competitive because that sense of value will translate into tangible resources that can make or break your career, or at least tip the scales. If you are an artist, you don't just want any chance, you want a *fair* chance. Fair chances come from creating situations that make the label feel they should value what they are signing.

So what does all of this mean? Do the right things—don't just hope to get lucky. Plan your luck. Do your homework. Try to take your career one step at a time and create the building blocks you need to succeed in the music industry game.

ZEN AND THE ART OF A&R

Justin Goldberg, *Farmer, 1995,* **watercolor on canvas, 14"x14"**

Long before Marshall Altman was an A&R guy, he was writing great songs like "California" and "Smile, Sadie" for Los Angeles based roots rock band Farmer, who were eventually signed to Greg Latterman's AWARE Records.

ARTISTS & REPERTOIRE, PRODUCER, SONG WRITER

MARSHALL ALTMAN
Columbia Records

First concert attended: Queen at Madison Square Garden in New York City

Best concert attended: Bruce Springsteen at the Brendan Byrne Arena, 1982

Top five album recommendations:
1. Bob Dylan *Blood on the Tracks*
2. Patty Griffin *Living with Ghosts*
3. Radiohead *OK Computer*
4. Randy Newman *Good Old Boys*
5. Bruce Springsteen *Born to Run*
6. Billy Joel *The Stranger*

Little known resume entry: Songwriter published by EMI Music Publishing, Record Producer.

Best project you were involved with that never made it big: Tsar

Recommended Web site: www.newyorktimes.com

Instruments played: Guitar, piano, engineer, programmer

Recent signings and upcoming projects: Marc Broussard, Jupiter Sunrise, Zebrahead (producing on all three)

SAY GOODNIGHT, THE PARTY'S OVER: IT'S ALL ABOUT THE HITS, BABY (WELL, AT LEAST THREE OF THEM, PLEASE)
SOME WORDS WITH MARSHALL ALTMAN OF COLUMBIA RECORDS

Justin Goldberg: How conscious are A&R people about bottom lines and budgets? Do they actually go through numbers sometimes at meetings and say, "This is what's happening this quarter..."?

Marshall Altman: I think everybody wants to think it could be a vast field of artist development, where we sign artists young and take our time. The truth is that none of that matters: all anybody wants is a hit. It doesn't matter if you're an indie band doing you own thing and you sell 500 records and some A&R guy hears your record and says, "That's a hit, we're going to sign you," or if you've just moved out to Los Angeles and you're playing at the Whiskey, and all of the sudden you write a hit and somebody hears it and says, "That's a hit, I want it." It doesn't matter to A&R people where they find you or where you came from. I think on the major label side, they're not interested in signing a band that can sell twenty five thousand records on their own unless they have a hit song.

JG: So, it's not so much driven by proven indie sales as it is by hit songs?

MA: I think there are some cases where bands will get signed without a hit. That does happen. If you have a hit song you will get a record deal, if you don't have a hit song the odds are going to be stacked against you. That said, the concept that turns the wheels are bands that don't care about major labels. They want to make it, they want to go out and play, they want to be able to sell records on their own terms and do what they want to do. That's how the business changes, at least on the rock/pop side. On the hip-hop side, I think it's a little different. I think there are fewer resources for a hip-hop band to go out and start touring without significant underground marketing.

JG: Let's say you get a great demo of a new hip-hop artist (as opposed to rock), what is some of thinking that relates to that genre in particular?

MA: The song needs to sound like it has money behind it, because money equals credibility and because it's such a track-intensive and production-intensive environment to get songs on the radio.

JG: What's the ideal ammunition needed to get people motivated at a label? Will one great song drive interest to the point of a record deal?

MA: Well, at Columbia it's three songs. I can't get anything signed unless there are three great songs. With the business being what it is, one great song doesn't guarantee that it's going to be on the radio. It has to be more than that, that's the kind of business we do here. A huge live presence helps, and the band having done their homework helps. But it all has to be part of a picture. If you're touring and you make a half a million on the road, but half of your set is covers, then the half a million you made doesn't matter. But if you can play shows and sell merchandise and kids know who your band is and know who you are, that's big. Usually, one follows the other.

Now, sometimes we roll the dice, sometimes you see something that's great and you hear potential but it isn't out yet or ready but I'll push to sign it because it's a competitive business and you can get lucky.

JG: What factors contribute to competitive situations?

MA: It could be a fart in the wind. Pretty much every situation is competitive, no matter what. It's rare that a band gets signed where only one A&R person knows about it. Because all of the managers, artists and lawyers are connected and have more than one relationship in the business. As soon as an artist gets an offer, they're virtually guaranteed to get another.

JG: Are there any hard feelings with that?

MA: It's business. It affects me, but that's the way the business is. I'd be just as apt to try to jump on somebody else's train as they would be on mine. In this business, we're all out to win. The thing about the business as an A&R person is, if you lose one band, there is surely another band to come along. I'm always looking for a way to ensure that I don't lose the band, to make it impossible for a band to go somewhere else if I want them.

JG: Let's talk about bands recording their own records in the hope that a major can pick it up and sign them and promote it. How expensive should it be to record? Do records need to sound a certain way? It does seem that indie records are often re-recorded when a band gets signed.

MA: The issue isn't whether a record costs $10 to make or costs one million to make, it's still going to cost the same amount of money to market and promote it if you want to really try to win big. And that's where the real costs lie. Even if you spend $500,000 making a record, at the end of the day that's gonna be 15-20 percent of the total cost to market and promote the record. To put a record out on a major label and spend 6-12 months marketing and promoting it actively can cost anywhere from $750,000 to $3-4 million just to keep it in the marketplace. And that's where the decisions get made. It's not, "Oh well, we spent half a million dollars signing this band and it's too much and we want to drop it"—that would be cutting your nose off to spite your face. It doesn't work like that. It's more like, "We've spent half a million making a record that we believe in and are spending another two million dollars to break this record because it is going to be worth it." That's how decisions get made.

JG: Any general thought on where music seems to be going?

MA: My hypothesis right now is that music is moving towards a more romantic place—rock and pop in particular are moving towards a more romantic era. The Smiths, The Cure, etc. Out of the ashes of the EMO movement will come bands like Jimmy Eat World and the next big band that breaks on that front will start to be exposed to the record buying community. I expect very emotional music that's going to bleed over into a more heartfelt sort of emotional soundtrack to people's lives.

I also think that the hard-core movement is softening up a bit, and they've started to become a part of popular culture as well. For urban music, for hip-hop in particular, I think it's gotten soft and I think it needs to re-digitize itself and get back to the days when it was a platform for change and for speaking out instead of partying, etc. It's a powerful enough force in pop culture where it needs to say more than it's saying, and I think the next twelve months will have a significant upswing of urban artists really having something to say.

· · · · · · ·

A&RT REPORT:
The Anatomy of A Buzz

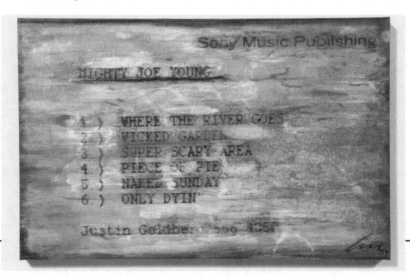

Justin Goldberg, *Early STP*, watercolor on canvas, 18"x27½"

Long before they changed their name to Stone Temple Pilots, Mighty Joe Young was a new hard rock band playing fairly regular gigs at the Coconut Teaszer on the Sunset Strip.

**Justin Goldberg, *Bidding War Live at Lingerie: The Presidents*,
watercolor on canvas, 13½"x19½"**

The year was 1994. The place? Somewhere north of Seattle with friend and
manager Staci Slater who managed two artists from the area—the inimitable
and now defunct 7 Year Bitch, and a new and odd recently formed trio of
characters calling themselves The Presidents of the United States of America.
While 7 Year Bitch was onstage (I think it was a high school auditorium,
actually) the PA went dead. The crowd was silent and confused. Then the
lights seem to have a problem. I was standing just by the stage watching
this with Chris Ballew, the guitar player of the Presidents, when suddenly he
said, "Excuse me for a sec," walked on stage, grabbed an electric guitar (the
guitar amps had not lost power) and flew into a completely impressive and
utterly hellraising four minute guitar solo that would have made Jimi Hendrix
himself smile. It drove the crowd insane. He came offstage just as noncha-
lantly, and I had no doubt this trio would bring the business down to its
knees. They were signed by Josh Sarubin after an A&R frenzied series of
shows at Club Lingerie.

**Justin Goldberg, *Anger Is A Gift: Rage Before Christmas '92*,
watercolor on canvas, 47"x34"**

Have you ever managed to accidentally electrocute yourself? Imagine that feeling for a forty minute set. That was what Rage Against the Machine was like live, from day one, even when they were performing at shows with fewer than twenty people at the now long defunct Los Angeles Club With No Name. Word spread immediately in the A&R community that a new and dynamic ball of fire was in town and would be a force to be reckoned with. Every player hit every note with a conviction they'd bleed for and you couldn't take your eyes off the stage for a second—it was explosive, it was raw, and it was real emotional energy that put all rap and rock related music in its place. Rage's early live shows ripped through public consciousness like wildfire—it was the kind of experience you were compelled to tell others about. Something was clearly going on if you were in the room, and being at a show was an initiation. Label interest didn't grow and awareness didn't build—it broke like a tsunami. After a bidding war, they were signed by Epic and Sony Publishing, with Warren Entner as their manager and Jamie Young as their attorney.

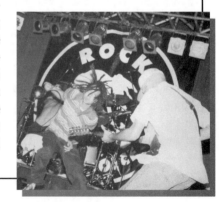

BIDDING WARS

*What is interesting to note is, and I'm sure others have said the same to
you, that 85 percent of the bidding-war bands never amount to anything.
It's usually the ones that are signed and created without fanfare that sort
of rise to the top.*

—*Jeff Rabhan, manager, The Firm*

What makes a bidding war? Simple. Other people with interest. Bidding
wars are an interesting phenomenon in the music industy. One would
imagine that with so much great unsigned talent in the world, there would
hardly be a need to crowd around a small precious sampling of it as if it
represented the last cool artist on earth. Surely there is enough music in
abundance for all the record labels and every A&R rep breathing air to go
through their entire careers without all decending upon the same small
pool of artists. Yet it happens so often with new talent that it begs a closer look at what the contributing factors are.

Certainly today's trend of lawyers and mangers working in concert to
promote new artists as they introduce them to the A&R community is one
important influence.

TRADING PLACES: A CAREER QUIZ

It is human nature to value what others want. And chasing after what others have, or are about to have, offers a challenge A&R people find familiar and strangely comforting—especially if that artist, once won, becomes
a disaster. Let's take a closer look at the equation:

Let's imagine for a moment that you are the Senior Vice President of
A&R for Who's Your Daddy Records. Your long day at the office (which
began at noon) is finally over and its time to put down your call sheet and
Blackberry and sift through your desk to listen to some music submissions. You grab a CD from the top of the pile, and it's a rock band from
England called Mobile Adapter. As you sit at your desk while the after-
hours janitor waters the plastic plants and dusts your hot twenty two-year-
old assistant's keyboard, you listen to the first track blast from your overly treble-y NS 10 speakers. Sitting there, you start to think—"Hey, wait a
minute: these guys are pretty great!" Every note screams platinum smash
hit. Looking through the liner notes, you notice the band photo of three
young men—and they're not bad looking either! You do some checking on
Google and find out that as good as they are, there's absolutely nothing

out there about them. You check your own company's submission/song tracking database and there isn't anything there, either. It turns out they were sent by an attorney in the U.K. via a mutual friend. There is no buzz. "Hmmm," you think, "I could sign them, but wait—if it's a total disaster— I'm the one who will take the blame." You put the CD down on your desk and pick up a music industry trade mag. A quick scan reveals the half dozen or so new bands on A&R community radar. One of those bands, you realize, is playing tonight. You know the competition will be there. You know the lawyer who represents this band, and many others with pending situations connected somehow to your business, will be there. It's far more career relevant that you be at that show than sitting in your office blasting the next potential hit. You know there could be changes pending upstairs (there are always changes pending upstairs). You know you only have a year left on your contract. You know that even if you love this little band, you are going to have to weigh your options carefully.

So...which band do you pursue?

JOURNALIST

RODEL DELFIN
Hits magazine

First concert attended: Santana circa mid '70s (with my dad)

Best concert(s) attended: Rage Against the Machine (unsigned at UCLA in front of fifty people), Prince (the Lovesexy Tour)

Top five album recommendations:
1. Herbie Hancock *Headhunters*
2. Beastie Boys *Paul's Boutique*
3. Nirvana *Nevermind*
4. Style Council *Confessions of a Pop Group*
5. The Clash *Combat Rock*

Little known resume entry: Mellon/Ford Graduate Economics Research Program at Princeton University participant.

Recomended reading: *The Last Mogul: Lew Wasserman, MCA and the Hidden History of Hollywood*, by Dennis McDougal

Instrument played: Piano

Rodel has worked with such artists as Stone Temple Pilots, Ice-T, Body Count, 2Pac, Ice Cube and Notorious B.I.G.

BIDDING WAR NOTES & OTHER WORDS OF WISDOM
AN INTERVIEW WITH RODEL DELFIN OF *HITS* MAGAZINE

Justin Goldberg: As someone who monitors the activity in the A&R community pretty closely, what are some of the changes that you've seen?

Rodel Delfin: I think what has changed significantly with the role of an A&R executive over the past, I'd say maybe five to seven years, is that music executives or talent scouts are less well rounded now. Back in the day, you had a guy who knew how to identify talent, brought talent and would also be well-versed in working in the studio—selecting producers, selecting engineers, selecting mixers, crafting songs, working with songs and developing the artist's career. And I think what you're finding today is that those specific roles, which used to be the responsibility of one A&R person, are now being divided among different people. So, what I'm seeing is that you're getting a staff that has low-level scouts circling out and seeking the talent, who aren't necessarily well versed in even closing the talent. You usually have to bring in the head of A&R or the president of the company to close the talent. And then it's being passed on to a veteran or higher-level executive to actually select the producer and work the record and craft and produce the songs. I think the problem is that there's been a lack of apprenticeship over the years.

JG: How do you think that affects the way that they pick music to sign?

RD: I think less raw talent is being developed. You brought up the fact that some A&R people are saying that there have to be all these elements for an artist in order for them to sign an artist. There has to be a story developing, or they're already far enough along in a development process for a record company to focus on and actually sign. With scouts going after acts on a data basis, rather than a talent basis...I think that creates a bidding war scenario, which is not necessarily the best way for an artist to get signed.

JG: Why is that? Why is a bidding war not in the artist's favor sometimes?

RD: Well, the obvious is there's too high an expectation from the label. If the artist doesn't deliver final product that the label thinks is going to sell hundreds of thousands of records the first week, then the chances of that artist being dropped are very high.

JG: What do you think of showcasing an artist in a rehearsal room or soundstage studio—at a venue like SIR, versus having a real gig at the Viper Room? How do you generally react when you get a call about a well-attended showcase at a rented rehearsal facility during the workday?

RD: Y'know, the funny thing about that is I used to feel that I would rather see a band at a live show—and I still lean towards that—however, I've seen cases where the showcase environment is much more advantageous for a band than the live show environment. My opinion is that it really depends on the artists. Whatever works better for them.

JG: So, if an act doesn't have a particularly great fan base or live show, a showcase is the best way to go?

RD: Yes. Particularly because you can control the sound at a rehearsal studio and know exactly what you need to do and fine-tune the sound quality, which you may not be able to do at a club.

JG: What are you thoughts for artists who gravitate towards wanting to release their own music and cultivate their own careers outside of the industry mainstream? Those who endeavor to be next Ani DiFranco or Martin Sexton, or at least want to cultivate a strategy for getting signed based on their own independent record?

RD: I think the number one compelling thing is the story you create for yourself. Whether it's a touring story or a sales story or a radio story, or what have you, create a name for yourself in your own community and expand upon that community.

I think that's always what most label people, right now in particular, are looking for. That's the thing I ask first when I get hit up by a manager or attorney about an act that they're representing. I ask, "Okay, what's the story? Are they selling thousands of records in their town? Are they

**Justin Goldberg, *Ten Thousand Dollars for Kathy Fisher*,
watercolor on canvas, 13"x20"**

Kathy Fisher was my first signing when I worked in music publishing, and it was an intense learning experience for all involved. Despite a hauntingly gorgeous vocal quality and a full set of commercially viable songs, getting attention at labels for this artist at the time proved to be like pulling teeth. It was hard to determine the source of the resistance—after all, she was beautiful, the material was well written and had a radio friendly pop sensibility. Sometimes it's just not in the cards. Nearly a decade later and re-branded as "Fisher," Kathy and her talented co-writer/producer husband, Ron Wasserman, would finally sign their record deal with Interscope after their own savvy online marketing campaigns garnered then-record levels of listeners.

selling out shows?" And, y'know, you look at some of the acts that have been signed, to use some examples, whether it's Howie Day or Graham Colton; these are acts in an indie singer-songwriter vein that tour two hundred to two hundred fifty shows a year and probably sell hundreds of CDs, plus their merch. That's compelling information and makes them an easier sell to a record company that is going to invest hundreds of thousands to millions of dollars.

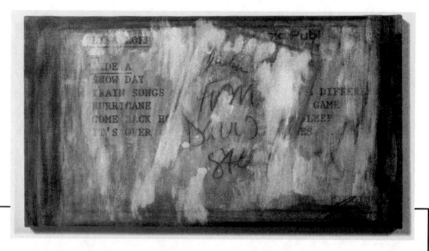

Justin Goldberg, *Lisa Loeb Post SXSW '94*, watercolor on canvas, 11"x19½"

Talk about leverage: when Lisa Loeb's neighbor, actor Ethan Hawke, had some of her music used in *Reality Bites*, the struggling unsigned New Yorker probably had no idea she was about to take a first and hugely lucky step toward having her pick of record deals. Typically, when material from an unsigned artist is used on a soundtrack recording released by a major, the label usually has the artist sign an agreement containing provisions for that label to have the first right of negotiation in the event the label is interested in the artist. In this case, someone probably got fired in the business affairs department: when the movie was released and the song's popularity soared from the soundtrack, Ms. Loeb found herself in the unusually cool position of being known, having airplay, and being unsigned while labels fawned all over her. When March hit of that year, Ms. Loeb found herself performing at outdoor venue Liberty Lunch in front of a standing room only industry crowd at South By Southwest, the industry's leading new talent showcase. Her budget for black-rimmed glasses went way up.

JG: Do you think there is some sort of key to getting signed today that didn't exist before?

RD: I think there's always been a key, and that key has always been great songs. Regardless of what people may say about record sales being hurt by Internet and by CD piracy from recordable CDs, I think that there's still an argument to be made that if an artist has three to four solid singles in their album they'll sell millions and millions of records. I think at the end of the day, if you've got three to four solid songs on your album—at least—you'll sell. You'll sell.

. . . .

TALENT SHOPPING 101:
YOUR OFFLINE PACKAGE

YOUR PROMO PACKAGE & KINKO'S PH.D.

So you went to Kinko's and have put together a most impressive twelve page promotional kit with your bio, several band photos and lyric sheets for all your songs in a nice clear plastic cover—just like that music industry how-to book published in 1971 told you to. Now walk on over to the trashcan and throw the whole thing away, except for the CD, from which we are going to remove all but your three best songs. And if there are only two great songs, or even one, then that's all that should go on the CD you plan to circulate. This isn't a high school book report and you're not getting a grade. You will not be needing anything with a spiral binding on it and this isn't time to be buying book report style folders in bulk from Staples. Save your money because these items are usually a sure sign that you have too much time on your hands and are not ready to deal with the mainstream of the industry. The best bet is to just stay focused on a clearly labeled CD and CD container (jewel box, digi pack, slim case, etc). Later, you may be judged on your organization and presentational skills but not now—the goal right now is to be perceived as someone onto something great.

THREE CHORDS AND THE TRUTH

Successfully assembling an artist promotional package is usually a game of less is more, and it should stay focused on the music (unless you are extremely attractive and young with a photograph that reflects this clearly in a tasteful way). Everything "else" in a promo kit should be considered a potential immediate interest killer. If your music is amazing but your photograph is mediocre, there's a good chance it won't even reach the CD player of certain industry targets who know all too well how difficult the modern artist signing and marketing game really is. Your package should avoid any baggage that can lead to an excuse to not listen and get into the music. Items like bios, "one-sheets" and lyric sheets may come in handy later, but in general for actual first artist packages, you should keep the contents to an absolute minimum. Usually a "one-sheet" style that lists the highlights of your project is the best option (depending on what you reveal).

WHERE TO FISH, WHAT TO USE FOR BAIT

You wouldn't fish for a shark in the ocean with a worm and you wouldn't fish for a bass in a lake with a side of beef. In other words, you must construct different packages for different targets. Reaching out to the press and asking them to take notice of something is a very different package than the one being directed to a radio program director, or sent to solicit interest from a music attorney/label/publisher/distributor and so on.

For one thing, people in the music business tend to receive a lot of packages. I've often wondered what the padded envelope industry would be like without the music biz; it would probably still be one dude stuffing bubble wrap and shredded paper at a stationary store somewhere if there weren't so many songs flying through the postal service. First, let's review the general mindset of those you are trying to impress and garner attention from: if they are very successful doing what they do, you can rightfully imagine that they are often the target of new music packages and are probably overbooked, overbusy individuals who hardly have the time to browse through your entire press kit. Thus the strong suggestion at the beginning of this chapter that you take the time to develop your online presence and electronic arsenal of music and press materials and make these available for review online at the time you request permission to send a physical package of material.

You want to be direct and connect them to what's special about you as quickly as possible. If there is some exciting piece of relevant industry progress related to your project, by all means announce it in your cover letter or a one-sheet with an overview. The main point of interest is going to be the music. Nothing else is going to have any impact.

Stewboss

22287 Mulholland Hwy #192 Los Angeles, CA 91302
krisa@peoplepc.com
ph: 818-988-8064   fax: 818-988-8065

- **4 songs from the first album 'Wanted A Girl' have been placed in independent and feature films.**
  1. 'Let's Go For A Ride' was in the Kevin Costner/Kurt Russell film "3,000 Miles To Graceland"
  2. 'Heaven Of Mine' was in the award winning short film "Jack And Jill"
  3. 'I Think She Wants Me Dead' was featured in the independent film "The Chocolate Fairy"
  4. 'A Walk In Spain' was in the independent film "If Tomorrow Comes"

- **The band has just completed their third tour of Europe in under two years, playing clubs, theaters and festivals of 2,500+ people.**
  1. Within 7 days after the band's performance in Holland, the distributor sold out of CDs and had to place another order with the label.

- **Veteran BBC2 Radio DJ, Bob Harris, has named the band on many occasions as one of his favorite new artists.**
  1. The song 'Fill Station' from "Wanted A Girl" was part of his TOP 10 songs of 2001 and was featured on his Bob Harris Presents compilation along with artists like Ryan Adams and Slaid Cleaves.
  2. Bob Harris was the first DJ in the UK to play artists like Bonnie Raitt, Jackson Browne and Little Feat when he began his career in the '70's.
  3. Stewboss has been featured (performed live) on BBC Scotland, BBC Wales, BBC London, BBC Newcastle and BBC Sheffield, and has received airplay on many stations in Belgium, Holland, Germany, Ireland and Australia. Their fan base reaches as far as Japan and Russia.

- **Their song "The Midnight Shift" placed as finalist in the 2001 John Lennon Songwriting Contest.**

- **Before leaving for their most recent tour of Europe, the band performed live on The Mark and Brian Show heard locally in Los Angeles on 95.5 KLOS and syndicated throughout the west coast from Seattle, Washington to Santa Fe, New Mexico.**
  1. The band was interviewed and played 6 songs over a 45-minute span.
  2. They received over 1,500 hits to their website, stewboss.com, and sold 250 cds via the internet alone, just from the one performance.

Single sheet "bios" outlining the highlights of your project make for clean, well-assembled first introductions.

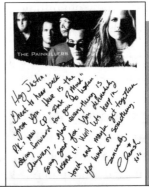

It's in the follow-up communications that some attention to detail with graphics can help create a good impression. These materials from Los Angeles based indie rockers The Painkillers have always encouraged me to consider them a unique combination of clever and serious about what they do.

Contact Person: Billy B
Shine Records: 213.673.7367

For Immediate Release
November 1, 2002

Artist: **the Painkillers**
New CD Release: **State of Mind**

The Painkillers are here to give alternative rock an **adrenalized shot to the arm with their latest release** *State of Mind* (2002, Shine Records). This LA-based band's highly-anticipated follow-up to *Medicine For The Soul* is "a deeper, more aggressive (album) that penetrates the soul," in the words of lead vocalist/songwriter Cherish Alexander. The band's self-proclaimed mission is to bring healing into people's lives through their music.

While the Painkillers deal with the same themes they did on their previous release, one thing that is different about *State of Mind* relates to the band's approach in recording the album. **"We took chances... recording (it) by incorporating newer sounds, edgier vocals, and experimental guitar noises,"** Cherish says. The band pulled out all the stops, revealing even more facets of their boundless musical creativity.

As heard in the relentless sonic avalanche of the title track, which opens the album with a huge dose of rock swagger, thanks to the dueling guitars of Alexander and lead axe-man Curtis Hooker. The radio friendly tune "Uncover Me" and the emotionally charged "Mistreated" reminds us to keep one's humanity intact, to the bittersweet ballads "Goodbye" and "Where You Belong," where Marco Montecillo's piano chords are poised to inspire a resurgence of raised Bic lighters in arenas around the world.

Having "Goodbye" featured in the syndicated television series "The Crow" gave the band a level of regional success and international exposure. It is not surprising that other songs on the album are also attracting some serious attention. "Mistreated" is already receiving regular airplay on Laurie Steele's "Homegrown" program at Las Vegas' KOMP radio 92.3 FM.

Indeed, *State of Mind* gives a major reality check to a lot of problems we all face in our daily lives, takes them head on, and offers a semblance of hope during a time that the world is in such a dreary state.

State of Mind is available at CDstreet.com and by mail order for $10.99 + $2.99 shipping and handling. The Painkillers, P.O. Box 7304 #347, North Hollywood, California 91603. CD's also available at selected stores. Check website for details.

Visit the Painkillers at their website,
www.thepainkillers.com

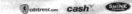

BATTLING THE PREDISPOSITION TO "NO"

The A&R game, from the label/lawyer/manger/publisher/agent/music supervisor point of view, is a process of elimination. The moment you begin to describe some exciting new music, the A&R mind will show subtle signs of tension: the A&R mind says to itself, "I'm already swamped. I already have a great project I'm committed to, I already have a pile of music that's prioritized according to my personal and professional relationships; I am utterly predisposed to saying, 'NO,' about whatever new opportunity is being offered me." Nevertheless, there are some simple ways around this, and it's best summed up with old adage: "You'll catch more bees with honey, and one drop of honey at a time." It's best to draw people into the music first and let them develop their own ideas about an artist.

THE PARADOX OF THE ARTIST PHOTOGRAPH
Video may have killed the radio star—but the cliché photo killed the shopping process.

Beware the artist photo! Although the right artist photo can be very helpful in shopping an artist, most photos are wrong—many artists and artist reps inadvertently taint a neutral listening experience long before a single note has been played. Remember what music was like before MTV—when you weren't really sure what an artist looked like? Many claimed that video killed the radio star for a good reason—artists who made unbelievable music but were not particularly visually engaging took a hit as the marketplace shifted, and vice versa—artists with the visual goods passed Go quickly and collected their $200. The entire meaning of pop music shifted with video broadcast; suddenly being fat and ugly and having hit songs was not as compelling to labels and publishers (or the lawyers and managers doing the shopping). This doesn't mean that genius level talent, without the looks to be mistaken for a model, can't still be treated like genius level talent, but it does mean that new artists should be aware of when and how to introduce themselves visually.

When you send in a photo with a package, you are exposing yourself to the possibility of rejection on a physical basis alone—a unfortunate and unfair but very real possibility if you are only marginally attractive. I can name dozens of artists who, in another era (before MTV), would be much further along in their careers based on their music. Similarly, tons of crap gets released and marketed based on image.

Photos can almost always work against you. There are a lot of pet peeves out there. You might have a tacky outfit or the wrong haircut—very few artists come away with their imaging completely intact.

ROCK OF AGES

In Hollywood, it's a matter of course to reduce your age by three to five years in an attempt to lengthen your shelf life. Lying about your age is practically a right of passage for actors and others in the limelight. For example, how is it that Cindy Crawford has no problem admitting to being in her late thirties, yet Naomi Campbell remains thirty-three year after year? The entertainment industry has always been paranoid about its stars and starmakers getting too old to be hip and bleed on the cutting edge. This is also true for the music business: stars like Mandy Moore, Jessica Simpson, Fiona Apple, Christina Aguilera, Britney Spears, Lee Ann Rimes and almost all of the boy bands were posing with platinum long before they could pose for a DMV photo. A&R folks may not feel particularly comfortable committing large sums of money toward a brand new band that is unproven, but they are even less interested in bands that have been around for too long. This can make for a very delicate balance when you are creating your press kit. Depending on your target, you want to create a sense of story, but you can't tell a story that makes you seem like you have been at this for too long. If your press kit has items in it from two or more years ago, you are showing your cards. "Why didn't something happen already with this act?" is often the first thought that will come to mind. Of course, every artist has his or her own story, and being on the scene for a certain period of time in itself hardly translates into hopelessness, but just be aware of the message you're sending. When houses are on the market for too long in real estate, it's a sign that something is up with the property. Same for artists, be aware of your own shelf-life. When you are shopping talent, or are in a new band being shopped, you usually have a brief—say, five to fifteen month period to be on the scene and have something happen. If you're around beyond that, you had better have a plan for sticking it out independently, or have something extraordinary happen because the bread is past the expiration date and A&R people are pretty adept at figuring this out. Changing band names is a good idea when too much time goes by without any action. Often bands think that it's a cool sign of their perseverance to stick it out and keep on keeping on with an existing project name—not so. Unless you're selling records or tickets independently, it's not cool, it's lame, and it only proves your perseverance at being stubborn. Of course it depends what your objectives are and what kind of band you're in, but if you're after major industry attention in a hurry, keep in mind this business moves fast.

TODAY'S DEMONSTRATION TAPES
(AKA These Are Not Your Father's ProTools)

Many years ago, the phrase demo tape came from artists and singers recording an example of their skills and talent so A&R people could get a rough idea what a potential record might sound like. The word "demo" derived from the idea of songs being recorded as sample "demonstrations," and not professionally produced recordings. Demo tapes were used primarily before the advent of inexpensive high-quality home-based digital recording devices; when it was cost prohibitive for unsigned artists to create professional quality recordings. But that was then. Music and technology have changed, and with these changes expectations have evolved to a point where the songs on your demo need to sound like they could—or should—be on the radio tomorrow. The driving factor of the industry is the overall quality of recorded music being circulated, and that quality increases with each passing year. So, what are the elements of a great demo?

THE NUMBER OF SONGS TO PUT ON A DEMO

There are artists who will say, "I've got a hundred songs." And you say, "Well, how many do you like," and they go, "Well, I like twenty." "Well, that's good, how many do you love?" "I love five." "How many do you think are going to be a hit?" "Well, I think this one here is good." It's all relative: I never cared about how many songs they had, I only cared about how many great songs they had.

—David Bendeth, President, Type A Records

NO TIME TO WALLOW IN THE MIRE

When I first arrived in Los Angeles and formed my band, The Bodhies, rock photographer and friend Lindsay Brice approached my partner in the band and announced she had some cool news: she'd played our tape for the producer of The Doors, Paul Rothchild, and he wanted us to come over with guitars for a private acoustic concert/audition. Our eyes nearly popped out of our heads with excitement, and we spent hours trying to determine the appropriate set list to play for him. Worried that we might leave him with a demo that wouldn't contain songs we'd overlooked that he might consider great, we ultimately decided that three separate ninety minute TDK cassettes would do the trick. It was essentially a collection of every song we had ever written. Today I cringe and chuckle at the thought of how pathetic we were, marching into his Laurel Canyon living room, gasping at his Jim Morrison mementos and shoving a list of thirty two compositions in his face. The late Paul Rothchild was an inspired gentlemen; he could not have been more kind to us, and he never let on that we were committing the first sin of introducing new music—not editing ourselves.

Today, I usually moan when an artist hands in a CD with more than three songs. There are many exceptions to this: for one, if it's an existing CD release and an existing artist project, then of course it's not exactly a "demo"—it's an example of what is already on the market. And of course, if you are working with someone creatively, such as a producer, writer, or even a manager or lawyer who is already leaning towards working with your music, by all means, open the floodgates of your musical world (within reason) and show off your different ideas. But if it's a talent evaluator, be careful! You must learn that limiting the number of songs on the CD you circulate is really only limiting the odds of having your work dismissed. Most music professionals do not have time to listen to more than a handful of songs unless you're in the process of working with them. Giving someone a CD with over a dozen tunes sends an unprofessional message.

OTHER CD TIPS: LABEL MATERIALS INDIVIDUALLY

Newsflash! CDs occasionally separate from their jewel boxes! I have actually been in a position where I wanted to license a song for a television show and couldn't, because the CD didn't contain any contact information and I couldn't recall who sent the package. *Label everything!* Always assume that the worst will happen to your package once it enters the chaotic maelstrom of a music professional's office. Always assume that your cover letter, press kit, disc, jewel box and whatever else you send will be separated from each other, and plan accordingly.

LABEL CD SPINES

The good: slim jewel cases look cool and are cheaper to mail. The bad: if you are sending material to music supervisors, or another music professional who may "catalog it" and refer to it or need it later, it might as well be invisible. CDs without "spines" *and spine labels* cannot be located when they're tucked into a few hundred other CDs on a CD library wall in an office. Always label your CD spine, CD jewel box and CD itself— always clearly mark your materials with:

> Contact name
> Email address and Web site address
> Telephone, fax and cell phone

You may get just one opportunity—won't it suck if they can't even find you?

Also indicate the track listing *on the jewel box*. This way the reviewer can make notes about the song titles while listening.

TARGETED PACKAGING TIPS
Music Supervisors

Music supervisors operate in a fast-paced, budget-driven business environment. Decisions need to be made quickly—which means that even the most appropriate creative musical choice can be ruled out in favor of a less risky or easier to clear alternative. If you are interested in having your music licensed, you should make that obvious by clearly marking all your materials with the following:

> "ONE-STOP LICENSING:
> ARTIST CONTROLLED MASTER AND PUBLISHING"

The above language indicates to a potential licensor that a single phone call can handle both "ends" of the necessary licensing arrangements—the master, which refers to the ownership of the recording—and the publishing, which refers to the songwriter's rights. (This topic will be covered in some detail later. So don't get confused just yet.)

Radio

Sending packages out to radio is an art form of its own and one that is usually dominated by label promotion staffers and indie radio promoters.

Generally speaking, you need to actually manufacture a separate CD with only one song on it. Of course, you can save money by simply highlighting the "radio track" or "single" on the CD, but that isn't the best or most professional way to go. If the industry has a short attention span, then radio stations might as well have no attention span at all—and assuming that a radio PD (program director) will bother to hit the forward button to the correct track on your disc is assuming a lot. Make your submission a no brainer by putting only a single song on the CD. Depending on which kind of radio you are targeting, it may also make sense to have them professionally mailed. The radio trade publication, FMQB (Friday Morning Quarterback) handles this service, and not only do they already have all the updated radio station mailing addresses and personnel, they also lend an air of credibility to your project when it arrives in their mailers. (Be prepared for them to try to tempt you into announcing your release in their magazine for a small extra fee.)

Keep your written materials to the point—no lyric sheets, no long press testimonials, no video EPKs. A single sheet highlighting some accomplishments that might be relevant to radio should suffice.

Press

If you are submitting materials to music publications, whatever written material you send will set the tone for how the publication will consider your project. Lazy writers (or those late with deadlines, like me) will simply reprint a great deal of what's already been written as a bio for the artist. Music magazines are the one target that will actually refer to your bio in detail, so take the time to make sure it's right. You will also want to include photographs with press packages—but make sure to send "real" photographs and not photocopies, color copies, half tones, or poorly printed dot matrix printer images. (Your printer's dpi setting should exceed 600 and truly look like a photo. Sending a black and white and a color photo is also a good idea, depending on the publication.)

SUBMITTING MATERIAL TO LAWYERS/MANAGERS/ A&R TYPES & EVERYONE ELSE

Again, A&R minds are already tilted, already too busy, already looking for a way out. Do not give it to them! Three great songs in a row followed by a mediocre fourth tune can throw off your balance. Restrict their ability to imagine the worst by keeping the music you circulate limited to the best material you have. The music, a friendly (and short) cover letter, a single sheet highlighting great things about the band and that's it!

INTERNET RELATED/JOURNALIST

GARY SAVELSON
Demodiaries.com

First concert attended: The Grateful Dead

Best concert attended: Jane's Addiction

Top five album recommendations:
1. U2 *The Joshua Tree*
2. The Cure *Disintegration*
3. The Verve *Urban Hymns*
4. The Police *Reggatta de Blanc*
5. R.E.M *Reckoning*

Best project you were involved with that never made it big: Twin A (but there's still hope)

Recommended films: *Fight Club* (20th Century Fox, 1999) and *Swingers* (Miramax, 1996)

Instrument played: Piano

Artist affiliations: Credited with getting Soil signed to J Records/BMG

PLAYING THE DEMO GAME
AN INTERVIEW WITH GARY SAVELSON OF DEMODIARIES.COM

Justin Goldberg: What would you say are the best tips for artists submitting demos?

Gary Savelson: Send three to five of your best songs burned onto a CD. If you have a full CD, include a note as to which you think are your best, or the ones that are getting the most attention. Send the CD in a padded envelope so the contents don't get broken or scratched. Do your best to email me ahead of time and brief me on your situation. Tell me to expect your CD, that way I'm now familiar with your name.

JG: Are there any do's or don'ts in terms of photos or demo quality?

GS: I don't really think so. I'm not picky about quality in the "demo" stage of an artist's career. If the vocals are great, with a solid song structure and a hooky melody, I'm going to follow up on it. But don't send a cassette tape, send a CD! Your photo should look hip, clear and be a definitive image of what you look like. A very short cover letter can't hurt.

JG: An official "press kit"?

GS: Personally, I don't need the press kit. In your cover letter you can list the top three magazines or radio stations that have reacted to your music, how many people come to your shows, how many CDs you've sold, and so on. There is no need to clutter your package with stuff that's just going to get thrown out.

JG: How important is it to have an attorney or a manager represent you?

GS: It's no lie that sometimes music exec people will pay more attention to you if you have a big attorney behind you. If your manager gets you where you need to go (label interest, radio interest, TV placements), then he's useful. Keep him! Managers promote you daily while you're busy writing music. They're supposed to open doors for you.

· · · · · · ·

THE TITILLATING EXTRAS INCLUDED IN DEMO SUBMISSIONS

The packages people send in have no influence on what I'll listen to first. I've gotten everything from underwear to cigarettes to liquor, candy, all sorts of stuff, crazy photographs. All that stuff, it just doesn't matter. It's just a good tape or CD, and maybe a photo. Maybe a little bit of press, but you don't need the nice folder you got at Staples. The songs are the most important. Then you have to have the ability to pull it off live, and have a certain charisma or star power or whatever "thing" that people who are successful have that you just can't put your finger on. You just know it when they walk into a room.

—Josh Sarubin, VP of A&R, Arista Records

INTERNET RELATED/ARTIST

CHRIS STANDRING
AandROnline.com

First concert attended: Procul Harem at Friars Aylesbury, UK, 1975

Best concert attended: Jeff Beck at Universal Amphitheatre in 2000 comes up high on the list.

Top five album recommendations:
1. Jeff Beck *Blow by Blow*
2. Pat Martino *Consciousness*
3. Pink Floyd *Dark Side of the Moon*
4. Coldplay *Parachutes*
5. Earth Wind & Fire *I Am*

Little known resume entry: Made sandwiches for eight months in 1980 at The Gingham Kitchen in Northridge, CA, to save up for a Gibson 335 (and a flight ticket back to the UK). I was just twenty years old.

Best project you were involved with that never made it big: Solar System, back in 1996

Recommended film: *The Jungle Book* (Walt Disney Pictures, 1967)

Recommended reading: *Hit Men: Power Brokers and Fast Money Inside the Music Business*, by Fredric Dannen

Instrument played: Guitar

HOW TO WIN FRIENDS AND INFLUENCE CONSUMERS
AN INTERVIEW WITH CHRIS STANDRING, ARTIST AND KING OF THE EMAIL NEWSLETTER

Justin Goldberg: You are on the receiving end of A&R packages, people looking for attention from record labels, connecting with the right source. What do people do wrong most often?

Chris Standring: Well, I'll tell you something, I can almost always tell you which package I may be interested in before I even open it. I can tell who's thought about something thoroughly, who is professional, and who is just throwing something at the wall. The type of artist who will probably have something to offer will send me a larger package with a proper press kit—it'll be completely professionally done, with press clippings, a professional quality CD with contact information on it, and a personalized typed-out introduction letter that also includes contact details. It's really not rocket science, but most people have no idea how to present something professionally. Presenting something professionally tells me that you've thought about your career long and hard and it's important to you. A CD in the mail with a scrap of paper begging for me to listen to it tells me you're not ready to be presented to record companies. You're just not ready.

JG: What is it that makes people ready?

CS: Experience, frankly. There is no getting away from it and there is no substitute for it. I can't tell you how to get experience apart from you just do it. One of things I advise people to do is: before you get signed, you have to exist in a marketplace; you can't possibly expect a record company to sign you if they don't know who you are. You have to know exactly who you are and exactly how you can be marketed before you even think about sending in a package. At the end of the day, if you're not ready, it's not worth it—*because you don't get a second shot.* So I tell people to go and buy *Radio & Records* and examine the charts and the radio formats and ask, "Where do I fit in to all this?" Look at the competition and play the songs in the Top Ten in all those charts, or in the specific chart that you think you're going to fit in to and ask yourself, "How am I going to compete? Am I ready?"

> You have to know exactly who you are and exactly how you can be marketed before you even think about sending in a package. At the end of the day, if you're not ready, it's not worth it—*because you don't get a second shot.*

• • • • • • •

ARTISTS & REPERTOIRE

JASON MARKEY
Immortal Records

First concert attended: Barry Manilow, 1981

Best concert attended: Bruce Springsteen's Born in the USA Tour at the LA Coliseum, 1984

Top five album recommendations:
1. Bruce Springsteen *Born to Run*
2. U2 *War*
3. Jim Croce *Greatest Hits*
4. The Beatles *The White Album*(obviously)
5. Nirvana *Bleach*

Little known resume entry: I was a coordinator in the Art Department for MCA Records.

Best project you were involved with that never made it big: Jude

Recommended film: *Swimming With Sharks* (Trimark Pictures, 1984)

Recommended reading: *The Operator: David Geffen Builds, Buys, and Sells the New Hollywood*, by Tom King

---

HONEY, I SHRUNK THE KID'S INTEREST IN POP MUSIC! DVDS VERSUS CDS
AN INTERVIEW WITH JASON MARKEY OF IMMORTAL RECORDS

Justin Goldberg: Jason, how has the signing game evolved as it affects your role of A&R?

Jason Markey: In terms of the signing game, I think that the labels typically are first asking, "Who's the lawyer, who's the manager?" Second is, "Let's hear the music." If the songs are great, then they want to see them live and then if it works, let's do the deal. There's no real thinking anymore. It's just basically bottom line versus overhead. How many records can this sell? That's the question. Not, "Oh my God, this guy's writing good songs now. Imagine what he's gonna be like seven years from now!" Nobody gives a shit about seven years from now. They care about September, and this is July. "How fast are you going to make this record so I can get it out for my fourth-quarter profits? Because I *really* think this is going to sell 3 million copies." It's really shortsighted because they're not creating catalogues anymore. They're creating one-record catalogues for these bands, or two records at the most.

JG: Let's talk about radio promotion briefly: would you say that from your perspective the modern industry trend has moved away from payola?

JM: I could probably go to jail for saying it, but I think that payola is worse than it's ever been. And it's hidden. It's not like me calling up Joe's Radio Station in Montana going, "Dude, I'll give you a hundred bucks to play this record." You have to go to a guy who knows a guy who has that radio station in his pocket and you have to give him a cut. And that guy's cut in with another guy who cuts in another guy, and the more records he gets played the more trips to Hawaii he gets. Basically. Or another Porsche. Or whatever the offering is. Today, the guys who are the radio promoters and the indie promoters, they have the twenty-five markets, and you're not getting one of those markets unless you're in bed with that person. So what has that created? It's created an extremely high marketing budget because these people want more. It's almost like an episode of *Miami Vice.* How many Ferraris, Porsches; how much blow can one guy do? It's insane amounts—I'm not saying the drugs, I'm just using that as a reference. It's not Honda. Now it's Porsche and Ferrari. How many of those can I get? And how many people can I siphon off of to get that?

JG: So how hard is it for a indie band—with high hopes and a couple of great songs—to release their own records and really make some noise?

JM: It's extremely hard. Unless you're willing to go on the road and spend your own money to develop yourself and create a fan base. Like a Dave Matthews or a Howie Day. I think that to get in bed with a major record company now, either you better have hit songs and know how to write a song, be really good looking and get on MTV, or you better have a fan base that you've created from the start so when your record *does* come out, you can sell an extraordinary number of records your first week. Then people will perk up and go, "Oh, I was wrong about this artist. It really looks like it can do something." And then maybe your major label will pay attention to you. If not, they're moving on to the next Neil Diamond greatest hits record, which is going to sell a million copies just by putting it out, and they're going to work that. Or they're going to work with an established artist like an Aerosmith. Whatever it is, they're going to do that because they don't have the time to develop you and they have a catalog. And they have to support that catalog because that's what makes them money, which pays the big salaries.

JG: And just how expensive is it to put out and promote a record? What does it cost to send a new band's first single off to radio? What happens if you just don't pay independent record promoters; you just say, "You know what, we've got the new Pearl Jam here. They have an amazing ground-swell of support."

JM: Pearl Jam is a different situation. You're talking about an established artist with extreme credibility.

JG: No, as an example—let's say it's a new artist on a career trajectory similar to Pearl Jam's early rise. Perhaps we should cite something more recent, perhaps a new White Stripes...

JM: Well, the White Stripes managed to create "a thing" and make people believe that they're cool; they toured and had two records out on their own. So there's a band that had two independent records, went out on their own, toured and managed to be selling out two nights of shows in Los Angeles at the Troubadour—all without a label. Then they moved up to the El Rey Theatre. They came and played the El Rey without a record deal—that theatre can hold 1,200 kids! Sold out in Los Angeles. They made sure that all the indie kids knew they were cool. They made sure that their independent releases were up to par, and made sure they were in all the cool stores and did all the cool in-stores and got on all the college radio stations. And people were like, "Oh yeah, this is a cool band to be associated with." So when it came time to get on the radio, on the mainstream alternative radio, they were "in" because people had heard so much about this band that they were like, "Oh my God, this is the next big thing."

JG: But were they on a label when they finally received commercial airplay?

JM: Yeah.

JG: So even though they were able to successfully work all of the key elements and position themselves properly in the indie community and reach all the right cool people, they were still unable to garner a mainstream alternative radio presence on a national level—

JM:—until they had that push from a record company.

JG: So what exactly does "the push of a record company" mean today? Does it mean cash for airplay? General industry influence from key relationships? All of it?

JM: Yes.

JG: What is the tab for that level of "push"—how expensive does it get? Let's say I have a lot of money, or I think I do, and I'm ready to just roll the dice on my own on a national level and start my own label, or some variation of that.

JM: Between a million and two million dollars.

JG: And that represents the cost to give a band a serious crack at radio airplay?

JM: Not just at radio, but to get into the record stores as well—it's all related. It's all one, big, giant pool of people swimming together and they all want the same thing—they want to sell records. And the space is so limited in the stores that if they don't think you're playing the game, they're not playing with you. Period. End of story. There's no, "Hey, it's Bob from Bill's Band. Can you carry twenty copies of my record?"

"Well, Bill, why would I want to carry twenty copies of your record?"

"I don't know. Just because I thought you'd do me a favor."

"No favors here, son. See you later. Get a deal, get 2,000 kids into a club to see your band, sell it out. Start something going on and then I'll talk to you about carrying your record."

You have to remember, the stores selling records today are Best Buy, Wal-Mart, Target and Circuit City.

JG: How has the online world affected everything? You said before that kids growing up with the Internet have supreme access and knowledge and are able to find unbelievable records that you can't even access in the record stores. So what does all this really mean for the record business?

JM: The bands that seem to break are the ones nobody knew about, and the smart A&R people are creatively trying to sign the bands they think are going to do well a year or two ahead, as opposed to right now. If you really get into the Internet and you get into where their heads are, the kids are out there dictating what they want in the future. If you're smart enough to pay attention to it, then you'll be able to creatively sign those kind of artists and develop them. Or not develop them. Or sign them and hope that they're going to happen at that moment in time.

I don't think the Internet's going to destroy the record industry. I think it's going to take a smarter and younger generation of people to come in and start marketing the records that understand the Internet and use the Internet as a tool, as opposed to the enemy. The good thing about the Internet is that it's like television. You can put the kid right in front of the artist as much as you want. If you can figure a way to get into their bedroom from Day One and make them feel like they own this artist over the course of two years while making and promoting the record, then maybe you're creating an almost nouveau-concert experience for them.

JG: Do you talk to other A&R guys about what they're signing? How competitive is that? When you're looking for new stuff and hearing about new stuff...

JM: It's *extremely* competitive. I think that back in the old times, you didn't have *Hits* magazine or everybody trying to be an A&R consultant, like we talked about with the lawyers. *Hits* magazine plays a big part into what the presidents of these labels want to sign, because nobody wants to be held accountable. It's like they can say, "Everybody tried to sign it. I can't believe it didn't happen." There's no ownership anymore. If they sign something, pay a million dollars for it—and it doesn't happen—they can blame it on the buzz factor.

JG: So it's easier to sign something that has a buzz factor because then it's harder to pin failure on one particular person? Is that a reason why labels typically don't take big chances?

JM: I think so. I think there are fewer chances being taken now than ever before. And when you do get a Strokes or a Hives or a White Stripes or whatever, for the most part, those are bands that created their own buzz. They've reached that point because they developed it. So now, instead of A&R people, labels are bringing in producers who have indie-rock credibility and who have been there, developed the sound and know what that sound is going to be. They're going to hire *that* guy as an A&R person, as a consultant, or give him his own label. Because they're expecting that there's this long pipe, and this guy has obviously figured out what's going to shoot down this pipe, and that's what we want shooting through our veins. The idea becomes, "Let's get this guy on our team." They'll hire someone like that, as opposed to some kid off the street who thinks he knows what's going to be hot.

JG: How important is a producer in the rock world?

JM: I think it's come full circle again. I think there was a point in the '60s and '70s when a producer specialized in a certain sound or genre of music and helped the artist fulfill their vision. The people who were producing those records all along were the people who were dictating what the future was going to be. And then I think we got to a point where people started understanding rock music so well, like in the early '80s, they felt like they could produce themselves. If you got all the modern rock artists of the '80s, like the Depeche Modes and The Cures, they knew their songs so well and they knew the technology that they wanted, and they could put it on tape. In the R&B world there's always been a Berry—there's always been guys like that for those genres that dictate what that sound is going to be in that flavor of music.

In rock, to get the sound you're looking for, you have to hire a producer you feel is going to accomplish that. And there are not that many great producers, so you go after the guys who are available and they're usually doing all the records that are successful.

JG: So having a producer with a proven track record can be something beyond name value in itself.

JM: Yeah, like, there was a band last year that I thought was okay—but they got what they got as far as money for their deal based on the fact that Don Gilmore was signed on to make the record. So they're betting on him as a producer to come up with the sound for the band that's going to break the band.

· · · · · · ·

ARTISTS & REPERTOIRE, PRODUCER

DAVID BENDETH
President
Type A Records

First concert attended: Jimi Hendrix

Best concert attended: Jeff Beck Group

Top five album recommendations:
1. Jeff Beck *Blow by Blow*
2. Rod Stewart *Every Picture Tells a Story*
3. Miles Davis *Bitches Brew*
4. Led Zeppelin *Led Zeppelin*
5. Earth, Wind and Fire *The Best of Earth, Wind and Fire*

Little known resume entry: Collector of Hornby Dublo British Electric Trains; avid freshwater fisherman (bass/musky/pike).

Best project you were involved with that never made it big: Sugarbomb

Recommended Web site: www.consumptionjunction.com

Instrument played: Guitar, bass

Recent or past signings: Elvis, SR-71, Vertical Horizon, Bruce Hornsby, Crash Test Dummies, Cowboy Junkies, Life at Sea, Exo, Parma Lee, Asi, Anna Lovles, Spiralling, Prairie Oyster

READING THE TEA LEAVES OF YOUR CAREER:
AN INTERVIEW WITH DAVID BENDETH, PRESIDENT OF TYPE A RECORDS

Justin Goldberg: Let's talk about the costs of making and selling records today. The complaint I keep hearing is that the entire cost structure is just astronomical.

David Bendeth: You can make a record for ten thousand dollars; you can make a record for a million dollars—it depends on who you're making it for and who you're making it with. The music dictates the cost of the record-making. If you're speaking directly to how much it's going to cost to break an act, that's another conversation. But, I think once you intertwine the two at a major label, you're looking at one million plus to even play the game.

JG: And that's for what? Just getting into radio, retail promotion, everything?

DB: Yes, and each time you go to another format, it's more: you go to modern rock, then you want to go to Top Forty—it's disgusting. Again, I think it was okay before because although there were a lot of expenses you were still selling records. It was different. Now, The Strokes, who have probably seen more press than most bands in the world this year, are really still just at a million records in America, which is unheard of really; two years ago that band would be at three or four million records.

JG: As compared to say, a band like Oasis who at a similar level of profile only a few years ago were already achieving multi-platinum sales?

DB: Correct, because that's what it is. They're such a great band but the fact of the matter is that people are downloading their songs and copying them, stealing the music. People are spending their money on different things; that twenty dollars is going to other places. To games, to their computer, to their monthly cable bill, to DVDs. I think that's part of the business. And the kids come out and say, "Hey, y'know what? Music is free. We can get it for free. We don't have to pay for it." And they're right. They can get it for free very easily.

JG: How do you feel about CD pricing?

DB: I think you can walk into Best Buy right now and buy any new band for $9.99, and Best Buy will take a hit on it to get people into the store. We might as well give the records away.

JG: There has been a trend away from the traditional A&R role over the last few years; the proliferation of online record labels began a new wave of thinking opposed to the very notion of even needing A&R people or traditional offline record companies. The idea suddenly became that if you had a Web site and a pile of cash you could go out, find artists and break them. Why do think that failed?

DB: That's pretty simple. A lot of the people who believed that record companies, or even A&R people, weren't needed anymore were basing all of their information on research. You research a band in an area and then research the retail store, you research the press, research the club and you break it down in some scientific way that allows you to calculate how much a band could sell: you really didn't have to be very smart, all you had to do was look at numbers. I think the whole plan fell apart because they saw bands like Hootie and the Blowfish sell eleven million records and then decided, "Well there's the template. That'll become our new formula: we'll find out who's big and we'll sign them and then we'll just trend," but the problem was that a lot of these acts were really happening on a local level and not on a national level; very few of them were making an impact in American radio. The fact of the matter is that there is still no replacement for great A&R, no matter what you do. When I say great A&R, I mean part old-school and part new-school—where you have somebody, whether it's a record company person, or just somebody who knows what they're doing—making a record with an act.

Making records is an art form. It cannot be done through research because it's got so much to do with feel and personality and intangibles. I think that making records is an intangible thing but I don't think making great records is luck. When Butch Vig sat down with Nirvana, I don't think there were a bunch of hackers in the room. I happen to think that you put Butch Vig in a great studio with a neat console and the right songs and Kurt Cobain and Dave Grohl playing drums, then you can get something pretty goddamn good. That's not an accident.

The other way is to sign something that's incredible and works at any time. Like those restaurants that serve breakfast all day—that's what I'm talking about. No matter what time it is, no matter what is invoked, the music is still pretty goddamn good. There are a couple of bands who fit into that category—Tom Petty, Radiohead—they're great at what they do and too bad if it's not the flavor of the month.

JG: It's situation-free music?

DB: Correct. So you try to find things like that.

JG: Is that because sometimes these regional explosions of talent don't necessarily translate into big national or international success stories?

DB: Most of them don't. Ninety-five percent of them don't translate because successful music is based on a reflection of the social, political and economic picture of the whole country, not on, say, just Raleigh, North Carolina.

Of course, it's great to see anybody sell ten thousand records anywhere on their own. That's a huge feat. But record companies can't build a business on ten thousand records. Now, when a band connects in Raleigh, North Carolina, and sells ten thousand records and then sells five thousand in Seattle at the same time, *that* is going to interest me.

JG: Do you think people aren't writing with the world in mind, they're just writing for an American audience?

DB: Yeah. I think more so now than they ever have. But I don't think that's such a bad thing. I mean, we're going through a period where out of this will come a change. I think everybody was waiting for the new U2, the new Nirvana, to come along. When it didn't, they were miffed. I think a lot of them were disillusioned, I think that they sort of had to reach further into music that was substantial. When I sit down today and I listen to Norah Jones or if I listen to even John Mayer to a certain degree, that is the new music of America. Those are up and coming artists people want to hear. And, y'know, they both have things in common. They're both really good singers and they're both very good instrumentalists, and they're both working with very talented people. Then you've got the punk scene, which has always been great, and you've got all these new bands like New Found Glory. And what they're bringing to the party is something that has been missing, which is the energy. You know, you miss that energy and aura. We keep forgetting that the kids of eighteen haven't seen, never got to see, a lot of the acts that we grew up with so to them [that energy] is brand new.

JG: You bring up an interesting point about the cycles of new music and how every few years a younger generation lays claim to their own artists: back when I tried to sign Stone Temple Pilots I was heavily criticized for jumping on the Pearl Jam bandwagon because the "true" music fans considered STP a rip-off act. Five years later when Creed came along, I cringed throughout their big Mercury Lounge New York showcase, thinking, "This band will never get a deal, and if they do, they'll catch hell for reinventing the Pearl Jam template," and I couldn't have been more wrong.

DB: It's funny—Los Angeles and New York are breeding grounds for punk and dance music, and all things culturally suave and debonair. But the fact of the matter is, in between those two areas—and all you have to do is go twenty miles across the street here to New Jersey, or if you're in California, you go to Las Vegas—and all of a sudden the whole landscape musically changes: you'll see kids wearing Motörhead and AC/DC T-shirts, and that's what they like. Never underestimate Middle America. Kids like great songs and whether you hate Creed or love Creed or whatever you think of them, Creed actually happens to write some pretty damn good songs. They might not be the hippest band. They might not be the coolest band, but that was never really important to sell records. We sit back today and look at Journey and REO Speedwagon. They're not that hip, but could they sing and play? Yes, they could, and so that's what that part of American music will always be.

JG: Let's talk for a minute about how the experience of introducing new music to the target audience has changed.

DB: Kids are turning to the TV. You could actually grow up through music with Nickelodeon. Nickelodeon used to be about Britney Spears and N'Sync, and now it's about Avril Levigne and Michelle Branch. You've got Nick Teen now. It's not just about eight-year-olds anymore. And when you go to the movie theater, you're completely immersed in all sorts of music coming through the movie, with soundtracks playing a huge part as well. Whether it's a clothing store, a movie or video games, kids are getting music in new ways. How many times have you heard someone ask, "What was the music on that Toyota commercial?" We don't know who the hell it is, but we want to go out and buy the record. That's us. Kids are getting this music, but they don't know us. "I love that song but I don't know what it is." So, the marketing has really fallen by the wayside. In fact, it's been very hard to put faces on these songs.

JG: Despite MTV, which really kind of turned that whole equation around twenty years ago where suddenly there were faces to the music and perhaps factors others than the music played a role in their popularity.

DB: Well, it's funny. People always talk about faceless bands, and they say, "Well, that band's not doing so well because they are faceless." I'm trying to think how many of the artists I know and love who are credible and are also not faceless. I'm sure that a lot of Dave Matthews Band could walk through Times Square and no one would know who the hell they are. Radiohead could probably do the same thing. See, I'm not necessarily sure it's about their face. I think it's way more about what they represent.

JG: It seems like everything in our business is rushed. It's a rush to sign the artist, it's a rush to get the album out—it's hardly an atmosphere where albums can take the time to build in the marketplace and artists can be afforded the time to stretch their legs and find fans. Would you say that artist development is dead?

DB: Absolutely. If you sign an act and they don't do the damage on the first record, you're not going to make another record with them.

JG: So I'm a new act. What kind of advice can you give me?

DB: You've got to be as self-sufficient as you can; you've got to go out and get the biggest following you can. You've got to read the tea leaves and pay attention to what's going on around you. You've got to make friends with every act you meet that's in your genre of music—if they get big one day and they might want to take you out there if they think you're cool. You've got to learn to tighten your belt. You've got to learn that there is going to be a certain amount of luck involved but it's not going to be all luck. You've got to be realistic about your time frame. You've got to write lyrics that mean something; for me anyway, I can't speak for anybody else, although with *American Idol* it doesn't seem to make any difference. I think you need to understand where you fit in the record business, musically where you fit. Ask yourself where you want to be in two or three years and what kind of records you want to be making, and whether you're prepared to get into a band with the guys that you're in a band with and live with them for the next three years. That's another huge problem, not being able to co-exist, musically and from a personality standpoint.

JG: A&R is often in the hot seat, being accused of a sort of lemming principle for signing similar sounding things. What are your thoughts on that—is it just one of those odd phenomenon, like prehistoric pyramids appearing mysteriously on different continents, or is it a conscious effort to sign something like the "next Avril Lavigne" because she's happening at that moment?

DB: Look, there are always so many great ideas musically, really. And you kind of lost me after 1973 anyway. Like, after I heard The Beatles *White Album*, The Sex Pistols' *Never Mind the Bollocks* and *Dark Side of the Moon*, I was like, "Okay! What else is out there?" Since then you can count the incredible records on a couple of hands. The Wilcos, Radioheads, Becks...how many are there? Way fewer than people think.

JG: Right, and worldwide record sales and catalogue sales would probably correspond more or less with that statement because classic catalog like the artists you just mentioned is what keeps labels in business, right?

DB: It is. When Coldplay comes along and everyone goes, "Wow! It's Coldplay!" Well of course they're fucking great, but then they always reminded me—and this is going to sound really jaded, maybe I'm still because I've seen Jimmy Hendrix and I saw The Beatles, I saw the Stones when it mattered—but you know when you go to a town and all the restaurants suck and then you go to another town and the food is really good? And you wonder whether it's really that good or is it just better than the food you'd been eating? That's kind of like what this reminds me of.

· · · · · · ·

A&R SERVICES: ARE THEY WORTH IT?

Taxi! Inside Sessions! Broadjam! Getsigned.com! Garageband.com!

Should you join? That depends upon your expectations and how much you already know about the business. Some of these companies make some pretty dramatic claims of guaranteed deal and industry access. Are they for real? Maybe. Depends who's offering what and how. Read the fine print. Most musicians' knee jerk reaction to "paid A&R" related services are negative. (In fact, I can recall a meeting with the CEO of one such company where he described the numerous death threats he had received from angry musicians over the years just because his company existed.)

But, artists and songwriters need to hear feedback about what they do. It is difficult to be creative in a vacuum and if you create music without ever hearing constructive criticism *from qualified players*, it can be difficult to improve. Getting professional feedback plays an important role in developing material that will work for your goals. Whether this means a group of friends with a requisite level of musical hipness and a generosity of spirit, or an independently paid A&R service or consultant, is up to you, your budget and your ability to be objective.

People often ask my advice about whether or not paid A&R related Web sites or companies are worth it. I have never been a client of any of these firms, but I have either received music or worked with some of them, and have been around enough to learn a few key things. Unlike managers and attorneys, paid A&R companies do not make money from your music making money, they make money directly from you. They do not have a financial incentive for your music to succeed; they are paid to provide you with creative feedback.

Has any single artist or song ever been discovered, launched and "broken" by one of these independent A&R services companies? Their flashy ads and Flashed up Web sites may proclaim otherwise, but I seriously doubt it. This is not to say that paid A&R services are a scam; but their value to you is really a matter of defining your own goals and expectations. You should also be aware that some of these companies are actively looking for reasons to justify their funding, which can substantially work in your favor: often new companies in this space are aggressively looking to "prove their business model" by helping an artist to get signed or get their songs placed. Occasionally artists can step into a company's contest-related system and find a warm welcome and true opportunity. It depends on the company.

Ultimately joining a paid A&R services company depends on your needs and the kind of reach that company has. It should go without saying that the odds are certainly against your being "discovered" via such services. Your artist project is not going to garner enormous response unless it's going to garner enormous response anyway. If you have the extra money to gamble on some opportunities, great. But don't be under any illusions. Do your homework and read up. Find some musicians groups online and network your way into finding out from existing or former members whether or not the opportunities were real or if they were disappointed.

CONGRATULATIONS! YOU'RE SIGNED!
(Now What?!)

Mazel Tov. You've signed a deal! Others think highly of your music and/or believe you can make them money. This is a time of celebration. It is also time to recognize that this relatively rare and unique opportunity can be fleeting and you should make the most of it in every way. When the ink on your contract and the bottle of Cristal from your signing party runs dry, it's important for you to realize that now *more than ever* you have got to stay focused and get to work. The machinery that surrounds you—your manager or lawyer or producer or creative partners are all probably in a high cycle with the recent good news, so you are on the up and up—your calls will be welcomed, your ideas will be listened to. May it always be so, but assume that it will not. Don't waste this precious period of your career with over celebration or fantasy—convert career aspirations to reality by doing all you can to cultivate and utilize key relationships that can give you the best opportunity possible to have a real career.

As we've already reviewed, so much can go wrong that has little to do with creative efforts and talent—anything from a scheduling problem in the marketing department to creative doubts over songs, production and budgeting concerns can derail all you have worked for. Of course so much depends on the particular variables of your career and genre, but shortly after an artist is signed is typically when attention is given to creating formal relationships and plans in the following areas:

CHOOSING THE RIGHT PRODUCER: DON'T JUST GUESS

The most common mistake newly signed artists make when they begin their careers is choosing the wrong producer. Artist and repertoire people and managers and presidents of labels will read the credits of a producer and say, "Oh, he did Linkin Park, so he could be good for you because your band is kind of like Linkin Park." But what makes records work is the unique personal chemistry between the members of a group, the musicians, the actual producer and the skill sets and the vibes and the sense of humor and love and everything that they all bring into that room when they are creating. Unless you know the producer and the people involved personally, you're really guessing. You're just guessing—and hoping and praying that something is magically going to happen.

—Ron Fair, President, A&&M Records

The premise is to put them in a situation creatively where they are comfortable. Whatever that means. Y'know, to work with people who are professional, who they feel comfortable with, and the best way to do that is by process of elimination. You put ten people in front of someone and you say, "You pick. You pick the one you think is the right person for you."

     Most people pick by looking for something that [the producer] has done that is like the artist you've got, which is the first kiss of death, because what you're doing is asking them to put something through a hamburger grinder again. I try to match personalities. I like to take things that are missing from someone's personality and find a producer who has all of the things the artist is missing. For example, if I've got an artist who is really anal and wants to dot every i and cross every t, I'll find a producer who likes to leave a mess all over the studio, and eat hamburgers while the artist eats granola bars. [Production] is like being married for four months, so you might as well bring out the sides that are missing.

—David Bendeth, President, Type A Records

SIGNING YOUR PUBLISHING DEAL

Publishers are, of course, focused on both the creative and financial aspects of songwriting. If you're an artist who is also a songwriter, with your own material that will appear on your forthcoming album, your songs just said K'ching—they have taken on new value. Depending on how much writing you do, it can be as if you were simply a songwriter who just scored ten "cuts" or covers with a signed artist about to release an album. Even the most successful "pure" songwriters would be lucky to have that many songs covered on major label releases over the course of a year. Receiving music publishing advance monies on potential future income to be derived from songwriter royalties has evolved into both a path for financial survival for new artists and a competitive industry for the publishers. We will discuss publishing in detail later in this chapter, but as a recently signed artist, publishing is a very significant item on your "to do" list—now that you have a record deal, your songs have value and you are poised to receive an additional advance, which in some cases can exceed your record deal monies. Meeting with publishers and cultivating the right attitudes and postures for shopping your publishing deal is an important process that should be attended to with the same attention given to shopping for a record deal. In addition to providing substantial interest free loans that outdo most commercial banking enterprises, publishers can also help create additional income by licensing your music for film and TV.

SIGNING WITH A BOOKING AGENT

Your A&R rep probably already has relationships in this area, and it's for good reason. Depending upon whether or not your music incorporates touring or having a live presence, connecting with the right booking agency is often part of a larger strategy that allows new artists to begin becoming part of larger tours and events, which will introduce your music to the appropriate target audience.

SIGNING YOUR SPONSORSHIP DEAL

Sponsorship deals are usually modest situations at the early stages of an artist's career, but even artists with indie record deals may be surprised at the free goods and/or opportunities potentially headed their way. Many equipment or instrument manufacturers are enthusiastic about establishing a connection with developing artists. There are also beverage company endorsements available to indie artists (check with certain energy drink companies, beer and liquor manufacturers for their artist programs—you'd be surprised how involved they get with developing artists).

SIGNING YOUR MANAGEMENT DEAL

If you do not already have a manager, now would be the time to lock in your management. Finding competent management once you already have a record deal should not be difficult, although it is possible that some managers will balk at not being able to commission the label's signing advance, which in most circumstances is the only actual payment they will receive for their services for at least a year, except perhaps for music publishing advances.

KEEPING UP YOUR OWN PROMOTIONAL MACHINE

Whatever you did to get to this point, you or someone on your behalf is doing something right. Keep it up. Don't stop just because you are "signed." You can be "unsigned" just as quickly. Many bands go to great lengths to cultivate a fan base and audience and then assume once they're signed, they no longer need to do all of the time-consuming and expensive grassroots promotional activities that got them to this level of awareness in the first place. That's short-sighted thinking that you do *not* want to encourage.

ON GENERATING YOUR OWN HYPE

I think now more than ever it's important to do stuff on the side, to start with having a base—whether it's playing clubs and building up a following and a mailing list, doing the Internet and having a Webpage, or whatever—so that when you get signed, you're not waiting for the label to take care of you. You've taken care of that first step. I think a lot of people make that mistake. That their getting signed is the end, when getting signed is barely even the beginning.

—*Josh Sarubin, VP A&R, Arista Records*

PAYING FOR IT

Every band I work with, *every single band*, I tell them: figure out a way to record music even if it's just really sort of rudimentary, not-the-best quality recording but a decent enough recording—and nowadays you can make a pretty sound for not nearly what it used to cost—and start selling those records at their shows. Get your fans used to paying for your music, because in our society we pay for what we value. So if you've got real fans, they will pay for your music. Get T-shirts printed up. Sell those T-shirts. Yeah, give some of them away, whatever, because you do want to have the advertising, but get people used to paying for them. Have fans who are willing to pay for your music. If you do that, and then you can expand your region of influence and your fan base. Then you've got a career, and who cares if a label signs you. You'll make more money selling your CDs at fifteen dollars a pop and keeping the five dollars of profit than you would at a record label where you'll get credited a dollar fifty to your royalty account that maybe you'll see someday—if you're lucky.

Getting signed is only an opportunity to spread out to a wider audience. If you abandon your core group of fans and the people who supported you before you were signed, they will notice! Fans are mercurial; they are smart; they are sensitive. They can tell when you go Vegas and decide they're not important anymore. Stay in touch with them, keep tabs on them and do not lose what got you signed in the first place. Stay connected to your audience. With the Internet, you have no excuse. It's too easy and cheap.

—*Pam Klein, Attorney, Serling, Rooks, & Ferrera*

MANAGER

JEFF RABHAN
The Firm

First concert attended: J. Geils Band

Best concert attended: REM and the Police in 1982

Top five album recommendations:
 1. Anything by Bob Marley
 2. Patty Griffin *Living with Ghosts*
 3. Bruce Springsteen *Darkness on the Edge of Town*
 4. REM *Reckoning*
 5. Beastie Boys *Paul's Boutique*

Little known resume entry: I once worked as the Maitre d' at the Gotham Bar and Grill, which was a big hangout for John Gotti.

Best project you were involved with that never made it big: 5 O'Clock Shadow

Recommended reading: *Stupid White Men*, by Michael Moore

Instrument played: Guitar

Jeff represents such artists as Michelle Branch and Trust Company

---

SIGNED, SEALED, DELIVERED I'M YOURS
SIGNING STORIES: MICHELLE BRANCH

Justin Goldberg: Jeff, you have been managing Michelle Branch long before she was signed. Can you fill us in on some of the specifics of the process—was there much fanfare before she signed her deal with Maverick?

Jeff Rabhan: It never was a sprint with us, it was always a marathon—week in and week out, we posted good numbers as opposed to having huge weeks in the beginning and sort of petering off. That was our model.

JG: So that strategy obviously worked.

JR: Well, it's not really strategy. It's what the market allows. If we could be selling 50,000 records a week, I'd love it. That being said, I'm happy to be in the position that I'm in now, going to the next record having truly set up this artist to have a career as opposed to perhaps having a shooting-star phenomenon where she comes out of the gate, sells four million records, and then it's over.

JG: Is that a danger people are concerned about, when an artist explodes like that?

JR: Without a doubt. At least on the artist side; I know the labels aren't worried about it.

JG: So how can you help ensure that your label is going to have that level of commitment? Is it a coincidence, just a matter of belief? Were there times when it could just as easily fallen off the map?

JR: I think in today's music business, many managers and labels have aligned themselves together and worked on several projects together because they like how the other one works. I think that managers don't want to take the risk anymore of signing to a guy and not knowing how that label works. A good example of this is how our company works amazingly well with Interscope: we have nine platinum acts with Interscope. With Universal, Jordan Schur and Jimmy Iovine, the compatibility factor is there. We know that if they're signing a band we're managing, they're going to give it 100 percent. I can't guarantee that with some of the other labels because I haven't worked with them before, but I know our bands are getting a shot if they sign with Interscope. This model is really the ever-changing model of the music business, but this is a model that I think a lot of managers are following now.

JG: So that's really almost a comment on where the management and label business has evolved to, in that you now have a well-oiled management machine specifically tuned to a large label's executive team and other resources. Does that seem accurate?

JR: This business has evolved: labels are having a very hard time; they clearly can't get the old model to work properly and they're bleeding cash. Managers have now taken the maverick approach of not wanting to rely on the record company to break our artists. We need to find other ways. We need to have our own marketing people, our own radio people; we need to package our own tours. And I think that by not relying on the label, and not expecting the label—you expect the label to support the artist financially—but you can't expect the label to break your artists anymore.

JG: What would you say is a good advice piece for artists who are looking to get started at Ground Zero? I mean, where do you begin? Do you invest money in making your own records, get a little regional following going, and then try to license it somehow?

JR: If it was 1992, I would say, "Without a doubt," because those were the days of the Mammoths and the Matadors, where the indie bands and the indie labels were as important as the majors in terms of taste-making and creating the next wave of acts. If you recall, a lot of those great indie rock bands went on to great major label deals and were developed properly. Two records on Mammoth or Matador, then you stepped up to Atlantic for your third or fourth record. It could and did happen. These days, there aren't many indie labels that are on the major label radar, and I think it's a lot harder to break through in that model. Listen, if you're selling out the Metro in Chicago, people are gonna take notice, but I think it is increasingly more and more difficult to really make it on your own.

JG: How did Michelle Branch get signed in the beginning? Did you specifically fly in, see her, and think to yourself, "This is something that I could get signed"?

JR: I was in Sedona, Arizona, for a weekend on vacation and I got roped into taking a time-share tour to buy property; the woman asked what I did for a living and I said that I was in the record business. She said, "Oh, you've got to meet my goddaughter. She's the little star of Sedona." Sedona is a town of 4000 people. So I thought, "Oh great, I put my foot in my mouth. Why didn't I just say that I was a school teacher or an architect? I could have enjoyed my weekend." So I said, "Here's my phone number, have her give me a call and I'm happy to talk to her." I take the tour and next thing I know, I come back from the tour and Michelle's standing there with her friend and her sister and her guitar; she had stolen her neighbor's golf-cart and raced up to see me. I thought she was a very sweet girl and she gave me a demo tape. We started working together then. I brought some people to Phoenix to work on some new demos for her, and I sent it out to a couple of friends just to try to get some feedback on the material, and one of those friends was Danny Strick, who signed her. She was fifteen or sixteen years old then.

JG: And how did radio respond at first to Michelle? Is that something that was an issue strategy-wise when you were initially conceiving how this record would be marketed?

JR: It was a complete uphill battle. With the first single "Everywhere," which ended up being a Top Five song, we had great resistance from radio because while there are a lot of great female artists out now, Michelle was the first artist in some time who was writing her own material, singing her own songs and playing an instrument. We did almost a month-long radio promotion tour where she went from station to station to station with her guitar—she played for everyone, so people could see that she was the real deal. And we got the shot at radio; we put the time and effort in at radio to get the shot and people responded. And that's how we fought with radio. But she writes very commercial songs, so it wasn't that much of a stretch for radio to give us that shot.

JG: Because the songs were great and you just kept up the pressure with the face-to-face meetings? It sounds like a big factor was her personality.

JR: A big part of it was, and radio wants to know that the label has a grip on the artist, just like a manager does, because radio doesn't want to take a risk on artists who don't have the support. They don't want to add songs to their playlists that are going to fall off in two weeks. That's not how you build research, that's not how you build your fan base, that's not how you build your current songs for current listeners. So the model is the same for radio although with a different end result.

JG: So what's your prognosis for the future of selling records?

JR: I think that, at the risk of sounding like everyone else you've interviewed, the model is definitely going to change. I think that the biggest travesty of the entertainment business or the music business in the last hundred years is having no handle whatsoever on piracy; the labels failing to come together to come up with a solution that works for all of them because they're so fucking proprietary—that they all decided to try to own the technology of watermarking instead of working together, trying to combat something that is killing our business and hurting artists and costing everybody money.

· · · · · · ·

PUBLISHER

KERRY MCCARTHY
Muzak

First concert attended: The Tubes

Best concert attended: Any Ben Folds Five or Moby Show

Top five album recommendations:
1. Blue Six *Beautiful Tomorrow*
2. Miguel Migs *Colorful You*
3. Simian *We Are Your Friends*
4. Nightmares on Wax *Mind Elevation*
5. Badly Drawn Boy *About A Boy*

Little known resume entry: I was a Foley artist in a London Film Studio.

Best projects you were involved with that never made it big: Melissa Lefton, 1Plus1

Recommended Web site: www.gohomeproductions.co.uk and www.AllMusicGuide.com

Instrument played: Car stereo

SIGNED, SEALED, DELIVERED I'M YOURS
SIGNING STORIES: BEN FOLDS

There are always stories about artists connecting with their musical champions—those key industry insiders who are able to spot the potential for world domination long before there's any semblance of an adulating crowd or a seven figure record deal. In the case of the early days of writer/artist/pianist Ben Folds before the formation of his phenomenal trio, The Ben Folds Five—I was able to observe it firsthand. My A&R partner for the majority of my time served in music publishing was the uniquely talented and dedicated Kerry McCarthy—who was absolutely convinced of Ben's potential while the young Ben languished in Nashville on a songwriter's salary and relegated to the rigidities of Nashville's song-driven universe. I asked her about her thoughts of the development experience with Ben and what elements contributed to the initial breakthrough:

Kerry McCarthy: Of course music industry folks had tried to help Ben Folds because he was so obviously talented, but things seem to click and accelerate when Ben and I started working together.

Certainly there were a few things acting against Ben up until that point. Most industry folks and A&R people could only see that perhaps he was the next Billy Joel or Elton John—A&R guys were asking me, "What is this? Is this alternative or Triple A?" This was during the time that the Triple A radio format was just becoming what people thought might be a serious outlet, and they weren't sure if he was a fit. Which sounds stupid, now. In the pre-record deal days for Ben, it was a bit "square peg/round hole," as a result of well-intentioned but unsure industry advice and direction.

It only took one meeting and one live show for me to realize that Ben had way more in common with Archers of Loaf and Nirvana than Elton or Billy. Having myself just returned from ten years in the U.K. music industry I didn't think so much in "formats" and was more open minded, and so slightly ahead of schedule musically. I found Ben Folds to be a highly refreshing way to shake off the grunge. Here are the things that worked solidly in his favor—but also, Ben Folds is just a smart guy.

A) He worked with Caleb Southern as a producer, to combine the raucous but pretty sound and capture the powerful live sound that was the "Ben Folds Five sound." Ben also found, not only the right bass player and drummer in Robert Sledge and Darren Jesse, but two guys who helped put the edge on the sound and on the stage. They are also stars.

Justin Goldberg, *When 3 Was 5: Ben Folds 1993-1999,*
watercolor on canvas, 13″x19½″

B) Signing to Caroline Records. This positioned Ben perfectly in the marketplace.

C) The power of Karen Glauber at *Hits* magazine.

D) The photo that changed everything—a black and white photo of Ben diving onto his piano. You don't even see his face, but instead you see his Converse All-Star sneaker in mid-air. To my mind, this photo helped to shake off any misconceptions and firmly implant the notion that this guy rocked the house.

E) He is an incredible entertainer and Ben Folds Five is an enormously entertaining live show that just won't quit.

F) Did I mention the songs?

So there's nothing kooky about this story, no putting cassettes in people's sandwiches—just one A&R girl schooled in England's music industry, one enormously talented musician/songwriter/piano god—and timing, sweet, sweet timing.

. . . .

ARTISTS & REPERTOIRE

TOM SARIG
Co-founder
The Shortlist Organization

First concert attended: Hall & Oates, Baltimore, 1976

Best concert attended: Prince, Washington, DC, 1985

Top five album recommendations:
1. Bruce Springsteen *Greetings from Asbury Park*
2. Donny Hathaway *Extensions of a Man*
3. Stevie Wonder *Talking Book*

Little known resume entry: I worked as a tax consultant at Deloitte and Touche in 1989.

Best project you were involved with that never made it big: Spookey Ruben

Recommended Web site: www.shortlistofmusic.com

Instruments played: Piano, guitar, trombone, voice

Recent or past signings: DJ Shadow, Eagle-Eye Cherry, Blackalicious

---

SIGNED, SEALED, DELIVERED I'M YOURS
SIGNING STORIES: BLACKALICIOUS

Justin Goldberg: Tell me about Blackalicious and their progress prior to your becoming involved.

Tom Sarig: They had a good following and they sold fifty thousand records on their own label, distributed through Caroline. They had built up a big touring fan base and I thought the time was right for them to cross over to a bigger audience, so we consciously made a record that was a bit more commercial, not alienating their sort of alternative hip-hop fans (85 percent of which are white, by the way).

JG: How do you usually find music—in general and with Blackalicious in particular—how did you first become aware of them?

TS: I was probably aware of them for a year before I signed them, and I just sort of watched their indie record. I find out about bands from the streets, sort of. I read tons of fanzines and magazines and talk to people at record stores and radio stations. I had heard about them, they were just becoming a big press thing and were a hipster thing, y'know? The press likes to write about them and they started getting better press in places like *Urb* magazine and that sort of thing. I was aware of their debut album that they put out themselves which came out and started to get some action. They were selling a thousand records a week for twenty weeks or so. They ended up selling fifty, sixty thousand records on their own label, which is pretty damn good for an independent act. I was living in Los Angeles then and they sold out the House of Blues, so they were selling-out thousand-seat venues on the West Coast. And I thought at the time that they're a tremendous live band, with great personality and also really soulful and unique—more musical than a lot of hip-hop stuff—and were really poised to move to a major label.

JG: And how did they manage to sell so many records on their own? Was it a really sizable indie or did it just turn into a phenomenon?

TS: They kind of just turned into a phenomenon, and the indie that they were on, which is called Quannum, is the label they own with DJ Shadow and a couple of other people. It was kind of a cult, popular label in the Bay Area. Adam [of Blackalicious] is a big media press artist as well, even more so than the band. His last album was on an independent label in England called Mo-Wax which is kind of an influential, hip, independent label also. So, yeah, Blackalicious comes from a background of really hip, cool, interesting hip-hop music.

JG: Would you say that deals with artists like Blackalicious represent the new paradigm for they way artists are signed to major labels nowadays? Where artists have created some excitement and sales on their own and then someone at a major steps in after there's some proven success?

TS: I find that major labels are generally not great at...we're not great at taking bands from zero to a hundred thousand. So yeah, if you can find an act that is really cool and has a good following and maybe has sold twenty, fifty, seventy thousand records, whatever it is, on their own or through an independent label, and they're somewhat commercial in that they can make songs for the radio, then a label is going to be interested. Labels are really concerned about needing gold and platinum records—and more. So I try to look for acts that are really interesting and cool, that have a following, have sold some records and have experience building their own careers—I look for bands that can cross the road on their own, y'know? And if they can do all that, and if they're somewhat commercial for some format of radio, then they're definitely a candidate. You've got to love them too, obviously.

JG: A lot of this book is geared toward people who want to put out their own record, people who want to create their own labels. What are some of elements you have in your mind to make something successful at that level?

TS: Well, I would suggest to any artist putting out any record to do it in the same but sort of smaller way, the same fashion that we try to do it at a major label, but do it for yourself. You have to get your record, whether it's local or regional, to all the important music writers and the press. Whether it's the *LA Weekly* if you're in Los Angeles, or any of those sort of outlets. Get your music to the local college radio stations or regional college radio stations. Get your music to the specialty shows of the commercial radio stations and maybe you can get some spins there. Just be playing gigs. I always tell bands that you should be not only playing in your hometown every month/six weeks, but you have to keep doing those concentric circles that get bigger and bigger, and keep repeating that pattern until something builds.

Say they're from Los Angeles, and they're playing there, then they do Orange County and San Diego—a couple cities in a concentric circle around Los Angeles—and they could do that circuit. Then, once they build up that base, widen the circle to include San Francisco and Phoenix. And build that way, regionally, and once they've got something going on regionally, that's really great.

JG: What are some of the things some of the labels are considering, in terms of maybe changing their business model?

TS: Shortening the album cycle: instead of having an artist put out a record every eighteen months or two years, we've shortened the album cycle. Have the artists put an album out every nine months or so. Have those albums be only eight or nine songs and then maybe we can price them at ten dollars instead of seventeen. It's kind of a different business model—maybe an artist will go in the studio and want to record twenty songs, then we have two albums and we put out an album and then nine months later put out a second album right after that, pricing them cheaply. We're definitely looking into a lot of that.

· · · · · · ·

WE'RE NOT ALL IN THIS TOGETHER
Different genres and their different rules

It's difficult to accurately address and describe the various components of the music industry when different genres really do in fact have their own rules and value different things. Rock music has always had more of an emphasis on the live music experience and overall posture and attitude; R&B has always been focused on production quality; country music is inseparable from the songwriting community.

And while great songs matter in any format and certain basics of music and human nature do not change from genre to genre, other things do. There are better genres than others for generating revenue independently. Certain musical styles are simply more or less likely to be responsive to grassroots efforts and thus directly impact the ability to establish a network that can operate well outside of the established music industry mainstream. For example, artists and industry critics often cite the wonderful independent achievements of artists like Ani DiFranco, whose meteoric indie success story is a tantalizing tale of hundreds of thousands of dollars in self-promoted record sales and concert revenue. Ms. DiFranco's success is indeed impressive, having sold over 400,000 copies of her various albums and grossing almost 2 million dollars in ticket sales from a rigorous performance schedule that has her doing several shows per week throughout the year. But it is important not to overlook the fact that a good portion of DiFranco's early success resulted from the connected and highly motivated lesbian community. Tapping into an existing network of people with similar values and social ties can be a key element that exponentially advances awareness and interest in an artist. Certain

---

It's the streak. Somebody no one has ever heard of can come out and sell five hundred thousand records the first week, when nobody had ever heard of them three weeks before, all because two or three artists think that they're great. The credibility factor is unbelievable. Rock can't do that. If someone like Fred Durst likes Puddle of Mudd, maybe they go on tour with Limp Bizkit for a year and *then* they break. That's nothing like the urban business. The urban business is incredible and it's always so tied to what's going on. The way I look at the urban and rap business is that it's like watching Fox or CNN: every time a song comes out, it's like a complete update of exactly the time stamp of the moment.

—David Bendeth, President, Type A Records

genres of music are predisposed towards spreading independently. Artists in the punk scene and the hip hop community also share a similar sense of grassroots power and reach, and both genres have their success stories that contain impressive sales figures reached without the help of the mainstream music industry.

SO YOU THINK YOU WANT TO DO A&R?

This could be a very short section, because there are so few A&R careers. Careers for executives are often as short lived as they are for the artists they sign. I guess there's some small solace in knowing that at least the business doesn't discriminate entirely against the creative side. As we've explored pretty deeply at this point, A&R used to be one thing and has turned into something completely different. This has a great deal to do with how technology has affected the business, because the paradigm of the purely creative and non-technical artist being guided through the song creation process by a producer and engineer who each perform separate tasks is really a thing of the past. Technology has placed the power of high-quality recording options into the hands of millions of artists, and with that evolution, the perceived value of having paid employment positions evaluate music for a living is vague at best. There are various ways to gain and maintain employment in such positions, which are—of course—coveted gigs, but in today's industry, really everyone does A&R. A&R today is not so much connecting the artist with the repertoire (the songs) and generating imaging concepts to help marketing departments sell records, it's a hipness factor, an awareness credential. It's a sign of taste, and it's something that everyone essentially can do and does in today's business. Anyone who works at a major music publishing or record company, from the assistant level on up, has likely already read and signed their employee handbook policies, and there's often an incentive agreement to encourage them to bring new artists to the company and a specified compensation package for doing so.

In short, anyone who makes it their business or hobby to find good music they want to let others know about, and somehow insert themselves into the equation, is essentially doing a modern version of A&R. Enter the modern music attorney. The reason this trend probably developed is economic in nature. Law firms tend to stay in business on the whole much longer than most other free agents and representatives of new talent. It's only natural that the momentum of success and the nature of relationships built over time would yield well-traveled channels for new talent to be shopped.

Not everyone agrees A&R is easy or is something everyone should be doing. Especially people doing A&R. Let's open up a dialogue here and weigh in with some responses:

ARTISTS & REPERTOIRE

JASON MARKEY
Immortal Records

LOTS OF LITTLE FIREMEN:
THE CASE AGAINST LAWYERS DOING A&R

Justin Goldberg: What's the hardest thing about doing A&R?

Jason Markey: Everything.

JG: Let's say I am determined to get an A&R position in today's industry. What would you suggest?

JM: I think the best way to do A&R today is find an artist you can attach yourself to and try to be the manager. You almost have to manage a product and get it to the point where it's ready to go, and focus on the kids who are likely to come to that artist's shows and proving an ability to understand how to make a record with the band and understand the development process. But that's a hard recommendation to give today. When I started in the business I got an internship, and I felt I had great taste in music and someone was going to take a shot with me. But I don't think it works that way anymore. I think that the A&R job you would get today would be working for someone who's going to take all the credit if you find a great act and you're never going to move up. That's just the feeling I get from all the major labels today. I think that if you want to do A&R and you have the know-how and the finances to do it, I'd say to try to open your own label and create for yourself a little roster of bands that people are going to want.

JG: That's almost how stiff the competition has become?

JM: Yes. The labels are downsizing tremendously. When I started in this business, I couldn't know all the A&R people, there were so many. The community is so small now, you can't hide anything. People know everything and lawyers have taken over the business, where it wasn't like that ten or twelve years ago.

JG: How have lawyers taken over the business?

JM: The lawyers end up dictating to the labels what bands they should sign based on how successful the lawyers are as their track records grow. Some law firms actually have A&R scouts working for them so they can find the next big thing, which is the weirdest thing I've ever seen. And they fancy themselves as talent scouts, some of them. It's kind of strange. But at the same time it's made the job a lot easier. It's made the job "who has the best relationship with what lawyer is going to get the band."

ARTISTS & REPERTOIRE, PRODUCER

DAVID BENDETH
President
Type A Records

David Bendeth (formerly of RCA) had a similar reaction about lawyers in relation to discovering new talent:

David Bendeth: Well, unfortunately, by the time the lawyer has the band and they're shopping it to an A&R guy, it's kind of over.

Justin Goldberg: In what way?

DB: Well, the A&R person can't really discover the act.

JG: How so?

DB: Because the lawyer's idea is to turn everyone on to it at the same time and create a bidding war and create a situation where there is more awareness than there needs to be, so you've got a lot of artists being signed prematurely, because everyone is jacking it all up and getting everyone all excited. Lawyers don't care whether the music is good or not. They never did. They care whether it's saleable.

JG: But they have to have some criteria for determining that on their own. Some of them have specific taste....

DB: I don't think so. I don't. I think it's like firemen, lots of little firemen. They go wherever the heat is.

JG: Does that mean that you prefer to find things on your own?

DB: By the time a lawyer tells me about an act, I feel like I haven't done my job or something, I don't know. It's very strange.

JG: How would you suggest someone get a job in A&R?

DB: Well, that's another thing—there's no farm system for A&R people. There's no farm system for managers. There's no farm system for the business: it's become a one for all, all for one. If I could give anybody advice, it would be to suck as much information as you can out of people you think know something.

THE CULT OF THE MUSIC BUSINESS: HIGH SCHOOL WITH MONEY

I'm not sure who it was that first pointed out the analogy, but somewhere along the path of my first year of experience in the music business someone said to me, "The music business is high school with money." An odd thing to say, I thought at the time, but eventually, a revelation—the gossip, the cliques, the In Crowd on the fast track, the backstabbing, the egos and the pettiness...it really *is* high school with money.

Perhaps the most surprising characteristic of the music business is the way it behaves almost as an independent body. When people interact with each other for a common (or at least related) goal, a group consciousness is formed with its own set of perceptions, rules and limitations.

People in music share many things in common, theoretically a love for music and a desire to share it. But there is a style and pulse to the industry that can make it appear to be full of glamour and the kind of freedom that many other businesses lack. Trust me, this is an illusion.

Artists have to remember that they are a corporation and that their success depends on what they do both creatively and business-wise. In terms of the business side, it's important to have talented, smart and good people around them so the artist can focus on the creative effort, because at the end of the day, if they don't write good songs and don't make good music, the whole thing crumbles. So, that's it. They're a corporation. They hire everybody. We all work for them.

—*Pam Klein, Attorney, Serling, Rooks, & Ferrara*

RECORDS AND DEALING WITH LABELS

Most books about the music industry place a great deal of focus on hiring the right team of music professionals to work for you. I hope that I have also made clear that the people you choose to represent your music can be as important as the music itself; the "industry" is really only a large web of human relationships with many intangible factors helping or hurting your career. If your focus is on writing, recording or playing music, you will not and should not have the extra time on your hands to learn every relevant legal angle that might apply to the documents you will be presented with throughout your career. But that should not translate into ignorance. You have to understand at least the rudiments of the business or you are asking to get screwed.

IGNORANCE IS BLISS
(But Get Your Bliss Elsewhere)

The price of ignorance for musicians who couldn't be bothered to pay attention to any of their business decisions is well documented (just turn to any random episode of *Behind the Music* if you need a quick reminder). This doesn't mean going to law school at night, but you should be aware of the decisions being made on your behalf. Make sure you stay involved and understand the general terms and industry circumstances related to your music and your rights will be affected as they travel through the cloudy maze of contorted and distorted rights known as a record deal. It's even more important to pay attention in today's business, because so much is in transition, and record labels are on the verge of altering the very nature of how they do business. If ever there was a time for artists to be paying close attention to their affairs, this would be it.

LABEL ANATOMY 101

Record labels have always had a certain sex appeal. The very words conjure glamour and magic; the notion of a dream factory able to transform rags to riches and raw talent into sonic enchantment ready for sale by the millions. Even in today's tentative market, new labels sprout up all the time. (May it always be so.)

But what exactly is a record company? How do you define it? The answer to that question, especially in today's industry, can be very confusing. For decades, recording and distributing music was a complicated and expensive technical process completely out of the reach of the general public. Today almost any professional musician has their own studio set-up and is able to output high quality sound recordings, and any metropolitan city has duplication facilities capable of manufacturing CDs, tapes, or even vinyl. This transformation has played a key role in the explosion of independent artists and record labels of every size and aspiration.

The truth is, for better and worse, a record company can be practically anything and started by anyone—from a single individual selling his or her own music out of the trunk of the car, to a multinational conglomerate comprised of hundreds of subsidiary record companies.

But once upon a time the classic organization of a record company had a well-defined structure with specific departmental functions, such as those below. (If you're starting your own indie with limited funding, be prepared to assume every one of these roles at one point or another.)

A&R

A&R stands (of course) for artists and repertoire, a reference to the days when most performers did not write their own material and the record company A&R man was usually the producer. Although there are still many in-house producers (a few in fact are interviewed here) doing A&R solely as talent acquisition has become its own role and today the majority of record producers are hired independently outside of the label. The responsibilities of A&R include everything creatively associated with finding and "developing" talent for making records and usually are charged with creating records within set budgets. Often A&R departments are divided into subdivisions according to genre: depending on the size of the company there may be separate departments devoted to urban music, country music, classical, or pop.

In terms of specific responsibilities, A&R is a role molded by the personality doing the job: there are those who find talent, help connect the project with a producer and essentially take a hands off approach with hope that the situation finds the autopilot button and some luck. There are also A&R people who see their role as direct and detailed, attending to every possible A&R related detail. If an artist does not have a manager, A&R folks often take on managerial roles as well—this can of course can range from analyst to agent, from producer to babysitter.

A&R ADMINISTRATION, ACCOUNTING DEPARTMENT, ROYALTY DEPARTMENT

Each of these departments may be quite different and separate at larger companies, but for indies, it usually all falls under a single job description for one tortured individual. A&R administrators take care of the nuts and bolts details related to A&R related activities, handle the billing, the label copy and generally make sure that all documentation is in order in connection with the recordings. "Admin," as they're sometimes called, can be a part of either the accounting department or the A&R department. The accounting department is usually a general description for those who tend to the traditional accounting functions of generating payroll, paying company bills and generating invoices and official company financial documents, such as profit and loss statements. The royalty department, if separate from these, is focused on tracking documentation related to providing royalty statements in connection with the contractual agreements for each artist.

LEGAL & BUSINESS AFFAIRS

Shortly after someone in the A&R department spots some hot new talent they want to sign, it's likely that their first order of business is to consult with an executive in Business and/or Legal Affairs, and this person is almost always a lawyer. Not only do the "outside" lawyers who shop new talent have an extensive scope of influence in the realm of A&R, but once a deal is first in the works, it's lawyers at labels themselves who will shape the actual deal and influence the long term business relationship that the artist has with the company.

But that's not all label atttorneys do; their role is extensive in both a basic and sophisticated sense. They may be involved at the highest level of decision-making for the company in terms of budgeting, staff organization, or distribution and usually represent the company in negotiations with major strategic partners, licensees and licensors, or target acquisitions. They are also responsible for churning out the agreements necessary to best protect and exploit the company's assets on an ongoing basis. This often positions the legal department as a central control center for the label's operations, as they monitor and service everything that might connect and affect quite literally, the company's legal and business affairs.

It's probably because of the extensive reach of this department, that often lawyers who have done their time in Business Affairs are considered uniquely qualified to run departments and eventually ascend to the highest positions in the business. If you run through a list of the senior executives at a record label or publishing company, it's a good bet that most of them were all once lowly attorneys churning out deals on the lower rungs of a business affairs department ladder. It's also one of the cruel ironies that so many creative departments are run by lawyers with little or no professional creative background.

PUBLICITY DEPARTMENT

In the music business, the best form of advertising has always been free—the radio. (Unfortunately, with the proliferation of illegal file-sharing on the Internet, now their product is free too, so there's a bit of an issue there.) The publicity department has a similar objective: to obtain free advertising in print by garnering press attention for artists on the roster who are releasing new product. Because Publicity represents the record company and its artists to the press, they are also critical when something goes wrong at a label and there is a need for damage control.

INTERNATIONAL

The existence of the international department is based on the size of the label. The world marketplace for music is enormous; finding out what American acts sell overseas is often a surprise. The function of the international department is to promote the company's releases overseas, and occasionally, to do the reverse—promote product from an overseas affiliate or licensor to the American market. Usually at big companies, American creative executives spend a lot of time fielding inquiries from foreign affiliates about U.S. releases for their roster—successfully penetrating the American market has long been the ultimate achievement for artists outside the U.S.

PROMOTION

Without promotion, there's barely a record business at all. Although they may do other things to help sell records, the promotion department is charged with charting the radio trajectory of a label's artists. They are the in-house version of the classic "independent radio promoters" of yore. The promotion department oversees the radio activity for their artists and initiates radio promotion strategies tailored specifically for the various musical formats at radio stations. Effective personnel in this area can look forward to an excellent shelf-life in the business; finding talented radio promotion executives has long been the mark of the most successful record labels.

ART DEPARTMENT, PRODUCT MANAGEMENT

The art department is just that—they create the art for everything related to the company's products from album covers to posters, postcards and advertising. Product managers are responsible for tracking an artists' actual release through the company's promotional machine from its raw recorded state to the finished album copy. They help to ensure the various elements involved in album preparation and launch are functioning effectively together. Often A&R people are the product managers.

SPECIAL PRODUCTS

One of the secrets about the record industry is that the real profits do not come from new hit records. They come from what's known as "catalog"— you know, the Eagles *Greatest Hits* album, James Taylor's *Daddy Loves His Work*, Fleetwood Mac's *Rumours* and Miles Davis' *Kind of Blue*. It is the special product department that often takes responsibility for repackaging albums, creating re-mastered and reformatted special box sets, or even creating new products as the result of a special joint venture with a strategic partner. When there is an initiative to imagine, assemble and market existing catalog to maximize revenue from a company asset, this department is at work.

SALES DEPARTMENT

The sales force at a record label is focused on selling a label's releases to retail. Often elaborate national networks, separate from the record companies' headquarters, sales departments can be divided into the division they focus on by both genre and level of distribution; some groups are focused on handling the major distribution chains, others on the independents. For the larger companies, this usually entails a sales force in certain regional areas where an existing warehouse stores actual record stock. Sales may also be focused on advertising initiatives, which, depending on the size of the company, can be extensive.

I'LL TAKE A DOUBLE DECAF NONFAT JOINT VENTURE WITH DISTRIBUTION TO GO, PLEASE

All record deals are not created equal, and nether are the companies from which they spring: artists such as Toni Braxton and TLC were signed to record deals and sold millions of records and generated millions of dollars in revenue for their labels. But despite their overwhelming luck and high level of commercial success, both multi-platinum selling artists filed for bankruptcy. How does that happen? Somewhere along the way they either trusted someone they shouldn't have and/or had no leverage when they signed their deal with a production company.

THE NIGHTMARE OF THE PRODUCTION COMPANY

Not all production companies are bad news. The truth is, like any business that takes a risk on unproven talent when no one else will, many more of them lose money and fail than succeed. And some production companies create fair deals with unique terms that often function as critical career launching pads for artists who might otherwise have been overlooked forever. But typically, when artists sign deals with production companies, they do so at the onset of their careers when they have very little leverage. With little or no material recorded to impress other potential suitors, they wind up agreeing to terms that virtually ensure they will never be fairly compensated even if they achieve the unlikely level of multi-platinum success. Production companies create a set of financial and creative terms that essentially bind the talent's services to the production company. When a deal with a record label is struck in connection with a certain artist, it is usually struck only between the production company and the record label. This leaves the financial arrangement where it began, with the production company. So while Toni Braxton sold millions of albums for her label, the label may not have been under direct obligation to pay her for her services *because she was under contract to a production company* whose responsibilities were limited. Record labels may take steps to prevent this and assist with these issues but you shouldn't count on it. They rarely litigate the hand that feeds them by going around production companies, as their deals usually specify otherwise. Don't let the same limo bill happen to you!

DIFFERENT TYPES OF RECORD LABELS

Imprints, Vanity Labels, Joint Ventures

Apart from the five major labels and their subsidiaries, there are several different kinds of indie labels. Imprints may function or be known to the public as a record labels but (essentially) imprints don't necessarily exist in terms of a staff or a physical location. So-called "vanity" labels are often imprints created especially for certain artists by their record labels as an incentive or gift. Vanity labels allow artists to sign other artists to their "label" and share in the profits. A "joint venture" is typically a partnership between two companies who have joined forces to create a separate profit-sharing entity. There are many variations to the joint venture, but typically joint ventures make use of a combined workforce, which may have different strengths poised to benefit by becoming strategically aligned. There are independent labels of every shape and size—many of which appear to be actually "independent" companies, but in truth are anything but and are either wholly or partially owned by majors.

Mini-Majors

The word indie label can have a variety of definitions. Typically, companies that are fully staffed, but have their distribution handled by a major, are known as "mini-majors." Labels like Maverick and Lava would be described as mini-majors.

True Stand-Alone Indies

"True" indies are not usually affiliated with major labels unless they are later acquired by them, which was a trend throughout the 1990s during an industry-wide effort to pick up market share and access specialized

FYI

THE MAJORS-NON DAIRY AND SUBSIDIARY

The Big Five majors and their important subsidiary record labels now include the following:

- UMG (Universal Music Group)—DreamWorks, Interscope/Geffen/A&M ("IGA"), MCA, Universal, Island/Def Jam/Mercury Group, PolyGram, Motown, MCA Nashville, Verve, Decca and Philips
- WMG (Warner Music Group)—Atlantic Records, Lava Records, Elektra Records, Rhino Entertainment, Warner/Reprise Records and Maverick Records
- Sony—Columbia, Epic, Legacy and Sony Classical
- BMG—J Records, Arista, RCA, Ariola, Windham Hill and Zomba Group
- EMI—Angel/Blue Note Records, Capitol Records, Priority Records and Virgin Records

The majors and their subsidiaries control about 80 percent of U.S. retail sales. Each major also runs its own fully integrated operations for affiliated music publishing, distribution and manufacturing companies.

markets. Examples of labels that began as independents but now belong to majors include Matador (now part of Atlantic) and Mammoth (now part of Disney). Examples of successful true indie labels include Vagrant Records, Righteous Babe Records and Epitaph. Usually true indies are investor-or owner-financed and distribute their albums through independent distributors, which control between 15–20 percent of the market. Independent distributors are smaller and usually better suited to catering to certain genres of music that majors either overlook or can't compete in effectively.

P&D Deals

Often an indie enters into P&D deals with a major. This means a major label will handle their manufacturing and distribution, but all other functions, such as A&R, promotion and marketing, are done by the indie.

RECORDING AGREEMENT BASICS: NOW AND ZEN

Recording agreements are strange beasts. Reading like a single one hundred mile long single sentence over dozens (if not hundreds) of pages, they are deliberately confusing documents of deceit; a willful minefield of hidden meanings designed to trip up artists and their lawyers and thus tip the odds even further in the favor of the label. That the scale would be tilted and the road rocky has always been a given to some degree, but within the industry, that has never been an unexpected or even unforgivable sin. Record companies have always gone to great lengths to ensure they receive most of the money from record sales; arguably and historically this has been allowed because they kept their hands out of other gilded pockets—such as touring and merchandising. Record companies take great risk on new talent and spend great sums creating imaging and marketing initiatives to propel sales, but once an artist is known to the public, labels traditionally do not get to share in revenues outside of the artist's recording activities. So when you consider the larger picture, labels spend a fortune creating a brand then they receive income only from a single specific category—master recording rights. This may no longer be the case. The Internet has changed the economics of investing in artists, and investors who get burned usually adjust their strategy. Record deals right now still incorporate the basic rights as laid out in the following section, but they may be reaching for much more sometime soon. Which may not necessarily be a bad thing—*if* they are willing to pay for extra rights and effectively execute the new business they want to create or take over.

YOUR OWNER'S MANUAL TO THAT NEW AND GLITTERY EXCLUSIVE RECORDING AGREEMENT

There are almost as many versions of this as there are recording artists. Record deals can vary tremendously, and do so for a very broad range of factors too long to list in this brief overview. There are several excellent books that go into great detail about the following contract provisions; fortunately for both of us, I'm not about to go into them here. The following is just a basic overview that should help you to know what's going on in A&R attorney meetings.

Territory—Simply designates *where* the record label will be permitted to sell the recordings under the deal—as deals may be specified to indicate virtually any geographical location (i.e., as in only for certain European territories, or only in the United States.) Often the territory is indicated as "The World," or to be on the safe side, "The Universe," (just in case Universal Records is one day in the unusual contractual predicament of being unable to sell their albums on a newly inhabited planet.)

Term—The length of time that the artist is to be held bound by the agreement where they furnish their recording services to the recording company. Many recording contracts indicate an initial term of one year, followed by "exercisable options" which almost always mean that the record label will have the option of determining whether or not they would like to continue with a particular artist and their recording contract. The word "option," obviously enough, indicates that they also have the option to drop the artist. Typical agreements with a term and options may indicate a term of one year plus anywhere from one to five options. This is an area to keep your eye on, because it is a seemingly innocuous enough category with potentially severe implications. The word "term" suggests a time period, but often a label will insert language that can distort time better than a Dali painting: if there is language that requires certain conditions be fulfilled (such as the delivery of recordings or the acceptance by the label of such recordings) then a simple term of "one year" can be doubled or even tripled. Often you hear of label and artist groups battling over something called the "seven year statute" which is directly related to this area. Artists sign deals that indicate a time period which winds up in reality extending beyond seven years. It just so happens that there is a lot of record business in the state of California, which *just happens* to have a labor law on the books prohibiting an employer from enforcing a personal service contract (i.e., anything beyond seven years).

Recording Commitment—This outlines how many recordings will be included in a particular agreement and lays out what the rules are (for both sides) in terms of delivering the recordings, and the rules for officially notifying each side about intention to continue or not with the deal. Naturally these conditions are usually written in favor of the record label. This section also defines exactly what a "master" recording is and usually indicates that the company will have the right to determine whether an artist's material is commercially satisfactory.

Advances & Recording Funds—An "advance" is what it sounds like, an advance or "pre-payment" of royalties. This is the most sought after chunk of money in the music business, because it's usually the largest. It's also non-refundable—advances are a gamble on the part of labels because they have no assurance that they will ever see a return on their investment. Once they hand over an advance, virtually anything can go wrong and put that money in jeopardy. If things go right (from a label perspective), that advance money will go a long way—usually toward making sure the artist doesn't see any other money for a while. Advances are "recoupable"—perhaps the most key word in all of the music business. Recouping costs is at the heart of any music operation; the idea being that once an advance is given, all monies earned by the artist are billed against that advance, and no monies are paid out until the entire amount advanced has been recouped. The specific definition of an advance can be murky as well, as often labels consider any and all payments made on behalf of the artist to be an advance. Also, artists also rarely realize that a huge portion of their signing advance goes toward the fees involved in actually making a record.

Royalties—This section of your contract outlines the specific formulas that will be used to calculate the monies owed to you from your record sales. The first problem is that records are sold to a variety of vendors under different terms and circumstances, some of which can be difficult to track. Records are also marketed, in part, by being given away for free at radio and retail, making the waters of how many records sold even murkier. The two big issues with royalties are what the royalty percentages are based on and what the royalty percentages are computed by: record sales royalties are either outlined in the agreement to be based on wholesale or retail, and subject to a long list of variables and potential deductions that reduce the overall number of records on which to base the royalty. Both wholesale and retail prices are essentially arbitrary, as retail pricing itself is usually described in the agreement as the SRLP (the "suggested" retail list price)—which can still be sold for much less than the record company "suggests." Wholesale prices are what the retail locations actually pay the record label. The royalty computation formula is filled with loopholes as it reduces the number of records royalties are even calculated on (as in "computed upon 90 percent of sales minus returns"). There are deductions everywhere, from the 10 percent packaging deduction I mentioned in the first chapter (to account for breakage during shipping, something that hasn't happened in 75 years) to singles, foreign sales and club-related royalty limitations.

Musical Compositions—How songwriters get paid for the use of their songs is a direct result of how the Copyright Act's guidelines are written; even when an artist writes and records his or her own material the Copyright Act legislates the way the artist is paid for writing the piece. The musical compositions segment of your contract outlines how the company intends to deal with paying "mechanical royalties" to the writer of the

---

WHY LAWYERS TRY TO MAX OUT RECORD COMPANY ADVANCES

You often hear artists complain that lawyers are overly interested in receiving upfront monies; this is partially because attorney's generally commission those upfront monies as part of their compensation for working on a client's behalf. I asked attorney Pam Klein, of Serling, Rooks, & Ferrera, to elaborate:

Pam Klein: There is no long term if you don't get to the short term. That I believe it's important to get the largest possible initial advance has absolutely nothing to do with how much money I might earn as the result— or even lining the artist's pocket. Sometimes it has to do with how much money the artist might owe to everyone who has spent money on them over the years that they now have to pay back, not to mention that they may want to eat. It's quite common for an artist to sign a record deal and then immediately have to pay over fifty thousand dollars of their hundred and twenty-five thousand dollar advance to people who, along the way, funded recordings, bought them clothes—all sorts of things. So, you need to max that out, but it also is an indication of the level of commitment that the label has going in. Having worked at a label, I will tell you that the artists who got the bigger deals were treated differently, not necessarily in an obvious way, but you hear about some artist being a priority. Well, how did they become a priority? They become a priority from the very beginning because the company had already put in a half a million dollars before they made a video or started with any promotions. For a label, a big dollar investment is always going to be the priority.

songs used on the album covered by the recording agreement. The word mechanical is derived from the very first mechanical devices that could reproduce music without live musicians; a law was created to pay the songwriters based on the use of the mechanical device. Today it's mainly used to calculate a set royalty based on actual record sales. There are few other key concepts and terms here:

The notion of "first use" of a song comes from the fact that when a song is first released to the public, the writer is allowed to charge any price he or she can get for their never before heard material to appear on an artist's record (even if the artist is the songwriter). This right is known as the "controlled composition clause." We are now in an era where so many artists record their own material that it's often a bit confusing to understand that the laws were developed to protect songwriter rights, which were traditionally separate from those of the artist. Once a song is "published," or released to the public, there is a law designating an amount of money that the songwriter is to be paid for the use of the song—it's a license the songwriter cannot refuse and the amount to be paid is a set fee by the government. This is called the "statutory rate." The statutory rate is another area that labels will try to whittle away, because they are loathe to pay the full amount seemingly owed in any category. Often the statutory rate itself is reduced down to what's often referred to as the "3/4 rate" because, well, mostly because they say so. The contract will be littered with items that have no real financial basis for being part of a deal other than the same items have been included for years, and are now standard to the industry's practices and represent the normal way of doing business. The upshot for you is that it amounts to an arbitrary reduction of the amount of money you will be eventually owed.

CD PRICING AND ROYALTY RATE CONSIDERATIONS:
A VERY UNBUMPY RIDE

A senior exec at a major recently told me that the most important factor right now in marketing new artists is the reasonable pricing of an album. His view is that the coming era of record sales is going to be geared toward a lower "developing artist" price and that artists with lower priced albums will be poised to sell more. I again asked Ms. Klein to elaborate:

Pam Klein: Having a low resale price for an album may potentially move more units, but as soon as you start any kind of marketing that competes on the basis of price rather than on the basis of quality, you've lost. As a lawyer, I would never want someone to hire me because my fee was more or less than somebody else's. I think it's a matter of basing the decision on the right criteria. You price a Bob Dylan record at top-dollar, and you're going to get that top-dollar. Now, in terms of breaking artists, I know many labels have had success with lower introductory artist pricing. For example, it's well known that Sony, "value-priced" John Mayer's recording as a "New Artist Series," to help market it and get it out there, and that was very successful. I think the most important thing, for an artist in negotiating their deal initially, is to make sure that the record label limits the number of those [value-priced] units they can sell. Those units don't count towards "bumps;" they don't count towards increases in your royalty rate because they're not "full-priced normal retail channel sales." Only [full-priced albums] count towards your bumps. Value-priced units are not full-priced, so you're not getting full mechanicals on them, not getting full dollars and cents. They are loss leaders for artists—and while it's important maybe for the first hundred thousand units, or maybe even two hundred thousand units—you want to actually limit the number that the label can do. You want to limit it—let's say an artist is considered broken at two hundred and fifty thousand units—then you want them to go back up to their normal price.

ATTORNEY

ED SHAPIRO
The Uberfall Group

First concert attended: Foreigner—the Foreigner 4 Tour with Billy Squier at Madison Square Garden, NY

Best concert attended: Miles Davis—the JVC Jazz Festival at Avery Fischer Hall, NY

Top five album recommendations:
1. Al Jarreau *All Fly Home*
2. Dave Grusin *Mountain Dance*
3. Elton John *Tumbleweed Connection*
4. Wendy Matthews *Stepping Stone*
5. Chaka Khan *Epiphany*

Little known resume entry: Semi-professional/sponsored adventure racer.

Recommended reading: *Standing For Something*, by Gordon B. Hinckley

Recommended film: *Amadeus* (Orion Pictures Corporation, 1984)

Recommended Web site: www.google.com

Instruments played: Piano, saxophone, violin, French horn, percussion, a little guitar

MECHANICAL ROYALTY CAPS:
ED SHAPIRO EXPLAINS IT ALL

Justin Goldberg: Mr. Shapiro, kindly explain to the other side of my brain what the "mechanical royalty cap" provision means as included in most recording agreements essentially sets forth.

Ed Shapiro: Well, typically in a record contract, the record company is responsible for paying what they call a mechanical royalty by law. A mechanical royalty is a royalty paid to the songwriter of that particular song for each actual, physical copy of an album or a single. So every time an album is pressed and sold, there's a royalty that the record company is required to pay the actual songwriter on that album or that single. A lot of times that is the artists themselves. So the record company is paying the artist who is also singing on that record. If you did an album full of covers, ten or twelve songwriters would be entitled to receive royalties. The record company puts a cap on how many songs, although they're required by law to pay the full amount, they may cap the number of songs they are willing to pay on that record before they end up charging back any over-age to that artist. So it's possible that a record contract will say, we'll pay ten times what the law prescribes, which is called the statutory rate. If you want to put twelve songs on your record, although the label is required to pay twelve by law, they are going to charge back two songs to your account. They feel that the quid pro quo, or consideration for putting you out as an artist, is that they get to cap and put a finite number, a dollar figure, on what their publishing or mechanical royalty outlay is going to be per record. Their rationale is, "We can't have artists who want to put fifteen or twenty songs on a record. It'll kill the model, the economic and financial model of selling records."

JG: And that's why artists don't put twenty-two songs on an album each time?

ES: Obviously there are creative reasons why you may not want to put twenty songs on an album. There's certainly a physical limitation, the size of a CD, of what it can hold. Although let's be honest, most CDs can hold a full seventy four minutes of music. But predominantly, the most important thing is, an artist who is also a songwriter is not going to get paid on more than the cap that's provided in the contract. If there's a ten-song cap and he wrote every song on the record, if he puts eleven songs, the record company would only pay him for ten.

JG: What if the song becomes a hit on the radio?

ES: Well, from a mechanical royalty standpoint, the record company is only obligated to pay for mechanical distribution. A songwriter has several different ways of making money. One of them is certainly from mechanical royalties. Another way is from performance royalties. Performance royalties come from performing live shows, money received from playing live performances. But the bulk of performance royalties comes from radio airplay; all the radio stations are required to pay, for each time they spin a record, they are supposed to pay a royalty to the songwriter. And typically a songwriter will enter into an agreement with a collection society, a performance rights society such as BMI or ASCAP, and the function of these societies is to go out there on behalf of the songwriter and the publisher to collect money on behalf of their members. They take that money and distribute it back to the songwriter.

· · · · · · ·

Release Commitment—Record labels tend to be rather commitment-phobic, so you can look forward to this section of the contract generally limiting the label's obligation to release material—even if it appears otherwise. Even the biggest artists will have agreements which essentially place the entire decision of what and when to release at the label's discretion. Most labels release a small fraction (less than 25 percent) of what they sign! The release commitment often appears to be a guarantee from a label actually committing to releasing an album according to a specific schedule of delivery, but careful analysis of the contract provisions usually reveal a chain of events that can keep the artist on a leash and the label well out of the liability zone.

Rights Granted—This section outlines further related rights needed or desired for promoting the artist, such as the right to use the name and likeness of the artist. Be careful here! We live in world of inexpensive video technology which in today's market often means DVD releases. Sometimes companies take a simple name and likeness agreement and combine it with certain recording rights, even very limited recording rights, and then choose to stretch the meaning of these rights into something altogether new. Recording rights, for example, when combined with the standard name and likeness language often included in a typical recording agreement can be argued in court to represent enough of a right to sell visual recordings in connection with the exploitation of a video release. After all, who defines exactly what a "recording" is unless a certain kind of exploitation is specifically excluded. Assume nothing! (If Bill Clinton can argue about what the definition of the word "is" is—anything can happen here.)

Accountings—This section outlines the schedule of financial accounting in relation to the record deal and the rules the record company will (theoretically) abide by if there is a financial disagreement.

Video—This area outlines terms for costs and arrangements related to the creation of music videos for sale and/or promotional use.

Warranties & Representations—This is basically where the artist confirms they there is no legal reason preventing him from entering into this particular deal, that the recordings are his to legally assign and that he will not be infringing upon any other artist, writer, or company by doing so.

Unique Services—The section wherein the artist acknowledges they are unique—as if they needed to be convinced!—and that since they indeed are unique, if they do not abide by this deal they cause irreparable damage to the company.

Governing Law—This section designates under which State's law both sides agree to have disputes related to this contract settled. This is a seemingly innocuous category in the agreement with broad ranging implications if your deal is ever subject to litigation.

Marketing Restrictions—You heard it here first—beware of marketing restrictions. What rights does a label have to exploit your masters and to change those masters without your consent? Can they couple them with somebody else's masters? Can they use them in motion pictures, on television, in TV, or radio commercials without your consent? Most first drafts of recording agreements say that a label can do any and all of the above, all without asking the artists permission. The other important consideration is how the masters themselves can be manipulated without your consent: for example, can they take your finished masters and remix it ten or twenty years from now, and then decide to release it at a different speed or with different instrumentation or vocals? Let's say they remix some part of your recording for a new artist or style of music that you don't particularly care for, or that impacts your career in a negative way. If you don't make sure that your agreement contains certain restrictions, then you don't have any say in the matter. Most labels are reasonable and will not go out of their way to piss off artists and or the powerful attorneys who represent them, but it's always smart to have such restrictions in writing.

PAY OR PLAY LANGUAGE: WHAT IT MEANS

Let's say that you're in a band and you're on a major label and your first album sold only a hundred thousand units. Not good, but you've got an A&R person who really believes in you, and he says to his boss, "I really believe in this artist. I want to make another record with them," and the record label says, "That's great, let's do it." Then, something goes a little wrong. Maybe you go into the studio and record some demos that don't impress, or maybe your A&R person gets another job at another label, or is laid off because the company needs to downsize—whatever—something goes wrong and all of a sudden, no one is interested in making your record. So you're sitting around wondering, "Am I making a record? Am I not making a record? Do I even have a label?" And pretty soon you say to yourself, "I don't think I like these guys anymore: I want off the label." That's when you look at your pay-or-play clause and follow the outlined rules regarding what your record company is obligated to do for you under the recording agreement if they are not willing to pay for you to make recordings. Usually they don't have to release any records that you make for them and they don't have to release anything in any particular territories. They don't have to do anything except pay for you to make the recordings.

But wait! I have a "release commitment!" you say. A release commitment says that if they don't release it, you can get out of the deal, if it's in the United States and it's the first record. You can get out of your contract, but they still own any masters anyway. But they don't have to put them out, because, remember, it's about a whole machine that goes into motion; they have to press up a bunch of records and incur money for creating artwork and maybe they have clearances to do and they've got to roll out those trucks and ship them and spend gas money and whatever else that is connected to the process. So, if they've already spent three hundred thousand dollars on a record and they're not hearing anything that's blowing them away, they might say, "Y'know what? We're not putting it out." The long and short of it is, they either pay—as in they either buy their way out of the contract and obligation to make the record, or you force them to actually put up the money to make the record.

—*Pam Klein, Attorney, Serling, Rooks, & Ferrera*

ATTORNEY

FRED GOLDRING
Goldring, Hertz & Lichtenstein, LLP

First concert attended: Leslie West & Mountain at the original Electric Factory in Philly (I was twelve).

Best concert attended: Live Aid 1985 (on stage); first and second Rock & Roll Hall of Fame Awards Dinners jams

Top five album recommendations:
1. Jimi Hendrix *Band of Gypsies*
2. James Taylor *Sweet Baby James*
3. The Police *Synchronicity*
4. Stevie Ray Vaughan *Texas Flood*
5. The Beatles *The White Album*

Little known resume entry: I was the opening act for Roger McGuinn in 1978 at a show in North Carolina.

Best project you were involved with that never made it big: Dakota Moon

Recommended film: *The Great Santini* (Warner Bros., 1979)

Recommended reading: *Protect & Defend*, by Richard North Patterson

Recommended Web site: www.comingsoon.net (the latest movie trailers online!)

Instruments played: Guitar, piano

Notable clients: Alanis Morissette, Will Smith, Destiny's Child, Christina Aguilera, Herbie Hancock, and No Doubt

....

COMPETING WITH FREE: EVOLVING RECORD COMPANY BUSINESS MODELS
A CCONVERSATION WITH FRED GOLDRING, FOUNDING PARTNER OF GOLDRING, HERTZ & LICHTENSTEIN

....

Justin Goldberg: How are record companies dealing with the changes in the market and how do you see all this shaking out? Has the shift in the market adversely affected what you do?

Fred Goldring: Well, I don't know that they've struck what I do other than that record companies are much more reluctant to front-load long-term deals than they used to be, because they don't know what the long-term means anymore. You used to be able to say, "Oh, I'll just front-load the deal, and give an advance spread over four or five albums." Now they don't know if that money will be there in four or five albums, so they're much more reluctant to do that; and they're also trying to cut costs wherever they can, so that impacts the bottom-line in terms of how the big advances are paid in a lot of those deals. That's probably the real immediate effect. I think the bigger question for companies is, "How do we compete with 'free'?" How do we compete in a world where music can be accessed for free? And the answer is: they can't. You can't compete with "free." All you can do is acknowledge that it's there and then try to give the consumer a better value than "free." I would argue that water is free, but there is a pretty big market in bottled water. The way that people access music by peer-to-peer file sharing and CD burning, it's not going away and no matter how much technology record companies come up with, there will always be technological workarounds that will enable consumers to figure out how to undo whatever record companies are doing. It's just a big tide and there's no way to really stop that. What companies *should* be doing, and I hope we are coming around to, is trying to figure out how to monetize that behavior. In other words, we're big advocates for compulsory licensing. Everybody should be able to trade whatever they want all the time, but there should be a little charge every step of the way in the process. Whether it's the guys who make the blank CDs, the guys who make the burning hardware, the ISPs, the phone companies, the computer companies, whatever it is...anybody who's in that chain...there's a little bit of money paid during the whole process that's put into a pool and goes back to the copyright holders, whether they be the record companies or the artists or whatever, much in the way that ASCAP and BMI work. Ultimately, I think that this is the only way it will ever work. You can't create supply-side solutions to demand-driven problems, which is what the record company was trying to do. I think that, over time, it'll eventually get to that. The other thing is, I think that record companies are really acknowledging that previous deals—which said, "We will help you create a brand that we don't own, as long as we can make almost all the money on the record side, but you make all the money on everything else," may not be the way it will work in future now that the money isn't all on the record side anymore. The labels feel like, "Well, we're helping to create this brand and we need to participate in all of the other income streams—that will undoubtedly occur as a result of [the label] making your records popular and making your music popular— whether it be touring, merchandising, publishing, whatever." It's great that the labels may want to participate in it but are they willing to be the sponsor of a tour, or a promoter of a tour? Are they willing to take the advances on merchandise the way a merchandiser would, and so on and so forth? It's not even so much that artists aren't willing to give up those rights, because they give them up to other people. If record companies can show that they'll pay just as much or more for it, and in fact very aggressively market in those areas, then it may make sense for artists to do those deals.

JG: Are you seeing deals already that are headed that way, where they are asking for those kinds of properties?

FG: No, not yet, but I can start to see that with the bigger deals, where superstars are becoming available, the companies are saying, "Well, maybe we'll make a new kind of deal. Maybe we'll make a deal where we'll put up a bunch of money and be your partner and everything." Take touring, for example. With new artists, they go out and want to create an audience but they have no demand yet, because no one knows who they are, which is where the concept of tour marketing comes into play. We're all gonna stay on the road because you know when you're out there building an audience—as people see you, and you're in these towns all along the way, getting reviews—it will all help eventually sell records. So, the record companies are probably sitting there thinking, "Well, wait a minute. If we're paying money to help an artist develop while touring, well, why don't we just promote the damn tour? Get in early and become part of the artist's touring machine? Let's help build it and let's help be a part of it." I think you're going to see more of that, because it just makes sense.

JG: What about artists who maybe aren't touring intensive? Do you think those artists are going to wind up suffering under this new system?

FG: It depends. I think in this brave new world, we're going to see all sorts of creative and novel ways of marketing artists. Madison Avenue is embracing new artists because they want hipper music, music that people will ask, "What was that?" You've seen Dirty Vegas, you've seen Moby— artists are really breaking out of television commercials and advertisers are getting them cheap instead of paying a gazillion dollars to some band everybody knows. They're paying for really cool music that no one's ever heard before. So it not only solves the problem of the music being cheaper for them, it also makes the product seem cooler and hipper because they're discovering music on the cutting edge and that makes them more interesting to the consumers. Two years ago, that kind of thing didn't even exist. You also see artists, big artists, who are embracing corporate

America in a way that they wouldn't have ten years ago. Aerosmith's doing commercials, and Celine Dion's doing her new thing with Chrysler. So to answer your question, I think the artists who don't tour will find alternative ways to market themselves that isn't dependent on touring.

JG: What do you think about the criminal prosecutions for copyright infringement that we've had?

FG: Well, the record labels are on kind of a slippery slope, there. I mean, they've got to very careful about right-to-privacy and invasion-of-privacy. It wasn't that long ago when Tipper Gore and the PMRC (Parents' Music Resource Center) were out on their campaign to not only label lyrics, but they were saying record companies shouldn't put out damaging gangster rap music because it was bad for kids to hear and damaging to society and blah, blah, blah. Meanwhile, the record companies were the ones saying, "You can't tell us what to do, it's our freedom of speech and freedom of choice," and now those same companies are saying that they're ready to invade your privacy and your choice under the guise of copyright infringement or protection of copyrights. When the roles were reversed, as they were in the early '90s, they were the first ones screaming about it.

JG: Why didn't we see artists being broken by Internet companies? What happened to all those well-funded Web sites intent on marketing and releasing music directly to the public?

FG: A lot of them went out of business or the record companies sued them out of existence. That's the first thing. Second, well, look at it this way: we had millions of music fans, for the first time, gathering in one place, whether it was MP3.com, or Napster, or whatever. For the first time in history, people who were anonymous in our business—the customers—were gathering in one place. But the industry, instead of figuring out how to market to those people, because now they're all in one place, basically told them all to go home. That's a big problem.

· · · · · · ·

ATTORNEY

CHRISTIAN CASTLE
Akin, Gump, Strauss, Hauer, & Feld LLP

First concert attended: The Rolling Stones at the Sam Houston Coliseum

Best concert attended: Jimi Hendrix Experience in Houston, TX

Top five album recommendations:
1. B.B. King *Three O'Clock Blues*
2. Miles Davis *Kind of Blue*
3. Billie Holiday *Lady in Satin*
4. Ella Fitzgerald *Duke Ellington Songbook*
5. Jimi Hendrix *Axis: Bold As Love*
5a. Billy Cobham *Crosswinds*
5b. Joni Mitchell *Don Juan's Reckless Daughter*
5c. Cream *Wheels of Fire*
5d. The Police *Synchronicity*

Little known resume entry: Was an Olin Fellow in Law and Economics; attended prep school with Prince Charles.

Best project you were involved with that never made it big: Wendy MaHarry

Recommended reading: *For Common Things: Irony, Trust and Commitment in America Today*, by Jedediah Purdy

Instruments played: Drums, guitar, piano, trombone

Notable clients: DreamWorks, Napster, Liquid Audio, Ark 21, Bob Dylan

A FUNDAMENTAL DISCONNECT: MUSIC, TECHNOLOGY, ROYALTIES AND CONGRESS (AND WHY NONE OF THEM ARE FRIENDS)
AN INTERVIEW WITH CHRISTIAN CASTLE OF AKIN, GUMP, STRAUSS, HAUER, AND FELD

Christian Castle: For those who criticize the record companies as being profit-driven and thinking of artists as products, it's the ultimate in hypocrisy to want to download one or two tracks and not pay for them. At the end of the day, the people who get the real short end of the stick are the songwriters. Because if you are a straight songwriter and the record doesn't get sold, then you don't get paid a mechanical royalty, which means you really aren't making any money at all. There's a popular misconception that, well, the artist can go sell another T-shirt and therefore everything's fine. But when the artist sells a T-shirt, the only person who makes money from that T-shirt is the artist; the record company doesn't make any money from it and the songwriters don't make any money from it. Young artists are hurt, and eventually the big artists are gonna get hurt because they're not going to be able to maintain the kind of income that it takes to support touring.

JG: Do you think the model will shift more towards live performance income?

CC: Well, there's a lot of download pressure on CD prices now and it's partly in response to the distribution of music through the Internet, file sharing and CD prices that have been high for a long time. There has been a lot of price-cutting, and we already have a segment of the music business that went through that process, which is classical music. Ten years ago there was a glut of super budget recordings of classical music that were put on the market because people who were not aficionados didn't really care whether it was the Berlin Philharmonic or the East Leningrad Gradial Orchestra, they just wanted to hear Beethoven. This compounded a trend that was already in motion, which was artists making more money from shows than they did from records and records being seen as more archival than a real source of income. Not a good sign. I think as the income stream starts to go down on the record side, record companies are not going to be willing to invest as much money as they once did in breaking [new acts] and you are probably going to see bands looking to tours and other channels as a way of keeping that income up.

JG: How effectively do you think the various agencies and the record labels have reacted to the online proliferation of music piracy and technology?

CC: I think there's an inherent problem with any sort of online exploitation of music in that there is virtually no way, at the moment, to account for anything. Even legitimate sound files that have come from a label and can be tracked don't really feed into anything at the label end. If they *are* sold, there is still a disconnect between the selling point and royalty accounting system. In terms of downloading as an online activity, until there is a way to figure out what it is precisely that's passing across the servers, it's very difficult to fit that experience into the traditional music business. You could say, "Well, let's not try; let's make everyone pay a certain amount for the files in bulk," and it sounds like a good idea. Verizon floated this as part of the KaZaA/Morphius litigation, there was a lot of talk about a compulsory licenses for songs and certain kinds of digital performing such a Web casting, but there is no compulsory license for copies.

With mechanical licenses there's a compulsory mechanical license for the song and the law says that if that song is going to be released in a record, the publisher cannot refuse to license that song and the law sets forth a rate that has to be paid. But what you *don't* have is the ability to make a copy of The Beatles singing "Love Me Do" and sell that. The compulsory license for sound recordings in a download situation would establish a licensing regime to do that. Such a compulsory license would essentially amount to allowing a compilation record, and there's never been such a license before.

JG: Is it likely to be granted?

CC: Well, that was what this Verizon idea was about a year ago. If an ISP knows what's going across their servers then the ISP, in theory, could have some kind of liability for copyright infringement; I think that's why the ISPs floated this idea. The problem is that it's like saying, "Well, I'm gonna come into your house and steal a Picasso, and I'm going to tell you what I want to pay you for it. I'm not stealing it, I'm just taking it, and I'll tell you what I want to pay for it." The problem you have with compulsory licensing is setting a value for individual and masters because the record business simply does not work that way: you pay more for something that is successful than you do for something that isn't. If you got a license for a film or TV program and you wanted to license The Beatles' "Love Me Do," as opposed to "Love Me Do" by Fat Freddy, you would expect to pay $1M or $500K to license the Beatles track, but you wouldn't expect to pay a comparable amount for a cover. So there's a big difference between the economics of the music publishing business and the record business. It's not all a bunch of widgets. Some widgets are more valuable than others. And so when you see something like this Verizon proposal where they're offering to pay X number of pennies for whatever it is, it really flies in the face of the way the record business has always worked.

JG: Do you think that that's part of the reason so much has gone wrong over the last four years?

CC: I do, definitely. It's still going on. Right now the Web casters are sitting in D.C. trying to work out a deal to allow small Web casters to stay in business. To me, if you have to pay for content, a component, or a good, and that causes you to go out of business, well, the world has not guaranteed you a right to stay in business. That is our capitalist system. For some reason they seem to think that they can say it about music.

JG: Do you think BMG purchased Napster to shut it down?

CC: No. I think Middlehoff had a vision and he felt that Napster fulfilled that vision. I was talking the other day to someone I'd consider a very sophisticated businessman, and we were talking about Sean Fanning and he said, "You know, whether you like it or not, Napster is probably one of the great innovations of the 20th Century." Sean got something started which has had a lot of negative affects, but certainly was innovative and certainly demonstrated that there was a market out there for the distribution of music online. When he went around to the labels and said, "I want to license tracks from you for download," one of the arguments that you heard before Napster was, "Oh there's no market there," now, I didn't believe this to be true and after Napster, *nobody* believed this to be true. If there's one good thing to come out of Napster, it demonstrated that there really was an online community who really did want to get their music digitally and that could be a business. *If* someone could figure out how to monetize it.

· · · · · · ·

ARTISTS & REPERTOIRE, PRODUCER, MUSICIAN

RON FAIR
President
A&M Records

First concert attended: Cat Stevens with Carly Simon opening at the Troubadour, West Hollywood, 1968

Best concert attended: Andre Previn conducting and performing Gershwin's *Rhapsody in Blue* with LA Philharmonic at the Hollywood Bowl, summer of 1969.

Top five album recommendations:
1. Nat King Cole *After Midnight*
2. The Jimi Hendrix Experience *Are You Experienced?*
3. Miles Davis *Kind of Blue*
4. Donovan's *Greatest Hits*
5. The Beatles *Sgt. Pepper's Lonely Hearts Club Band*

Little known resume entries: I trekked to the top of Mount Kilimanjaro, Kenya in 2001; I mixed the album *Hell Awaits* by Slayer for Metal Blade Records; The first act I ever signed was Armored Saint; I was a Fender-Rhodes-fake-book-playing wedding singer for years.

Best band that never made it: Wild Orchid

Recommended reading: *Far From the City of Class,* short stories by Bruce Jay Friedman

Recommended film: *It's a Wonderful Life* (RKO Radio Pictures, 1946)

Instruments played: Piano, organ, vibraphone, harmonica, guitar

Upcoming projects: Black Eyed Peas; Mya, Jonny Lang, Butterfly, MXPX, Joanna

IMPOSTER BEES AND BLOUSES AT THE BOTTOM OF THE DRAWER:
A CONVERSATION WITH RON FAIR, PRESIDENT OF A&M RECORDS

JG: Let's talk about A&R and how people find new music.

RF: With the name A&R, the dichotomy begins—because one thing is the signing of the artists and the other thing is making a record. Between Artists and Repertoire, there you have a huge difference. There's often a nightclub with a line of record executives standing in the front watching a band, all tripping over each other because there's a buzz. Or, there's a basement somewhere with a talented kid in it, or there's a hairdresser who knows a woman who has a son whose cousin.... There are any number of crazy lanes that lead to the discovery and the development of talent. There is no set rule to it Sometimes talent walks in the front door; sometimes it lives next door—in the case of The Calling, Alex, the lead-singer, lived next door to me for many years. In fact, the band used to be called Next Door because we didn't know what else to call them. I met him when he was thirteen, signed him when he was sixteen and when he was nineteen, he sold two million records and had the biggest hit of the year with "Wherever You Will Go". I don't know who said this to me, but it certainly resonated: "Take the hit when it comes knocking." A hit record can come from anywhere and you have to really have your wits about you and be completely open. There have been plenty of examples...where there has been tremendous excitement and buzz on an artist and a competitive signing atmosphere with labels coughing up fortunes to get involved in the career of an artist—and then nothing happens. You can name many, many examples, where a guy comes out of nowhere, captures everyone's imagination, and [the bidding] gets into the millions of dollars—and then nothing ever happens with it. There are plenty of other stories like Christina Aguilera who was passed on by several record companies—she came in, made a very modest little demo deal to begin with and then we stumbled into the *Mulan* soundtrack, and from there "Genie in a Bottle" and eventually ten Number One records, two Number One albums and three Grammys. So, I guess my attitude is to remain open and to try to put my own musical taste to the side when assessing or trying to assess how deep someone's talent runs, because it could be a band like Rage Against the Machine that I stumble onto tomorrow night, or it could be an artist like Jill Scott, or it could be a band like Radiohead, or it could be, y'know, Mark Chestnut. I don't know. All I know is I have to be able to recognize talent in whatever form and be able act certainly and decisively.

JG: I didn't realize that Christina actually began as a development deal.

RF: A kind of amazing set of circumstances surrounded it. I got a call from Chris Montan, who runs music for Disney, and they have an animated film called *Mulan* about a Chinese girl. It's kind of a nice, tender little story and they had a rangy, rangy song called "Reflection" that Matthew Wilder and David Zipple had written for the end title. Chris had come to the realization that the type of song that it was—which was kind of a straight, conventional ballad—that there were very few singers who could really get on the radio with a "conventional ballad" anymore. So, the artist pool for what he was looking to do—you're not going to get Mariah, you're not going to get Celine and you're not going to get Whitney. Who are you going to get? He was really looking to get ideas and I had just heard Christina's tape, so I said, "Well, I have this girl. I haven't signed her yet, but I have this girl who's capable of singing in this range," and he said, "Well there's a high E—an octave above middle C at full-voice, can she hit that note?" I said, "I don't know." I called her and I asked, "Can you hit the high E an octave above middle C?" She said, "Mom! Can I hit the high E an octave above middle C?" "And if you can, sing it on a little crappy cassette and get it to me." So she did and I got it to Montan. I flew her in to audition for the song with Matthew Wilder and Chris Montan and David Zipple. She basically sang the first three words of the song, "Look at me," and her tone was magnificent and they gave her the gig right there. So, we had been negotiating the development deal and we just switched it to a record deal. She got the *Mulan* gig, she got her record contract and it all happened at the same time. And it was a little risky for me because I could have lost her. I didn't have her signed when we did the *Mulan* thing. But still, her original contract was very modest. There was no other competition, there was nobody bidding for her services, there was me and her and her first manager in a room. That's how it began.

JG: OK. What is it that makes one artist take off over another? What are some of the elements—are they all just intangibles like luck and timing, or what?

RF: If I knew what went into that cocktail, I'd be the richest guy on the planet. For one thing, phenomenal luck. Karma, God-given talent. Sometimes, the lack of talent. I mean, you can look at something like— who's that guy who had that record last year? "...because I get high, because I get high..."?

JG: Afroman.

RF: Not to be insulting, but it ain't about musical talent, he just had a catchy little song and caught the world by surprise; it was a gigantic hit. I think, certainly, there are a lot of qualities—like look at Norah Jones, for example. I think when they made the Norah Jones record, they probably thought, "Well, we'll sell a hundred thousand. It'll be nice, it's a cool vibe." I don't think they were expecting to sell ten million records. That's the beauty of our business. It's one of the last businesses on earth where you can come in with a whole in your jeans and a crappy cassette, a burned CD and a half a beat—and a year later be a millionaire. You can't do that in a lot of businesses. You can't do it in the movie business because you can't make a movie for less than millions of dollars. And, home recording is so available to everybody now that somebody talented can walk into a bedroom and make a song that will generate millions of dollars for nothing. So aside from the cosmic aspects of luck and timing and all those things you can't control, what brings success to a lot of these projects consistently is having a great team. Experienced people, people with connections, people with clout, people with friends, people who are owed favors. Teams that exist behind the artist that, just like a sports team, work together to achieve victory. It's more than just a guy with a guitar out there. The team and the strategy behind, "Do we do this tour or not, do we do this TV show or this commercial, is this our first single, is this our second single, do we do this video? Should we do this duet? Should we wear those clothes?" All those strategic decisions along the path are huge contributors to success or failure.

JG: So does that create an equation where someone in your shoes looks for a good team in place when you first find an artist?

RF: You see the Hollywood cliché all the time where a brand new artist comes in with a manager who may be a parent, or a buddy from college, someone who maybe has invested money—they arrive together at the beginning of a career and very quickly it's obvious that the manager doesn't possess the skills, connections, or ability to really manage an artist's career. And there are so many lanes where an artist's career is exploited and developed—whether it's movies, television, advertising, sponsorship, touring, or press. The management thing is crucial, it's just as important a job as that of the artist in a lot of respects; it's more than just saying no, and most of the people who manage artists are, I think, unqualified. They are going to say the same thing about us too—that most of the record company people are unqualified. It's a problem, but you end up dealing with whoever it is. You have to honor the artist's choice of manager, but it makes a big difference if it's somebody good.

JG: This business seems to have as many unpredictable turns for executive careers as it does for artists.

RF: I'm just lucky that I've been around this long and I've been able to keep showing the people with the power above me that I'm valuable and I'm able to keep playing. It's a hard thing to do. There was a point when my career was so cold, I hadn't had a hit in four and a half years. Every single thing I did was a failure. Every song I endorsed, every band I chose, every singer I worked with—everything was a miserable failure, and frankly, four and a half years is a very long cold spell. Bob Jameson, God bless him, he never gave up on me even though it was highly un-fun to be on a team and not scoring any points. And then, all of a sudden, changes in my life occurred and I was able to reinvent my viewpoint and slam-dunk Lit's album, which was a Number One record for four and a half months and sold two million albums, and I followed them with Christina Aguilera who sold twenty-two million albums. So, although I had four and a half cold years as an A&R guy, when I did get back going, the music that I generated in working with these artists, in its gross form, earned about eighty million dollars.

JG: Wow.

RF: So, people got rich and recoupments were made and I was able to live yet again.

JG: What is it that kept you going? Did you think that you were going to have to leave the business?

RF: No, never. I produce records and I make music. I was able to gravitate toward, and be accepted by, several mentors throughout my career, but they were all musicians—whether it was Bill Conte, who was a huge, huge influence and impact on my life, or Mike Chapman, or Terry Ellis, or Chris Blackwell and now Jimmy Iovine. I've been able to be worthy of their training and it continues now as I pass the torch. You have to be realistic about yourself in this racket. None of us have a hundred percent batting averages. It's like baseball; did you know that the greatest hitter of all time basically hits the ball only about 30 percent of the time?

The main thing is, don't believe your own hype. All of the big, big, big, big, big, big, producers who get hot through history, whether you go back to Hugo and Luigi, or Stock, Aitken and Waterman, or Nile Rogers and Bernard Edwards, or Mike Chatmore, or Gavin Lewis, or the Neptunes, Phil Ramone, or whoever, don't go on forever. It doesn't go on forever.

There's a timeframe where you are channeling, you are reflecting and interpreting the beat that is in people's hearts and souls with music, and it resonates and it works, and then it ends at some point. So, it doesn't last forever and you have to be very honest about it, about yourself.

JG: What do you think is happening now with the business? Fred Davis made the apt point that the music business is healthy just as the television business is healthy, citing that it's network television having the hard time while HBO is doing well. Is that appropriate to say about the music business?

RF: I've heard every cliché. There were obviously some serious, unforeseen, and huge problems when the CD was created; the record business did not see the vulnerability of the sound recording itself. But a few things that have fundamentally changed in the landscape. One is that technology and things like ProTools and the availability of cheap recording equipment can take a marginal musical performance and, through editing, make it sound like a strong musical performance. The ability to manipulate music and performance on record cheaply and in the home has created a tidal wave of mediocrity. Because, before, if you couldn't play, you couldn't pursue it. You were out of the game. It's like being in the five-man pick-up basketball team. If I go on a five-man pick-up basketball team and I can't run, jump, shoot, or dribble, then I can't play. I'm out of the game. But if you get ProTools you can fix that out of tune note. You can sing it out of tune, and then you can fix it; you can edit it, you can time stretch it; you can pitch correct it; you can fly it; you can take something and reanimate it. What it does is it's a massive invitation for a lower level of musical talent to get in the game, which completely gluts the market and fills the beehive with imposter bees that don't produce honey—so, singers who can't sing that well who are about an image. But, it's so pervasive that it affects the entire culture, where now we accept the fact that J.Lo is not a great singer. But she's cool, she's great, she's gorgeous, she dances; it's a vibe and people like the records.

> ...it's a massive invitation for a lower level of musical talent to get in the game, which completely gluts the market and fills the beehive with imposter bees that don't produce honey—so, singers who can't sing that well who are about an image.

JG: Right, so it's a personality-driven project. But certainly twenty years ago it would be difficult to imagine her as a star singer.

RF: Y'know, Fred Astaire was not a great singer. Gene Kelly was not a great singer. They were great entertainers, but that was the movie business. That wasn't the record business. Y'know, the record business had Sinatra and Johnnie Ray; it had people who did what they did. Music no longer plays the same role. It doesn't galvanize things except in cases like Eminem, 50 Cent—music that's part of a cultural thing. Music that is offensive. Music from artists who are edgy, artists who are bold, artists who are weird, artists who threaten. Or like a Limp Bizkit—that's why these things work on such a big level, because they penetrate, they go further, and the rest of the stuff that we do, all the other records—or even Norah Jones. Norah Jones is like Eminem in the fact that it's so bold and weird. It's so minimal. There's nothing else that is that minimal. Norah Jones threatens all this fabricated pop shit because she just sings the song. In the meantime, everything else on the chart is crowded in the anthill, in the big middle pack, which is very hard to get out of. Now, you can make a living in the middle pack. You can entertain in the middle pack; you can touch a lot of people's lives in the middle pack; you can have a record business in the middle pack—but very, very few things can capture that kid who signs on except for acts like Eminem, 50 Cent—the artists who are really become something meaningful. Britney Spears was that meaningful. People signed on. Kids signed on. Now, they've passed through it. Anybody who comes on the scene now, bare midriff, dancing and moving like Britney Spears; get it out of here—which is really regrettable and unfortunate if you're Britney. Christina was able to move away from that because she was just this fucking amazing singer.

JG: Right, so she was able to transition from one phase to another.

RF: But, that's the fundamental difference to me today. And then you add to that all the artists who are going to Washington and saying that the record companies are stealing their royalties. Which artists are saying that? The ones who are multi-millionaires. And then there's the lobbyist who represents Clear Channel who's on the ropes in Washington; their lobbyist said, "Hey, we're not homogenizing radio. The problem is the record companies don't sign enough new talent." That's what he said in Washington to senators and congressmen. We don't sign enough new talent? We are spending millions of dollars on stuff that will never be heard.

JG: Of course—the problem has always been getting radio to be responsive to those new acts.

RF: That nobody cares about. So you add that to it. You add the radio consolidation to it. The fact that one giant chain owns everything. You add the economic conditions. Then you add the fact that maybe this particular crop of artists at this moment aren't that compelling, which we can't control. Somebody walks through the door like Fred Durst one day, and he's really compelling. The next day someone else walks through the door, and he's good. He's just not that compelling. So we can't control that, and you add in Xbox, which is really compelling. Y'know, if you're a kid, and you have the choice of, "Hey, Grandma! The Eminem or the System of a Down record, I really want that, and that's sixteen bucks—but this new Grand Theft 3.5 is really cool. I'll take Grand Theft 3.5 and I'll get System of a Down at school. I'll get that for a buck." So, when you add it all together, you have a quagmire: you have a business that is hemorrhaging, where the only thing that they can do, because of money involved, is stop spending.

JG: Which is what seems to be happening.

RF: What stop spending means is not just fire the executives, which they are doing, or eliminate record companies, which they are also doing—it means get rid of the artists. Every artist who isn't at X level, chop it off, get rid of it. Which means, get rid of the limo driver who took them to the Grammys, get rid of the guy who makes the little peanut butter Ritz cracker things on the video shoot, get rid of him. Get rid of the video shoot. Get rid of the video director. Get rid of the messenger who's taking this cassette across town. Get rid of the secretary. The food chain of "get rid of" is huge and it affects thousands and thousands of people. Having said all that, it's life, and it's a survival of the fittest. So, it makes us, as "marketeers"—which I don't like to call myself—but it makes us, as marketeers, do less and make them count more, which pressurizes it, because you know what? The beauty of this whole thing is that no matter what we do sitting around in a board room and trying to crunch down our numbers, there's a guy in Salt Lake City who's playing a gig tonight in a shitty club with sawdust on the floor who's going to be the next Dave Matthews Band, and somehow—without radio, without promotion, with a van, a little CD burner and his laptop—he's going to reach millions of people. We don't know who that is, but I know he's out there. We all know it's out there and that's the beauty of what we do. Stuff just appears. And right now, the trend is branding. Two to three years ago, it was synergy. Everyone was talking about synergy. Get the guys from the book division to talk to the guys from the cartoon division to talk to the guys from the pencil box division. But nobody knew each other and they all had turf wars. It didn't work. Those kinds of synergies are based on friendships that didn't exist. They look good on paper but if you don't have those people, y'know, skiing on Thanksgiving holiday together, those deals never come to pass.

JG: Why is that exactly—is it because certain departments are simply too self-contained?

RF: Yeah. If you have friends who work in different areas, then you do, but it doesn't just happen [without relationships]. The other trend right now, which is very interesting to watch, is what they call branding, which is putting Enrique Iglesias with Jeep. Sting with Jaguar. Sheryl Crow with American Express. U2 with Microsoft. Mya with Coca-Cola. Jessica Simpson with Redken, Beyoncé with Pepsi and blah, blah, blah. Celine and Chrysler. Because [the big corporations] think that those artists represent public segments and they want to tap into it, which makes sense.

JG: And the artists are agreeing with it and the labels are agreeing with it. Why? Because of the power of the marketing?

RF: Because the record sales are down, and the other lanes are shrinking. They figure, "Hey, this is new real estate. You can get on TV. You can get all these impressions."

JG: And even artists like Macy Gray, who only a few short years ago might have been too cool, cred and hip to be pushing Mercury SUVs now say to themselves, "I guess I've got to do this"?

RF: No, they say, "I *want* to do this: I get four hundred grand, I get an SUV *and* I get exposure? Why not?"

JG: Right. So it's fair to say that this represents a massive shift in acceptable artist exposure?

RF: Massive. A massive shift. It used to be that artists would say, "Hey, I'm not putting my image on anything. I'm about the music." Now we have entire departments in the company whose job it is just to put Oakley sunglasses on Marcus Houston. Just to put Nike tennis shoes on Mya. And it isn't just our label. Every label's doing it. Every label's got a deal with AT&T.

RF: The audience, I think, is going to get sick of it.

RF: Are [consumers] going to buy, y'know, Playtex rubber gloves because Gwen's wearing them?" Maybe if it was just Gwen. But when it's Gwen, Pink, Christina, Mya and Mariah; when it's every single one of the music figures and they are all a product, I think it's just going to be annoying.

JG: It's overkill and over-marketing.

RF: It's the over-marketing of everything. And then something comes up which actually gives us hope, like Queens of the Stone Age which will come out of nowhere and just have a great rock song and all of a sudden there are a million kids who want to have that record and they don't do any of that. That's what keeps it all healthy.

· · · · · · ·

SONGS AND MUSIC PUBLISHING: AN OVERVIEW
Brill Building and Brylcreem

Throughout this volume, you've read references to the olden days of the record business—the days when the A and the R in A&R actually meant what they stood for—the artist, say a Frank Sinatra, being connected to the repertoire, the song. And the song was controlled by the music publisher. These grey and grimy early prewar days conjure up a an era of snappily dressed record men who drank black coffee in fedora hats and ate big meals at the Automat for a dime. They climbed the echo-filled staircase of a mythic New York brick edifice called the Brill Building where songwriters with Brylcreem slicked into their hair sat around pianos smoking filterless cigarettes, doing smoky, sexy backdoor deals with the softer side of the mob in order to fund the new doo wop hit of the day.

At least, that's how I always imagined it. The industry has been pretty much radically transformed since then, but the basics of music publishing have pretty much remained the same. It's like this:

Time to Make Some Cash...

When you write a new tune, even right this very moment as you read this sentence, as soon as you start humming the tune—go ahead and take a second, let's actually write a little section of a song right now at this moment—got it? Okay now, go ahead and turn on your tape recorder—sing it with some lyrics. Congratulations!—you now own a new copyright (and I'm taking 25 percent)....

Seriously, though, you just now technically and literally created a "copyright," as you have converted your creative idea into a fixed and tangible medium—the tape you recorded. Any rights that apply to anyone with a copyright now apply to you and that "song." Sometimes people worry about circulating material without it having an official "copyright." Frankly, I'd worry about something else more worth your energy; people at record companies or publishing companies have better things to do than try to rip off your song. Any writer runs the risk of having their material inadvertently stolen. Most of the legal remedies however, should disputes arise, are related to the copyright holder's ability to prove that they in fact are the first and rightful creators. This is where the U.S. Copyright Office can come in handy. (Visit the link provided on the enclosed disc.) They key issue is timing. If a dispute arises and three people separately claim authorship to the song, the person who filed the last copyright has the burden of doubt.

But make no mistake, when you send off your material to Washington D.C., no one is sitting around a table comparing songs and stamping them with official copyrights. In fact, if you were to send in the entire Beatles catalog and claim you wrote every song, no one would be likely to catch it there because your package doesn't even get listened to, it just gets filed with a number proving you sent it on X date. When it comes to copyrighting your material, the main issue is one of legitimate proof—again, visit the Library of Congress online.

Music publishing concerns itself with anything related to songwriting rights and the revenue associated with such rights. There are many formulas for determining how and when this money comes to whom and for what, and there are some great books that examine and describe in detail various components of copyright law and publishing, including royalty structure, licensing and publishing deals. This volume will focus on how the publishing industry has changed and is continuing to evolve in today's industry.

For new artists, the main equation in music publishing is one of financial security and long term vs. short term financial considerations. If you own a credit card you are employing this concept right now—allow a company to charge you a premium for giving you money up front. Of course there is no finance charge per se in music publishing, but you are giving up a percentage of your potential future income for cash up front. Cashing in on your publishing, also allows you to take advantage of what's essentially a tax-free loan from a bank that understands your business in a detailed way with a creative vision. People often complain about publishers, but thank God they are out there—can you imagine going into a traditional bank as a recently signed songwriter or artist, with little or no documented income, and walking out with a loan *you never need to pay back* of hundreds of thousands of dollars?

In the new music industry, the music publishing rights of songs recorded by new artists is not unlike the stock at new companies, which may dramatically rise according to a variety of market factors. There is a direct connection between the value of song copyrights and the value of the artist performing them—all the more so if they are one and the same. If a recording becomes wildly successful, the associated music publishing rights are valuable by direct association.

Since my own background is in music publishing, I am often approached by new artists or new artist reps asking to have their unknown, unsigned material considered by music publishers: "This is an amazing songwriter—she should be signed with a music publisher." Such comments usually indicate a lack of understanding about publishing, because today's music publishers are not as concerned with finding great unknown songs to pitch. Among other things we will explore throughout the next several pages, they are interested in locating potentially explosive or exciting situations already in place that will help to make the song itself have value.

Music publishers used to control the business by controlling the great songs and songwriters, and as such were often the active link between the A and the R that made the whole industry tick. The difference today is that most artists perform their own material, and this trend has altered the nature of music publishing's focus, to the point where music publishers are just as likely to be focused on any material appearing on an album that has exposure or sales rather than specifically concerned with "great songs."

Music publisher, as a term, simply refers to the ownership of the portion of the song's copyright designated as the "publisher's share." The publisher's share traditionally refers to 50 percent of the copyright. Interestingly enough, when you do a traditional "co-publishing deal" you are really only going into business on that half of the song so the new company you're doing a deal with is usually only acquiring 50 percent of that publisher's share—which only amounts to a 25 percent interest in the entire copyright.

Right now the song you wrote earlier already has a publisher—it's you, because you have yet to assign it to anyone else and have not done a publishing deal involving that copyright. There are many ways for this to change. If you included this song on your debut album slated for release on RCA records for example, you would probably get a call from your lawyer asking you (or telling you) how to handle the publishing. Let's say he had already received a call from a big corporate music publisher who thinks your record is going to be huge and has offered a high six figure advance.

There are a few ways to handle this news as you ponder the realities of the music business and your potential music publishing revenue. In a perfect world, if you knew that your record was going to be huge, you would probably decline the music publishing offer. Why? Because then you would receive the full amount of music publishing—related revenue without that big corporate music publisher taking their cut.

But we hardly live in a perfect world. Much can go wrong with any artist's career—and the world of music publishing deals can represent a measure of security or opportunity to your career. In this chapter we will hear from five music publishing related players, each with a different focus on today's evolving music publishing landscape.

MUSIC PUBLISHER, ATTORNEY

SCOTT FRANCIS
President
BMG Music Publishing

First concert attended: Sly and the Family Stone. with The Staple Singers at Madison Square Garden

Best concert attended: Paul McCartney at Staples Arena (it was as close to a Beatles concert as I'll ever get!)

Top five album recommendations:
1. Any Beatles album
2. James Taylor *The Best of James Taylor*
3. Coldplay *Parachutes*
4. Everclear *Scenes From an American Movie (Volume 1)*
5a. Matthew Sweet *Greatest Hits*
5b. Freedy Johnson *This Perfect World*
5c. Any Motown Hits package

Little known resume entry: I started out as a white collar criminal defense attorney.

Recommended reading: *High Fidelity*, by Nick Hornby

Recommended film: *It's a Wonderful Life* (RKO Radio Pictures, 1946)

Instrument played: Guitar (terribly)

....

MUSIC, MEET BLING-BLING: HOW THE MUSIC PUBLISHING GAME HAS (AND HASN'T) CHANGED
AN INTERVIEW WITH SCOTT FRANCIS, PRESIDENT OF
BMG MUSIC PUBLISHING

....

Justin Goldberg: How has the music publishing landscape changed?

Scott Francis: It's really not about the music anymore, it's all about the money. And that thought process—from the lawyers to the managers to even the writers and the artists themselves—has changed every piece of the business. In today's world, there's really no room to develop an artist. Record companies say, "We want to develop artists here," and, "We want to develop long-term career artists." Publishers say they want to develop long-term writers and help them write better songs. But the fact of the matter is because most of the companies are owned by corporations; it's all about the dollars and you have to have a return on your investment quickly. And how are you going to develop if you have to have a return on your investment quickly? How can you advance someone some money and let it sit on your books for a long period of time without the corporation saying, "Hey buddy, where's the return?" It doesn't work: Having a creative business in the hands of a corporation just doesn't make sense.

JG: How has the Internet impacted the industry in your view?

SF: Years ago, everybody was still living off the revenues from consumers replenishing their record collections with CDs. Everybody was asking at that time, what's going to be the next format, how are we going to keep this business going? Well, lo and behold the next format became the biggest pipeline of piracy that you have ever seen. So the difference now is that the business is not in a good place, and the money's not rolling in like it used to, and therefore the corporation takes a harder look at your numbers because they're not what they were. So, if I had a hit record, say, five years ago, it would stay on the charts a long time, get a lot of money in on the performance side; it would sell a ton of records. Nowadays, you've got guys streaming, maybe not listening to the radio stations as much; people aren't listening to radio stations like they used to, ad revenue's not going to be as high, so there's less money to be split up among the publishers and all the various other royalty-earning parties. And then on the other hand, people aren't buying records because they can get it for free. You've got a whole generation of kids who have no clue that they're actually stealing property—that's what they're doing, and that's the difference. You've got all these things going on and it puts more pressure on you because the money is just not rolling in like it used to.

JG: Is some of that perception as opposed to reality, or is the reality that record sales are down considerably?

SF: I would tell you that it's probably a combination of both. Record sales are down because of the Internet—people can just get it online and it's easy to do. Record sales are also down because the world has changed. Young kids, ten to twenty five, are really the major record buyers, and there are all these other things out there for them to do now, like video games. It's amazing to me, I bought my son this new video game the other day and I heard some music in the background that sounded so familiar to me—I asked, "What is this?" and he said, "It's the Good Charlotte single; it's in the background of the video." Now, the music to this kid and to a whole generation just like him, is not the music, it's this other thing, the video game. There are these alternative media and entertainment that kids would rather have, it's a more in your face thing than sitting back and just listening to music, everybody multi-tasks now and music is not "the" thing to do—it's just one of the things that's going on while you're doing other things.

JG: Do you think that's partly because the quality of music has gone down? Some of our colleagues feel strongly that today's music quality overall has diminished.

SF: If you think about it, go back forty or fifty years, Elvis comes out, your parents at the time said, "This is the biggest piece of crap I've ever heard! How could you possibly listen to this?" Then as you move on, there's The Beatles—same thing—the young kids buying records replace their parents. Now they're the ones who are saying that the music is bad. Popular music is supposed to be music loved by the masses, but that's not really what it is, popular music is loved by the kids, the people who are actually buying the music, and most kids buy the music to piss off their parents. The music you buy as a kid is music your parents don't like, it's very simple. So when we sit here now and we say, "Oh my God, how can these kids be listening to Dre," and stuff like that—white Jewish kids who live on Long Island, they're buying all this stuff, how could they possibly relate to it? Well, let me tell you something, they're buying it because it's music that is their own and their parents *can't* relate to it. I really think that's how it works, I don't think that music is getting any worse, it's just different, and if it's not appealing to you, most likely you're just out of the range, the age range.

JG: So you would characterize the shifts as a matter of business evolution and format changes—not representative of a cultural shift in whether or not there's a Rolling Stones for the next generation.

SF: Absolutely not. Everyone says, "We need the next best thing to save music,"—it's not going to happen. What's happening now is a convergence of all these different things: technology, maybe some music piracy, all these different things that have just converged at one point in time—maybe if one thing had happened without all the other things, the industry could overcome it, but all these things have hit at once. All these guys I speak to in the business who have been around a while, they say they've never ever seen anything like this.

JG: As a business, as a publisher, are overall different avenues of revenue down? Has publishing been affected as much as records, just because of the obvious relationship that publishing has with the record side?

SF: Publishing revenue as a whole is not down yet, though for some companies it may be soon. What has happened is different types of revenue have decreased while other types of revenue have increased, for example, mechanicals are down because fewer records are being sold, however, more people are using music in audio visual material, sync is up—sync is skyrocketing and has been skyrocketing for the past few years, and if you think about it, it's almost what I said before, all these different types of media are using music more than ever to enhance their products. Movies, all of a sudden people who are making movies realize that you can really show an emotional moment or move the audience by having different types of music.

JG: What piece of a large publishing corporation's income is tied to record sales as opposed to revenue streams?

SF: I would say that record sales represent probably 50 percent, at least 50 percent of your overall revenue.

JG: So the fate of the record business is unavoidably tied to music publishing?

SF: You've got to sell music, whether it's on a record, a hard piece, or whether it's through digital delivery of a song; you've got to sell music, that's what the music business is, it's the sale of music.

JG: What kind of approach does a company like BMG publishing have toward licensing material to new forms of media?

SF: As far as new media goes, we license everything, as long as it is copyright protectable. We will make a deal with anybody, that's what we do here.

JG: If someone is in a band and they're going to start shopping for a new deal, could they come to a publishing company first?

SF: Absolutely, we do it all the time. We help artists and bands that aren't always ready for record deals—perhaps they need to develop themselves, sometimes they need to write better songs, sometimes they need to write better songs because they need a co-writer or maybe they don't know how to structure a song properly, so they come to a publisher. They may not be able to get a record deal yet, but there may be a publisher out there who is willing to invest in them. Sometimes a music publisher can help and be a bank—of course, everyone's heard that—give them some money that allows them to go on and play small clubs and survive so they can get a record deal and have a successful career as a recording artist. We also help bands that write their own songs by affording them opportunities; you can have a band that's written one great song, and get a sync opportunity. You can be off and running when that happens, because it exposes a song, a recording and a band to an incredible number of people and helps them get a deal and get noticed.

JG: Let's say somebody gets a record deal, does that automatically entitle them to getting a publishing deal? Are they suddenly much more likely to get a publishing deal?

SF: Different publishers have different goals, but all of them want to make money. If a band has a record deal, and the likelihood of their record coming out is strong, then their likelihood of being more successful than a straight songwriter is greater. Because you've then got an outlet for those songs, you don't have to search; the band is a self-contained outlet for those songs. Get the record out, get a song on the radio, the money's gonna come in—as opposed to a writer, where you have to work harder these days to get their songs recorded and that's because almost every recording artist wants to record their own songs. I mean The Beatles were a great thing for the business and a bad thing for the business in that Lennon and McCartney were two guys who were not only great recording artists and great performers but who were exceptional songwriters, and therefore every other band that followed wanted to be The Beatles. "We're gonna write our own songs," "We're gonna get our own message across," and 80 to 90 percent of them cannot write songs.

JG: Historically in the music business—long before the Beatles era, the publisher has always had a great deal of clout. Why? Is it because they controlled the best songs and they cultivated songwriters and owned their material?

SF: In the old days, recording artists didn't write their own songs, before 1960 or 1965, I would bet you can't name ten successful recording artists that actually wrote their songs. They didn't write their songs, so they had to go and find songs from the publishers. You couldn't record without the songs, and who owned the songs? Publishers. So there you go, publishers were very powerful. Publishers were very powerful people because they controlled the songs.

JG: So what really began as an industry of catering to songs, now caters to recordings and recording artists.

SF: Absolutely, except in Nashville, where they still understand the importance of the song. You watch an awards ceremony, you watch the Country Music Awards; they often thank the songwriters. But when you watch the Grammy Awards, they never thank the songwriters, even if they didn't write the song themselves, they never thank the songwriters. I think you can have someone with a great voice who's very talented, but if you have them sing a horrible song, it's still horrible; you can also have someone who doesn't sing as well but if you give them a great song, it'll sound a lot better. Like everybody says, the song is the foundation to a good recording.

JG: You made a reference earlier to a "straight songwriter." What does that refer to?

SF: When I say straight songwriter, I'm talking about someone *other than an artist* who writes his own songs and a producer. Right now, pop music is producer and production driven, almost every time you take a look at a song, one of the writers of the song is usually the producer. And writing a song these days is a lot different than it used to be. Writing a song used to be someone who wrote the lyrics and someone who wrote the melody—now you've got a track writer. A song will be built around a track; a studio guy/producer goes into the studio starts messing around, comes up with a nice track or maybe some beats and hands it over to somebody else who will put a melody through it or chord progression, and then somebody else will add some words; it's not like it used to be. The way a song is written today is entirely different than it used to be, in the pop world. Not in the country world, but in pop and R&B—definitely R&B—right now, it's funny, you have a guy behind the board and he's just messing around and he thinks he should have a piece of the song. It's why the R&B world is so producer driven, and we have claims on songs all the time; a large part of a music publisher's day is spent trying to settle song splits and song claims.

JG: That brings up an interesting point: let's say I create the backing track to a song that would be great for Toni Braxton, and she cuts it while four other people are in a room adding in bits and pieces of lyric or melody— how do I determine what my percentage of the song is?

SF: If you and four other people are in a room and all of you add to the song...

JG: Even if one person wrote 90 percent of it and three other people were just in the room?

SF: Right, well in the room and maybe someone had a lyric idea and maybe someone added a couple of notes, but if these five people are in a room working on a song together, regardless of how much each of them added to the song, they would own an equal share of the song, 20 percent. Absent an agreement to the contrary, they share the song equally.

JG: How is there an agreement to the contrary? Let's say someone comes in with a track, and he says, "This is a great track, but before I even play this for you guys, I want you to know this is 90 percent my song."

SF: If I'm the artist, and I'm in the room, it's likely I'm going say, "You know what, you can take your track," but it's not the way it usually happens because the person with the track wants the song recorded. What usually happens is a room full of people and nobody's really talking about what piece they control, they get in there and then they walk out of the room, they have the recording. Then when the record company goes to license the song, you end up with people claiming pieces that add up to 200 percent, and a deal has to be struck.

JG: Now, when you say the record company goes to license the song, why do they need to do that and what specifically needs to occur? Fill us in a little bit on the basic sequence of events in terms of how publishers interact with a label on a first album release.

SF: Here's how it goes: there's something called the First Use Doctrine, which indicates you can't record a song for the first time without a license from the copyright owners. After a song is recorded for the first time, anybody can re-record the song as long as they adhere to certain steps set out by the copyright law. Those steps are very hard to follow, and they require

FYI

Harry Fox Agency, Inc. was established in 1927 as a musical copyright information source and licensing agency for the music industry. HFA currently represents more than 27,000 music publishers, and is the premier licensing resource for the mechanical use of music reproduced in all formats and media.

certain reporting requirements, accounting requirements, on a monthly basis—all these things that are too hard. So they end up going to the publisher and they license it from the various publishers, or they go to Harry Fox which represents all the music publishers. The first time around the record company will go to the music publisher and request the license for their share of the song. Either the music publisher will direct-license it to them or more likely it's done through Harry Fox, so the record company has to find out who the actual publishers are first; usually that information is supplied by the artist and often it turns out to be a mess, because there is usually more than one person involved in writing. So people will file a claim or they'll call up the record company or they'll have music publishers call on their behalf and say, "Wait a minute, my writer wrote part of this song; we control 20 percent," and the record company will say, "Well, this is the information we have," and then the license doesn't get issued and no money gets paid out. Records companies love that situation—they get to hold the money.

JG: In issuing mechanicals?

SF: In issuing licenses, the actual license—mostly mechanical licenses, which gives one the right to record a song—can only be given the first time around by the music publisher, the second time around anyone can record a song *if they follow certain rules set by the copyright law.* That's Harry Fox, Harry Fox is a mechanical rights licensing agent. SESAC, ASCAP and BMI are performing rights societies, which means they deal with the performance of songs—anywhere you hear it, you hear it on the radio, you hear it on the television, in certain countries you get paid directly for that when it's in a film; when you hear it in a restaurant, certain restaurants, performance of a song whether it's over the radio or just somebody has a copy of the CD and they play it in the restaurant—all of these are performances of the songs, and each of these places in which a song is performed pays ASCAP, and BMI, and SESAC a certain annual license fee to use the songs that are controlled by each society. So how did the society get the rights to these songs? Well if I'm a songwriter, I want somebody out there collecting money for each time my song is performed, so I join SESAC, BMI, or ASCAP. If you are gonna ask me which one is better, I'm not able to tell you because better means different things to different people—for young songwriters who don't have let's say, a publishing deal and they need the support of an agency, they may join BMI, SESAC or ASCAP because there's a certain person there who believes in them and will help get their careers off the ground, for someone more established, certain people believe that ASCAP or BMI may pay better in certain genres of music. I think that always fluctuates.

JG: I would imagine that the answer to that can be factually determined?

SF: It can, and the way it is factually determined is as follows: if a band came to me, let's say a duo, two people are recording artists who record together and they both write their songs together; they come to me and ask, "Scott, we want to sign at BMG, should we join ASCAP or BMI?" I might tell them to split up—one of them should join ASCAP, one of them should join BMI—this way, they can compare their royalty statements and the one who got less can go to that performing rights society and say, "I don't understand this, the other performing rights society paid my co-writer, who writes the same percentage of the songs I do, they paid him more." So I always tell people to do that.

JG: Okay, new topic: people are so often curious about actual numbers: How high can public performance money go?

SF: Okay, a Number One song: Nelly's "Dilemma"—right now Nelly's at 3.5 million units.

JG: So he's made roughly how much per unit from his label?

SF: Let's say $1.10

JG: So let's say around 3 million generated from the label side, not counting what he had to recoup...

SF: So, he could make $500,000 or more on the performance of his song, a hit like that, on all performance royalties, radio, television. It depends: an urban song will tend to make more if it is also sort of a pop song and fits a lot of different formats, because then it will be performed more.

JG: So formats are key?

SF: Well, one of the keys is obviously how many times your song is played, and if it's played across different formats, it's going to be played on more radio stations, and if it's played on more radio stations, you're going to get more money.

JG: How does the word "reversion" fit into your world? Do most major artists get "reversions" of their copyrights so the company doesn't own the songs forever?

SF: With reversions you don't own an asset, you kind of rent it. We'll do reversions if it's something we have to do to get the deal. Sometimes we do partial reversions, which means that we keep our share of the copyright and hand the writer his copyright share along with his writer share—he then has the ability to administer his share and we just keep our 50 percent copyright share and we administer our share. From a monetary standpoint you make the same amount of money in a partial reversion, but what you don't have is control and that means there is more than one person licensing the song. Sometimes that makes it difficult.

JG: Overall do you feel that the music publishing business has become more about renting copyrights and receiving income for a set period of time than about long-term ownership?

SF: Let's flip it, let's say that the goal of a recording artist and a writer is controlling the product from those careers. Music publishing is always about assets, and retaining those assets for life of a copyright. Right now the competing interest is the recording artist and the writer who want to own their rights later in time, and get what I like to call a second bite of the apple. Later on in their careers, or after their careers may be over, they still have an asset that they can sell again.

· · · · · · ·

ARTISTS & REPERTOIRE/PUBLISHING

JIM VELLUTATO
Senior Director of Creative Affairs
Sony/ATV Music Publishing

First concert attended: The Beatles (in Las Vegas, Nevada: My dad talked the guard at the door into letting my brother and I in for the last three songs. I think the last song was "I Wanna Hold Your Hand". I couldn't really hear it over the screams.)

Best concert attended: The Jackson 5 at the Sahara Tahoe Hotel or Elvis' comeback, also at the Sahara.

Top five album recommendations:
1. The Beatles *Abbey Road*
2. Peter Gabriel *So*
3. Fleetwood Mac *Rumours*
4. The Eagles *Greatest Hits*
5. Michael Jackson *Thriller*

Little known resume entry: I wrote two musicals at UCLA which were developed and given a three week run.

Best project you were involved with that never made it big: Angela Via

Instruments played: Drums, guitar, piano, and recorder

Recent or past signings: TQ, Paula Cole, Angela Via, Wild Orchid, Puff Johnson, Marti Frederiksen, Sam Watters and Louis Biancaniello, Billy Mann, Jon John Robinson, Steve Diamond, John Gregory and KB.

THE TRADITIONALIST:
PEEKING INTO TODAY'S SONG MARKET—
A CONVERSATION WITH JIM VELLUTATO, SENIOR DIRECTOR OF CREATIVE AFFAIRS FOR SONY MUSIC PUBLISHING

Justin Goldberg: How long does it take to find out whether a song is going to be worth your time after you pop it into the machine and press PLAY?

Jim Vellutato: Musically, you can probably tell in the first eight or ten notes whether the person is a competitive music writer.

JG: So, just from the sonic quality of the production, before you even hear the song's full melody or even vocal, you can usually tell whether or not they're "in the game."

JV: From the production. And then, if it's a name writer who's been in the business for a long time, you would listen for the melody and the lyric of the song and find out whether it's just a rough demo they've put together. But if it's a serious songwriter who is trying to break in, the material has to be top A-quality. You know very quickly.

JG: One of the main themes I'm exploring is how the business is evolving in various areas. Now, you operate in an area of publishing that has become relatively unique over the past few decades because you deal primarily with actual songwriters, correct?

JV: Yes, songwriters and developing artists.

JG: And how has that landscape changed in the recent past?

JV: I think it's changed where...if it doesn't sound like a hit, it's not going to get used. And most of artists are writing or co-writing their songs, so trying to get an outside song placed is really difficult. What ends up happening a lot of times is a songwriter will write a song that excites an artist, and instead of cutting that song, the artist will want to co-write a song with that particular writer, so the artist can get a percentage on the album and get publishing. That's happening quite a bit.

JG: So song choices and collaborations can be driven by music publishing considerations, because of the potential income?

JV: And how much they contribute is always different. I think what's happening is you have several writers who are consistent hit songwriters, and for the major projects those A&R people go back to those big songwriters to try to get co-writes with their artists, rather than spending hours and hours going through hundreds and hundreds of songs. They'd rather go back to that writer's track record and get their artist to co-write. That's the biggest change that I've seen.

JG: Can you describe the process of looking for material for a new artist?

JV: You just try to get someone interested in one of your writers, in one of your songs, and then that will lead to co-writes and getting a cover on the artist.

JG: Is it really just a "name game"? Do unknown writers who might have great songs stand a chance against the established big name songwriters?

JV: Well, everybody's looking to either co-write or to get a song from the person who had the last big hit. It's always been like that. It'll always be that way because there's a certain quality of music or genre of music that's going on out there. If a writer hits it and the song becomes a big hit, everybody looks for something similar to that. I need something like Avril Lavigne. I need something like Mariah Carey. I need something like this. The easy thing is to go back to the writer who wrote that big hit for that artist. The Matrix, a year ago, they had a bunch of records coming out. And music changed and a lot of those albums didn't come out, but now they have Avril out. And it's exploding, so now they're the hot property again. It's just goes in waves. But if you're a writer and you're consistent and you can take chances, not be too different but be different enough, to move music forward in a different place, that's what you want. That's the key.

JG: Since you're really in more of the traditional A&R role in terms of putting artist with repertoire—do you feel like there are fewer opportunities to place that material with outside writers? I mean, a lot of people who are outside the business see shows like *American Idol* or *Popstars*, and come to the conclusion that the music industry is one big audition—if they're good enough, they'll get "picked" and be handed a bunch of hit songs. How realistic is that?

JV: There are hundreds and hundreds of people who are talented, who are very good. I think what everybody looks for is someone who is beyond "very good," someone who is just exceptional in some way. Something above the mold. And you never know who that is going to be. I remember there was a producer named Laney Stewart out of Chicago who had a kick drum that was just undeniable. If you heard this kick drum, it would just move you, and he got a lot of records just because of that kick drum. I remember there was a singer who came in here that sang just a cappella, without any instrumentation. But her voice was so good that you wanted to sign her on the spot. We ended up signing her, and getting a record deal. Everyone is looking for above average.

JG: How often are there disputes about splitting song ownership—disputes over the "splits" in the publishing percentages?

JV: All the time. If it's not discussed beforehand, then it's split between the parties in the room creating the song. That's why songwriters have to be very careful who is around when they're writing a song. There was a situation once where a song was written while an engineer was in the room, and they had to make some changes in the song. The engineer made a suggestion that they ended up using, and he sued for a percentage of the song. Writers have to be very careful. If there are more than two writers and you don't feel that one writer participated as much as the other writers, you must discuss it *at that time* and come up with a reasonable solution, or else a writer can stake a claim on the song later on down the road. My suggestion is to have a form for the writers who are there to sign stating what their particular percentage is of the song. (Visit the LSN Web site, there's an agreement like this to download.)

JG: So if somebody does the track, say, and then says, "I don't have any lyrics or a little bit of a melody," then there's no automatic...

JV: Usually the track is 50 percent. That's kind of the going rate right now, that the track person gets 50 percent. And then the melody/lyric person gets 50 percent. At least mostly in R&B music. In pop and rock music, that can vary a little bit because the melody and lyric seems to be a lot more important in pop music, whereas in R&B music and rap music, the track is very, very important.

. . . .

PUBLISHER

HARRY POLONER
EMI Music Publishing

First concert attended: Cheap Trick, the Dream Police tour, at Madison Square Garden

Best concert attended: Sigur Rós in Iceland

Top five album recommendations:
1. Elvis Costello
2. Randy Newman
3. John Lennon
4. Nirvana
5. The Who *Quadrophenia*

Little known resume entry: Co-founded Airwaves, the Icelandic Music Festival.

Best projects you were involved with that never made it big: Quarashi, Regia, Smile, and Wondermints

Recommended reading: *All You Need to Know About the Music Business*, by Donald Passman

Harry has signed and/or worked with such artists as The Mighty Mighty Bosstones, Cake, Flaming Lips, and Incubus.

TALENT ACQUISITION &
THE BY ANY MEANS NECESSARY DEPARTMENT:
EMI'S HARRY POLONER DOES SOME EXPLAINING

Justin Goldberg: You are primarily charged with dealing with new recording artists who have publishing rights, correct? From your point of view, what are a publisher's responsibilities?

Harry Poloner: Well, it's primarily talent acquisition—but what a publishing company does is eventually enter into a joint venture for co-ownership of the copyrights of those songs. So, it's our responsibility to exploit those songs in a good way. And what that means is, yes, there is a function of collecting money but also becoming much more aggressive in radio promotion, marketing, and we act as a true partner with the labels and we are the by-any-means-necessary department. So if that means trying to put our bands together on tours or helping out the labels and hiring independent radio promotion or helping out the labels and hiring publicists—all independent from what the label is doing—it helps get us with end goal, which is selling more records. That's where publishers make their money.

In addition to that, the most important function of the publisher certainly over the past three to five years, has been the growth of synchronization. That has really been a source of revenue that has dramatically increased and has really helped keep the publishers in a better position with a decline in sales over a period in time. So it is no longer taboo for bands or writers to allow their songs or music to be used either in television commercials or on TV shows or soundtracks or what have you, and as a result that's an entirely...it's not a new revenue stream, but it's a revenue stream that didn't exist and wasn't being fully exploited, although now it is.

JG: It's odd, because the rest of the business seems to be crying that the sky is falling, yet synchronization seems to be up.

HP: Synchronization is up and if you turn on the TV, it's quite apparent. It really sort of turned with the Stones or even with the Verve being used in Nike commercials. It was no longer viewed as the huge corporate sell-out that it was in the early nineties—when you had artists like Nirvana, and Rage [Against the Machine] and Pearl Jam, and certainly Neil Young waving the banner of anti-corporate America rock, and not allowing their songs to be used in any form. Now it's acceptable and you can use [a song] if it's done tastefully and even not so tastefully. If you go back to any of the contracts there always seems to be a clause in there that under no circumstances can [a song] be used in any X-rated material, and now it seems that every other band I have in here wants us to get their music into porn movies! So the times have certainly changed.

JG: I'll say. What criteria do you have for getting involved with new talent's publishing rights? Let's say you have two bands both signed to record deals. What makes one more worthy of investing in their music publishing than another? What are some of the telltale signs that you consider when you look at a new artist with a record deal?

HP: Certainly if you're signing a new artist at a record label, you have a certain amount of control over that band's trajectory—what you try to do is essentially map out the plan for their future. With management and with the band's label, of course, but the ball is in your court. When you're a publisher, you don't have that element of control. Not that you're completely out of the picture, but publishers cannot in and of themselves break a new artist. They can assist in the breaking of a new artist, but we're not going to be able to do it independent of a major label. So as a result, your perspective and the different criteria that you use to determine which artist you should be investing in, will vary: you have to take into account the label's success rate, you have to consider who it is at the label. The further along you get in the process, the more variables get eliminated. For example, do you sign an urban act to a label that doesn't have an urban department? Well, that would be somewhat risky. So, that's the first round. So what's the label? How hot is the label? Is it an artist who is playing into the strong suit of that particular label? Who signed the act at the label? Then you get into the sort of internal workings. Is it a person who is about to leave? Is he staying? Is he in good graces with everybody? Is that person a senior enough person—because there's always a battle for internal priority—is this person most likely to have his artist win out when there are finite dollars to be spent on marketing and promotion? Then you take into account the songs, which are a huge element. If we're saying that all songs are equal in comparing different artists, assuming they all have the same songs, who's produced the record? Is it a person who understands the current commercial climate of radio? Who has the band been able to align with, personally or through management? Certainly, we've seen the sort of internal machine that is The Firm, Geffen, anything that's related to Jordan (Schur) or Fred (Davis). They keep everything very insular, and at the same time they're able to get the people they want and get the sort of promotion they want and get the attention they want at the label. Is it fair? I don't know what fair is, but if you're standing on the outside looking in, trying to determine what increases an artist's likelihood of a commercial success, you take all things into account. Certainly a huge element of that is radio promotion department: strong, not strong, who's there, is anybody coming, is anybody going, and what's their internal read on the record? Is it something that they think they'll have a relatively easy time with, or is it going to be a long haul, a grind it out sort of thing? Different labels have different sorts of approaches when it comes to different types of music. For example, Aware Records: they grind it out, they put the band out on the road, they say get back to us in nine months to a year, and then we'll discuss whether or not we'll go to radio. So whether it's John Mayer or Train or Five for Fighting, it's a very methodical, long-term approach—whereas there are other labels where it's all about your first two weeks at radio: how many ads do you get, and what's your first week's SoundScan number? Again, these are all variables that you need to take into account. The theory being, the earlier you get in, the less expensive the deal should be because you don't know the outcome of a certain number of variables. The closer you get to that second or third week of SoundScan when you have a better idea what the album is, in fact, going to do, you should be paying a premium for those acts that have survived the first round of cuts. There are plenty of acts that have been huge priorities and have fizzled at radio prior to their first week of sales. It's very difficult for a label to then resurrect a project like that. Is the label going to pull the plug, or are they going to hang in there and keep fighting it out with second and third singles? I think if you're going to choose a label that's happened more often than not...probably Universal. Universal Records, over the past few years, has been all about your first couple of weeks at radio. Do you have success? What are the first-week SoundScan numbers like? At that point, they'll decide whether or not they want to commit more marketing dollars to the project. If you win, you survive—and if you don't, you're essentially done.

JG: Yikes. So let's say I'm in an act and I come to your office and you want to do a deal with me. What am I likely to hear from you?

HP: The first thing that I generally have to do is explain why bands do publishing deals. I think, for whatever reason, there is a different attitude towards publishing as opposed to a record deal. There is the perception that artists don't need to do a publishing deal, which is true, they don't need to, but that it is almost a negative thinking. The songwriters generally get a bit more guarded when it comes to the joint venture of a copyright as opposed to the joint venture of master ownership, which is essentially what they have with the record label. The '30s, '40s and '50s are over. The publisher no longer takes 100 percent control of the copyright, gives the songwriter twenty bucks and says, "Have a nice day, and don't let the door hit you in the ass on your way out."

JG: So today's music publishing deals are often fairly complex in terms of rights and permissions and often favor the artist?

HP: Yes. Certainly it's a better split than what they might get from a record company. Generally speaking, your traditional co-publishing deal is a 75/25 split, with seventy five being owned and controlled by the songwriter. Flip that around to the label side, where the artist is getting fourteen, maybe fifteen points in a perfect world. That is obviously significantly less than the seventy five points that they would be getting in a publishing deal. It's a matter really of education, first and foremost.

JG: Should a band wait to do a publishing deal?

HP: It depends on what they are looking to get out of it. If it's strictly a matter of money and you're looking to maximize the dollars that you get, you have to wait. The songwriters have to understand, you're essentially playing a game of double or nothing. The longer you wait, the greater your opportunity to double your money, that being your advance money, but the risk being that at any given time during that period, you could end up with nothing. I could never put a quantifiable number on what that's worth: ten grand, fifty grand...I don't know. If somebody offers a nickel more, it's a nickel more.

JG: How has the A&R scene changed in the last few years?

HP: With fewer and fewer acts being signed, and the consolidation that has taken place—not just within label groups, but within labels—there are fewer and fewer signings, and with fewer signings, there is greater pressure for each of those signings to not just recoup but actually to make more money. So there are fewer A&R people and there is significantly less artist development, because of the time constraints that are placed on the label and on the A&R community. If you talk to any of the older A&R people, they'll tell you they were working on six or seven projects in any given year. Now they're lucky if they're working on three. That's just the way it is. That's what consolidation is. That's what cutting down your overhead is, that's the nature of the beast today. It presents a tremendous opportunity for indie labels, because there is a void that's there, there is an opportunity to jump in there and be profitable selling twenty or thirty thousand records rather than not breaking even at 250,000 or 500,000 records.

JG: If you were in a band now, what are some of the steps that you would take to get your music heard?

HP: You always put your best foot forward. As difficult as the experiences have been in the industry, or as they continue to be today, the opportunities are still there. The shift has really been from the labels to artists and managers and indie labels. You have an opportunity now to record incredibly high quality albums, CDs. You have the opportunity to make great-sounding master recordings and get those out there. Today, it's all about coming to a label with a finished product. I find that's a model that works. Labels are looking for bands or songs that they can hear on the radio this quarter, not next year. And that shift has created a burden on labels, artists and managers to not submit demos per se, but to actually submit finished product in the form of a demo. The labels don't do any development anymore and the artists no longer have that incubation period to kind of get their shit together. And there are so many more bands and artists recording and putting out albums now. It's an unbelievable amount to try to listen to and try to keep straight. We're doing it better than we ever have, but we're being significantly outpaced by the kids, as we should. This whole industry is being significantly outpaced by the kids—that the Internet is a bunch of pot-smoking college kids kicking the ass of the major labels. That's it—and on the one hand that's great, and on the other hand, it's really causing the major label infrastructure to re-examine the way they do business and their business model, which may or may not work anymore. So, if my brother's in a band, I tell him to take his LSATS or his MCATs and make sure that everything is okay there and *then* you get the best possible recordings you can. You do your best to create the story locally, and if that means sending a CD into BDS and getting it registered so the major label infrastructure can then discover you, so be it. If it means getting a barcode so all your sales can be SoundScanned and you can do it at the venues so that we can then discover you, go ahead. But the shift is now toward the bands to do the things they need to do in order to be discovered; it's not about a hand-written note and a three song demo-tape that nobody's going to listen to. It's about, "What the hell is the band that's getting spins in Birmingham at RAX and seems to have something going on in the local indie stores?" We'll find you if it's out there.

· · · · · · ·

ARTISTS & REPERTOIRE

JASON MARKEY
Immortal Records

ROCK'N WRITING:
AN INTERVIEW WITH JASON MARKEY OF IMMORTAL RECORDS

JG: Is the rock world in general opposed to accepting help with writing material? It seems that, unlike the country market, you rarely hear someone saying, "I've got a great rock act but we're looking for one more great song."

JM: I think that's starting to change a lot.

JG: That's starting to change? So it's no longer, "Whatever Cobain writes and performs is holy," regardless of whether or not the whole record is going to stick?

JM: Not everybody's a Kurt Cobain.

JG: And that's just kind of a judgment call creatively throughout the process, is that right?

JM: Yeah, and I think it takes a good A&R person to understand that and convince an artist that there is no shame in working with a co-writer.

JG: Have you ever done that—set up some of your bands on co-writes?

JM: Yeah. I have two of my bands right now who fought me on doing co-writes and now they are absolutely thrilled.

JG: So you're Lisa Loeb, you write your own songs, or you're Dave Matthews the same—you sing what you write. And that's because spiritually and soulfully speaking, you want the whole project to fully represent whatever that artist is trying to say to the world, right? Is that sort of the overall idea of why the general notion of outside material for such acts is viewed as a kind of sacrilege?

JM: I would say that's pretty true. I think that rock artists always have this holier-than-thou attitude.

JG: And then you have bands that are kind of on the edge of that, like say The Calling—are they a rock band, or are they a pop band? Do they have credibility as rockers and are they really trying to say something, or are they primarily concerned with writing hit and, do the two concepts need to be mutually exclusive?

JM: I think you have to look at it this way. If somebody had a mandate to develop nuclear power and one guy sat in a room and said, "Fuck you all. I don't need your brains. I'm gonna be the guy to develop nuclear power," and didn't rely on other engineers to help him out, there would be no nuclear power. It's a collaborative effort. Science is maybe one of the fields that music people should borrow from a lot more—you put a group of smart people in one room with a compound or a problem to solve, and people come up with ideas and have numbers flying all over the place until they put it together and invent something. In country music they understand the process. You look at a country song or an R&B song and there will be sixteen co-writes on one song. That's because maybe one guy had an idea that worked with another guy's ear, which worked with another guy's ear to come up with the theory of relativity.

Rock bands have this attitude like, "We don't need the help." And that's why we end up with songs that always sound the same because they're only listening to what's out there. They're not collaborating with other people to come up with something fresh and new. I think, sometimes, there's no shame in asking for help with anything in life. I'm building a house, and I don't know how to put the 2x4s into the wall, what am I going to do? Do I just say, "Fuck it," and leave it hanging from the wall? No, I call a carpenter to help figure it out—that way, the next time I do it, I actually understand how to do it right.

· · · · · · ·

PERFORMING RIGHTS ORGANIZATION

SUE DEVINE
ASCAP

First concert attended: The Police

Best concert attended: Arlo Guthrie and Pete Seeger at the Wolftrap, 1990

Top five album recommendations:
1. Joni Mitchell *Blue*
2. Arlo Guthrie *Alice's Restaurant*
3. Hamell on Trial *Big as Life*
4. Mikel Rouse *Dennis Cleveland*
5. Josh Ritter's 2003 demo release

Little known resume entry: I once worked as a personal assistant to Lauren Hutton.

Recommended film: *Amelie* (Miramax, 2001)

Recommended reading: *Jane Eyre* by Charlotte Brontë

Recommended Web site: www.orbitz.com

Instruments played: Oboe, flute, piccolo, mellophone, cello

Notable clients: Dave Matthews, David Grey, Mikel Rouse, Martin Sexton, John Alagia, Josh Ritter, Lori McKenna, Carter Burwell, Howard Shore, Elliot Goldenthal, Angelo Badalamenti

---

ASCAP VERSUS BMI: WHAT IT ALL MEANS (ROUND 1)
AN INTERVIEW WITH SUE DEVINE OF ASCAP

Justin Goldberg: Let's start off with how is ASCAP different from BMI, because most people probably have no idea what the fundamental differences are.

Sue Divine: ASCAP's essential purpose it to collect performing rights royalties, which is the same as BMI. We collect those license fees from broadcasters and we pay the license fees out to songwriters as performance royalties. ASCAP is different from BMI in that ASCAP is a membership organization that has members who are writers and publishers, and our board of directors is made up of twelve writer members and twelve publisher members. BMI is a corporation. It is Broadcast Music Incorporated. It's owned and run by the broadcasters and, as a corporation, they don't have members, they have associates; their board of directors is composed of broadcasters, which are the people who pay the license fees for the music. ASCAP's board, which are songwriters and publishers, are voted into places on the board of directors by other songwriter and publisher members. Writers and publishers set the direction for the company and make sure that ASCAP remains at the forefront of protecting songwriters' rights. We make sure that we do that by maximizing our license fees and maximizing our payments on public performance royalties. We also work on legislative issues. We are at the forefront lobbying for different legislative issues; for example, the life of copyright issue, extending life of copyright, and other legal issues. So we have a certain freedom to take on legislative pursuits to protect songwriters, because our board of directors is made up of songwriters and publishers.

JG: One of the great mysteries of the music industry is how exactly the money gets split up and distributed by a performing rights society like ASCAP or BMI. Can you shed some light on this? How are you able to find, monitor, tabulate, map out and then disperse payments to songwriters from all the songs that are played all over the nation—from small town dive bars to football stadiums?

SD: Yeah, let me dive in. There are different parts of a copyright and one aspect is the public performance royalty. If your song is on the radio, or if your song's on a television show or in a film that airs on either television or in the theaters internationally or on television internationally or radio internationally, or if your song is in in-flight music on an airplane, or maybe it's played in an amusement park, maybe it's played in a club, maybe it's played in Gap or in a restaurant—any of those things count as public performance of your song. Maybe the best way to look at the basic model of why and how you get paid is to look at radio: a radio station's sole source of income is advertising revenue, and they're generating that level of advertising income based specifically on the songs they play. They choose songs, they create a demographic, they create the market-share, and based on all of that they sell advertising and raise a certain amount of advertising income. The idea is that the songwriters who write the songs, which is the product the radio stations use to generate advertising income from, should get a slice. So ASCAP will negotiate with all of the broadcasters of music—film, TV, radio, amusement park, live concert venue, airplane music, restaurants, retail stores like Gap, etcetera, etcetera. We negotiate with those broadcasters, and there's a specific formula for each of those areas that tends to be related to the amount of income generated. So, in general, the amount of advertising income you're bringing in, based on the use of a song, is going to reflect the amount of what your blanket license fee will be. So we can go for example to radio, our share when we do Billboard research tends to run, depending on genre, 60 to 70 percent, maybe 55 to 65 percent. In R&B, we're often 70 percent. Sometimes in country we're below 50 percent, say 45 percent of the market share.

JG: Meaning half the writers are with you and half the writers are somewhere else?

SD: Yeah. So we run 55 to 65 percent, sometimes up to 70 percent in certain genres. The remainder tend to be BMI. When we do our chart research, SESAC doesn't actually score a percentage point, typically, so we'll leave them out of it, which makes the remainder BMI. So we can go to the broadcasters of music at radio, and say, depending on the genre they're in, let's say 55 to 75 percent of the music they play is ASCAP, therefore they should pay us this amount of money in a blanket license and they can use any of our writers' songs in the ASCAP repertory. For this amount of money you can use any song for this amount of time, and then after a couple of years, we renegotiate that because our market-share might have changed, or their ad revenue might have changed, or whatever. So all those license fees come in, and then we have overhead taken out. ASCAP has one of the lowest overheads in all of the performing rights societies in all the world, approximately 15 percent, and then everything else is paid out in performance royalties.

JG: So how do you figure out whose songs are getting played?

SD: It depends on the genre of music, but there's a "follow the dollar" principle where monies that come in on radio, go out on radio. Monies that come in on country music go out on country music. Money that comes in on TV goes out on TV. We're very transparent and open about our earnings each year and about our payment system; if you get a check, we can answer specifically how we came up with the credit value and the dollar amount. How we figure out who's getting paid the royalites...there are over twelve thousand stations in the country, and there is no technology in place yet that can successfully, representatively, accurately, or anything else, listen to all twelve thousand stations twenty-four hours a day and identify the music. We are at the forefront of building a technology of fingerprinting and/or watermarking, and experimenting with those technologies to get something in place that will do that, but it's not completed yet. So what we do is we build a survey—all different kinds of stations, all different genres, all different sizes of stations at different times of day—then an outside firm actually builds the survey and makes sure that it is representative of the whole, so that the smaller group represents the larger group. And, as you're picked up in the survey, you'll earn a credit value. You'll earn more credits on a large commercial station that's paying a higher license fee than you'll earn on a small public station paying a lower license fee, but you will get included. A credit value is approximately five dollars and change, so say you earn twenty credits, then twenty credits times five dollars and change equals the payment for that particular song.

JG: So how exactly would my check for a song I co-wrote that got some radio airplay be tabulated and processed?

SD: Well, let's say one hundred dollars or one hundred thousand dollars are allocated for a certain song based on the credits earned in that quarter. Every songwriter, one, joins as a songwriter and a publisher, and two, gives us a title registration form that shows the name of every song they've written that might be getting a public performance and who the writer's share goes to and who the publisher's share goes to. So if a hundred dollars comes in for the "Red Shoes" song, we look up the title registration form and see that "Bob" gets 50 percent of the writer's share, "Tom" gets 50 percent of the writer's share, and Bob's and Tom's publishing companies may also split the publisher's share. For television, it's a much more finite group of stations, so most stations are on a census survey, which means if your song has been in a TV show, you'll get paid every time. ABC, NBC, CBS, the major networks are all on a census so any song in a TV show gets paid for. Warner Bros., Fox, UPN, same thing, and all of the major cable stations. As more and more cable stations come into existence, we start licensing them and we move them on to a census as soon as we can. Some of the smaller ones remain on a sample...if the licensing fee is too low, it makes more sense to keep them on a sample survey and not spend all of the income doing an exact census.

JG: What about the Internet?

SD: I'd have to check the number, but I believe it's approximately a million dollars coming and going on the Internet at the moment. Which on the one hand sounds like a lot, but ASCAP collects over six hundred million dollars in license fees a year and pays out over five hundred million dollars in license fees a year. So, relative to the whole, it's still a small amount. ASCAP is also legislatively on the forefront of making sure, as the Internet performances become defined, that the appropriate downloads or streams are able to be licensed where it's appropriate.

JG: Are small establishments that play music publicly ever exempt from paying performance royalties?

SD: Some are exempt, if they're small enough and if the use of music is small enough and if the money generated on that use of music is small enough. ASCAP has a licensing department that licenses radio and film and TV and all these different venues, so we have a team of people who will go out to the different clubs, and there's a formula based on how big the venue is from the number of seats, and what the cover charge is, how often is music played, and so on. It could be as low as four hundred dollars a year or it could be much higher than that. Many club owners might feel that they don't have to pay it because it doesn't actually go back into the hands of the writer. But it does go back into the hands of the writers: when those license fees come in, they're part of what's called a general licensing allocation. ASCAP has a program called ASCAP Plus, where monies from the general licensing allocation go back into ASCAP Plus and other areas. They go out to writers on every statement. On every check you get as a writer, you'll see an amount of money because of your airplay and then an amount of money because of a general licensing allocation. With that program, any writer earning fifteen thousand dollars or less on public performance monies can submit, once a year, an application—the deadline's always April 1—you submit an application and you say, "I wrote all these songs. I recorded a CD. I toured all these different venues. I got airplay on all these different stations," and it's to acknowledge, one, if you toured all those venues who are paying license fees, this is a way we could pay those monies out to you as the writer, and two, if you got played on all these radio stations that typically, at the beginning of your career, you're getting played on smaller stations, you might not have been picked up in the sample survey. Sometimes that award will exceed what you would've gotten paid had you been picked up on the survey. It's too administratively cumbersome and it would cost more money than we bring in to do an exact census on every live performance venue, so this is our way of addressing that issue.

JG: When does someone need to start joining or think about joining ASCAP?

SD: People join ASCAP sometimes well in advance because they know ASCAP is out there and they know that the membership department at ASCAP does a lot of creative events for emerging writers, like showcases or songwriter workshops or grants or whatever. There are a number of

events that on our Web site, and you can take a look at what creative
events are open to our developing artists. So, some people know about
that and join early. Some people don't know about it and find themselves
on a record label with their new deal and their new CD coming out when
someone at the label asks, "Are you ASCAP or BMI?" and they haven't
thought about it yet. Then the label sets up a meeting with us and we talk
to the writers and they decide if they want to join. In our membership
department, we do artist development with writers at every level of experience. I'll have a writer come in who has written a bunch of songs and
the best thing they can do is get their first gig. That would the next logical step. I have another writer come in who is doing really well in some
genre and maybe they need a manager or a lawyer, or maybe I have another writer come in who's already had two major label deals and is now
writing talk-show operas or whatever. Everyone comes in at a different
level of experience and a different track record and a different goal of what
they want to do next.

JG: What's a cue sheet?

SD: Let me go back to something else we said earlier, which is how we
know who to pay. We did it with radio with the title registration form.
With film and TV, you fill out what's called a cue sheet; the film production company or the television production company fills out a cue sheet
and that indicates all the different pieces of music used throughout the
show, who wrote them, who's the publisher, is it ASCAP or BMI. When
we see an episode of *Will & Grace* aired on TV, we can look up the cue
sheet and know who the monies should be paid out to. In film and television, a public performance in the United States is anything that airs on
television, but a theatrical performance in the United States—a theatrical
film playing at the local cineplex this week—isn't going to pay a public
performance royalty because of a strange loophole based on the way the
music and film business grew up. So in the U.S., a film playing in a movie
theater is not a public performance, though technically it should be.

JG: But soundtrack-related income from mechanical royalties from sales,
and public performance money if there were airplay would still be generated, right?

SD: Yes. If the soundtrack has a single that goes to radio, public performance monies on that single at radio would generate money from ASCAP.

JG: But the actual public playing of the movie with a writer's music in it does not generate money here?

SD: Not in the United States. In every other country, it does.

JG: Since ASCAP is in the business of closely monitoring revenue from music, albeit mostly public performance music revenue, what kind of impact have changes in our business had on your organization's overall revenues?

SD: If CD sales slow down by twenty plus percent—that's not going to affect ASCAP. What's going to affect us is if the economy is down and advertising revenues are down—if advertising is down as an industry, and so ad revenues are down, then our license fees might take a dip, though maybe to a different degree than the dip that CD sales are taking. There are different variables.

· · · · · · ·

PERFORMING RIGHTS ORGANIZATION

CHARLIE FELDMAN
BMI

First concert attended: Sam & Dave

Best concert attended: Jimi Hendrix

Top five album recommendations:
1. Astrud Gilberto *Girl from Ipanema*
2. Les McCann *Pump It Up*
3. Maria Callas *La Mamma Morta*
4. Rolling Stones *Brown Sugar*
5. Led Zeppelin *Black Dog*

Little known resume entry: Songwriter for Muscle Shoals Sound publishing.

Best project you were involved with that never made it big: Smith Perkins Smith

Recommended reading: *Tuesdays with Morrie* by Mitch Albon

Instruments played: A little guitar and piano

Notable clients: Tony Joe White, R. Kelly

ASCAP VERSUS BMI: WHAT IT ALL MEANS (ROUND 2)
AN INTERVIEW WITH CHARLIE FELDMAN OF BMI

Justin Goldberg: At what point do I need to find BMI if I'm a songwriter?

Charlie Feldman: Technically, you don't need to be with a performing rights organization in this country until you have music coming out on the market—being released in a CD that is going to go to a radio station, or if you compose or publish music that's going to be synchronized in a film or on TV. Because with films, they don't get paid for performances in the movie theatre, but when they go to cable TV or network TV, that will generate a public performance royalty for the composer and the publisher. This country is unique. In Europe, there is only one society and they represent public performances and mechanicals and synchronization. In the U.S., there are three performing arts organizations: ASCAP, BMI and SESAC, and they deal specifically with the performance. No mechanicals, no synchronization.

However, part B to that question...when do you need to be with BMI? Because of our showcase programming, our educational programming, our networking with lawyers, A&R people, creative publishers, agents, managers, people want to be with us before they have product coming out because we help them further their careers. It's such a competitive, service-driven system in this country, and we provide certain services that can help serve as a catalyst for writers and artists who write their own songs.

Also, we're really the last bastion for listening to unsolicited material. As you know, if you send [publishers and record companies] a CD in the mail blindly, it's going to come back to you unopened. They will no longer review unsolicited material. You need to get an attorney or manager who knows someone at those companies to get an ear. With performing rights, with BMI, we listen to all the music that finds us.

JG: Regarding the Internet—shortly after I founded and launched The Online Music Channel, I received an unsolicited notice from BMI saying, "We noticed you have this site. Please send us a check for a few hundred dollars. We'd like to know which songs you're streaming," which I thought was great. Was that a nice boon in revenue for a while? Or was it just an administrative nightmare to figure out who and where all these people were who were streaming music like I was?

CF: It's been a rapid growth curve from very miniscule licensing fees to small licensing fees. It is a burgeoning business, a growing business. It is going to offset some of the other areas that have maybe felt the pain of what's happened economically. I mean, certainly radio and TV advertising revenues are down. When their revenues are down, our revenues are down. It hasn't really been an administrative nightmare. It's been a challenge. It's still a challenge to get the right documentation and to be able to license everybody out there who is using music on the Internet, but we've grown. It's grown pretty exponentially, and it will continue to, and it's just a matter of staying on top of it and focusing on it.

We've been really proud of our technological advances. One way that we probably found out about you is—we coined the phrase "Music Bot," and it's technology that gives us the means to go out and roam the Internet and identify sites using music.

JG: And it would troll through the Web looking for music files?

CF: It would surf through and find sites that had music. You know, there are so many of them cropping up, and there isn't any way to get them all. But we've really tried to work with our "customers" online and not put a gun to their heads, but just get them licensed because that's the right thing to do. They really shouldn't be using music without getting permission because it is public and it is a performance. It's a transmission.

JG: Let's talk a little bit about the writer...you're probably in a terrific spot to see an overview of the business and how a lot of the exchanges work. What would you say to a young writer who has some material that's being covered—maybe he's gotten a couple of cuts, he has some sort of licensing activity, and he's been approached by some publishers—but he doesn't particularly need the money. And he decides he is going to depend upon BMI to collect his royalties and maybe a lawyer to do some kind of administration. What would you say to a person like that?

CF: Certainly we're friends with the publishing houses and we would never suggest taking business away from them, but if someone has the intelligence and the drive and the perseverance to do it on their own, then self-publishing would be an option. I can think of several people right now who are having a lot of success in similar situations and that's great because they control their own destinies.

JG: So, the reason to really think about doing a publishing deal is because there is more than just money involved?

CF: Well, with publishing houses—some are better than others, but they are all departmentalized. They have synchronization departments exploiting music for commercials, which is a very lucrative end of the business; they have people full-time pitching music to get synchronized in television and film, which can also be very lucrative; some of them have good executives in the copyright departments who manage their copyrights well. It can be a good way to go. The people who are really maximizing their situation are the people who are leveraging their catalogs, or they've got enough leverage to get a lot of money in advance payments from publishing houses.

This is my opinion, but if you don't need the money and if you know how to exploit your songs and you've got a track record and a history and you've created a demand for your creations, why not own them? At some later point you can always make a publishing deal. Different people have different needs.

There are a few writers, I won't mention their names, who hooked up with record producers and they're guaranteed they're going to get their own cuts. They're just having someone administer their copyrights. They don't need a big machine.

JG: What kind of general advice comes to mind when you sit with a talented writer or artist just entering the game who wants to hear about some productive first steps?

CF: To use your metaphor, it *is* a game—you don't want to go and put yourself in the big leagues and not know anything. In this day and age, you have to educate yourself. You have to be industrious. You can't think somebody is going to do it for you, because there isn't enough time in the day for somebody to do it for you. You have to know who your competition is. You need to know who the different teams are; you'd better know who's running the team, and you better know what positions the team players are playing. It used to be that you could go hang out in the studio and create something wonderful and then somebody else would do it for you, but it's not like that anymore. In this day and age, you can go record something that's mediocre, get CDs pressed and it looks like a great album. That's all frou-frou stuff, man. If it isn't in the grooves, as they say, it's not going to happen. I don't care how nice your J-card is or your graphics or any of that stuff. You'd better have great music, and you better compete with what you're hearing. You know a lot of people say, "I hear junk on the radio," and the truth of the matter is, there is some junk on the radio, but there's also some great music on the radio. It wouldn't be getting played over and over if it wasn't. Music is either good or bad. You better be able to know the difference between good or bad because most of the people I meet who are just getting into the business, their music is bad, and they think it's good.

I have people call me all the time to ask me questions that they didn't need to waste their dime to call me about. They just needed to think. You're coming to a music market and you want to know who will listen to your songs? Well, find out where the hot clubs are, find out where the talent scouts are going to be. Look in the Yellow Pages. See who the record companies are, see who the publishing companies are. Look under artist management. You gotta hit all sources. I'm pretty intense about all this because half my day could be spent talking to people who are never going to get to first base because they really aren't realistic about it. They think they're great, but they don't want to do any of the leg work. It's, "What can you do for me?" when it should be, "What can I do for myself?"

· · · · · · ·

5

NOT GETTING SIGNED:
a blessing in disguise?

Having always considered myself to be a performer, I actually had a hard time transitioning into a career doing A&R. At first I imagined that I would collect a paycheck at the office just long enough for someone to discover my own music, and then somehow I would get back to what I had always planned on doing—writing, recording and performing music. Fate however, would have something else in mind. That something was called Martin Sexton.

Martin Sexton

Sometime in 1991, my then song-writing partner (and now big time Hollywood writer-producer) John Zinman phoned to invite me down to see a play in which his wife, actress Amy Goddard, was appearing. There was a singer-songwriter from Boston playing guitar between the scenes, and, knowing I had recently taken a gig officially scouting for new talent, John insisted I come down to check out the guy. Knowing that John is usually a tough person to impress

Justin Goldberg, *Martin Sexton, Black Sheep*, watercolor on canvas, 19"x30"

musically, I went to the play. Ten seconds into the guitar player's between-the-scenes performance, I knew I was seeing and hearing one of the most talented solo artists of my generation; his every guitar riff was straight from the soul, his vocal ability dropped the jaw and chilled the spine, and his poignant lyrics brought audiences to their knees in nostalgiac revelation. It was as clear as day: this guy was tapped into something great. I became determined to do my part in seeing to it that he was not overlooked. When the company I had just started working for two weeks prior expressed some doubt and hesitated to sign him, I stole my rent check out of the mailbox and used the money to pay for some acoustic recording sessions at the studio where I had just completed my own demo. Armed with fresh evidence of pure genius, I vigorously lobbied my new employer to put up a modest cash advance to sign him to a development deal. Thrilled I had not only just inked my first deal but had done so with someone I was convinced would redefine the very genre of singer songwriter, I set upon my Mission from God to land him a suitably large record deal and make everyone from the company to the artist proud we took the gamble.

But a suitably large record deal did not lie ahead—what *did* was my education in the music busines, where I would endure unimaginable frustration while learning how even the most undeniably moving music can be subject to the deafening silence of absolute indifference. Over the course of the next twenty four months, I would witness one amazing show or event after the other that should have generated serious label interest but did not: there were sold out shows at L.A.'s Troubadour, standing ovations at ASCAP showcases, private auditions at labels, accolades from rock stars and music critics, and me, running around taking meetings from coast to coast on Martin's behalf in an effort to move his career forward...all with no results at all. What should have been an easy task that quickly escalated into a bidding war for his artistic services, was instead like pulling teeth everywhere I went. I was utterly dumbfounded at the total lack of interest or respect for his music. Martin Sexton would not get a record deal for seven years.

But I would argue, and he himself might even agree, that not getting signed at that stage was probably the best thing that ever happened to him. Had he been given a shot by one of the majors, or even one of the larger indies, his career may have very well taken a very different course. And if that course wasn't focused on cultivating and maintaining a live following throughout the country, he would not have the singular and wholly independent success he has today.

It's possible that if he had been "lucky" and been signed to a record deal early on, with no real fan base to speak of and only a single self-recorded album, a label (along with a manager and lawyer) would likely have persuaded him to record with a certain producer and come up with a certain sound or song(s) best suited to gain radio airplay in order go for a "hit," so he could sell records. This may have jumpstarted him to where he is today, but it's not likely, because he was not fully formed as an artist then. Perhaps the efforts of a label would have sent him in a very different direction, one that might have eluded the kind of fans he now has, and the artist he has become.

TORI AMOS THE DOMINATRIX

Most of us think of Tori Amos as a fresh breath of creative air who took charge of her own destiny and redefined the notion of female singer songwriter at the piano. But have you ever seen one of her early press phots, of her clad in leather and chains? Do they exist? You bet. Look them up and have a laugh; it was from her first album when she was first signed, called *Y Kant Tori Read*. And she is one lucky genius—there are plenty of other creative folks out there who never escaped the crushing weight of their first awful imaging choice. Of couse it's indeed hard to imagine Martin Sexton, the soulful troubadour and inspiration for the likes of John Mayer, to be in any equally artistically compromising situations, but you never know.

As his fans today know well, Martin Sexton's appeal as an artist is that his music and performances touch the soul in a way that most pop artists do not. There are no tours built around key markets based on radio activity, there isn't an increase in attendance because his video got added to buzzbin or his songs added to someone's playlist. Sexton's fans show up to hear his genuine talent and they spread the word because it's real. Had he not been forced to play music without a label and take care of the basics out on the road himself, he might not have developed the muscles necessary to achieve the kind of independent success he now enjoys. He might have been so spoiled by a major that he might have expected the label to develop an audience for him. Instead he now tours through America, as he has done for more than a decade, entertaining the fans who have grown along with him as his audience continues to expand from one converted believer to the next.

The irony is that when he did finally get the major label deal he thought he'd always wanted—directly from legendary Atlantic Records founder Ahmet Ertegun—it's likely that his deal was structured with far better terms because of the independent success he already had behind him. The label was stepping into a potentially lucrative situation that had

---

THE IMPORTANCE OF CREATING AN AUDIENCE

I asked manager Jordan Berliant of 10th Street Entertainment (formerly known as The Left Bank Organization), what he felt was the single most important area of focus for new bands wanting to advance their careers:

Well, I think it's creating an audience and having as close to a direct relationship with your audience as possible, because it's the audience ultimately that's leveragable. More so than even the talent, because without ears, without people paying attention—you could write the greatest song in the world, you could be the greatest artist in the world, but if nobody cares to listen or bothers to listen, it doesn't mean anything. So, artists who are successful understand that their currency is their audience, and it's amazing the way that audiences can affect, and should affect, how record companies market records and the decisions that record companies make. For a long time, and still to this day, a lot of the marketing and promotion that goes on at a record company is not directed towards the consumer. I think less than 10 percent of the marketing promotion budget that a record company has is actually directed toward the consumer.

—Jordan Berliant, General Manager, 10th Street Entertainment

little to do with its own efforts. Similarly, when artists like Dave Matthews and Offspring were first signed, there were already recordings circulated and fan bases percolating. (And the labels that signed both artists paid a premium for that sales base insurance).

He built it and they came. So should you.

THE D.I.Y. UNIVERSE

As this book has hopefully made abundantly clear, it is increasingly becoming a DIY dominated universe. DIY stands for **D**o **I**t **Y**ourself and has, in the music industry, historically been the phrase attributed to those in the artistic community who took fate into their own hands and recorded, released, or played music live—without depending on, or interacting with the mainstream music industry. With consolidation in radio and at the labels, the embrace of things DIY is not only on the rise, it has become a veritable revolution. Companies that sell independent CDs online, such as CDbaby and CDstreet (these and many others are linked to from our Web site and the enclosed CD-ROM) have increased their market share considerably. There is a viable market for selling independent music, and everywhere there are inexpensive or free channels to expose indie music to new listeners—you just need to know where to look.

YOU WANT A RECORD DEAL? GO GET ONE!

Musicians everywhere seem to be endlessly chasing their tails in pursuit of a deal. They remain convinced this magic treasure chest lies just beyond their reach, and from there it's Easy Street. I hear it everyday as I field the calls that come in: there's an artist on the phone from such and such, referred by a guy or a girl who knows so and so, and when the banter subsides they fill me in on their unique situation and mission—surprise! they want a record deal. Even my dog wants a record deal (and he's a better singer than most).

The reality is, most people want a record deal without having read this far into a book like this—they think a deal is something that it's not. And when they don't get what it is they think they wanted, they assume it's over. Meanwhile, they may actually have releasable, desirable product that could find a home with an independent in the U.S. or abroad that can generate revenue, create live touring revenue possibilities, and even generate interest in a major—ostensibly the goal of many in the first place. What most people *don't* realize, even musicians who have been signed to a major, is that there is an entire galaxy of independent labels all over the world in virtually every genre.

It may take quite a few miracles at the Viper Room on the Sunset Strip to get signed to Warner Bros. for a three firm record deal, with a half a million dollar advance, based on a bidding war that's been egged on by *Hits* magazine. *But* if you own your own masters and have a compelling story to sell, there could be revenue you're missing out on—and that, my friends, would suck.

If you are savvy enough, willing to take the time, do some work for your own career, and take control over your release, you can probably find yourself cashing some checks and feeling proud of the fact that you can actually derive revenue from your own recordings that you license to a third party. If you went to the trouble to get a bar code and create a

CD-ROM

releasable, professional, commercial package for retail and your material is good, you should seriously consider pursuing a variety of domestic and international independent labels who might just be really interested in signing you to a deal. Start by clicking on the Artist Marketplace section of your CD-ROM.

THE STARTING YOUR OWN LABEL CHECKLIST
First Things First: Gathering the Gadgets

The music business has always been driven forward by new gadgets. It's probably some kind of irony that the ultimate gadget—computers accessing each other via the Internet—now threatens the entire industry.

If you are going to function effectively as an independent label (or some variation thereof) it's critical that you get an updated computer system, because this is going to be your base of operations for most of what's outlined in this book.

GO GO GADGETS & OTHER TECH ESSENTIALS
Basic Music Business Office Set Up

Most of the tasks mentioned in both versions of Talent Shopping 101 outline the basic computer functions you'll be handling regularly: you are going to need a computer capable of burning CDs, making MP3 files, connecting to the Internet, and of course, generating and printing documents. Although many readers are undoubtedly technically proficient and may be reading this volume perched over a new laptop while wirelessly connect-

What you're finding right now is the independent record scene is healthier than it ever has been. What happened, and it's still happening, is a lot of kids form a band to get a record deal. That's the wrong approach, and an unhealthy approach. If I were advising them, I'd say do it because you like the music. Realize you're a business and go and hustle a business like everybody else, but don't expect to get married on your first date. It's like you have to earn your relationships: you have to earn the record deal, and it shouldn't all be about getting the record deal with the major label. If you set that out as the goal, you'll be screwed from day one. Do it because you love the music and you want to leave a message with other kids, and go out and hustle like every other entrepreneur does in the business. That is a mind-set that people have lost. It's got to be a burning desire to go out and play music in a gig, in live-in hellholes...like any other single business in the world, it's hard work in the beginning. It's not all about getting the magical record deal and becoming Number One. That happens one one-thousandth of one percent of the time, but it became the goal for everybody. When did that happen? Do boxers when they box, or basketball players, do they aspire to work up to become the big NBA contract? Sure they do—but don't forget the process of the training and the hours spent in the gyms, and everything it takes to get there. Somehow, in the music business, we thought we'd go from three gigs at [New York club] CBGB to MTV stardom overnight. That's the mentality that you have to get away from.

—Fred Davis, Attorney, Davis, Shapiro, Lewit, Montone & Hayes

ed to a high speed Internet connection, you might be surprised at how many musicians avoid computers completely. As savvy as most musicians are about computers and technology today, many are just plain convinced it's someone else's gig to be connected to the Internet and they don't need or can't afford a computer. Not true. You can't afford to be *without* a computer connected to the Internet in today's world, period. Whether purchasing discounted airfares or retail items, or finding new music, players, or professionals, there is simply no excuse to not have a computer. You can buy a cheap and highly functional machine on auction sites such as EBay or Half.com. Regardless of whether you own (or plan to own) a Mac or a PC, you should consider purchasing or borrowing the following:

WORD UP—LETTERHEAD, LABELS AND BUSINESS CARDS

For basic word processing and spreadsheet solutions, Microsoft Word®
and Microsoft Excel® are the standards. There are other word processing
programs but "Word" has evolved into the most commonly used program
for contracts, business plans, letters, resumes and other documents often
exchanged via email. Once you get your word processing situation together, one of the first documents you should consider creating is your letterhead or stationary. Regardless of how small your new label might be,
every small exchange of information with others should be viewed as an
opportunity to "brand" your company and create an impression about
what you are doing professionally. Letterhead is usually as simple as a
company name, address, phone number, fax number, Web site URL and
email address with single line spacing at the top, or at the left, of a document. You can limit your letterhead to type or use one of the programs listed below, such as Photoshop, to create a logo that can be pasted into a
template. Once you have created the look of your letterhead, you should
use the same information, font and logo to round out your tools by generating business cards, mailing labels and return mailing labels. This will
come in handy when you do mailings or even hand off packages and need
to quickly label some of your product. If you happen to be reading this
chapter at Staples or Office Depot, pick up plenty of extra mailing labels.
The format I choose for small, address-only sized mailing labels is Avery
size 5160 (thirty labels per page), and for larger mailing labels with a
preprinted return address I usually purchase Avery size 5164 (six labels
per page).

    Random computer tip for Macintosh zealots: If you are emailing out
Microsoft Word files, you need to save your document as a "Word 95" document. Other versions often have trouble being viewed on PC machines.

LITTLE SHOP OF PHOTOS

For graphic processing, Adobe Photoshop®, Illustrator® and QuarkXpress®
are pretty much essential if you are going to be designing several different
projects throughout the year. If you are unfamiliar with these programs, I
recommend that you take a course offered by Adobe in how to best utilize
their platforms. Adobe programs tend to be rather intuitive, and if you
have the initiative to start somewhere, I'd recommend starting with
Photoshop. The time you invest learning the ins and outs of Photoshop
will pay off again and again. It is an extremely versatile program that can
have you designing virtually anything with professional precision in a rel-

atively short time. Once you master Photoshop, however, and begin using it for various graphic projects, it's likely you'll soon realize that some production houses, graphic printers and CD manufacturers do not accept Photoshop files as final documents for printing. Localized print shops such as Kinko's can print anything, including Photoshop files, but most professional-level printers require the files to be delivered in either Illustrator or Quark, both of which make use of Photoshop files but have more detailed layout capabilities. (You will want to purchase a scanner to use with these programs. Make sure it's one with a USB connection—it's faster and easier to use.) Visit www.adobe.com

DIGITAL VIDEO

Shooting and editing high quality digital video with audio has never been cheaper, easier, or more accessible to nontechnical people. Depending on your budget and available time for learning new software, there are a number of options available. The professional standard for video editing is the AVID® platform and software, but entire feature films have been edited and processed with such consumer level software tools as Final Cut Pro®, Adobe Premiere® and Macintosh's iMovie®. (Digital affects programs such as Cinelook® and Adobe AfterEffects® can really soup up your production too—check out www.cinelook.com and www.adobe.com for details.) For compressing video (Mac users) I'd recommend Media Cleaner Pro®—a great software tool for transforming videos into any size and format.

DON'T FONT WITH ME!

All computers come with a limited number of fonts. Fresh looking fonts can make all the difference in presentations—whether they are on posters, documents, or album covers. Purchasing hundreds of extra font selections is cheap and easy. Purchase a program like Font Manager from www.greenstreet.com to give all your material a visual boost.

MUSIC ATTORNEY ALLEN GRUBMAN SAYS: "IT'S NOT ABOUT THE MONEY—IT'S *ALL* ABOUT THE MONEY"

CD-ROM

And he would know. He didn't mention anything about recommending that you purchase Intuit's QuickBooks Pro® to handle your financial records, but I will. This may be the most important investment in your business that you will ever make. What exactly does it do? Everything that relates to your money and financial records. It will help you file your taxes, create official company financial statements, write checks, reconcile your bank statements, transfer funds, keep track of individual project costs, revenue forecasts and much more. Simply essential for keeping track of your expenses, revenue and inventory. This program can save you thousands of dollars in accounting fees and last minute income tax anxiety if you enter your data in on a regular basis. Visit www.intuit.com

If you have Excel® installed on your machine, you can open the Excel file on the enclosed All Access Passport CD-ROM, which contains a pre-formatted budget with formulas already in place to add in various expenses typically incurred in the recording process. Transfer the file to your hard drive and keep it handy for easy budgeting during recording projects.

BURN BABY BURN

For making MP3 files and burning CDs, there are many software options, ranging from free to under $200 for more elaborate systems. Mac users gravitate toward Toast® which burns discs (and more—visit www.macworld.com), hip PC users swear by Adaptec's EZ CD Creator®, which also burns discs (and more—visit www.adaptec.om for details); other solutions include: WinAmp (www.winamp.com), Music Match (www.musicmatch.com) and Real Player (www.realnetworks.com).

FREE PROGRAMS YOU NEED

Often Web sites, emails and companies present their documents in a PDF format. PDF files can be opened by a program called Adobe Acrobat®. The full version is well worth purchasing if you need to create PDF files and exert detailed control over your documents, but the free version of Acrobat suffices for most basic viewing and printing functions (www.adobe.com).

Similarly, you are going to receive compressed materials and will likely need to download an "unstuffing" program such as WinZip (www.winzip.com).

HARDWARE ESSENTIALS FOR YOUR COMPUTER

Scanner—In a world where a café latte can exceed five bucks, it's nice to know that scanners have joined the ranks of tortillas and rolling papers in the category of essential "everyday items that could be priced higher but aren't." Make sure you avoid SCSII connector-only scanners; most new scanners are USB compatible. USB connections are easier, smaller, faster and better for a variety of reasons.

CD Burner—Most new computers have CD burners built into their hard drives. If yours doesn't have one, purchase an external burner drive. You will need CDs to burn back up data discs of your information as well as music CDs. Again, stick to burners with USB cables.

Zip Drive—Zip disks are a great, reliable data storage format that can be used many times over. If you have a CD burner, a Zip drive is not essential; the biggest Zip disk can only currently hold 250 megabytes, whereas a typical CD holds at least 650 megabytes. CDs are also a cheaper medium for storing your data.

HARDWARE ESSENTIALS FOR YOUR OFFICE

Fax Machine—Try to go for a plain paper fax (no rolls! Your faxes will need to be ironed otherwise). Make sure you purchase extra paper and printer cartridges—you will always run out of ink or paper exactly when you need it most.

Telephony on a budget—If you have set up a business name and have accounts operating under that business name, such as a telephone line, beware—most phone companies charge you higher rates for local and long distance service just because you are listed as a business. One way to escape this evil plan is to get a better evil plan, that is, obtain a cost effective local and long distance cell phone plan and use your cell phone for what you might typically be charged a premium for if you were to be using your regular phone. Most cell phone plans include digital one rates for certain areas and times that make long distance calls a nonissue. (Keep in mind that regardless of your telephone set up, you want to have separate lines for your online service so you can be online and on a telephone call simultaneously, if your system uses a "dial up" connection to get online via a modem.) I would also recommend looking into voiceover IP services—visit a Web site called www.vonage.com—this is a tip that can save you a telephonic fortune!

YOUR GROWING INDIE EMPIRE

Now that you're armed with the appropriate tools—your stationary, labels, computer programs and gadgets, you are ready to wheel and deal your way into a universe of opportunities that will hopefully continue to build into something you deem worthwhile, regardless of whether you are setting up shop to release only your own music or if you're aiming to be the next David Geffen.

RECORDING INDIE RECORDS

When I first started Laundry Room Records, I sold my Isuzu Rodeo to finance the recording of my first signing's album, Walkie Talkie's *School Yard Rhymes*. I was also the producer on the album, and it was a terrific experience in the studio. We had high hopes for the material and as such gave careful attention to every detail of the recording process; analyzing each song's various instrumentation needs, arrangements and sound effects. We hired a variety of professional players and recorded at some of LA's best facilities to do the tracking and mixing. But when we were finished making the album, I was almost completely broke—our marketing budget had been eaten up by the recording budget, which kept expanding to keep pace with the creative ideas and momentum of the album's creation. The album remains one of my all time favorite records (take a listen at www.MP3.com/walkietalkie), but it would have probably reached more ears if I had been more cautious about the money spent on recording, which could have been put towards marketing and promotion. It was to be my first lesson in how to make indie records: you've got to keep it cheap.

There are ways to make money releasing music independently. But unless you are cashing out a lucky ticket as part of a major label buy out/record deal, you are likely going to be seeing revenue in small increments—from licensing, regional distributors, synchronization income from film/TV or advertising—all of which can add up to a tidy profit *if* you are willing to keep your own overhead down.

Of course it depends on the style of music you are recording and releasing, but generally speaking, your recording costs should be very low—if you are a truly indie operation without funding above, say, $50,000, your album budgets should be well under $10,000, and possibly below $5,000 or even $3,000. Don't gripe that it can't be done—it can be; just find someone with a home ProTools set up. Maybe you can track somewhere high-end for a day or two and then scurry the tapes back to a cheaper facility for overdubs and mixing. Just keep your recording costs down!

PROMOTION: WHAT YOU REALLY NEED THE MONEY FOR

The main reason for keeping your pennies away from your recording budget is promotion: in all of its forms, promoting your music is going to eat up a serious percentage of your available money, regardless of whether your budget is a thousand or a million dollars.

What you should be spending money on in connection with your indie release depends in part on what your goals are. Some indie releases are actually geared towards remaining independent by selling records while others are really a vehicle for A&R awareness, with no real marketing coming into play in terms of releasing the material to the public via retail or the Internet. If the former is the case, you should determine where it's most likely you will be selling your albums based on your genre. If you have an impressive live show or following, your efforts and expenses should be focused on selling your records to your audience and generating additional opportunities to play in front of, and expand, that audience. Research music festivals (check our calendar section on the Web site, www.labelservicesnetwork.com for listings) or try to contact appropriate booking agents to book additional live appearances. Locate Web sites that cater to your genre of music—this is where you will find like-minded artists and industry-related ears that may be open to what you do musically. Aside from activities related to cultivating an online presence, the big promotional angles that most releases focus on include press, radio and retail—and each one of these categories will gladly accept your money for promoting your albums. Some details about these categories are just up ahead...

RETAIL PROMOTION

Newsflash: not every release from a major label makes it into every major retail chain. That's right—just because Band X got lucky enough to cash in a six figure advance check after their big showcase—they may very well not even be included in their rightful section at Tower Records. Why? Yes, that's right, it's time for another music industry dirty secret: labels pay for shelf space and different levels of visibility at actual stores. It's called retail promotion. It's perfectly legal for stores to charge labels for prominent visual placements of new releases. This creates a competitive situation where even the majors have difficulty trying to justify paying for retail placement of their releases—so you can imagine that indie labels, especially those at the self-release level—can have a hard time squeezing their records into the picture.

INDIE LABEL A&R PHILOSOPHY: HOCUS FOCUS

The most common mistake small labels make is signing too many acts. It is certainly the mistake that I made at Laundry Room; I was excited by a few different projects which were fairly inexpensive to acquire the rights to and before I knew it we had half a dozen artists with records to release, promote and pay attention to. I had wrongly assumed that our label would come across as more legitimate and established to investors, major labels and distributors if we had more artists on the roster. Perhaps it did make us seem a bit further ahead than we really were at the time, but that was also part of what made the whole idea of too many acts such a big problem. For a small label with a limited number of employees, it was nearly impossible to effectively respond to the various issues, needs and opportunities for each artist. Even major record labels with dozens of staffers, hundreds of thousands of dollars worth of promotional activities and massive retail distribution support find it difficult to devote equal time to several artists at once. (Thus the notion of designating certain artists as priorities.) Ultimately, a distributor and your bank account would prefer to have 50,000 copies sold of a single artist than three different artists selling 10,000 copies each. Not only is there 20,000 album copies worth of additional revenue in your pocket (which could be between $120,000 and $140,000) it's also cheaper to achieve those additional sales—with only one artist to focus on less time is wasted on coordinating the various promotional activities of two other artists, which can have a taxing effect on a small company.

CHOOSING "BREAKABLE" TALENT FOR YOUR BUDGET

Signing too many acts is often a common problem because people who start indie labels are usually either music lovers or well-connected to opportunities for discovering new artists who have been overlooked. If you are new to the A&R game, you are likely to discover a heartbreaking fact about unsigned music makers that those of us in the A&R community have known for a long time: there is an enormous amount of great unsigned talent out there—but not all of it is equal in terms of return on your investment. Some talent is easier to see money coming back in on than others, and often it's not what you'd expect. Certain genres of music that have large independent followings—such as punk, hip hop, or folk, for example—can create a great deal of grassroots awareness via their live shows and clever street marketing. The various components of the scenes around those genres of music are conducive to selling a relatively small but stable number of albums with a modest promotional budget. Ironically, it is the "mainstream" sounding artists, in genres such as pop and R&B, who require the promotional muscle of a major label machine to make any money at all; it's simply too difficult to gain traction at the independent level with artists in such categories. Try to avoid burdening your label with responsibilities you do not have the personnel or financial means to handle—it may drain you of the very resources that could be used towards breaking one single great artist or record. It's equally important to focus on the kinds of artists you have the best resources to promote.

MARKETING, PROMOTION & PUBLICITY
Download This: Your Internet Marketing Department

CD-ROM

Because you have purchased this book with the enclosed disc, you now possess within your arsenal a powerful and wide range of tools for spreading your music or music-related mission to dozens, hundreds or thousands of companies that might be able to help you move your project forward. The key section you should review in connection with your marketing and promotion efforts is located within the "Virtual Music Biz Team" section of your CD-ROM. Once clicked, you will see the category titled "Promotion Department," and within this category the options pictured below will appear.

COLLECTING AND CREATING YOUR BASIC ARTILLERY

Before you even start clicking around, it's important to collect some basic materials related to your project. You have before you, in the form of this CD-ROM, virtually the entire music industry at your fingertips. It's an industry comprised of small start ups, large conglomerates and every kind of company focused on every kind of genre. But before you go off into cyberspace and start attempting to connect your product with the people, it's worthwhile to take the time to focus on what it is you intend to accomplish and what materials you will be utilizing to present yourself to these new potential business contacts. Go back to Talent Shopping 101 if you still need to assemble the online and offline materials necessary for your promotional activities.

CREATING EFFECTIVE WEB SITES:
This Brand Is Your Brand, This Brand Is My Brand....

Remember that even if you are promoting a simple three piece rock band, you are basically creating a brand, and that brand should be afforded the same considerations that a large company about to launch a marketing campaign for their new product would have. Your Web site is going to be your primary tool for accomplishing this branding, as it is a direct channel for displaying your talents, story or wares via audio, visual and/or text-based materials that are related to your project. It's an opportunity to choose fonts, colors and graphics that best represent your project; you should create a logo and imagery that is consistent, so people will connect your promotional materials back to you and recognize them if they see them again. There are many variations to the artist Web site, but aside from being visually engaging, it should also accomplish the following goals:

1. It should feature music that can be listened to (but not necessarily downloaded into someone's hard drive).
2. It should link to a location where people can purchase your CD.
3. It should clearly indicate the structure of the site, and where to find what on the Web site itself.
4. It should feature a schedule of any live performances.
5. It should link to other sites hosting some of your music, where listening statistics can be verified (such as IUMA or MP3.com).
6. It should prominently feature a contact form or email sign up list indicating where fans or industry can reach the artist.

YOUR BASIC GUIDE TO CREATING ONE SHEETS

What is a "one sheet?" A one sheet contains sales oriented information as presented by the label and distributor to retail. It's called a one sheet simply because this information is typically presented on a single sheet of paper. It's a critical sales tool, and the first place that important people in the music industry's sales chain see information about your artist and/or release—the retail buyer. The buyer is the individual at retail whose job it is to sort through the many one sheets presented by distributors and labels and choose which releases to stock and which to not stock. Ensuring that your release is chosen and thus able to sit on a shelf in a store available for purchase is in part dependent on your ability to create a convincing sales story within your one sheet. It also needs to have a particular format and contain specific information about your release.

One sheets also aid in the imaging of your label, and help to position release in the marketplace. Remember, buyers look at hundreds of releases and one sheets each month, so make it visually appealing as well as coherent and interesting.

ONE SHEET TEMPLATE—INCLUDE ALL OF THE FOLLOWING:

Main Info Section:
* Artist, Title, Catalog Number, UPC Code
* List Price, Album Art, Street Date, Parental Advisory (Y/N)
* Configuration, Sales Territory, Label Logo & Address,
  File Under/Genre
* Short, Concise Bio of Artist
* Web site URL
* Picture of Artist
* Distributor Logos

List "Key Selling Points" information in bullet point summary:
* Producer and Credits of Interest
* Past Artist Projects of Interest/Discography/Previous Success
* Sales or Chart History or Hometown Success or Strong Markets
* Guest Artists on Album

List "Support Points" information in bullet point summary:
* List/Hype Degree of Servicing Involved in Release
* List Press Targets (fanzines, national publications)
* List Retail Targets (mom & pops, chain stores)
* List Radio Targets (college, commercial stations)
* List/Hype Touring Information or Plans
* List/Hype Video Information or Plans (director's credits, etc.)
* Consumer Advertising Plans (list of targeted publications venues)
* Indicate Any Participation on Samplers or Listening Booths
* Indicate Willingness to Participate In Co-Op Advertising
* Indicate P.O.P Materials Available (P.O.P. Materials are "point of purchase" sales tools provided by labels and/or distributors that encourage sales at retail)

(PLACE DISTRIBUTOR LOGO HERE) **New Release**

Artist:	Sharon America
Title:	Free2BU
Cat. #:	LRR9610
List price:	$13.98
Format:	CD
File Under:	"S"/Rock

6 07714 60062 7

TRACK LISTING:
1) 1. Pastoral, 2. Paradise Pond, 3. Intro Extro 4.) Shoot The Moon 5.) Trashman, 6,) Celeste 7.) Mind The Gap,
8.) Pleasure Seeker, 9.) 04 10.) Sharon America, 11.) Punky Bleach Kit, 12.)Wrythe 13.) Courtney Taylor

Kevin Colgan is a rock star, and that's the first thing you think or say when you hear him or see him onstage –
Magnetic and irrestistible and whatever it is that makes the few among us tick with allure and danger is simply what
he is. Some say he used to rob banks; others tell second hand tales of *their* Sharon America story - There's the time
famed producer George Massenberg "discovered" Mr. Colgan only to have him walk mid-project upon him feeling the
sound was too contrived; there are sordid tales of fistfights and love stories-some of which have become lyrical scars
on this album with clever references to Mr. Colgan's past differences with the pretensions of other local-at-the-time
outfits like **Everclear** and **The Dandy Warhols** –both cleverly assaulted in song on **FREE2BU**. Undaunted by the
task of helming the signing and recording of this explosive three piece was the determined Laundry Room production
team of Barrett Jones (**Bush, Nirvana, Foo Fighters, Presidents Of The USA**) and Justin Goldberg, who helped
discover and develop the likes of **Rage Against The Machine, Candlebox, and Martin Sexton**.

POP
12 x 18 perforated full color posters
36x48 foamcore display posters

PROMOTION/MARKETING HIGHLIGHTS
• Record produced by Barrett Jones (**Bush, Nirvana, Foo Fighters**) and Justin Goldberg (**Martin Sexton)
  Talkie**)
• Mixed by Tom Smurdon (**Pearl Jam, Satchel & Soundgarden**) at Seattle's legendary Laundry Room
  Studios
• Barrage of stickers, posters, and 10,000 samplers with CD Rom video footage of Vans Tour
• Full CMJ & Specialty Radio Show servicing handled by AAM
• Print Ads in Resonance, Velocity, Flaunt, Paper, AP, Spin
• Intensive Internet and Street marketing campaign
• Upcoming National Tour with 17 Reasons Why - dates in SF, LA, NYC and

PLACE DISTRIBUTOR INFORMATION HERE
INCLUDING CONTACT INFORMATION

Sample one sheet

CREATING EFFECTIVE NEWSLETTERS—ONLINE AND OFF
Come Gather 'Round People, Wherever You Roam, And Submit Your Email Addresses

At every point of contact with the public, whether it's online at your Web site, or offline at a live performance, you should have a clearly marked station where people can join a mailing list or emailing list to receive a newsletter. Newsletters are an inexpensive and effective method for branding your project in the minds of your audience. If properly executed, newsletters can offer a great opportunity to solidify the connection between the audience and the artist.

Newsletters are usually focused on notifying fans of upcoming shows, CD releases, or other events relevant to the audience. It's important to keep them clever and to the point so they don't get thrown out and fail their purpose. If your primary purpose is to send out newsletters built around certain live appearances, be sure to break down your list by region and only notify those who live in the area where you are headed to perform; no sense in driving everyone on an email list nuts if they're all over the country and you're only doing small local shows for a while.

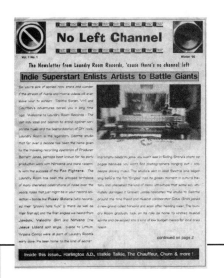

Online newsletters are so common now that it's actually nice
to receive a printed version now and then.

INTERNET RELATED/ARTIST
CHRIS STANDRING
AandROnline.com

As someone who receives a few hundred emails per day, many of them artist newsletters, I feel confident in declaring Mesa/Blue Moon recording artist (and AandRonline.com CEO) Chris Standring the email newsletter king. His emailed newsletters always come across as upbeat, visually engaging, highly personal and straight to the point.

Justin Goldberg: I thought it would be interesting to hear your thoughts about newsletters and online marketing because you are known, in my mind at least, for two things: being an incredible self-Web-oriented marketer, and also for being a musician who has managed to survive during a difficult period for the industry. What are some of the strategies and things that have worked for you?

Chris Standring: Well, I'm in a lucky situation, because I've always had record deals. So I have the luxury of a label spending dollars on me that I don't have to spend. But, at the same time, I'm always afraid that at any given moment that luxury might end and I will find myself in a situation where I'm going to have to sort out my career, just like every other independent artist. Even though I've got a deal, I understand that it's up to me to do the grassroots thing and pick up new fans at every single gig. I have always focused on building a massive email list so that every time I get a record out, I can blanket mail all my fans personally—right there I've sold a few thousand records. Email is a great thing to do whether you have a label situation or not. The label is never going to be interested in making sure you have a loyal fan base. That is absolutely up to you. So, I think it's a matter of being incredibly hands on—every gig you do, grab email addresses and names of fans and make sure you build a personal relationship with every single one of them. I know that sounds bizarre, but there is nothing more exciting for a fan than feeling like they know you personally. It's not about being distant and putting up walls so you create an element of mystery; those days are gone.

JG: Let's say I want to send out a newsletter. What are some tips?

CS: I think if you send it out any more than twice a month, you're shooting yourself in the foot, because you want to make things special events for people and you don't want to oversaturate your fan base. But let's assume that you're going to send out an email once a month or once every two weeks, depending on how many gigs you've got: you need to get yourself a list server, which is an online mailing list service. Get yourself a mailing list server—and there are tons on ways to do this, you might have to spend a little bit of money, but not too much—and just get to sending broadcast emails over the Internet.

JG: And a list server is what?

CS: It's basically an online method of bulk mailing people. It's not something that you could do at home because you'd have ISP problems. Your dial-up service or your DSL or however else you connect to the Internet, is very protective of how many emails get sent through their server. So you have to go to a specific company that will allow you to send out large amounts of mail. And if you're very successful, you may have several thousand people on that mailing list, so you need a company that can handle that.

> The label is never going to be interested in making sure you have a loyal fan base. That is absolutely up to you.

JG: As a musician who is very familiar with the Internet, are there any particular sites that are worth posting your music on for people to discover?

CS: My feeling is you shouldn't really be concentrating on drawing fans to someone else's Web site. It's much more beneficial if you have your own dedicated band Web site and draw people to that. Who knows when that third party company is going to go out of business? All of a sudden people don't know where to find you. So you've got to have your own dot com or dot-net. But at the same time, I'm not saying don't do it because I think you need to make your music easy to find so people can hear it.

However, I don't think that you should spend all your focus directing people to a third party Web site. You've got to spend your time directing people to your own.

. . . .

MARKETING PLAN

What's a marketing plan for? A marketing plan puts all the pertinent information for a label and distribution in one place—so people working on different ends of the same project can be on the same page with a release. Even when the "label" is really just you and your multiple personalities, it's helpful to have an actual marketing plan. Typically, there are two versions of the same marketing plan for a release—there's the version for your own "in-house" use (that will include costs and potentially sensitive company details you may want kept only for internal use) and then an official version for public consumption furnished to your distributor(s), sales staff, and anyone else who is part of the project. On the internal version, be sure to tally up all related costs so you know your real budget. Realistic budgets make for good business! Establish your limits and set realistic goals. The "public consumption" version of the plan should make the most of your promotional plans and efforts; in other words, in the true spirit of marketing and promotion, stretch your reach a bit and sell your plan. For example, if you know you can only afford to hire an indie publicist for a four-week stint, you should include the timeline in your internal plan, but not in the version being sent out to all involved. An example of a marketing plan is included below (it can be found in electronic form on your CD-ROM, located in the Promotion Department file).

THE ALL-HOLY MARKETING PLAN TEMPLATE

CD-ROM

The following are the basic elements of a marketing plan. By following along and filling your own information into the template below, you will have generated a standard industry marketing plan. Good luck...and remember to budget!

PLACE LABEL NAME HERE
MARKETING OVERVIEW FOR _____

Artist Title Cat. #

Street Date:

Format:

List Price:

Discount: (List any pre-order discount that you might want to apply to your release here)

Track list: (List all songs on the album here)

1.	6.
2.	7.
3.	8.
4.	9.
5.	10.

A&R Overview
In this area you should describe what makes the artist compelling and a brief sales "sizzle" on why this artist in particular is headed for success. It's almost the description that an A&R person would provide to a record label to encourage the label to sign the act in the first place. Describe the sound, history and target audience. Make references if there are similarities or actual connections to other artists—the music industry, as you likely know by now, is a very small world—you never know who may get an idea from your marketing plan to help propel your artist and your release toward success. Also provide pertinent music business information, such as booking agent and/or management details (especially if there is a well-connected manager involved) and what other artists these professionals work with. The A&R Overview section can also function as a "mission statement" or "executive summary" and as such you should state the general goal of the release's marketing plan and a brief outline of how the plan intends to achieve that goal.

Calendar
List critical dates (such as public appearances, contests, concert appearances, in-stores, release parties, etc.) that directly or indirectly involve the artist and the release.

In-House Awareness

Even small labels should schedule awareness meetings to review sales angles and information. Listening meetings and artwork review meetings generate overall confidence in a release.

Distribution Awareness

A month or so prior to the street date, schedule a presentation to be made to the distribution company's sales staff. Generate a brief meeting agenda covering key sales info and release information.

Focus Tracks

Generate a list of focus tracks. What are focus tracks? Focus tracks should be either the single or specific songs selected for their ability to convey what is unique or compelling about the release and or artist. You may want to designate different focus tracks depending on the target audience (e.g., clubs vs. retail vs. radio).

Marketing

- With a series of bullet points, you should list here *who* you are targeting, *why* and *how*. This is the overview section of the marketing plan itself.
- List all your promotional angles and what image you are going to use for visual marketing objectives.
- List all servicing ("servicing" refers to the promotional copies you send out). You should also list if there are any variations on the actual release, such as an interactive CDROM or vinyl copies that certain demographics will find more useful or interesting than others.
- Below are the main sections of the marketing plan, which for most music business marketing plans focus on Press, Radio, Retail and Video. Other than these main four, are there any other unique promotional targets? If so, list them here as a bullet point.
- Make the most of any celebratory event surrounding the artist or release as well in this section, such as if there is to be a nightclub kick off party or gig marking the release date.

Press Campaign

- Publicity: List who is handling publicity and for how long—in-house or outsourced. The publicist is perhaps the single most important choice in terms of awareness for print. List previous success and clients. List targeted publications. The following list is a fairly comprehensive publication listing for most rock/alternative/pop and hip hop releases:

NATIONAL PRINT TARGETS

Alternative Press
Axcess
Bikini
Billboard
Blunt
Brutarian Quarterly
CMJ
CMJ Monthly
Details
Detour
Down Beat
Entertainment Weekly
Heckler
Hits
Hollywood Reporter
Indie Cent
Los Angeles Times
Magnet
Massive
Mean Magazine
Mean Street
Milk

Mixmag
Moo
Oculus
On the One
Option
Paper
Pitchfork
Playboy
Puncture
Radio & Records
Request
Rolling Stone
Resonance
Scoop
Seconds
The Source
Spin
Streetsound
Stop Smiling
Swing
Synergy
Thousand Words
Urb
Vibe

Wired
XLR8R

TV

Entertainment Tonight
MTV NEWS

FANZINES

Baby Sue Music
  Review
Backwash
Big Takeover
BPM
Digital Artifacts
Fix

ONLINE

ABC. com
Allstar.com
Billboard.com
Launch.yahoo.com
MTV.com
RollingStone.com
Spin.com
UBL.com

- (For the in-house version of the marketing plan, it is advisable to include a budget line and associate all costs involving publicity and mailings.)
- Again, restate your objective and why targeting such publications support the goals of the plan.
- **Postal Plan**: List target dates for all mailings and the quantity of mailings, list the key recipients who will actually implement servicing of mailings. Outline costs associated with mailings and any associated printing needs.
- **Advertising Plan**: List consumer (*Spin, Rolling Stone*) and trade ads (*Billboard, Hits*, etc.), street dates, the names and contact information of the people booking coordinating details, and any applicable graphics details such as file formats and sizes, films, etc. Be sure to include the graphic designer's name and contact information as well.

(Also include associated costs for advertising for the in-house version of the marketing plan.)

Video Campaign

- List video venue targets and rationale for targets.
- Briefly describe the video concept (and which song).
- List the director and his/her credits.
- Describe expectations for MTV play (if any).

Radio Campaign

- List type of stations and format that will be targeted (RPM, CMJ Top 200, Commercial, etc.).
- List a calendar of radio goals.
- What type of stations are targeted? Calender-ize radio schedule, especially if you are going for more.
- List who is handling radio promotion, in-house or independent promoters (list previous successes).
- List who is servicing stations, create postal plan.
- Determine and list "add date"(date record is added to radio playlists).

Ad/Merch./P.O.P.

Create a listing for all merchandising materials and a matrix documenting the details around each item (i.e., the specific graphic dimensions, when will each item be available and in what quantity). Keep track of all internal costs!

1. Stickers
2. Postcards
3. T-shirts
4. Banners
5. Bin cards
6. Posters
7. Flats

Retail Campaign

- Create goals for quantity of records to ship out to retail. Create list of which retail locations to focus on and briefly describe reasons.
- Briefly describe who is handling retail promotion, in-house or outsourced company. Create a list of ad materials being created for different publications.
- List the date advance copies of the album are being serviced—again, create a list of who is being serviced, and how many copies are being furnished to each location.
- Describe advance copy mailing plan and describe which stores will encourage in-store play and if in-store play will in fact be encouraged.
- List any retail promotion (i.e. flyers, contests, etc.) target accounts, and dates such promotion will be running.

- Designate a co-op budget, if any. (Co-op budget may be the one budget related item that you *do* include in the public consumption version of your marketing plan as it is typically an item for distribution to discuss openly with the label. Co-op ads can be purchased at a discount rate made available by the bulk rate discounts available to the distributors.

Touring

Successfully releasing albums, on either a major or an indie, is almost always predicated on strategically planning live appearances or touring. Getting your artist on another successful artist's tour in the same or a similar genre has become routine strategy for the industry's introduction of new artists to established audiences for known acts. Successful indies manage to get their artists on regional tours and pickup dates with major headliners. Even if you do not have a major tour for your artist, nothing connects people to new releases like live appearances—get them on the road! Generate a detailed touring information spreadsheet listing the following information related to your artists' live appearances:

- List the agency handling the act.
- List a rough itinerary, even if it's simply target dates for when the tour begins.
- List target or actual markets.
- List any dates from previously successful tours or live appearances.
- Outline costs related to tour support (for internal version).

RADIO CATEGORIES
College Radio, Commercial Radio, Independent Radio

Reaching a nationwide radio audience has always required a substantial and risky investment in radio promotion. Major labels, indie labels and even the federal government all begrudge this—but it doesn't look like it's about to change. If anything, consolidation in the broadcasting industry could make it even worse. If you are operating on an indie budget, however, there is still some consolation to be found within the college radio format and the Internet. College radio and online radio are some of the most efficient, cost effective and often the easiest ways to get independent music heard; they can also provide the following:

- Targeted marketing: college radio is supportive of local bands and those that tour in their area; if response to the music is positive, it is generally added to rotation. College radio listeners are the same young music devotees who seek out new releases and routinely purchase records on independent labels.

- High potential reach: as with commercial radio, any radio listener can potentially listen to airplay, depending on the strength of the signal of the station.
- A bastion for independent label music: just as independent labels search out new sounds and unknown bands to distinguish themselves from the major labels, college radio stations play independent music to distinguish themselves from commercial radio.

PUBLIC RELATIONS

ALISSE KINGSLEY
President
Muse Media

First concert attended: Carole King in Central Park, 1971 (the *Tapestry* album—a friend's parents took us)

Best concert attended: Patti Smith at the Roxy

Top five album recommendations:
1. Van Morrison *Moondance*
2. Patti Smith *Horses*
3. Joni Mitchell *Blue*
4. The Rolling Stones *Exile on Main Street*
5. Anything by Sinatra

Little known resume entry: I do volunteer work for Guide Dogs for the Blind.

Recommended reading: *Quiet Days in Clichy*, by Henry Miller; *Doubletake* magazine

Recommended Web site: www.Salon.com

Notable clients: Joni Mitchell, Paul Simon, Rickie Lee Jones, Iris Dement, Peter, Paul & Mary, Dee Dee Bridgewater, the Chieftains

---

A FOCUS ON RELATIONSHIPS (EVERYTHING YOU NEED TO KNOW ABOUT PUBLICITY IS IN THIS INTERVIEW!):
A CONVERSATION WITH PUBLICIST ALISSE KINGSLEY

Justin Goldberg: Why don't you lead us through some of the basic tools and steps in the PR process.

Alisse Kingsley: The basic tools are the projects—the CD, DVD or tour. The final result is the music, which can take the form of any one of these.

Those are the three things that might be taken into consideration. You're also going to need to do a press release and/or bio about the project, and make advance copies of the project because you want the press to know about something in advance of when it's actually happening.

JG: What's typically the timeline for that?

AK: That would be three to four months for "long lead" publications and one to two months for weeklies. Copies of the copy itself, such as a bio, press release and photo, are always helpful. Great photographs are always useful and anything else that's relevant: for example, is there merchandising? Is there a Web site? All these other elements can be important tools. You can also get into other things like satellite press tours, listening events, kick off parties; there are so many developments that can occur and directions that a project can get into.

JG: You have some clients who are simply icons—Paul Simon and Joni Mitchell, to name just two. But let's say you were to take on a completely unknown but equally talented new artist before they even had a major record deal. Let's say you had an independent release that you wanted to publicize. Is it critical to have distribution for your record to go out there and start looking for press coverage?

AK: I think it's more difficult without it, but I don't think it's impossible. Ani DiFranco is the perfect example of somebody who started her own label and who has done very well and a lot of it was through the 'net. She is absolutely in record stores now, but in the beginning a lot of her sales were online.

Touring also plays a part. If there is a tour accompanying the release, a lot of times you can create a groundswell through tour press and start in individual niche markets and build that way. It depends upon the publicist and his or her personal relationships with journalists. You've got to decide who you are working with—is that person connected in terms of having good relationships? In other words, is he good at getting people to come down to shows—at saying, "Hey, I've got this great new band, I really want you to hear them"? If he has a strong relationship with these people, they might come out regardless. I think in the music industry relationships are just key, they are instrumental to the process of evolving a record.

JG: Would you want to reach out to local press at first for an indie band?

AK: Absolutely. I think sometimes you will go through three to four different servicings. I want to take into account what dates are being done around the country or in a certain local region. I want to hone in on those outlets, those that coincide with the tour, but at the same time if I think the record's great I may want other people on a national level to hear it. Even if they don't listen the first time, I'll send it again, maybe they'll remember and say, "Oh yeah. She sent it a few months ago and now look, there's some chart action," or, "Look, now there's a tour happening." And they'll get it again. I've often sent out two to three mailings to the same person before that person actually takes a listen. Sometimes you just have to do that.

JG: Would it be impossible, for instance, to take something on for just a few weeks or a single month and go on a publicity blitz?

AK: Virtually impossible. When people come to me and say, "We want you to work on something for a month," my answer has to be no. I spend the first month or first few weeks of the campaign just setting everything up: analyzing, listening, creating my plan, having artists go over it with me, if we need to do a photo shoot for stills, etc. A lot of times we've created an EPK, which is a video version of the press kit. That's a great tool for TV outlets to have, whether it's national or local television. Let's say they are going to do *Good Day Atlanta* and they want footage, great, we've got it on Beta and can FedEx it to them the next day. There's so much that goes into campaign preparedness and readiness. To do something in a month is impossible, really. Maybe if you are a huge name, you can get something done, but for a new upcoming band you need a lot of lead time.

JG: What is a publicist's function on a day to day basis?

AK: Everything from helping to define the image, to creating the press materials, to being the spokesperson for the project to the world, to choosing what interviews the act should or should not do, to damage control if something comes up that is not pleasant. It's all of those things. It's also babysitter, personal shopper—it's a number of things. Predominately you are the spokesperson to the world about this project and you have a hand in creating all the materials that go along with it, which are in effect, your tools for getting the word out to the press and the world at large.

JG: Where are the materials distributed and how are they interpreted and put out to the world?

AK: Okay, let's start with print. There are short-term print outlets, which consist of newspapers and weeklies. And there are your long-term outlets that consist of major magazines, which have a three to four month lead time. That's why you want to be careful to have your press materials prepared and ready to go.

JG: How many copies do you need?

AK: Well, that depends upon the genre of music. Typically, in terms of advances, I will send out somewhere between 300—500 advance copies of the project. And that's keeping into consideration print, radio, online and TV. So, the print is the short and long lead.

JG: When it comes to TV, is that an off limits realm for new artists?

PRESS OUTLET TARGETS: RADIO, TV, PRESS

Then there is radio/talk radio. It's great to do syndicated radio pieces, for instance like Westwood One or AP Radio. Then there are also wonderfully influential and thoughtful radio outlets such as NPR's *Fresh Air, All Things Considered* and *Morning Edition*, that always find help getting the word out; NPR does amazing interviews with artists. There are local stations in tour markets, which can be great when you have a band that's on the road. There are different components to radio as well.

Online, you have dedicated sites for the artists, you have label sites, chat rooms about the artists, you have links to sites that are not necessarily about the artist, but be deemed relevant to the artist. There are so many different things you can do now online and it's a very effective tool because a lot of fans are searching for information about the artist online. There's a whole wonderful world in and of itself. The Internet has its own magazines, it's own radio and TV.

Then you have TV outlets such as the major morning shows—*Good Morning America, The Today Show, Good Day New York, Good Day Atlanta*— that are all crucial, particularly when you are doing a tour—some of these are very effective. Then you have your late night: Conan, Leno, Last Call, Letterman, Jimmy Kimmel, SNL, all of which are wonderful exposure. There are a lot of outlets available for music and they all have slightly different demographic bench marks to think about.

—Alisse Kingsley, President, Muse Media

AK: Not off limits, but certainly more difficult. Late night considers new artists, Conan considers new artists at younger stages than SNL or Letterman. It seems like the later the show the more possible consideration a newer band might get.

JG: With the advent of high quality, inexpensive digital video, many new artists have made their own low budget music videos. Are there cable outlets that accept videos from new artists? Do you even handle furnishing/servicing videos out to masses? Or is that a whole separate art form?

AK: It is a separate art form, in fact the labels have video promotion departments that handle that; not only do they service MTV and VH-1, they reach out to all these little fringe cable shows and local cable shows on a national level in various markets. That's usually not handled by the publicist per se, although sometimes again it crosses, just like with radio.

JG: What are some cost effective ways to promote yourself if you are releasing your own record?

AK: If you are a new band and you don't have a lot of money and you want to try to get the word out, touring is essential; you can call and invite people to come to shows. Maybe creating your own materials to start is a way to keep costs down. It's an industry built on relationships, so it's a lot tougher when you're going at it alone. Is there a friend you can call in to help out, do favors, call the press on your behalf? I think there's a method to the madness in terms of getting word out about the music and having materials go out with it in some way, shape, or form. I think that things have to happen. Yes, online chat rooms are great, links are great— but you still need somebody to call the press' attention to you. Whether it's somebody who is doing it on a very grassroots level or someone you've hired. It's been done with very limited funds before.

JG: Let's say you have a big list of media outlets, do you just go and randomly send it to a whole bunch of people?

AK: Well, if you don't know much about these people, it's going to be more difficult. It's better to narrow down that list and say, "Okay, now this is an alternative country band, so I'm probably going to send it to my general pop writers, my folk and country writers and my entertainment writers." I probably wouldn't send it to my jazz or alternative rock lists, although in some cases it might cross over. So, you have to think about what is the subject matter and then break your lists down from there. I do a custom list for every project. So, yes, a band could have a list and just send their project out, but if they don't have a relationship with anybody at that outlet, who knows if it will ever get listened to?

JG: How important is follow up to all this?

AK: Follow up is very important. Most press people are very busy and they receive a ton of packages; to make yours stand out you *always* have to follow up. Make sure they received it and then ask them if they have any questions. It also depends on your own priorities: do you want press to attend a certain show, or are you trying to achieve a feature interview or an album review? You have to have certain goals when you send out a package to somebody. I also think the human voice is still the best way to connect and contact someone. I know it's not as efficient as emails and faxes, but I think people like hearing from someone personally; they don't like being hounded by a machine, whether it's a voicemail or email. I do everything, I email, phone and snail mail.

JG: Are there any tricks of the trade in terms of pictures press are likely to run? A sexed up picture of a female singer? Is it important to get a professional photograph?

AK: Yes, the last thing you want to look is boring. You want to look intriguing and interesting: what sets you apart from somebody else? Sex, of course, sells—it always has, it always will. It's important to spend some money on a good photo.

JG: When you see a photograph in an article about an artist and it seems like a different photograph than everyone's running, where is that coming from? Does the publication choose it or is the publicist smart enough to furnish a couple of different shots?

AK: Both. Sometimes a publication will pay for their own photo shoot because they want something different, sometimes a publicist will go through photos with the artist and put aside those to be used for exclusives for magazines that demand something different than what every other publication across the country is running.

JG: What's an exclusive?

AK: An exclusive is a photograph that's only used for one particular publication for a period of time. After the publication runs, the photo usually becomes a non-exclusive. But sometimes a publication will command their own photo shoot because they want to own the pictures and don't want them reverting back to the publicist.

JG: If a magazine wanted to run a feature about an artist, they might hire their own photographer to shoot their own pictures. Why would they do this?

AK: Well, *Vanity Fair* is a good example. They want a look of their own, indigenous to their magazine. A lot of publications have a certain sense of style. They have a certain look that they create in their magazine that they want followed. They don't want to use a photo that everybody else across the country is running.

JG: Do those photos then become the property of the magazine?

AK: It depends upon the agreement that the magazine has worked out with the individual photographer. Sometimes the publicist and the label might negotiate if it's going to be a buyout—are you going to own the photos or does the photographer own the photos? What rights have you negotiated? Is it for publicity or are you also buying out for advertising and marketing?

JG: When you say advertising and marketing, what do you mean?

AK: Ads. When you negotiate with the photographer, are you doing a total buyout so that you own the photos, or are you just buying them for publicity purposes?

You're going for stories about your artist—reviews, interviews, TV appearances. The more information as you can give to an outlet beforehand, then the more informed they are about the project. One thing I find that artists hate is when an interviewer is uninformed. So another tool that we do is called a "Track by Track" or a "Words in Music," which is a detailed written piece about the actual project which goes track by track and talks about each song. Each track might have a little particular nuance that's of interest to somebody doing a review of the record.

JG: What are some of the important considerations to weigh when hiring a publicist to work on a project?

AK: Consider things such as:

- How long have they been doing what they've been doing?
- What are their contacts like?
- Who else do they handle?
- What is their track record?
- Where are they located?
- What are you looking for in a publicist—are you looking for a huge firm, or are you looking for a small indie publicist? Sometimes it's just a matter of personal taste.
- Who will be handling the actual pitching at the firm? What is their experience? Their preferred type of music? How busy are they? Who works for them and with them?

I think you have to meet with your prospective publicist. The most important thing is the meshing of the minds. What's most important is how do they view your project and what their goals are.

JG: Is it advisable to consider hiring an outside publicist if you already are signed to a record company? Do people do that?

AK: Yes, all of the time. Sometimes the artist pays for it, sometimes management pays for it and sometimes the label pays for it. It varies case by case. A lot of artists have outside publicists. They are there for a lot of things, around for the long haul.

JG: Do you try to keep your eye on the ball in terms of promoting actual product for sale, a tour, etc?

AK: Yes, but sometimes it's a long time between projects for an artist and something comes up that's a great opportunity for that artist and you definitely want to present it to them. I never make a final decision about anything, I always consult with the artist.

· · · · · · ·

INDIE LABEL

KURT DEUTSCH
Sh-K-Boom Records

First concert attended: My parents took me to John Denver, Barry Manilow, or Neil Diamond—I can't remember which one was first.

Best concert attended: Bruce Springsteen's The River tour (8th Grade), U2's Joshua Tree Tour at the Carrier Dome (college freshman year at Syracuse University).

Top five album recommendations:
1. Randy Newman *Sail Away*
2. Bruce Springsteen *Born to Run*
3. Joni Mitchell *Blue*
4. Bob Dylan *Nashville Skyline*
5. Tom Waits *Small Change*
6. David Bowie *Hunky Dory*
7. Ricki Lee Jones *Pirates*

Little known resume entry: I was the original Faust in Randy Newman's musical *Faust* and Randy Newman sang at my wedding!

Recommended reading: Donald Passman's bible: *All You Need to Know About the Music Business*

Instrument played: I act and sing (if you can call it that).

Recent or upcoming projects: Adam Pascal, Sherie Rene Scott, Alice Ripley, Michael Cerveris, The Broadway Inspirational Voices, and a bunch of Broadway and Off-Broadway cast albums.

FILLING A NICHE: HOW KURT DEUTSCH TURNED A LOVE OF THE STAGE INTO AN INDIE THAT MATTERS
AN INTERVIEW WITH KURT DEUTSCH OF SH-K-BOOM RECORDS

Justin Goldberg: Kurt, there are a lot of people out there who have started record labels or are thinking about starting a record label. This is something you have done and are relatively new to. How did you do it and why are you succeeding?

Kurt Deutch: I did it because I found a niche that was completely being overlooked, and that niche is New York theater stars and composers who, in an ideal world, want to bridge the gap between rock 'n' roll and theater. I've been an actor all my life; I'm married to a Broadway musical actor; all my friends are Broadway actors—and major record labels never really gave them the time of day. And the independent record labels that dealt with these people were really only interested in showtunes, which have a very limited audience and are ultimately kind of cheesy and never really make any money unless you go and play live. So, I started it with my wife, for my wife. Because she was presented a record contract that was the most ridiculous thing I'd ever seen—because she doesn't write, she would never have seen any money from that contract, so I thought, "Well, she's playing to 15,000 people a week on Broadway. We can put her Web site in her bio in the playbill and if people like her, they'll buy her record." She was doing *Aida* then; we made her record with a Grammy-winning producer, and we did it for under fifty grand. We figured we had to sell five thousand records to break even. I knew nothing about the music business so I was like, "Whatever," and then I started thinking, "If I could do it with her, why can't I do it with my other friends who don't want to make Broadway showtune records, who want to make rock 'n' roll records?" And so I got in touch with Adam Pascal and Alice Ripley, and a couple of other Broadway people who are really amazing songwriters, and who have a really strong following because of *Rent* and *Rocky Horror* or *Sideshow*. I made their records for pretty cheap, but in terms of quality they were really great, with people who believed in this mission of bridging the gap between rock 'n' roll and theater, and we just kind of went from there.

JG: How did you find a way to distribute your records?

KD: Well, initially, we just did it online, through our Sh-K-Boom Web site. I also purchased (with the artists) their domain names. So, if you went to see *Aida*, in Adam Pascal's bio in the playbill, it says Adam was in *Rent*, and he was in this, and he was in that—but he also did this record on Sh-K-Boom Records, if you want additional information, go to adampascal.com. So people could go to Sh-K-Boom or people could go to adampascal.com, and if they went on to adampascal.com, then they would be led to the homepage of the record label site.

JG: And what happened? Did it work? Did people buy records?

KD: Yes. Initially we sold around eight thousand copies in the first few months.

JG: So in terms of cash revenue to you, that's, what, eight thousand times ten?

KD: Better—times fifteen, plus shipping and handling.

JG: Wow, so that's over a hundred thousand dollars.

KD: And that was just for Sherie Rene and Adam Pascal. Sherie didn't sell quite as many, she sold probably five or six thousand; Adam sold about eight.

JG: How were you able to find distribution outside of your Web site?

KD: Well, then the theater—owned by Disney, they really liked the show—so the theaters sell the CDs and when you walk out of the theater, you can buy their solo CDs...people buy at the venue. People buy on Amazon.com now. People buy on the homepages of the artists and the label. So, traditional retail distribution is great if you can get it. If you're a major and you have major promotion behind you, that's wonderful, but what was important to me was to maintain control of my own Web site, my own in-the-theater sales, so that's what we did: we found a distributor who wouldn't take as much, who was strictly for retail sales, so it's only retail and I have to manufacture my own CDs.

JG: Is that something that you recommend doing—to manufacturing your own CDs? I know some indies are skeptical of distributors doing their manufacturing "free" as part of the deal because they will charge the labels much more on their account than they actually pay for it themselves.

KD: Yeah, they're going to mark that up. At this level, with distributors, everything they do is going to be recoupable. For me, if I had a record that I knew was going to sell two hundred thousand or five hundred thousand copies, maybe it would make sense for me to have somebody else pay for manufacturing initially. But if I know off the top that I'm really going to be selling ten or fifteen or twenty thousand units, then I would rather pay for that and control it, so that I know specifically what's going on when I send that number of CDs to the distributor. It also depends on how much money you have. And I would rather press the first fifteen or twenty thousand units myself, and maintain the control—because you make more when you sell it and control the units yourself. The less you have to give away, the better. And for an independent label, especially for niche artists, when you know you're not going to sell initially, unless it catches on or unless it's that one huge hit, you want to try to keep everything as close to home as you possibly can.

JG: Let's talk for a minute about how Internet piracy might be affecting a smaller, niche-focused independent label like yours. My guess is that the Internet is not likely to be plaguing you the way that it's ravaging the revenue streams of the majors. Why is that? You don't think that people are downloading and trading...

KD: I'm sure that they are, actually. I'm sure that with CDs being able to be copied, it's hard, but the interesting thing about theater people as a group is that they are collectors. They want to own something with the picture of the star. And a lot of times with a cast album, you want the lyrics to the songs, because a lot of musical theater students want to be able to sing along. They really want to know all the right words, and I think that they want to have a piece of what they just saw. That's why there's a Disney store right outside of the New Amsterdam Theater. They want to go and buy something connected to the experience they just had.

JG: What are some key start-up lessons if someone were to tell you that they were about to start an indie label similar to yours—what would you advise them, based on some mistakes you made the first time around?

KD: I spent too much money at the beginning. I overestimated what the audience was. I definitely spent too much money.

JG: Recording?

KD: Recording, yes, and marketing. My stupidest mistakes were in advertising and marketing. Here's a great story: in the very beginning, I didn't know much, so I hired a publicist when I released the first two records. The publicist was like three thousand dollars a month. Expensive, okay? She said, "We got this great hit. CNN's *Showbiz Today* wants to do a piece and Adam's going to sing a song, then Sherie's going to sing a song. Actually two different shows, but they're going to do it on one day, they're going to tape it, and they'll show the Web site." I didn't have distribution at this time. They were going to show the Web site when they're singing and I said, "Oh, this is fantastic," but you have to pay for the musicians to come, you have to pay for a sound system to be there because they don't have a sound system. You have to pay for everything, so ultimately it was ten grand that I had to pay. But it was going to be two shows, it was going to be on CNN in front of millions of people, and I said, "This is great, you can't beat this. It's national, it's international television exposure and then we're going to sell so many records off of this one thing. So I paid the money for the set up, and I think we sold maybe twenty CDs!

It was so depressing. But I learned that with advertising and marketing; it has to be so repeatedly put in front of people, over and over and over and over. I think I also learned that I can't sign an unknown artist and try to break him or her. The artist has to have some kind of a following. At least what I'm doing, the fact that they're playing every night, eight shows a week, to a thousand or two thousand people—even though they're not singing the songs that they're necessarily singing on their records, they're in front of an audience. Unless they really have that built in audience, I don't have the marketing and advertising dollars to spend [to break them]. So I look to the artists to really help. I also produce these concerts which have been an amazing branding tool; it's not necessarily an amazing money-making thing, but it's really helped to brand the label and the roster.

JG: So you've incorporated a live venue that the artists on your label play regularly?

KD: Yes, it's artists on my label but it's also Broadway or theater artists who have a similar vision. It's building a sense of community. It's building a group of artists who want to be a part of this mission of bridging the gap between rock 'n' roll and theater. So, late night Thursday nights and sometimes Monday nights, at a place called the Cutting Room—which is downtown, and we also moved it to a five-hundred seat off-Broadway theater in the Village which is the old Village Gate Theater—we do these concerts. And the reason we do it late night Thursday night is because it's after Broadway shows are done. It's a place where the audience and the artists can kind of come together and we just put on these shows. It's been great to brand the label, and also to brand the artists, and to get the artists out in front of people, and it's called the Sh-K-Boom Room. So people get to learn what everything's all about.

JG: Any final words of advice for those just starting up their indie labels?

KD: I think another key is being specific with who you are and what you want to do. If you're just starting a record label, and you've got a whole bunch of different artists who do a whole bunch of different types of things musically, I think you're going to shoot yourself in the foot if you aren't specific about what niche you're trying to fill in the marketplace.

ARTIST

PHIL ROY
Or Music

First concert attended: Johnny Winter/The James Gang at The Spectrum in Philadelphia, PA

Best concert attended: Bridge School Benefit (2000)

Little known resume entry: Future Political Candidate

Best project you were involved with that never made it big: Carrera and World Citizens

Recommended film: *Guess Who's Coming to Dinner* (Columbia Pictures, 1967)

Instrument played: Guitar

MISSION CRITICAL: DISTRIBUTION
AN INTERVIEW WITH RECORDING ARTIST PHIL ROY

Phil Roy has always been a songwriter's songwriter; the kind of genius with just that delicate turn of phrase and melody to chill your spine and rouse just enough memories to change the mood of your whole day. Most writers would envy any one of his achievements, having seen his songs recorded by a an impressive array of legends and stars, including Ray Charles, Joe Cocker, Aaron Neville, Paul Young and Widespread Panic, just to name a few. But Phil Roy was never one to rest on laurels or shun the spotlight—he wanted to sing his own songs. But as sucessful as he was as a songwriter for others, he couldn't get a label to give him a deal as a recording artist in his own right. Not one to take rejection lying down, he gave naysayers the finger by releasing and promoting his own recordings and hit the pavement with his own money. Those doors aren't closed anymore, in fact they could be flying off the hinges: his new album, *Issues + Options*, is being released on Or Music, a label that signed him largely based on the success he had with his self-released debut album, entitled *Grouchy Friendly*. Roy's warm, worn, uninhibited vocals and vivid lyrical tales promise to make him an independent force vital for years to come. He's also the only person to encourage my efforts in courting and promoting Martin Sexton. "That kid's the real deal. I'm telling you—just wait," he would say, and he was right. I thought Phil's perspective and story were especially appropriate to this section so I asked him to contribute some thoughts about the important details of independent releases, such as distribution:

Phil Roy: There's a big difference between being a self-released musician and being an indie. The difference between being self-released is that you manufacture your CDs yourself. You made it, you're putting it out there yourself, you have no staff, you have none of the infrastructure to really take on the business of getting your music to a national audience. Even if you have the good fortune of getting on the radio and having a demand for your CD in certain markets, it still comes back to distribution. Are you able to get your music in the stores? I've found that there's a big difference between being on an indie label like Hybrid, Vanguard, or Ryko, and being self-released. So I think that when people talk about how they are an indie, I think they should really clarify whether they are self-released or indicate exactly what is going on. I mean everyone, basically, can buy a Web site for thirty dollars, call themselves my record company dot com, call it whatever they want, and they're a record company.

Part of the problem right now is that everyone with a computer, three hundred dollars to buy a four-track and a program like Illustrator or Photoshop, can make a record and an album cover. And the market's just saturated with these discs out there. That's why it's so hard to get people to pay attention to those little discs, because there are too many of them.

Justin Goldberg, *Phil Roy's Early Nineties*,
watercolor on canvas, 15¾"x24½"

JG: But you managed to break through the fog in a fairly substantial way—even at one point managing to be heard by Starbucks. How'd that come about?

PR: I actually had a song in an independent movie called *Love and Sex*, which did very well at the Sundance Film Festival. It was one of the early things that was happening from releasing the *Grouchy Friendly* record. A publisher who had put together a compilation of music from the festival gave me a contact at Starbucks, and the guy actually listened to my CD and programmed four songs from my album into every Starbucks in North America and Canada. So that was the first indication that maybe I had something that people would react to. And then KCRW started playing it and then the guy from KCRW sent it to XPN in Philadelphia. Then [stations in] Philadelphia and New York City started playing it. Then Pittsburgh started playing it, then Austin, Texas, and suddenly it was all over the country, and I became a staple at the World Café, which is a nationally syndicated show out of Philadelphia that goes out to over a hundred and fifty affiliates. So what happened was something very rare—that without any kind of infrastructure at all, the radio program deemed my music vital—it was almost a small miracle. But then again, as great as that was, and how precious that radio airplay is, even for a Warner Bros., or a Sony, the records weren't in the stores. I mean, sure, they could come to my Web site and buy it from Amazon.com, but I would go into little mom and pop stores in the area and they'd say, "You're Phil Roy? I could have sold hundreds of your CDs if I'd had them!" And they didn't have them.

JG: So the moral of that story is really that exposure and promotion are only as valuable as your distribution, right?

PR: Distribution is key. Now, of course, there are a lot of people who have the problem of their records being in the stores, but no one knows about it. It was very rare, what happened to me; the amount of radio attention that I got. So the moral of the story is, yes, you can be self-released and be successful, but you are going to have to have some kind of distribution to sell records. If things start taking off, people need to be able to find your music, other than a Web-based place to buy it. Because only a very small percentage of people buy their music exclusively from the Web. As much as we might be all Web savvy and go to Amazon and different places to buy our CDs, it's still only maybe 4 percent of where music is sold.

JG: So you struck out on your own with your own dime—a gutsy thing to do, and perhaps a path many in your shoes would not have taken. What advice would you give to a another songwriter or artist looking to release their own music?

PR: Remember: if you are going to put your own music out there, you're not just competing with other indie artists: you're competing in the triple A format. The day I chose for my release date Peter Gabriel, Jackson Brown, Ryan Adams and Steve Earl all came out with albums. Every one. If they're not playing Peter Gabriel or Ryan Adams, if they're giving you a spin at the radio stations, then the big labels are losing that precious air time. So you have to be very realistic about what you're putting out into the world. And it has to be as competitive as anything that the major labels are pushing. When it's all said and done, if you're going to wait for permission from anyone to make your own music, you're fucked.

· · · · · · ·

6

RADIO RULES

Most kids don't even know what radio station to listen to—they just flip around till they find something they like. They'll go from the rock station to the modern rock station to the pop station to the rap station, and they'll just keep going. But I also know that radio sells records more than anything else, and if that's the only way we can get the kids, then we have to deal with radio. That's just the way it is. I'm not a radio guy, but I think dealing with radio is like just doing business with everybody else except they've got this stranglehold on the airwaves, and they know that 95 percent of the records we sell are through their formats. So their job is to sell advertising and our job is to sell records, and the two clash like crazy. It all culminates and ends in radio. Radio guys spend most of their time trying to find out what their sound is and just about when they nail it to the wall and decide it's Ozzy Osbourne, it's time to play The Strokes. So you can't really chase it, y'know. It's just there.

Radio promotion people listen to something that's extremely timely and they'll say, "This is a great band, go sign them," and then KROQ isn't playing that kind of music anymore. And, y'know, I understand what they have to deal with—but I think at a certain point radio promotion people don't understand what A&R people really do because if they did, they would never try to get you to sign anything like what's on the radio right now, because we don't turn records around that quickly. It's basically the dog trying to catch his tail.

—David Bendeth, President, Type A Records

RADIO PROMOTION

DAVID LEACH
Big Three Entertainment

First concert attended: Sly and the Family Stone

Best concert attended: Bon Jovi/Springsteen/Southside Johnny at the Count Basie Theater

Top five album recommendations:
1. Joni Mitchell *Hejira*
2. Neil Young *Harvest Moon*
3. Roseanne Cash *Introspective*
4. Van Morrison *Poetic Champions Compose*
5. Traffic *Low Spark of High Heeled Boys*

Little known resume entry: I have played sixty of the top ranked golf courses in the world.

Best band that never made it: Dan Reed Network

Recommended reading: *High Fidelity*, by Nick Hornby

Recommended film: *Being There* (United Artists, 1979)

Instruments played: None, thankfully!

Upcoming projects: Cheap Trick, Aja, Courtney Love

AN IDIOT'S GUIDE TO RADIO FORMATS, CROSSOVER HITS & 'TWEENERS
AN INTERVIEW WITH BIG 3 ENTERTAINMENT'S DAVID LEACH

Justin Goldberg: What are radio formats? Why are they so important?

David Leach: For our business, it's an opportunity to expose an artist to literally hundreds of thousands of people at once. It's just the easiest way to reach the greatest number of people.

JG: And what are the biggest markets? What's the dream situation for an artist? To cross over, right? What does the word "crossover" mean, when you have a crossover hit?

DL: When you have a crossover hit, it means you go from one format to another. You reach an even greater number of people who are now exposed to your record and who hopefully will become fans of your music. So when you go from one genre of music—whether it be rock or urban or pop or whatever—and go onto another; it increases your sales base along with it, because now those people become potential consumers.

JG: So what are the biggest radio formats? There's urban, there's rock. What are they called?

DL: There's country. There's urban/Black. There's rhythm and crossover, which is a blend of kind of pop and mostly urban/Black, skewed more towards a pop audience. There's pop. There's adult contemporary. And then there's Hot AC, which is hipper adult contemporary.

JG: Is it important before I go in and record my record to know where these songs might be aiming towards, in terms of radio format?

DL: Oh, I think so. I think that with any piece of music or with any piece of art—because music is art—you have to have some sort of vision of who it will appeal to. Male/female, black/white, young/old, hip/not. When you finish a piece of art or piece of music, when you look at it you think, "That should appeal to this," or, "That should appeal to that," it's not always the case, and you don't necessarily want to be locked in, but the fact is that everything starts with the demographic you think will most likely appreciate it.

JG: And how specific is it? Are there times when something is just a great song, but it's not ever-so-slightly *something* enough to go on a certain format?

DL: Sure, it happens all the time. They're called "tweeners" in the sense that it's not a direct hit on any one format, but it's a little mish-mosh of this, it's nooks and crannies. Those are the harder records, but they could also be the biggest records. Norah Jones did not start off being the huge sensation she is. That was a record that found itself a home in certain portions of radio formats, but not one specifically, until it really started to catch on with the public. She had to find her audience, or more likely, her audience had to find her. And that was done via a lot of critical acclaim and some champions at the various radio formats. But no one format embraced her initially. It was bits and pieces until the sum effect was this huge thing that started to break through and connect with the consumer; at that point, radio had to start paying attention.

If you want to be in touch with your audience, you've got to serve them, and that means giving them what they want to hear. And if they are buying that record that means they want to hear it. If you don't play it on your radio station, they're going to go find it somewhere else when they're driving in the car. Or they're going to put the CD in their car and not listen to your radio station. So it's a matter of serving your consumer base, which, in this case, is the listeners of certain radio stations.

JG: So I guess radio functions a little bit like the A&R community does, where they're always trying to get ahead of the curve, to find something that no one else has and champion it.

DL: Not really. Quite frankly, radio is the opposite. There is no huge upside for radio stations to lead the way in breaking new music. They're more of a mindset to play the hits—to play what's familiar and not take chances. That's kind of the current climate at most pop and adult stations—they want to play safe bets so they're not losing listeners to other stations because the competition is a little bit fierce on the pop and adult side. Other formats, like rock, may be looking for the next big thing that'll hook the kids in, and they have to have their ears to the street a bit more.

JG: You always hear about radio stations as some kind of impenetrable gate that you can't get past when you're trying to get new music played. How responsive are radio stations to people calling in and requesting material? There's this perception that it's all kind of wired and someone's paying somebody and it's all figured out; that it's all just bought and paid for. Is that true?

DL: It's true in certain cases. It's not true in other cases. There are certain stations that put more emphasis on their active audience, which means the people who call in requesting records, the people who buy records on a local level. But, most of radio now is very research driven, which means they'll give a record a certain number of spins and put it into research, if it doesn't show potential, and doesn't show that it's gaining some traction with their customers, they're usually quick to dump it.

JG: And how do they find that out?

DL: They play an 8-second hook. They'll take a sample, and it depends on the size of the market, but they'll take a sample of a couple hundred people and they'll play eight seconds of a hook, and they'll say, "Do you like this? How much do you like it? Do you want to hear it more? Do you want to hear it less? Have you heard it enough? Do you need to hear it more?" And they'll come up with a formula to show them how a record is performing with their audience. Unfortunately it's a limited sample, it's a limited way of gauging a true audience passion for the record and all that, but it's what they have to go on. And unfortunately, more and more program directors are relying on that to help them program.

JG: The word "payola" seems to be misunderstood concept—most people don't realize that it's completely legal to pay radio stations in connection with promotion so long as it's disclosed.

DL: Correct. These days, an independent will get a contract signed with either the general manager or the head of the chain, and it's done on a very antiseptic level. It's a business transaction, unfortunately. I think record companies would rather put their monies to use really marketing their artists on those stations that have passion to play their music.

JG: Whenever people start a dialogue about radio today, you hear about the various corporate movements of Clear Channel. How has that changed the landscape of getting records played? Is it harder because radio is more centralized now?

DL: It's not really centralized to that extent. It's harder because Clear Channel shares research, so therefore, negative research tends to spread quickly because it's readily available. And it's very hard for new music to get great research early. It's a growing pain that every young record has to go through; I think music needs to be exposed a lot before people end up taking to it. The early days in a record can kill a record. Good programmers know that. Good programmers won't research a record too early. They'll go with their gut if they really feel a record is going to benefit them.

JG: Is the Clear Channel database an accessible one that you can reference in your work?

DL: I can't. Only program directors have access to it.

JG: So there's no way for you to instantly check on research and see how it might be affecting a record you are helping to promote?

DL: Nope. You can only try to overcome it by getting stories in other markets, in other areas, in other radio stations or formats that are positive.

JG: What would you say to a new artist who is about to record an album for a label, in terms of radio formats? Should they be thinking about radio formats before they even go into the studio?

DL: I wouldn't necessarily think about a radio format before going into the studio. I think that the band should think about making a great record—as good a record as they can possible make. If it's meant to find a home, it will. If there's the right level of passion within the company that's promoting it, it will get its shot, and hopefully, it will get traction and take hold. I wouldn't be concerned with trying to fit into this category or into that category. I don't think that works. I think that you gotta go and make the absolute best record you can possibly make, and hopefully nature takes its course.

JG: So even beneath all of these structures and huge financial transactions for music, there is a general sense of awareness of what's a cool record and a band that's going to happen?

DL: Yeah, there's good music and there's bad music. I think most of us can tell the difference, especially radio guys. They get trained to tell the difference between great music, good music, okay music and bad music.

JG: Is there ever something you hear that is just an unstoppable single? Where you just say, "Oh my God, this could be absolutely huge on radio," but it maybe has other drawbacks and you second-guess yourself? "Well, I don't know. The rest of the record sucks," or, "They're terrible live, and I don't know about this artist."

DL: Well, they're not necessarily mutually exclusive. You can have great music get on the radio from bands that can't play live. You can have great live bands that have great careers, but don't get on the radio—like a Phish or the Grateful Dead. These guys sell out major arenas no problem at all and they'll *never* be big on the radio. Jimmy Buffet hasn't had a record on the radio in years, and he sells out [live shows] every year. Radio isn't the end-all. Radio is the quickest way to reach large numbers of people. Unfortunately, it does cost a lot of money to do it. There's a reason for it.

The system unfortunately is sort of set up in such a way that you want to cut through the clutter and position the record as the best new record out there. And everyone else is trying to do the same thing. So everyone tries to one-up each other and outspend each other, and do this and do that. They're also realizing that doesn't necessarily make a hit record. You can spend thousands of dollars to get it all over the radio and it still isn't a hit.

JG: Let's say a label like a Wind Up is launching a new album from an artist like Creed. And they've got certain relationships with independent promoters, and they're paying them, and everyone's launching this new record. It's kind of tough at first, but then eventually it gets pushed through, and certain key stations start playing the record. Then it's a hit and then other stations just pick it up, but maybe were not paid directly or indirectly—

DL: Again, no one pays stations directly. You don't want to say it's all pay-for-play because it's not. There are stations that play local music. One thing I would do is to get in bed with their local radio station, because most stations will still try to help a local act—if it's credible and if they've got credible music. All you need is one success story to spread it to get signed, or spread it to other stations, or other formats, or things like that. You need a success and a win to hang your hat on, and hopefully from there, other people will get hip to the trip with it.

· · · · · · ·

JOURNALIST/INTERNET RELATED

SAT BISLA
Clear Channel Communications A&R Network

First concert attended: Judas Priest (1978)

Best concert attended: Faithless in San Francisco, 1997

Top five album recommendations:
1. The Beatles *The White Album*
2. Faithless *Reverence*
3. Rob Dougan *Furious Angels*
4. U2 *Achtung Baby*
5. Depeche Mode *Violator*

Little known resume entry: I once worked as a club promoter and concert booker in Fresno.

Best project you were involved with that never made it big: Alabama 3

Recommended Web site: www.xfm.co.uk (one of the best alternative radio stations in the world).

Instrument played: The turntable

Sat played a pivotal role with many notable acts long before they were either signed or known in the U.S., artists such as Dido, Faithless, H-Blockx, Uncle Ho, Frou Frou, Rob Dougan (Warner Bros.), Soul Kid #1 (DreamWorks), Revis (Epic), Cherie (Lava), Bonnie McKee (Warner Bros.), Acroma (Republic/Universal), Missy Higgins (Warner Bros.), The Hiss (Polydor, U.K.), and Adema (DreamWorks).

PROACTIVE VS. REACTIVE: HOW THE U.S. DIFFERS FROM THE INTERNATIONAL MUSIC INDUSTRY
A CONVERSATION WITH SAT BISLA OF CLEAR CHANNEL COMMUNICATIONS A&R NETWORK

Justin Goldberg: How have the changes in the music industry affected what you do?

Sat Bisla: Since there are fewer labels in the business, it has gotten more difficult to help find unsigned talent places to sign. In addition, with there being less competition in the label, radio and touring side of the music business, there are fewer avenues to expose new talent. It's ironic that in a market such as the U.S., which has thrived on capitalism, there seems to be less and less of it. Competition is healthy; take that out of the equation, and we're taking steps backwards. Our business needs to become more creative, innovative and competitive.

JG: How is the international market different than the U.S.?

SB: The international market is different depending on what part of the business you're talking about. As it pertains to radio, I'd have to say that the international market is healthier from an ownership angle. For example, the U.K. has limits on market share and format any one broadcaster can have in any given region. From a label angle, it seems there are more opportunities for artists to break from independent labels. With independent promoters not having the kind of control they do in the States, that allows the little guy an opportunity to develop talent and have a relatively fair shot at getting the act played on radio. From a creative standpoint, I feel the international market is a lot more proactive when it comes to nurturing and defining new music trends, genres, production techniques and the marketing of music. Press, new media, TV, club culture and live entertainment seem to have a much bigger impact overseas in a shorter time span than the States—the countries aren't as big as the U.S., so it doesn't take as long for the ripple effect to make an impact.

JG: How is radio in other countries different?

SB: Most countries abroad have a national radio that is governed by the political system. For example, in the U.K. you have the BBC, in Australia you have the ABC. Both governing bodies encourage their stations to serve the needs of the public at large. Also, these stations broadcast to a national audience. Having the ears of millions of listeners around the country allows you much more strength to help kick start an artist's career and create new music trends. You get a lot more innovative programming from outlets like the BBC and ABC because their charter requires them to serve the listening needs of the mass public that are not necessarily being fulfilled by commercial broadcasters. Musically, I feel that the international market is a lot more proactive than reactive when it comes to exposing music. Foreign radio also tends to be more localized and less homogenized than it is in the States. Interaction with a live on-air personality and the audience is a big part of a radio station's creed in most overseas markets and most foreign radio seems to be a lot more localized.

JG: What would you recommend to someone trying to get signed to a major in the U.S.? Would it differ if they were, say, in the U.K.?

SB: There really is not much difference from what I'd recommend to an artist wanting to sign to a U.S. major versus a U.K. major. By definition, majors on both sides of the Atlantic have similar tactics for signing and developing artists. I recommend any artist wanting to sign with a major make sure that the label is sincere and passionate about the artist and the music. Make sure that the label and the staff you'll be working with have a creative vision that will help take the music to its maximum success. Also, find out as much as possible on the label's track record for breaking similar artists and also find out what level of commitment (in writing) the label is willing to invest. Of course, I always recommend a competent manager and a savvy lawyer to oversee the contractual side of matters. These days it's also important to make sure that the A&R person at the major label has the backing of the label head and CFO. Those that have decision-making power and hold the purse strings control a large part of the artist's ability to get the tools necessary from the record label.

JG: Where do you see the business going—do you suppose there will be more deals where labels take a percentage of revenue from touring and merchandising?

SB: Absolutely. In today's business climate it's no longer business as usual. Record companies are going to have to come up with innovative ways to generate new revenue streams. Technology has played a part in reducing sales via downloads, burning, etc. The record business spends millions on developing artists, but they limit themselves to the artist's income stream via record sales. Record companies should tap into publishing, merchandising and touring if they're helping create that cash flow

---

MAKING MUSIC CONFERENCES WORK FOR YOUR CAREER

I think over the past few years, there's been much more focus from the A&R community to attend regional music conferences, and I think they're helpful in the sense that an A&R person can get an idea of what the talent is in a particular region. For some of the unsigned acts who are clever, what I've seen work is that they have sent packages to select A&R people at various companies and basically said in the package and in the follow up calls, "Hey, we're not sure if you're coming to our music conference in the next month or so but here's our music, this is where we're playing and here's our story—if you can, come and check us out." Most of the scouts who do go to the conferences put together a list of all the artists they want to check out, and that has been an effective strategy for some of the acts to get noticed by some of the labels.

—Rodel Delfin, A&R Editor, Hits *magazine*

for artists. Obviously, labels will have to offer artists greater incentives in signing to these types of deals. The label and artist should have a similar vision (partnership) in terms of business success. No business partner is going to be happy if only one is reaping the financial rewards. It's smart business to offer incentives for all partners to reap the rewards of a business situation.

· · · · · · ·

SOUTH BY SOUTHWEST! NORTH BY NORTHEAST! CMJ MUSIC MARATHON! IN THE CITY! MIDEM! WINTER MUSIC CONFERENCE! NEMO! ATLANTIS!

Which one features the best unsigned talent? Which are truly worth attending? Which draws the coolest people or is the most fun?

Take a good look at the Music Industry Trade Conferences section on the LSN Web site and you will quickly realize that there are lot of notable music conferences to consider attending. Music conferences, or conventions, are big business: when you consider that the vast majority of artists playing at these conferences are unknown and paid a nominal fee to appear, and that as many as 5,000-15,000 attendees turn over anywhere from 300-800 dollars for registration fees, the numbers add up to some serious business. In fact, music industry festivals have a better track record for profitability than most record labels.

Should you enter an application to play or attend some of these music conventions? Probably—but how do you chose? Usually by genre, budget and career purpose.

All Access Passport

CD-ROM

The conferences listed above represent most of the music industry's major annual gatherings (although I would encourage you to review the full and updated worldwide conference listing in the calendar section of the LSN Web site at www.labelservicesnetwork.com). Generally, each conference has its own consistent character in terms of regional flavor, level of talent expectation and industry executive attendance level. The Winter Music Conference is focused on dance music and electronica-related culture—it occurs in and is defined by Miami, Florida, to a large degree with its late night dance clubs and rave event spectaculars. Conferences like New York's CMJ (College Music Journal, a college radio trade publication) are focused on emerging pop and rock artists; MIDEM is a massive international event with some live performances but far more focused on business meetings as an event for dealmakers representing new and established artists of every caliber from all over the world. Austin's South by Southwest New Music and Media Conference probably has the longest standing reputation as an annual event for the broadest U.S.-based industry group; few gatherings seem to be as effective at drawing both new emerging artists of every genre as well as all levels of established industry executives and lowly scouts. Every year in March, for the last decade and a half, the streets get blocked off in the small town city of Austin, Texas, and the clubs fill with musical notes and noise from every genre of music from groups making the pilgrimage from their hometowns in search of career attention. Several other U.S.-based music conferences offer variations of the same with different backdrops and expectations for industry attendance. Most conferences usually consist of a daytime itinerary of panels comprised of industry "experts" and professionals offering their opinions up against each other on a long laundry list of topical industry subjects—as you can imagine, there are many similar topics and faces from year to year.

Be realistic about your expectations in attending music conferences, and place an emphasis on accomplishing some homework long before the date of a conference performance arrives. There are always signing stories emerging from the aftermath of music conferences, but they are usually like lottery ticket winners—they are the exception and hardly the rule. The acts that reap the most rewards from conferences see their participation in them as only a well-scheduled step to show off their own momentum and career progress. Most music convention attendees are overscheduled lawyers, publishers and A&R executives who actually spend only a small fraction of their time in clubs hearing musicians perform; they tend to use their time at conferences to mostly network (and party) with their own colleagues, and to attend a short list of presanctioned hot acts with great word of mouth. The industry types actually looking to hear exciting new and available music are usually either junior scouts without signing power or at the independent level. But hey, you never know.

FOUNDATION

NIKI ROWLING
Co-Founder/Program Director,
Austin Music Foundation

First concert attended: Huey Lewis & the News

Best concert attended: Rage Against the Machine (I was crushed in the mosh pit)

Top five album recommendations:
1. Jimi Hendrix *Axis: Bold as Love*
2. Miles Davis *Sketches of Spain*
3. Jeff Buckley *Grace*
4. Public Enemy *Fear of a Black Planet*
5. Anything by The Clash

Little known resume entry: I spent six months in Southeast Asia, where I received a tattoo by an Indonesian tribe.

Recommended reading: *Rules for Radicals*, by Saul D. Alinsky

Recommended Web site: www.austinmusicfoundation.org

SXSW
A CONVERSATION WITH NIKI ROWLING OF THE AUSTIN MUSIC FOUNDATION

Justin Goldberg: What's a brief overview of South By Southwest these days? Is it worth going to if you're a new musician from out of town, or a new band trying to break? Can you give me a general overview?

Niki Rowling: I think that as a new musician, to say that you've played at an exclusive event like SXSW—which receives thousands of submissions—is a great notch in the belt. So, if you make the cut and get in, it's a great thing to say you've done it. As far as making career connections, I really think that is mostly up to the artist and how hard they want it to work. It's not like you're going to play at SXSW and suddenly someone's going to discover you and sign you to a record deal—that really is very rare. That's not the kind of expectation artists should have about SXSW. But, if you are willing to work really hard and hustle your stuff at the convention center and work it in every way you can, you can usually meet people just due to the sheer volume of industry people who are here.

JG: So it's still fair to describe it as a really good starting point or networking opportunity?

NR: Right, and like anything else, if you do make it in you would do well to put some thought into how to create a buzz before you arrive in Austin. Consider various ways to market yourself and your upcoming showcase. You will be fortunate if you get two people who are industry leaders to come to your showcase; it doesn't normally happen so easily.

JG: What are some of the things you can do to ensure some sort of awareness at the event?

NR: Well, what I would do is—if you are an attendee, if you actually register for the conference—is use the access you will be granted to the list of other registrants so you can target specific people you think might be interested in what you do. Start trying to build those connections months before you play down here. If you're in any other business that goes to trade shows, what they're going to do is check out the list of attendees ahead of time and target specific people in order to try to set up one-on-one meetings and work those opportunities. As a musician you should do the same thing. Really, it's just a matter of being intelligent about your target marketing.

JG: What are some of the best places to play in Austin if you're a new act and you're playing the festival?

NR: Well, SXSW is odd because a lot of restaurants and other entities that aren't normally live music venues get used for SXSW. If you can get into one of the more established clubs here, then that's great. Antone's, Stubbs, La Zona Rosa, those are all really good places to be able to play. Emos is another good one depending on the kind of music you are. But those are also really hard to get. You have to know somebody or have a big buzz going on already in order to wind up playing at those venues at SXSW.

The other thing that you can do is take a look at the other musicians who are getting in and try to build relationships with other bands that might work with you, and you can partner up and help each other out. I think that's one of the most effective things that bands can do at a conference like that. Network with each other—with other musicians.

JG: How easy is it to tour your way through Texas to get there?

NR: Not easy, because everyone's trying to do that. Usually, Dallas, Houston, San Antonio, those areas, the bigger acts are likely to fill up shows at venues in those cities.

JG: Even though SXSW has evolved into an international event, it seems indelibly stamped with the soul of Austin's year round musical spirit. What are some of the unwritten rules about being a musician in Austin?

NR: Well, the unwritten rule is that you have to pay your dues. And a lot of artists really hate that reality, but it's true. The truth of the matter is you have to build your own audience, build your own fan base. And once you do that, then you start getting the kind of gigs that you want and start getting the attention of managers and of radio.

We actually have a really open radio market here—a locally based company owns five radio stations so we're not all Clear Channel or Infinity. You actually *can* get on the radio here. It's unique in that way. It's great for Austin musicians. But you've got to pay your dues.

JG: Any tips on somebody submitting music to SXSW and how they would better their chances of being chosen?

NR: I couldn't even give you a word of advice. Obviously, if it's a band they've heard of or a band that they know of, then that's better. The best thing I can say is, submit the best demo you've got so that they hear the very best of what you have. If you've got good press about you or if you've played with bands they would know of, that's all good, too.

JG: Would you say that it's perhaps more beneficial to release your own record and have that press and presence as opposed to just having an amazing demo?

NR: Well, for the submissions for SXSW, I don't think so. Having a record in the submissions packet versus a demo in it doesn't guide them in either direction, I don't think. If you don't get in one year, you should keep applying. If you don't have anything rolling, you're going to have a hard time. You need to have a good story to tell to get a shot, simply due to the volume of the number of submissions they get. I think about 1,000 acts wind up getting to showcase at the event, but they receive more than 8,000 or 9,000 submissions. So, the odds are low. The other unwritten rule about SXSW: if you want to network with industry people, the best place to be in the whole city is at the Four Seasons bar!

· · · · · · ·

PLAYING MUSIC LIVE

If your goal in music is to eventually be playing, singing or both in front of a live audience, then you have only one basic mission above all else: start playing live now. Feeling confident and comfortable in front of a live audience is something that doesn't just happen because you are inherently talented (although that certainly helps); it's a process that will take time to evolve until you are able to hone in on what kind of live persona and presence works best for your music. It's something that can and should change as songwriting subjects and moods evolve. It's something that just takes time and a zillion rehearsals and uncomfortable learning experiences in as many dive gigs as you can stand to play until the dots start connecting and you're able to widen your circle of live appearances.

In the beginning, there is typically and unfortunately little to lean on in the live show booking department: it's usually something that new artists eventually come to realize they have to deal with directly on their own. There are some early level booking agencies in New York and Los Angeles (visit www.webookbands.com in Los Angeles for example, they're pretty cool) but for the most part, this is where the musician's game most closely resembles the actor's routine: it's about cold calls, mailing music with some hype (reviews, bio, photos or video) and often even colder follow up calls.

Of course there are different paths to go down depending on your goals and musical genres. There is lucrative live work for venues that require "entertainment" that I would consider off the radar for developing variations of "pop" music seeking the kind of momentum designed to lead to record sales. If your goals fall into that area of hotel and cruise ship gigs, you should skip directly to some of those booking agents, as you will find them relatively open to new artists if you have the kind of professional package they deem worthy of that level of work—and there are many thriving and different kinds of booking agencies that handle different kinds of artists for different venues, ranging from cruise ships to the college circuit, from hotels and casinos to vacation resorts and amusement parks. But realize that there is little hope for your developing recording career if you find yourself sidetracked by making money on a cruise ship or playing in the lobby of a hotel in Puerto Rico.

Within major booking agencies located in the major music industry cities, there are different departments devoted to handling specific areas for different artists, who may be focused on international markets, arena work,

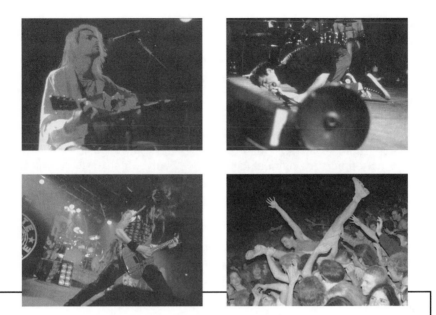

**Feeling confident in front of a live audience takes time,
because it can get a little crazy up there.**

or regional domestic bookings. Once a band is at the level of promoting a nationally distributed album, or managing to draw sizable crowds routinely enough to warrant regular, revenue generating shows, a booking agent can be an essential piece of an artist's puzzle. Established booking agencies typically have long term relationships with the more reputable venues, and thus usually have methods for saving money that could elude an artist with either no or limited agency representation. Due to consolidation in the touring industry, there are also fewer promoters in the market, which leaves a smaller pool of dealmakers to negotiate with. Once a competitive market open to entrepreneurs and truly independent promoters, the U.S. market is now dominated by three main companies, Clear Channel, Concerts West (which houses Goldenvoice) and House of Blues.

ARTIST

GREG SARFATY
Lead singer of Stewboss, on Stewsongs Records

First concert attended: AC/DC

Best concert attended: Bruce Springsteen and the E Street Band

Top five album recommendations:
1. Rolling Stones *Exile on Main Street*
2. Bruce Springsteen *Born to Run*
3. Van Morrison *Moondance*
4. The Jimi Hendrix Experience *Are You Experienced?*
5. Led Zeppelin *Physical Graffiti*

Little known resume entry: I am an ordained minister.

Best project you were involved with that never made it big: Coal

Favorite/recommended media: Singing telegram

Recommended Web site: www.stewboss.com

Instrument played: Guitar

Favorite unsigned artists: Gary Jules, Minibar, The Amazing Pilots, Renee Stahl, Alexi Murdoch, Wobbleshop, Two Dog Garage, Trespasser's William, Leslie King, Ernie Payne

---

"LOOK, MA, WE'RE HUGE IN EUROPE!" EVERYTHING YOU NEED TO KNOW ABOUT HOW GRASSROOTS NETWORKING CAN PUT YOU ON TOUR IN EUROPE:
AN INTERVIEW WITH GREG SARFATY OF STEWBOSS

Stewboss is an unsigned, Los Angeles-based rock trio categorized as Americana or even "alt. country," with some modest independent sales from their Web site and a small but growing loyal following. So how exactly did these guys manage to profitably tour Europe three times, get their record distributed throughout Europe and sell nearly ten thousand copies? Aside from crafting one of the finest independently produced albums I've ever heard, *Sweet Lullaby* (available on www.stewboss.com), I figured I would extract some of their secret formulas for your benefit:

Justin Goldberg: How does someone like you—armed with only some great songs, players, and their own record—get to go on a European tour?

Greg Sarfaty: A major part of it was the Internet—that was probably the most useful tool in the beginning. [We were] on local radio with Bob

Harris and the BBC. That initiated some initial buzz and interest in the band. And we started selling some CDs abroad via the Internet. We didn't have any distribution there at the time. They just went to our Web site to check us out and there was a link to buy the CD. There was a DJ who really "got" our music and began some of the initial interest in the band. So after selling some CDs, we started getting some emails from people asking, "Hey, when are you going to play here?" and we really thought that getting to do a European tour was out of the question, until we had a deal and support and all that other stuff. But at some point we just said, "Hey, let's check it out and see what the reality is." So we priced out tickets and—step by step—we set it up. Because we knew we were going to do it ourselves, we set it up four months in advance and really started doing the work.

The first thing I did was send out a mass email to everyone who had bought a CD online, because we had their email addresses. And we said, "Hey, we're thinking about coming out and doing a tour, and if we do, we want to make sure we get to your area. So can you recommend a local venue that you really like and where you think we'd go over well?"

The email was just an attempt to get some contacts and see what the interest really was—to see who would even write back. And what happened was, a lot of people wrote back and said, "Well, yeah, I know a venue. And here's the promoter's name. And you can stay at my place." So we received all these responses and it started us thinking we might actually have some meaningful contacts.

There's a bit of a club circuit there that we were able to tap into. We picked up some foreign publications—*Mojo* magazine is one where they have ads for touring bands all the time. We looked for like-minded bands, bands in our own genre, and did some checking on what clubs they were playing. And there are phone numbers right there on all the advertisements in the magazines for the clubs. So, we started there and contacted the venues. We would call on odd hours; Kristen [Greg's wife and label chief] did a lot of the calling. At three in the morning, we'd be calling these places. We'd book a show at one venue and they would recommend calling another one and suddenly there was a tour. Suddenly, there were twelve dates. While we were doing all that, we were offered a licensing deal with a company—they called us initially about licensing one song for a compilation, and when they realized we didn't have distribution, they invited us to sign on and license a whole record. So they set us up with a bunch of radio appointments every day while we were there; we did the shows at night and radio during the day.

JG: So it really sounds like one thing just lead to another as soon as you kind of gave it some energy and followed each lead?

GS: Once you get into it, stuff kind of starts to show up. That's the fascinating thing about it. Once you really commit to it, everything kind of falls into place a bit. And it was a serious undertaking. We really had to sort out what our money situation was. We had to ask ourselves, "Do we have enough for renting backline?" Europe has different power configurations and we weren't really going to fly in amplifiers or drum kits or anything like that.

JG: How about the travel expenses?

GS: On the first trip, there were airline fees. Thankfully, we're a three-piece band so we were able to fly relatively cheaply. Including Kris, who acted as tour manager, it added up to four of us altogether. So for four tickets...I think it was something like $650 roundtrip because we went in the summertime when it was a little more expensive. You can get better tickets at different times of year.

So there was that investment. Then there was renting the van, which we actually rented from another band that wasn't on tour at the time. Sometimes if you network enough, you can find a band there that isn't touring and will rent you their van. The upside to that is that you get a much better rate. The downside is that they don't have roadside service or anything like that. So it has to be a good van. It's got to be in good shape. You really have to check it out when you get it and make sure they've changed their oil recently and whatever.

But then there are also plenty of companies that have vans for rent. Although, if you're renting from a company, it's anywhere from $80 to $100 bucks a day.

JG: So do you need a van to tour? What part of Europe were you in?

GS: The first time we were throughout the UK, so all through England and Scotland. This last time we took the ferry across and actually played in Belgium and Holland. But you need a van for all the equipment, for luggage, and there was certainly enough room for us. You could make it work with maybe a minivan if you're small enough. Certainly someone who's just traveling as a singer-songwriter with an acoustic guitar, they could just rent a car and be ready to go. I don't think you need a tour bus necessarily. Actually, a tour bus would suck because there are so many small, tiny streets.

JG: What kind of backline did most of these clubs have?

GS: Most of the clubs really just provided PA and a sound engineer. Almost every club there, though—and this is a great thing about Europe— is that most of the clubs will put you up overnight if you ask. They'll sort out accommodations for you. They'll either put you up with friends of the promoters or they'll get you a hotel room, depending on what kind of level the club is. And most places will even get you dinner, because there are a lot of clubs that actually serve food. So we were guaranteed at least one meal a day and somewhere to sleep, most of the time. And then also there were some places where fans were willing to put you up. When you're working on that kind of grassroots level, that's kind of the way you do it.

> I don't think you need a tour bus necessarily. Actually, a tour bus would suck because there are so many small, tiny streets.

JG: Would there be a fee to the band for the show?

GS: And they pay you, yeah. What we were able to work out at most places was a flat fee, plus a percentage of the door. So they gave us a flat fee that was lower than normal, but there's a risk on both parts. You want to make sure that you don't bury the promoter, because if you do, you'll never get invited back. So you want to make sure it works on both sides. You want to make sure they're happy with the night, and you want to make sure that you're actually making some money for your time to get there. It's kind of a delicate balance.

But what we found to really work was the guaranteed flat fee so we know we're getting paid something. And if there's a great draw, then we both win. We get a good percentage of the door, they keep a percentage, plus they get a percentage of the bar, or if they own the place, the whole bar.

JG: What would you say is the most difficult aspect of this kind of grass-roots touring?

GS: I think the most difficult part is a lot of the basic logistics. Especially when we were doing radio interviews every day. Just having to find places—directions get confusing, and there are so many bizarre streets and you may be dealing with language barriers, too. You've got to give yourself extra time to arrive at locations. You learn that if they say, "Hey, it takes you only three hours to get there," it really takes about five because you have to deal with another language and places you've never been before. You need ample time to make sure you can travel places.

JG: What did you do about travel visas and official documents? Did you need to obtain an actual work permit to perform?

GS: Absolutely. You have to get work permits when you go into England, though we got work permits sorted out for us. Sometimes a venue will help sort it out and kind of vouch for you and get you permits. So a venue can do it. Or a label. With us, the label that did the overseas licensing deal actually worked out our work permits. And there's a home office in the U.K. for work permits. (That number is 011-4-269-3710.) You can call them for information. You have to sort out work permits for any country. And I think you can find them online actually, through government offices. Every country, they ask you to have a valid work permit if you're going to be receiving any money for services, so you have to have a work permit. It wasn't really a big deal. When you come through and they check your passport, you can say, "Hey, not here on business, here on vacation," but most clubs have to file all their payments, and once they say that they pay you, they're going to come looking for you, asking you why you were making money when you didn't have a work permit. And most places pay you cash. Oh, and it's always better to convert the money when you're back at home. Use the money you make there along the way and save the rest. Any money you come home with, convert it when you get here. One of the best places to convert money is at the American Express booth at the airport. Most conversion places, they take a percentage; American Express only does like $5 flat fee or something like that. It's great.

JG: Did you sell CDs at the shows?

GS: Yeah, absolutely. We shipped CDs and T-shirts over there beforehand, stored them with one of our contacts there and then picked them up. That was another cost, the shipping of the CDs and T-shirts. But then, all your merchandise is yours when you're touring at that level, so that's good.

JG: Did you reduce the price of the CDs for different countries?

GS: We tried to keep things consistent all the way through. We tried to keep things simple and with the least amount of change. You don't want to be dealing with a lot of change. So with England, we just charged a flat ten pounds. And then when you're in Holland, you just charge ten bucks. And when you take it out of conversion, the English are probably paying an extra buck for a CD, but it was just easier for us and no one really had a problem with it.

JG: Is there anything else you might suggest for a new artist who is considering or planning on staging a similar touring effort?

GS: I think one of the things to be conscious of is that you need to go into it to really build for the future. The first time we went, once everything was paid—like the telephone bill and the flights—we actually lost a little bit of money. But when we went the following year with the new record, we came home with money. For most bands I know, it took until about the third tour to see any profit. You build up enough momentum and more people start coming to the clubs, and the word-of-mouth gets around. It's very difficult at the club level to *really* make money. Some nights the soundman gets paid more than you. The person we're renting the van from got paid more than we did once we all divvied everything up on the first tour. And some nights you make out like bandits. You just don't know.

JG: So like anything else, it's a long-term proposition.

GS: It is. It's not a go-in-there, it-all-kind-of-works-out, come-home-and-retire thing. Not at that level. You have to have some kind of momentum before you go. There's this common music business logic that has always said it's important to really build something in your own backyard first. And I get that, but that's not really always the route to go. And I think the other thing is that a lot of bands really resist being attached to some sort of niche or some sort of genre. They want to say, "We're our own thing. We're brand new. We're not rock. We're not this." And I think in the very beginning, it's really important for a band to kind of find a community. Let yourself be called rock 'n' roll. Let yourself be called bluegrass or Americana or alternative rock, whatever that is. Because there are fanzines, the press and DJs who like specific genres of music; if you can get yourself in a niche, it is easier at the very beginning. When I first made our record, I didn't really consider us an alt-country, Americana band. We just were guys making music, but at some point, you start to look and you say, "Oh, well, other people making this kind of music, they're kind of like-minded. They make music for the same reasons we make music, so maybe we are part of that niche."

Oh, and one last really good piece of advice: before you start calling all the clubs overseas from the States, to book shows and call promoters, make sure you've set up an international calling plan because you're going to be making calls for the next month, two months, while things are getting put together. You'll save immeasurably. There are a lot of calling plans that if you're calling just one specific country, you get a really reduced rate just for those few months. And then you can cancel it. And then you can come up with another plan. But before you make those calls, set it up with your long-distance phone carrier or you're going to see a bill that's going to make you fall on the floor.

· · · · · · ·

ROAD RULES:
ON THE ROAD AGAIN WITH WILLIE NELSON & FAMILY

In a musical landscape that typically defines artists' careers in terms of single digit album releases, or one or two hit songs in so many years, Willie Nelson is an artist who defies any and all boundaries of music or business. His consistent stable of musicians and his genuine, smalltown generosity of spirit and sense of accessibility belie the fact that he has sold over 32 million records, ranking up with the likes of The Beatles, Prince and Eric Clapton in the zone of all-time multimillion sellers. He has released well over a hundred albums and written some of the best and well-known standards in music. The list of celebrities, legends, geniuses (and even American presidents) he can count as close friends, fans, or collaborators is astonishing: Dylan, Sinatra, Cash, Bono, Wyclef; Paul Simon, Keith Richards, Ray Charles, Neil Young and on and on. They all know something is up with this guy—this deceptively simple guitar god and lyrical master. His appeal crosses every demographic and his concerts summon believers from often incongruent walks of life—in any given audience one will always find plenty of cowboys, both real and imagined; there are hippies and yuppies alongside Hells Angels, and punk rockers alongside great grandparents with their children's children's children. With fervor I've seen only at religious gatherings and Grateful Dead concerts, his fans travel far and wide with a dedication that suggests hearing the music and being a part of the energy are indeed filling a spiritual void. Ever conscious of his role and the importance attached to his person, he stands for hours after almost every performance to greet fans and graciously sign autographs and pose for photographs. It's tough for even the nicest rock stars to compete with Willie when it comes to selfless fan time.

Past seventy years old now, and on the road for the better part of the last forty years, gigging on more nights than not, Willie Nelson's life has been defined by live performances. I caught up with Willie shortly after his gig at this year's SXSW convention (where his show was easily the most anticipated event of the week) to hear his thoughts on his ever-increasing popularity, choosing record producers, music industry changes, Farm Aid, performing live and what sustains the energy of his creative spirit and those around him.

Justin Goldberg: At this point in your career, it seems you are simply bigger than ever: did you ever imagine that you might have this kind of success this late in life?

Willie Nelson: It seems that through the years, it just gets a little better every year. There have been many times that we didn't have airplay, but we were still drawing packed houses. And now, with a little airplay, even that's getting better.

JG: I wanted to ask your thoughts about the importance of performing live; in today's music business, a lot of artists don't play much live before they get out to make their first record with a label. Do you feel that early on your live performance experiences played an important role in how you eventually developed as a performing artist?

WN: Well, I think so. I think it has to help you if you're doing songs live even before you go into the studio. I enjoy doing them live in front of audiences just to see if they like them as much as I do, and if it's an immediate thing or if it's something that's probably going to take a while. But I think doing them in person is very important if you want to get the real feel of how people look at your material.

JG: I've heard you warn about the danger of adding too many musicians to a recording session because of the risk of losing the feel of the session—why is that?

WN: Because if everybody plays at once, inevitably, you're not going to be able to hear the guy who's singing. So, for someone like me, who depends entirely on lyrics, that could be a catastrophe—and has been. It all has to do with the way that [the songs] are mixed and the way that they're produced. You can take a big band and do it right, but it really takes a special guy to know how.

JG: When I spoke with Ron Fair, over at A&M Records, he said that the number one mistake musicians make after signing their first deal is choosing the wrong producer. Any advice on how artists should choose producers?

WN: Well, the way I do it is that I listen to things that the producer has done before and then I try to picture doing some things with him. A lot of times you just have to say, "Well, y'know, I'm just going to turn it over to him." It doesn't mean that you're throwing your whole career at his feet, but for this one album, if you really like someone and you really need a producer on a particular project, that's the way I judge it.

JG: So you feel at ease turning over the reigns to someone like a Daniel Lanois, who may take more control of the overall sound?

WN: Yeah, Daniel Lanois, Matt Serletic, James Stroud—these are guys who I feel know what they're doing and I feel comfortable with just turning it over to them.

JG: Let's talk about your tour bus for a minute: I think some people would be surprised to learn that you don't usually check into a nice hotel room when you tour; rumor has it you prefer the confines of this bus, the Honeysuckle Rose III, when you're not onstage. Is that difficult sometimes to share an area that has to function as both your office and living room?

WN: Well first of all, I enjoy the privacy of the bus and having it really does help more than it hurts. Before a show or after a show, if I have time, I'm always glad to say hello to some folks. But during the day, I have it to myself for several hours. When I go to work, I know and I expect there to be people there—if I really didn't want that to happen, I shouldn't go to work that night.

JG: You have an outstanding crew of dedicated people who make your touring operation run like a well oiled machine. I asked your daughter, Lana, and your friend and tour manager David Andersen what makes this group work so well together and they both cited genuine respect and love for the bandleader as the overriding principal that sustains the group. Especially curious is that they mentioned that somehow that your low key approach actually makes everyone work that much harder because you aren't imposing a lot of demands on people. Is that something that you think about consciously?

WN: Well, again, I think that for the two to three hours at night that I work the length of the show, everyone has got to be very good, and everything that leads up to that point has to be good. From the time that the stage guys and everybody gets there in the morning to set up the thing, these guys have to be real good at what they do or they wouldn't be there very long. I've been very fortunate to have good guys who know what they're doing and who show up and do their job and are dependable—I really don't have to start in the morning yelling and screaming about a lot of things because I know that when I get ready to start "Whiskey River", everything's going to be working. If it isn't, I look around and I see what's wrong with it and I try to fix that immediately.

JG: It's well known that you maintain a rigorous, high-cycled schedule of performing. What sustains your interest in performing so much—is it looking forward to just getting out there and playing? Is it not wanting to disappoint fans? What's the feeling that you get when you know you have to perform yet another show? Is it still exciting for you?

WN: Well, for instance, we're going out tomorrow night and we head out to New Orleans, where we'll do three stages at the House of Blues. That's going to be a lot of fun and I'm looking forward to it. But I admit, when I've been out here for three months and haven't had a day off, it's a little harder to start the day and know that, well, here comes another night. But once I hit the stage and watch the fans start letting us know that they're enjoying it as much as we are, then that's what sustains me and I think the rest of us. We play two and a half to three hours, but there's another whole length of time there that we're not playing and those are the hardest hours. After I've caught up on my rest and sleep, then I'm hard to live with. I'll start looking for a place to go and something to do—I don't get into as much trouble as I used to, but normally, for me, to have something to do every night is a good thing.

JG: So is life today on the road really very different from the American road of forty years ago when you first toured with Ray Price and the Cherokee Cowboys?

WN: Well, the money is better. The mode of transportation is better. The hotels that we do stay in are better, but other than that, the fans have been there all the years. When I was playing with Ray Price, he had some of the best fans in the world and still does, and the same with our fans. So that hasn't changed. The enthusiasm has been there from the fans ever since I played the first shows in Texas many years ago.

JG: But certainly America has changed. This might be a good opportunity to ask you about Farm Aid—a very worthy and ever-relevant cause you have been at the forefront of for years. I would imagine that simply as someone who travels so much within our country, it must be a very different world to perform, to see how the actual landscape has changed, how the farming communities have changed.

WN: Well, you see a lot of old, run-down, empty, vacant, farmhouses if you look out the window, and a lot of rusty pickups and tractors, things that will never run again. And you remember that there used to be millions and millions of small family farmers out there doing well and now there're very few and they're not doing that well at all. So all those things are very obvious or else we wouldn't still be doing Farm Aid. We haven't solved the problem. I thought it would be fairly simple. We did our first Farm Aid and I was just naïve enough to think that our Democrats and Republicans would say, "Oh my goodness. We're not taking care of the backbone of our country, the small businessman, the small family farmer." But then I realized that it's not that way anymore. They could care less about the small business man or the small family farmer, because they have their factory farms now. They have their big corporations and they have come to the conclusion that fewer is better and you little guys go find something else to do. That's the worst philosophy I've ever heard and it's taken its toll on America. When a young couple could get out of high school, college, or whatever, and go and buy and couple of hundred acres and make a living at it, those were the best days. Now, all the raw producers in this country are suffering, and it's because of the big corporations that have put them out.

www.farmaid.com

JG: So the corporations step in and take control of the land. I've read that it's only a small group of corporations that have really just taken over a huge percentage of the market.

WN: Yeah. And you don't realize it until you look out there and see all these vacant farmhouses and then wonder what happened.

JG: The music business has obviously had a crazy past few years. There have been huge losses from all the illegal Internet-related music piracy, and a lot of people are having a tough time staying business. Some labels now are aiming to dip into touring and merchandising to make up for that lost money. Do you have any thoughts on where all this might be headed?

WN: Well, I can see how the record companies could be a little nervous because their revenues have dropped considerably. They blame it on the Internet and the ability to download free music, and that may be true. But the reality is it's here and it's not going to be that easy to stop it, so you have to figure out a way to use it. I think a lot of the big record companies and some of the small companies and even the artists themselves are finding out, "Well, if the big record doesn't need me, I'll go on the Internet and I'll market my own stuff. I've got a little old CD player that I can record on and you won't be able to tell the difference and I can do it in my garage." So this has hurt a lot of studios. In fact, I own a couple of studios and I know business has been hurt considerably by people being able to go on their own computer and record. I do it myself and I'm amazed continually at the quality. I don't blame them for doing it. I just think it's something that record companies are just going to have to figure out a way to accept: "If you can't beat 'em, join 'em."

· · · · · · ·

ROAD MANAGER, PRODUCER

DAVID ANDERSEN
Willie Nelson & Family

First concert attended: The Monkees (my Dad took me)

Best concert(s) attended: Jethro Tull/Elp/Pink Floyd and Cirque du Soleil

Top five recommended albums:
1. Aqualung *Aqualung*
2. Yes
3. Mike and the Mechanics
4. Anything by Journey
5. Willie Nelson *Stardust*

Little known resume entry: Produced *Red Headed Stranger* and Farm Aid (1 and 2).

Recommended film: *2001: A Space Odyssey* (MGM, 1968)

Upcoming project we should look forward to: Willie Nelson and Friends *Live And Kickin'*

ON THE BUS AGAIN WITH WILLIE NELSON & FAMILY
AN INTERVIEW WITH ROAD MANAGER DAVID ANDERSEN
AND LANA NELSON

Justin Goldberg: I've been seeing most of the same faces around this bus for close to twenty years; clearly this is a team that works together better and lasts longer than most marriages. What are some of the traits that it takes to get along well with each other on tour?

Lana Nelson: You have to go with the flow. You have to have a positive attitude.

David Andersen: And a desire to do it.

LN: And a sense of humor. You have to have a sense of humor, kind of make fun of all the things that are going wrong—that somehow makes it easier.

DA: But, if you don't like doing it, it doesn't matter what you do.

LN: Yeah, you have to really love it or it's going to be miserable.

JG: What's the longest you guys have been out at a time? What are the long stretches?

LN: Six months in Branson [Missouri].

JG: Six months?

DA: Two shows a day.

LN: A slow death. A miserable, choking death.

JG: What's so bad about it?

DA: Two shows a day, every day. Different audiences.

LN: And you're not moving. You're just kind of stuck, but you're not home—but you don't get to move either, so that's really a double negative there.

DA: And an eight-hour day becomes a sixteen-hour day.

LN: I don't know how people would do the Vegas thing and all that. That wouldn't make this group very happy. You've at least got to know you're going to be rolling pretty soon.

JG: Are there people who haven't worked out on a tour? What do you do when something like that happens?

LN: Everybody does it different. It's all different circumstances. A lot of times people just don't work out. I would suspect that probably most bands, they put up with it until one day there's a big flare up and everybody's got to make a big decision. Then it's made and they go on until the next big flare up, but usually everyone tries to make peace as long as you possibly can.

But what I think really and truly keeps it all together, is that this particular group of people loves the band leader as much as they do. If they didn't love Dad as much as they do...it would be a totally different crew, it would be a totally different job and I don't think that everybody would be working as hard. It wouldn't go as smooth. It's kind of like he's everybody's Daddy and everybody wants to please him and they want to make him proud of them.

DA: Because he doesn't have any demands, so you want to do more. I think the bands that put on these demands, it kind of wears on you and then you're like, "Well, fuck you," after a while. He is just the opposite so you want to keep him happy.

JG: You always think of the archetypical bandleader as a guy bossing everybody around.

DA: He can and he has and he will again—but he doesn't want to. Everyone knows what they need to do and if someone is sick or whatever, someone else just picks up the ball and runs with it because it's a team.

JG: And you guys prefer to travel by bus? How does that work out with sleeping and showering and stuff?

LN: Well, usually the bunks are a lot more comfortable than the beds in the hotels. Still, I enjoy it when we do have a hotel. But the guys, they can just shower at the gig. It's not that important to them.

DA: Well, also, we get rooms every day.

LN: Yeah. People will go in and take showers but you're going to sleep on the bus anyway. And leave after the gig. Instead of waiting 'til in the morning to leave, always leave after the gig, because it's so much easier to travel at night. It's a lot less traffic. You don't have rush hour. You don't have a lot of the stuff that you have to contend with. It always works out better.

JG: To leave at night.

DA: Yes, because if you break down, you've got time to deal with it. Otherwise, you've got a flat or whatever, you're going to be late. We just wake up and we're there.

JG: Alright. Let me ask one last question. What's the deal for people getting in and out of the bus? Do you stress out about private time? Who coordinates who gets on and off the bus?

LN: Dad's bus is his office and his living room and so all the meetings that he would be having in some office, he has on the bus.

DA: And most of the people, again, have been with him for so long—we know everyone who is doing business with him. If anyone says that they are and they aren't—it's easy to pinpoint them and say, "Thank you. I'll give it to him," and shut the door. How did you get in by the way?

JG: I crawled in through the back. There was an open door on top.

DA: Security is a key issue, I think. Not having it, that's how things like this happen.

· · · · · · ·

7

THOSE GOLDEN WORDS: FILM & TV

Why are they golden words? Mostly because of their flexibility in delivering two other golden words—revenue and exposure. Creating music for, or having your music used in, film, television, or advertising projects, can be a substantial source of revenue without the typical limitations of all things connected to the rest of the music industry. An artist, songwriter, or composer doesn't need to have a record deal, publishing deal, agent, album, or a band to necessarily have success. The focus is generally on music and whether it is appropriate to a particular project. Many of the intangible factors that can contribute to success or failure in music—such as physical appearance, press, live performances, etc.—are (fortunately) cast aside when it comes to working music into film, television and advertising. It's a project-focused activity concerned with finding music that will complete a project; it's not about an artist. For many creative music makers who have either outgrown or evolved away from an "artist based" mentality or career plan, creating music for film, TV and advertising projects represents a creative and lucrative second lease on life in a business usually associated with a short career run in the fast lane.

Getting your music used in media projects should become part of your list of target goals; but it's not something you need to invest a lot of time or money pursuing. While there are surely many former rock stars, or almost former rock stars, who now find themselves at Starbucks in front of their Macintosh G4 computers composing television music in ProTools, there is no reason you shouldn't be spending the same promotional energy you are already expending to others in the music business toward some of the influential forces involved in getting music into film and TV.

THERE'S SOMETHING ABOUT MARY (AND BRET REILLY)

Never heard of Bret Reilly? Add his name to the top of the most talented people you haven't heard of—yet. It's likely, however, you have already have heard his music. As an unsigned artist based in New York City, Bret's music has been featured in films like *Dumb and Dumber*, *There's Something About Mary* and *Me, Myself and Irene*. How does a guy without a deal manage to cash checks larger than some major label acts pock-

et as signing advances? "I focused on the relationship with the filmmakers. I took the time to stay in touch and keep them aware about what I was doing." Visit www.bretreilly.com for more information about Bret. Remember, you read it here first.

Like everything else related to the entertainment business, a buzz is a buzz and can help move your possibilities forward at any level of opportunity. If you are a developing artist, your story is of interest to music supervisors and others who may use your music in a project because as you develop, so will your relationship with key creative people who may have a hand in choosing music for projects. The life of the project too, may take on new meaning after a developing artist has developed. (Think of the key creative person involved with the now classic film *The Graduate* who pushed for using the then-unknown artist and writer team of Simon and Garfunkel for the music in the film—he certainly started looking like a genius when that film's soundtrack began flying up the charts).

TV AS THE NEW RADIO

As we've learned in previous interviews, corporate consolidation at radio has had the cumulative effect of decreasing the available airtime for new music; this is partially the reason you often hear that in today's business, "TV is the new radio." Once upon a time, long before Celine "drove all night" in her Chrysler, or Sting cruised through London in his "Jag-u-ar," credible recording artists generally shunned the idea of having their music used for advertising purposes or even in television shows. Obviously, times have changed: with fewer channels available to new music, the industry has shifted towards a model where such television exposure is viewed as a welcome opportunity for exposure, revenue, or both.

STICKER TIP

Your promo package can be a key factor in getting your music listened to or placed by a music supervisor, as it is an indicator of how easy and professional doing business with you will be. The most important factor to indicate in submitting music to film and television music supervisors is that you can easily and quickly clear the master and the publishing. If you created and own your own material or have a good relationship with those who do, then you should clearly mark this on your package. Placing a sticker on your CD that says "100% ARTIST CONTROLLED" or "100% SYNCH & MASTER CONTROLLED" indicates to a prospective licensee that the music can be cleared for use with a single phone call. As you will read below, music supervision related decisions happen quickly and change often. A clearly marked professional package will hardly guarantee a response or a use, but if it's nearby when a critical moment hits—perhaps when a track "falls out" or doesn't get cleared, your package may be in line to save the day. This is especially true when there is little time to wait for a larger label to go through several layers of written approval. You should also make sure that your CD indicates song titles, song length and your contact information on both the disc *and* the jewel case. If your music is being reviewed and noted for use on a particular project, your titles, times and other important information need to be visible while the actual cd is being played in a player. Similarly, never use "slim" cases, CD "sleeves" or any other "spineless" CD packaging when submitting music to supervisors—your music will be filed on a big wall and you don't want it to be invisible when stacked with other CDs.

For a detailed analysis of various "music in film" agreements, visit www.ascap.com or www.bmi.com—both organizations offer excellent and informed descriptions of the nature of specific deals and compensation guidelines.

PUBLISHER/FILM & TELEVISION RELATED

RON BROITMAN
BMG Music Publishing

First concert attended: Van Halen

Best concert attended: Oingo Boingo

Top five album recommendations:
1. Anything Zeppelin.
2. Anything Bauhaus
3. The Waterboys *The Waterboys*
4. The Waterboys *A Pagan Place*
5. The Waterboys *This Is the Sea*

Best project you were involved with that never made it big: Louie Says

Instrument played: Guitar

SYNC INTO CASH
AN INTERVIEW WITH BMG MUSIC PUBLISHING'S RON BROITMAN

Justin Goldberg: You were saying that this is a good time for unknown, unsigned artists to get sync uses in commercials. How has that evolved over the last few years?

Ron Broitman: In the last five to seven years, songs used in commercials have really peaked; I think it's still ongoing. It started out with the well-known songs—there was equity in the recognition and association with such songs that was valuable and that went on for a while. There were a number of years where there were continually more songs being licensed each year, but they were always the big songs and prices started going up. This helped the publishers and the writers as well.

Then, about three years ago a backlash began to develop. A couple of the ad agencies, on behalf of certain clients—one being Volkswagen—considered the prices too high. It was basically a battle of who could afford it and who could get it. There wasn't anything creative in it for them once they've got to that point, it was just, "Oh, great, another really expensive obvious song use," and that's how they were seeing it. So they started looking for music nobody else was using. They were a little more open to a song that wasn't recognizable, but it felt right, it set the right mood, and perhaps it worked well with the visuals—yet was a fraction of the cost.

Now, that kind of thinking actually goes contrary to what I do to some degree—but it doesn't have to, if I play it right on behalf of my lesser-known writers from other countries. Then it becomes a volume game; it becomes more focused on getting them exposure. So, I can still win. But I really think VW was the first. VW was using these electro-bands from France and the U.K. and then you had Burger King running these commercial factories every thirteen weeks with every familiar Motown hit—it was almost like some kind of dealing counterpoint thing was going on, so it was really kind of funny.

Now it's gotten to a place where certain ad agencies, on behalf of certain clients, are open to this and actually want something that hasn't been released yet in the U.S. or something that's going to be coming out at a certain time or even something that was only released in another country. They want to find something cool, they want to find something new, and to them that's the true creativity—that's the value of using a song in a creative way. It's not so much the obvious association with a specific lyric, it's more about this is something new, this is something different, we were the ones that found it and that brings us to today where we are with Mitsubishi. Gap used pretty well-known songs too, but songs that maybe we'd forgotten about. But Mitsubishi is the cool brand right now—with the Wise Guys, Dirty Vegas and a new French band called Tele Pop Music—they are literally breaking bands and that kind of affects how I negotiate with them.

JG: So advertisers at this level are capable of helping to break bands?

RB: Yes. They are breaking bands. The labels are tying marketing campaigns, print campaigns and they're using the value of a song being in a commercial as much as Mitsubishi is using the value of a song that works in their commercial—they are really working together. Now, Mitsubishi knows this, so they go out on a hunt for things that haven't been licensed, things that haven't been released; but then they also want broader rights for less money because of the reciprocal value. So that's what we have to fight out and balance out, but it's a good place to be. Here we are with one of the biggest commercial campaigns around, with one of the largest media spends around, specifically looking for something that no one else has used.

JG: At what point do advertising agencies conceive of music in the development of their ad campaigns? Is it early for something to be done and air four months later? What's the timeline like in these situations?

RB: Well, corporate image campaigns take a lot more time. In most cases it can be a few days before they ship, and they may still be having song issues. Song ideas come from the creative departments when they can see the spot, then they have to sell it to the client; or the song ideas can come from the client before the spot is even conceived, or after they sign off on the creative for the spot, then the song ideas come flowing. Music really comes at any point in the process. It comes from the guy editing the spot at the production facility who just had it in his car—you hear these stories, and they do actually happen. I pitch to editors and have them on my mailing list because they're the guys who say, "Hey, I just heard this song," and they pull it right out of their pockets; it really happens.

JG: Can you lead us through the steps of how music is considered and then paid for? Let's say I wanted to use say a Beatles song or something with a very high equity value, is that something that would need to be part of the budget from the earliest conception because of its very high cost?

RB: Right, well if it's coming from the agency and the agency is putting it in the creative concept—which includes the song and the song is integral to it—they'll pitch the creative to the client at the same time they are also giving them budgets. So, during that process if they are good and smart, they reach out to us and ask for ballpark estimates. So once everything is factored in, they come to me and get a ballpark figure. If they use the master they go to the record label, if they don't use the master then it's just the publisher and it's at that point that we start tossing it around and giving them estimates and it's a huge negotiation.

JG: How much do the rights vary in terms of compensation? Are there typically any royalties involved when material is used, say, in television, or are deals typically buyout uses of songs?

RB: Well, the sync license fee is what I would collect for the use of the song in the commercial for a certain set of rights. Then, just like a song used in a TV show, the writers get performance royalties based on the commercial airing on network X times a year—or on cable, or whatever. Depending on what TV medium it appears on, it gets weighted and there are performance royalties.

JG: And does the publisher share in that or no?

RB: I think typically on the performance side, the writer receives his or her performance portion directly and the publisher gets a piece of the performance income as well. But the whole point in all this is that you don't need to be signed to a major publisher or a major label to get your music in commercials, and you can be represented by a number of different people who represent independent catalogs. So for an independent writer/artist reading this, there is a way to get your stuff heard.

JG: What are some of the best ways to get your music out there? What are some of the ways that I can reach the people who make these kind of decisions?

RB: There are independent music reps who will represent you—ideally if you are signed they'll be able to represent you by way of publishing and master, or if you are signed to an indie label. Those reps will go out there and pitch your stuff to the appropriate possibilities. Another way is to just do it yourself. A lot of this is basic marketing, and traditional marketing still works. You put together samplers, you do your research, you find out who the music people are. It's not hard to do. You can read the advertising trades and find out which agency did which spot and find out who the producers were on the spot—it's public information. Make contact with them. The flip side for artists and writers signing with majors, whether it's publishing and/or label, they shouldn't be put off by the fact that the label is so damn big and such a big machine. People like me listen to this stuff and pitch it when we can. Now that the ad agencies are opening up to this, your major label can be more effective than you think in landing your stuff even though you're not what's on the radio right now.

JG: So, you might take something unsigned if there's a really appropriate track?

RB: Maybe we sign them to a publishing development deal and there's no label yet or maybe there is a label, and it's just come out but no one knows what it is. The point is, for an unknown band the likelihood of me pitching it is greater than ever before. Therefore I'm going to make sure that I know what I have and I'll pitch it when appropriate. You don't need to be a well-known song to get any attention from me or a publisher.

JG: Let's go through the role that you play as a publisher and who some of the key players are in this game of film and TV.

RB: We take songs that we represent, whether it's catalog or new writers or whatever it is, and we go out there and market them in order to exploit them for any sort of audio-visual work. Whether it's TV, film, trailers, commercials, or video games. So we are out there actively pitching song ideas. We make new relationships, we find out who is working on what and we pitch our ideas. The flip side to the creative end of what we do is when somebody finds a song they want to use—they find out who owns the rights and if we happen to control the publishing, then they have to come to me for licensing rights and we handle the business side of it. We deal with the clearances, we deal with putting together a quote, we deal with the negotiation, ideally the licensing and collection of the money. So that's the double sided coin of what we do. There's the creative component and then there's the business component.

JG: So, do you have to go to the writer?

RB: That's contractual. It just depends on the catalog and the writer. Then you go to the person requesting the studio, the music supervisor and you give them your quote. Sometimes you have to negotiate things and send more quotes around to get them to where they need to be for their budget. So you create options on the back-end, etc. and you issue your quote. Then they may use it, if you get a license request, and you issue a license and collect the fee.

JG: Is that a standard thing, that you spit out a license?

RB: Absolutely. Yes, once we know the song is used. Sometimes for TV, you find out after the fact and that's fine. They'll say this song has been used, please issue us a license. What we're talking about is more of the normal practice where we've already gone through this whole negotiation—I've already sent them a quote, this is approved for what you're asking for, for this specified amount of money. They have it in writing, they have the approval and sometimes you find out after it's aired that it's confirmed. It's normal practice.

A lot of news program shows that air once without repeating claim that they can use limited amounts of music without having to pay for it. That claim falls under the Fair Use Clause, and since they are not re-airing it, they are not technically making a copy, therefore they don't need a license or permission; that is kind of a gray area.

JG: How have the changes in the music industry affected your particular area?

RB: It's made our area more important. Record sales are down, so bands look to us to be the marketing team, and to get their music in TV and film.

I think—because the buyers are using more music, because there are more TV shows and soundtracks—that there is a heightened awareness to

TV and film and commercials. I think the bigger artists are blowing off the old stigma of selling out and letting their songs go, which has helped roll that along. But as far as what's been happening in music, the whole industry is down. Sales are down and have been for two or three years now. So writers and artists look up to us generate income, generate exposure and help push record sales, whereas before it was more the traditional radio and MTV. It's a balancing act. I can't say concretely that certain sync uses affect record sales—the shows present it one way, the labels present it another way. I think it's somewhere in the middle. If it's a priority for me, say, a band that needs the promotional value, then we would take that into account. You kind of weigh it all. If it's a career artist, yes, this is their next single, but it's not so much an issue of promotional value, it's more an issue of I'm giving you content. If I can gauge those two, that's how I decide where to go on the fee.

JG: So film and TV are jumpstarting careers, that happens?

RB: Absolutely. In the TV area, there were a few shows that were instrumental. Shows like *Dawson's Creek*, which I think were the ones that started the ad cards. I think they have actually been able to document spikes and sales after the airing because the shows and the music are targeted to the same audience that would then go out and buy this stuff. If it's an Internet-friendly audience, people email shows, people email ad agencies or commercial brands and are finding out what music's being used.

JG: It certainly seems that your end of business is doing quite well despite the bad time the rest of the industry is having.

RB: There's almost this inverse relationship. These departments become more important because sales are down and radio and radio play is hard to get, so they look to us for the marketing value. Because of the current willingness to use lesser-known music, I can adapt to that easily. So you adapt.

My talent is to know what I have and to know when to pitch it. A writer who personalizes the process, I will look to for help. We can't always make up the creative around a song that exists, yet we have to give a client what they need. So, if a writer works with me and personalizes the process to where I know what they have, I know what they've written, I know what's in their catalog and I can respond quickly—getting more choices to a client who has a specific need at a specific time, I will be more effective.

· · · · · · ·

MUSIC SUPERVISOR

MAUREEN CROWE
Senior VP
MGM Music

First concert attended: The New York Philharmonic

Top five album recommendations:
1. Norah Jones *Come Away with Me*
2. Puccini *La Bohème*
3. The Beatles *Rubber Soul*
4. Alice in Chains *Greatest Hits*
5. Sesame Street *Rubber Ducky*

Little known resume entry: Music supervisor on the film *True Romance*.

Instrument played: Some guitar, piano

Some recent and past projects: *Chicago, The Perfect Storm, Dangerous Minds, Dead Man Walking, The Bodyguard, Wayne's World*

WHAT MUSIC SUPERVISORS *REALLY* DO ALL DAY
AN INTERVIEW WITH MAUREEN CROWE, SENIOR VP OF MUSIC, MGM

Justin Goldberg: Your role as a music supervisor is focused on feature films. How do you typically begin a new feature film project? Who does the hiring and how early in the filmmaking process do you get involved?

Maureen Crowe: Ideally, I'm hired before the film starts shooting. Sometimes you're hired after the movie is shot if there aren't a lot of musical needs up front. And you meet with the director and producer. When you are a music supervisor, you are really hired by three different people: the producer, the director, or the studio. The studio is basically hiring you to look after what they consider heavily music-intensive projects or a producer-director team who need a lot of attention because they are doing a lot of different films. They need you to take care of it, keep them informed and basically take care of the needs of the film. You're there to bridge the gap and try to bring the appropriate music into the film for the producer or the director to choose. If there is a lot of pre-recorded material, like a wedding or a dance scene or this or that, you may also get involved in the hiring of the composer and relate it to other elements—like a soundtrack deal, or whether, for example, a single is needed. At a record company, their agenda is to find films that take care of the needs of their artists. So they are looking to match up their artists with films that they think are going to be very successful—meaning making at least fifty million dollars or more at the box office. For about ten years soundtracks were a big focus, and it kind of wore out the industry a bit. Now they are really looking to consolidate their efforts towards the big hits, and the studio is involved in getting a single out to help market the film, market the movie, market the soundtrack. In television, a music supervisor takes care of the needs of an episodic show. Those are usually lower budgets and a very quick turnaround, so you really need to be focused on the show and go through a huge quantity of music.

JG: And as with most ambassadors bridging cultures, I imagine your job would have some moments of tension. What are some of the common misconceptions that each side—the film side and music side—have about each other?

MC: I think the most common misconception is the actual cost of music, putting the cost of music into the film. I think that most people, because they're out there listening to radio, they can just turn on their car radio and listen to music, they go into malls and listen to music—it feels like it's free, or it should be free. There's a general tendency to ask, why does it cost so much money? For the record companies, it's a big source of revenue; for the artists it's a big source of revenue. Consider a band like the Doors; it's not like they're recording new albums to sell, so a very large segment of their overall revenue is derived from licensing their music, in addition to the income that is generated from those songs. Often such artists are not willing to negotiate. It doesn't matter to them that it's a ten million dollar film. They want two hundred thousand, four hundred thousand for their song. One of the big misconceptions in this field is the cost of music and how, even though a new song can be fairly obscure, it doesn't mean that it should be less expensive. It really is a buyers-sellers market in terms of what the seller is willing to sell for and what the buyer is willing to buy for. And so, while everything is negotiable, at some point the people who own the music can walk away from it if they don't like the content of the film, or if they feel like the use of their song will ultimately hurt their copyright, or if they don't like the image it puts on the song. Some artists are very open, some are not. They feel like it could hurt them and they're not sure it's the image, and they don't want to feel like they're selling out, and all this kind of stuff. For me, I think airtime is airtime and everything is pretty much good unless it hurts the copyright or hurts the image of the band—but if it's in a record store and it's just playing, I don't see how that hurts the band.

JG: Let's talk about what your role is on a daily basis. I'm sure there are plenty of aspiring music supervisors out there who imagine you coming to the office and getting to listen to music all day. What's the reality?

MC: That's another big misconception—people think music supervisors get to sit around and listen to music all day! It would be wonderful if we did, but during much of the day, you're listening to stuff and you're getting stuff pitched to you, while the director and the producer are coming up with their own ideas and the editor and what have you...you're trying to sort through all that, while trying to help define the musical direction of the film. You're also dealing with everyone from attorneys to marketing people, and constantly trying to get people what they need. It's a lot of administration, and a lot of business skill, as well as ears. It's all those things together.

JG: Let's talk for a moment about when a record company might enter into the equation of making a film. At what point is it determined whether or not there will be a soundtrack album release of music in a film? Do most films have soundtracks in today's market?

MC: The best soundtracks are the ones that have a strong theme. The music is very consistent in that the music itself is building a subtext to the story. If you take the music out of the film and listen to it, you're going to recall the movie, recall the scenes; it's an intricate part of the storytelling. Not every film should have a soundtrack. Sometimes the music is very eclectic, or there's no strong musical style to the film, it's just kind of small snippets of music here and there. A record company becomes involved in a soundtrack if it's a big summer movie or a big Christmas movie, such as a *Charlie's Angels* or a *Spider-Man* or something like that. In those cases, the interest of the record company will be immediate, and there will probably be competitive bids in terms of acquiring the soundtrack rights because a big movie will have a big fan base, something that's going to attract a wide audience of young teenagers to adults twenty five and over. Record companies are interested in selling albums; their focus is on looking for movies that are going to throw the broadest possible net, so that if the music single hits and the music sells then they can sell across the board to a lot of people.

JG: If a priority act has written a song for a film, is it mostly the case that the artist's label will also release the soundtrack?

MC: If they are interested, yes. I mean, ultimately the most important factor is to find whoever can deliver the biggest artist with the right song for the film, with the most marketing potential. The ideal scenario is to have all things working together at once, so that it works for the film, it works for the studio, it works for the marketing effort, and it works for the record company in terms of the airplay and subsequent record sales. If you hit all those five points, everybody's happy and everybody wins—but a lot of times, you don't hit those points: it might be right for the film but not right for marketing the film. Maybe the song in the film is a ballad, maybe the marketing people think they need an up-tempo kind of action thing to help sell the movie. Now the record company isn't happy, they don't have as many sales, they don't have impressions going out to help buy tickets and fewer people are happy in the process.

JG: How does the independent artist or unsigned artist reach a music supervisor? How does new music at that level reach someone like you?

MC: I get music from a number of different sources. I get music directly from independent labels, sometimes from individual bands, through managers. I recently had a manager, I was talking to him about one of his major bands, but at the same time, we were talking just about needing particular songs, and he had a writer-artist who he was managing and hadn't gotten signed, but he was like, "Listen, if you want to use some of his stuff, use it," and I listened to it. I ended up not using it in the film but I introduced him to MGM. MGM really liked him, and now there's the beginning of a potentially long-term relationship. A lot of it's luck, timing, and just having the right material. So if all of a sudden you can have a situation where someone might say, "Hey, what about that guy...," or whatever and you end up pulling it off the shelf.

The *Hollywood Reporter* has a listing of music supervisors who you could try sending material to. I would not send a lot of material; I would not send a whole album. I would send maybe three key songs and then follow-up with some other songs in three or four months, so the music supervisor can get a sense of them. You're not asking someone to sit down and listen to a fourteen cut album to get to know you. You just ask them to listen to one or two tracks and let them know that they can expect to hear from you down the line. Again, that's a lot of legwork, but you don't want to overwhelm people. It's a long-term relationship that you're trying to establish.

JG: How does somebody become a music supervisor?

MC: I think everybody takes a different path. If you're interested in being a music supervisor, and you know people who are in production—an editor or a television show, or whatever, anybody involved in it at all—you want to let them know that you're interested in providing them with music. There is a guy right now who is just finishing college, and he goes around and picks up new bands. He picks a couple of tracks and he has lots of energy and calls me and says, "Let me know what you're looking for; I'll just keep feeding you new artists and new bands I see around. I'm going around all the time hearing new music and I'm really into it." And there is no doubt in my mind that this guy is going to be, if not running a record company, absolutely music supervising one day because he understands that it's subject and tone related. If I'm working on a jazz movie, there is no point in sending me hard rock material. If you do send me material I'm not looking for, it means you're not paying attention and you're taking up time that I can't afford to spend right now listening to hard rock music. If I'm working on a hard rock movie, then great, I'm going to want all that you have in that genre.

Another way to break into music supervising would be to really be in the industry, working as a PA for a director or a producer. That's not an easy thing to do either, but again, it's just trying to be around film people, being around television people. When I first started out, I volunteered for a lot of AFI movies and movies at UCLA and USC as a way of meeting people, my peers who were going to do this stuff. You want to be around people who are doing what you want to do. Once you learn the business of clearing music and things like that, and you go to independent film festivals and you meet the business people, you have to let them know, "This is what I want to do. If you know of somebody who is looking for someone, let me know." They may give you a chance, you don't know, but you have to get to know people. That's it. You just have to work around the industry, wherever you are.

· · · · · · ·

MUSIC SUPERVISOR

KEVIN EDELMAN
Metalman Music

First concert attended: Iron Maiden

Top five album recommendations:
1. Bob Marley: *Legend*
2. Journey *Greatest Hits*
3. NWA *Straight Outta Compton*
4. Eagles *Greatest Hits*
5. The Mambo Kings soundtrack

Little known resume entry: Music supervisor for *Thunder in Paradise* with Hulk Hogan.

Best project you were involved with that never made it big: September Red

Recommended film: *Waiting for Guffman* (Sony Pictures Classics, 1996)

Recommended reading: *It's Not About the Bike*, by Lance Armstrong

Recommended Web site: www.kontraband.com

Instruments played: Drums, guitar, keyboards

Some recent and past projects: *Boston Public, Providence, Baywatch*

TV CAN BREAK YOU (IN A GOOD WAY)
AN INTERVIEW WITH MUSIC SUPERVISOR KEVIN EDELMAN

Justin Goldberg: Since the focus of your work as a music supervisor is mostly on episodic television series, I would imagine it would be different than that of someone focused exclusively on feature films. Describe for us how the process of licensing music for television unfolds as it relates to what you do.

Kevin Edelman: The process of music supervision for television, and in general, for that matter, is ever-changing because it's different on every project. A big part of a music supervisor's job is learning and discovering what each particular project needs, because every project needs a little something different. Sometimes the role of a music supervisor can become very involved and take on the appearance of a producer in some respects; where you're involved in a lot of decision-making, and the music is very integral to the picture. Other times, it's a more of a post-production orient- ed series of tasks where songs may simply be dropped in at the very last minute. But I feel it works most efficiently when the music supervisor is involved as early in the process as possible. Most of the projects that I've worked on have had me involved early enough, usually at the script level—because if there's anything scripted with music, that has to be cleared before it's shot. Licensing has to be addressed with any scripted lyrics or scripted songs. Other than those obvious licensing situations, you also want to address any scenes that feel like that they could be underscored or simply benefit from an appropriate song. In television, everything is quick. Everything happens very quickly, especially as compared to feature films. It's a different process, but I wouldn't say it's a more difficult process than with films. Feature films have their own difficulties. Television is just a faster process when it comes to the clearance of songs and your production timetable; everything is condensed.

JG: How does music find its way to you?

KE: Music finds its way to me from every source imaginable. I am serviced by pretty much every major label, as well as most indie labels. Actually, I wouldn't say most indie labels, because there are a lot of indies that actually don't explore film and TV, so I'm sure there are many I don't know about. But a good number of indie labels do try to exploit their artists with film and television.

JG: How can independent or unsigned artists without labels find their way into film and televison projects?

KE: A lot of independent artists who don't have a label can still find people to represent their music. I have proudly coined the term "indie consolidators" to name a growing trend and group of people focused on finding just that—indie artists and unrepresented indie labels, those indies who don't have a film and television person—and they kind of consolidate the music all under one place, under what's usually a one-stop shop. You know, a place that controls the publishing, or can help facilitate the publishing as well as the master clearance. So these indie consolidators have really helped both sides of the music supervision business. They're really a huge part of the music supervision business these days, because of the tightening budgets over the last few years. Indie consolidators provide music supervisors with a great service, in that they consolidate a lot of great sounding music that sounds like it could be on a platinum selling record or on the radio; what you'd call "record quality" material. And they can provide it at a much lower price, because the indie artists and labels don't have the overhead that the major labels have, and indies can be much more flexible than the majors. [Indie consolidators] provide a great service when you're on these tight budgets for television. So, I guess to answer the question of how the music finds it's way to me, when you factor in these other sources, it's really the U.S. Postal Service, UPS, FedEx, Airborne Express....

JG: And MP3s?

KE: And MP3s. Pretty much any method to get the music over here, that's what's used. It's fairly overwhelming, but we try to do what we can to stay on top of everything, although we have to go through music quickly because of the volume that comes into the office. We do try to listen to everything that comes through, to see if it's appropriate for any of our projects.

JG: Let's talk about some of the issues that come up when you're trying to license something for a TV show. There are two parts to the licensing game, right? There's the master side, which is the rights to the actual recorded music, often owned by a record label; and then the publishing side, related to the ownership and control of the actual song and copyright, which may be with either the songwriter, a music publisher, or both. How does all this begin, with request letters for the license being sent out to each?

KE: Correct. Sometimes it's the same person, and that's where some of these one-stop shops come into play; they have the rights to license both the master and the publishing, because the artist may own everything.

JG: I would imagine that would make the process move more quickly, yes?

KE: It makes our lives a lot easier as music supervisors, to be able to deal with one person—usually one fax, one phone call, for a quick turnaround and reasonable fee. Those people really help us on a daily basis. Not that the regular channels of clearing music through the major labels and major publishers are so difficult, because they're not. It's the same process, but often the major labels and major publishers need certain approvals; they may need artist approvals or writer approvals. So our fax to them is just the first step in the process, which then takes on a whole life of its own, and has to go through several other steps before it makes its way back to us—while we're anxiously waiting for some sort of answer before we can allow the production to proceed with airing or risk nixing the song from the show. We fax our request to the record company for the master. A synchronization request will go to the publishing company. At that point, if it's an artist where the record company needs artist approval, they usually then contact management and fax the request through to them with their notes of, perhaps, how much they think this should go for or how much they would like to quote. I've learned that every label has a different process and procedure they use with management and the artist. But I think it's fairly standard that they go to management. Management may have something to say about a particular use. It may or may not even get to the artist—sometimes management has the right to basically speak on behalf of the artist. The request then makes its way back to the label, and depending on the label group, there may also be label approvals: someone at the record label may have to also approve the use, such as the head of the record label or the A&R person, the product manager. There are a lot of people who may be involved, depending on the label group, there may be multiple layers of clearance that you need.

JG: And politics...

KE: And politics and things that may be involved with that artist at that particular time. They may have just appeared in a commercial and they're worried about overexposure. That label may have just put a soundtrack out with that same song on it, and they don't want to overexpose that song. There are a lot of intricacies that could help or hurt your chances of getting an approval to use the master. On the publishing side it's a similar process, and it's usually a little less complex with fewer layers toward approval. Although, certain publishing companies do have high clearance standards, and they have people involved who have to approve every single use.

JG: Are there times when one side says yes and the other says no?

KE: It happens. If I had to guess which scenario happens more often, I would say that more often you'll clear the publishing, but you won't clear the master. Because often the artist may not have written the song, so the songwriter, who may be a professional songwriter and whose living is based on exploiting their songs, is happy to license the song. And therefore the publishing company is happy to grant you permission on behalf of their songwriter to use the song in your show. But the artist, for whatever reason—label approvals, management not wanting this artist to be overexposed, whatever feeling that the artist may have about it, that perhaps they've grown too big for a certain type of licensing, which can happen when an artist starts to break—sometimes they no longer like to license for television or they only want to do movies of a certain magnitude and style. The master may get denied although you've got completely approved publishing on the song. If the song works perfectly, but you can't clear the record, you may want to consider re-recording the song with your own version. So that's something that production sometimes— it's a way to get the song you want, even though it might not be the artist you want.

JG: We were speaking earlier about a situation we shared recently where we had a very famous rock band turn down an opportunity to have a track briefly in a scene of a new TV show because their lawyer said no without consulting with his own artist. And it was worth 75 grand! That is certainly a frustration I've faced when making label and publishing offers—that lawyers or managers will sometimes essentially determine the fate of these offers on their own.

KE: Yeah, that's one of the hurdles of the job. One of the frustrations is that sometimes the artist never even knows. Something can get denied without the artist ever knowing, and you wonder if the artist would have been fine with it if they actually got the chance to hear what the opportunity was. I do believe that most managers act with their best intentions and they're acting according to what they think is best for their artist. I just don't always agree with it because, being in this side of the business, I see television and film as a brilliant vehicle to open doors and open more ears to an artist's material.

JG: So since you've been working in the film and TV area, how have you seen business trends shift?

KE: Well, it's been a slower shift than people think, but, in the ten years that I've been music supervising, it's become a recognized branch of the film and television business, and of the music business. Whereas when I started, there were only a handful of people doing music supervision. There was this tight knit group, but it wasn't widely recognized. People didn't know that there was someone who actually had to compile all the music for the soundtrack, make all the licensing deals, creatively work with the director and work with the producers on music. It didn't register with people that there was actually a position there, and at one point in time, there *wasn't* a position there, but it has evolved. During the last five years I'd say it's quickly evolved into a known role recognized for its importance. I've also noticed that more and more television productions and films use music supervisors. That's another result of the shift in using more popular music, more "needle drops," as we call them, you know, song placements, in television shows and films. That's been going on forever, but in films in the forties and fifties, most of the time, if there were songs in the movie, they would have been written for the movie by the movie's composer, or by a songwriting team hired to write the songs for the movie. Probably in the seventies and really in the eighties is when, you know, a lot of songs started getting licensed into television and film, and now it's become an incredibly dynamic area. As you said earlier, it's the "new radio," right? I think a lot more labels, publishers and artists have opened up to film and television as a large-scale vehicle from which they can access a wider audience and yet a specific audience. There is no other vehicle out there that I'm aware of, that can immediately access ten million sets of ears.

· · · · · · ·

MANAGER/FILM AND TELEVISION RELATED

RICH JACOBELLIS
First Artists Management

First concert attended: Europe

Best concert attended: Stone Temple Pilots

Top five album recommendations:
Anything by Pearl Jam

Little known resume entry: My nickname in high school was Roach!

Best project you were involved with that never made it big: The Frequent

Recommended film: *Caddyshack* (Orion Pictures Corporation, 1980)

Notable clients: Lalo Schifrin

YO! REPRESENT! REPRESENTING COMPOSERS FOR FILM AND TELEVISION
AN INTERVIEW WITH RICH JACOBELLIS OF
FIRST ARTISTS MANAGEMENT

Justin Goldberg: As an agent who represents composers, you connect the composers you represent with new film and television projects. Perhaps you could just describe the landscape of what players are typically involved in the process of putting music to a film or TV project?

Rich Jacobellis: On the composer side, the players are the director, the producer, the music supervisor (if there is one) and then all the studio people involved if it's a studio film, such as the heads of music at the studio. So as an agent you're calling on these films trying to get to the producers and directors. Sometimes they hire somebody early, it varies. What you're trying to figure out as the agent is what, exactly, they are looking for. When it's early in the process, a lot of things can change from the time they start shooting to the time they actually see the film—the music may change, so what you are trying to do is get an idea of what they are looking for, so you can put the appropriate composer forward.

JG: Let's talk for a moment about the actual role a composer plays. Do most composers work in a similar fashion? Often people assume the composer is the person who sits in front of an orchestra with a conductor's baton or writing down musical notes for violin parts. I would imagine today's composers rely heavily on computer programs like ProTools. How do most of your clients work?

RJ: Everyone is different and may work differently on different projects. With some of the scores—depending on the budget, with the computer programs they have now—a composer can sit there in a home studio and bang out the score. Every situation is different. Some do small ensemble things, most of the time guys do it on guitar or write the score out and come in after and finish it.

JG: Meaning that the composer will look at the action on screen and literally play along to it?

RJ: When a film is done, they will sit down with the music editor, the editor of the film, the director, and maybe the producer and they will spot the movie and decide where the director wants the music to be. Then they time out the film and the composer goes back to his studio and writes the music to fit the scenes.

JG: Let's say I've always wanted to be a composer. Or I was in a band and now I feel I am qualified to be a great composer for film, television, or commercial projects. How do people who aspire to be film and TV composers get their first break? Where do they start?

RJ: The best thing for a young or new composer to do is meet directors— go to festivals, go to places where directors hang out, especially film schools. Start scoring student directors' films with the hope that those directors will go on to have a career and do bigger films. To just go and try to get an agent right out of school without having any credits, well, there's not much an agent can do for you at that level so you have to be realistic. There are huge composers who have done fifty and sixty successful films, so it's very competitive and difficult. The best thing to do is to go and establish yourself with filmmakers, if you can manage to be "their" guy then you are cemented into a valuable relationship.

Relationships with directors are the most important thing for a composer because if those directors keep making movies and you're their guy, you'll continue to score those movies. And the bigger that director gets, the bigger you're going to get. If you start doing some cool independent films that people are seeing and hearing, then that will be able to get you the agent who will hopefully be able to open some additional doors on the studio side so you can get the bigger budget films.

JG: What about the financial aspect of the process? Can composers make substantial royalties on performance income?

RJ: Yes, certainly. Especially when a film does very well overseas, that's when composers can make a lot of money.

JG: If an actual soundtrack recording is made out of a score, then the composer could also get additional royalties?

RJ: Yes, if a composer writes a song with somebody, he'll get royalties for the song. If a cue from the movie ends up on the song album, he'll receive royalties there, which I would commission.

· · · · · · ·

RECORD COMPANY/FILM AND TELEVISION RELATED

KEVIN WEAVER
Lava Records

First concert attended: Twisted Sister at Radio City Music Hall, 1980

Best concert attended: It's a tie between Boogie Down Productions at the Hollywood Palace in 1987 and Paul Okenfold on New Year's Eve, 2001, on Hollywood Blvd.

Top five album recommendations:
1. Boogie Down Productions *Criminal Minded*
2. Tool *Undertow*
3. Souls of Mischief *'93 'til Infinity*
4. Pearl Jam *10*
5. Eric B. And Rakin *Paid in Full*
5a. Wu Tang Clan *Enter the 36 Chambers*

Little known resume entry: I worked as a video deliveryman for a mom and pop video store on the Upper West Side of Manhattan in 1986. In the middle of winter, in a blizzard, on a bicycle. After pedaling thirty blocks with a six degree windchill to bring some old perv his porn for a seventy-five cent tip, I quit. It was my second day.

Best project you were involved with that never made it big: Angela Via

Recommended viewing: *The Shield* on FX

Notable clients: The Lava Roster includes Uncle Kracker, Kid Rock, Sugar Ray, and Simple Plan.

THE LABEL MAN FROM PLANET CHYRON
A CONVERSATION WITH KEVIN WEAVER OF LAVA RECORDS

Justin Goldberg: Explain to us what "chyroning" is and why it is important?

Kevin Weaver: Chyroning is the MTV-style credit: it's that credit that goes at the bottom of the screen before and after you see a music video played on any music video outlet or television channel, usually indicating who the artist is and what label they are on. Through strategic marketing and through placing our music and tying our music into other companies' media, regardless of what that is—whether it's a TV show, a radio or TV promo spot, we have found that it has substantially more value to us to barter our license fee in exchange for an MTV-style, or chyron credit. So if we are piggybacking a hundred million dollars of media, for example, with, let's say, the Six Flags Theme Parks nationwide advertising campaign, and I have a song they're going to use in a series of sixty second TV spots that they are going to play intensively for six months straight across the country, it has much more value to me to have the name of my artist, the name of my song and Web site information show up at the bottom or in the center of the screen as predominantly as possible during the commercial or TV spot. That has substantially much more value to me than another ten or twenty grand in licensing fees. It is much more important for us to break an artist, in that we are shifting towards a trend of genuine artist development, similar to the way it was fifteen or twenty years ago, versus the way many labels today just throw stuff out there musically and see what sticks. We work our artists and our records in every area of media possible, and we don't give up easily. Our band Simple Plan is a perfect example of that: the Simple Plan record has been tied into about twenty or thirty different media opportunities, and I'd say more than 75 percent of those had the MTV-style, or chyron, credit.

JG: That makes sense, because most of the music that is licensed and supposedly has such a great promotional impact probably doesn't register if the public doesn't know who they're hearing, right?

KW: Exactly. If you hear a song on the radio, but they don't announce who the song is, or you hear the song on a TV commercial and there's no credit for who the song is, that's all great—but at the end of the day, if nobody knows what the song is or who is performing it, they can't go out and buy it.

JG: As a licensor of music, you are really coming from a very different perspective than the licensing departments of most major labels, whose basic function is typically to generate as much revenue as possible from their roster and catalog—with less or no focus on breaking artists—especially if the master recording in question is from an artist no longer living. Tell us about your "pre-clear" program and what pre-clearing is.

KW: I have this pre-clear program, where I pre-clear a select group of masters every twelve weeks for a list of a hundred and fifty TV shows, and within that, if I get an ad card—which is even better than a chyron credit—

JG: Hold it. What's the difference between an ad card and a chryon credit?

KW: An ad card appears at the end of a TV show and includes the actual artwork from the album onscreen. It basically is an ad: they play a snippet of the song played in the episode, and then a voiceover comes on and says something like "Tonight you have heard music from Simple Plan which is available on Lava Records," or whatever. Having something like an ad card is what I need to break acts. And with respect to catalog material, we like our catalog stuff as well, but that material has a different agenda. With the catalog material, I essentially have the same licensing role and agenda as a music publisher, which is to recoup the monies already spent, or make money on an artist who is not a current priority. But I spend the majority of my efforts and energy working on current priorities, knowing that these other areas of media are so valuable to us and that the amount of exposure and impact we can get from them is so substantial: being able to get twenty million impressions from an episode of a TV show like *Smallville,* with an ad card, for a current single that's a priority act—that is worth taking a reduced license fee of fifteen hundred dollars, versus five or ten grand, or whatever I could possibly get for it. The publishers are also starting to see that a little bit more on the emerging artist side. They have an investment in the emerging artists as much as we do, so I've found that working with the publishers is getting easier on this kind of stuff. When it comes to catalogue material that I control here at the label, I just work with the publisher and we quote whatever we think is fair. But at the end of the day, it has much more value to me to place an emerging artist with a substantial marketing credit.

· · · · · · ·

8
—
CAREER CALAMITIES:
when the ship hits the fan

At some point in your travels it is more than likely you will find yourself faced with considerable adversity and things will just plain suck. In the music industry, it can be all the harder to take because so often disaster strikes as a result of intangibles or people who cannot be directly controlled—such as when an artist is dropped from their label without warn-

---

HOW BADLY DOES IT HURT A BAND IF THEY'RE DROPPED?

It depends on the band mostly, but it's absolutely not the death of the band. Absolutely not. I am working right now with a band that had moderate success at a label, but I don't think they've had a record deal for two years. They made another record on their own, shopped it, got three labels interested and now they have another record deal. Remember The Wallflowers? They were on Virgin, got dropped from Virgin—and no one knew who the hell they were when they were on Virgin—and they went on to major success with Interscope. You can get dropped for different reasons; maybe it's just not the right team to work the project, maybe someone somewhere at the label just isn't feeling it. It's about people and their individual personalities at the end of the day. Every record company is made up of individuals and it's about whether or not they believe in your product and your music at that time.

—*Pam Klein, Attorney, Serling, Rooks & Ferrera*

ing, or an artist's representative acts without your best interest in mind. It is with this cheery idea that I present the following two interviews with artists who managed to creatively overcome their misfortune by turning their career calamities into positive experiences.

ARTIST/PRODUCER

GUY GARVEY
Lead Singer of Elbow, on V2 Records;
Producer, Duke of A&R, Skinny Dog Records
(a Manchester collective and haven for the temporarily unsigned)

First concert attended: Ride at Manchester Boardwalk, 1990 (my friend lost a shoe and never found it).

Most influenced by: Late Talk Talk

Least influenced by: The fuckin' Eagles

Favorite project: Producing I Am Kloot's *Natural History*

HOW TO GET DROPPED WITH MANNERS AND GRACE (AND LIVE TO RISE & ROCK AGAIN):
A CONVERSATION WITH GUY GARVEY OF V2'S ELBOW

Justin Goldberg: Guy, your band Elbow was signed by a high profile A&R man at a major label—but shortly after making your record, strange things started to happen—like getting dropped amidst a big company merger, and then an attempt by that same label to get your recordings back. Can you describe what happened?

Guy Garvey: Well, before signing our deal we basically had won the English equivalent of South By Southwest, which is called In The City over here. It's an annual event held in Manchester, organized by Tony Wilson of Factory Records fame, and there wasn't actually a winner, but the buzz bands that year included a few different bands—Kay, Muse and another sort of pop outfit called JJ72, and we all played a sort of winners gig with all the industry's A&R people present. A guy named Nick Angel, who worked for Island Records at the time, liked our band and decided he wanted to do something with us, so we signed there in February of '98. We went to the studio with Steve Osborne at Peter Gabriel's place, Real World, and we made the album in about three or four months. And then, little by little, people starting getting fired at the label—including Nick—because they'd been taken over by Universal. We were eventually dropped in January of 2000. Three months later, in March of 2000, we released two of the recordings we'd made with Steve, and two recordings we'd made ourselves, as an EP, which we called the "Newborn" EP, and the critical acclaim was such that record labels started looking at us again. And that's when Island decided to let us know that we couldn't use the album that we'd made with them.

JG: So even though they didn't release your record, dropped you and gave you your rights back, they decided to claim they still had some right to it?

GG: Yes, they did. Because they had actually broken their deal by without releasing anything, they had just said to us at the time that we could keep the rights to our recordings as a kind of compensation for them dropping us. Then they decided against that once they realized that it was probably going to embarrass them that they'd dropped us.

JG: So they essentially dropped you, then added insult to injury by going back on their word to give you control of the record?

GG: In the contract, I think it's a pretty standard clause stating that when a record company employs a producer, there's a re-recording restriction, whereby if anything happens between the band and the label then they are prohibited from using the same producer for a period of about three years. This is obviously to stop material being stolen at source, because that's exactly what we were going to do, we were going to go back into the studio with Steve Osbourne and we were going to twiddle the work we'd already done and pretend it was a new recording and release that. But they enforced the recording restrictions, which meant we couldn't work with Steve and therefore couldn't get away with it—so we instead made the whole thing from scratch, which was pretty tough as you can imagine. Then EMI started courting us, and they said all the right things and they offered us a deal and they told us they were going to nurture us over three or four albums, and then about three weeks before we were due to sign, while the contract was being negotiated, they changed their minds and pulled out of the deal.

JG: How did they tell you that they were pulling out of the deal?

GG: Radio silence for three weeks, not a word, and then a brief phone call to our manager. We've been let down by various people over the years in various ways, and I don't trust my own opinion to the tune of 3 million pounds, so it doesn't surprise me when people are edgy about trusting theirs. I mean, you squander enough label money and you don't work in the industry again. I've always made a point of leaving a voicemail for whoever it is who made the decision whenever we've been dropped saying, "Nice nearly working with you, don't let it put you off coming to gigs, see you soon." I always try and leave on good terms because if you don't have that kind of attitude then it's very difficult to carry on. I've seen many bands fall by the wayside, I have recordings of music that I've actually made myself—knowing that no one else is ever going to record it because the band is sick of going through the treadmill. So yeah, the world loses a lot of great music because of how intrinsically fucked up the process is between writing the music and getting it to the public.

> We've been let down by various people over the years in various ways, and I don't trust my own opinion to the tune of 3 million pounds, so it doesn't surprise me when people are edgy about trusting theirs.

JG: Do you think it's better or worse in the U.K. than in the rest of the world and in America?

GG: It's a lot easier in the U.K. than it is in the rest of Europe, especially countries like Spain, where there's just no infrastructure in music. But in America I'd say it's exactly the same, the same sort of chances, the same sort of thing—everybody wants the next flavor of the month, whatever it is, and if you don't fit into one of these money-spinning categories, nobody listens to you. You have to learn to make what you're doing sound like something else.

JG: Now, in your particular case, it would seem that the music press in the U.K. played a pivotal role. I wonder if the American press would rally around an unsigned or indie artist in the same way that might lead to a similar happy ending. How and why is the music press in the U.K. so influential?

GG: It is very influential and can have a big impact on indie bands. If you are a traditional indie band, just because of the size of the country, I mean you can tour the whole thing on relatively a low budget. You can tour England three times and not spend too much money, so local press is important—even the student magazines are important. To be honest with you, I think record companies trust the press more than they actually let on, and if the *NME* [*New Music Express*] is supporting you, that translates into sales—not just in this country but a small percentage of America as well. I guess you've got Anglophile kids in every small town in America who follow English music, so it does translate abroad—especially in a country like Japan, where there's obviously a far greater number of people: what would be ten people in a small town in Kansas, would translate to maybe 100,000 people in Japan.

JG: So it's a powerful factor.

GG: Yes. I think the English press is a powerful thing. The radio here is just sewn up with dance music; you can't get your music heard at all on radio—I mean, our record went gold and we still weren't getting on playlists. Pretty crazy. And there's only one radio station here that people aim for, so that's what, ten DJs that the entire industry is trying to get the attention of?

JG: So, how did you happen to get signed to V2 records?

GG: Well, we have a very good manager—we were the first band he ever managed, so, he came in asking a lot of questions and being very enthusiastic. I think that may have appealed to them somewhat, plus, we'd already proved that we could do this without a major label. We could have found the investment elsewhere, but I think it would have taken a lot longer, perhaps four or five years instead of one or two, to get to the level we're at now. But we were willing to do that if nobody came forward with a deal that we liked. More than anything, if a band can grasp what's involved in releasing a record by doing it themselves on a small scale, then they'll feel a little more in control where the big picture is concerned. I think you have to have a hands-on approach: you have to know that first of all, your band is impenetrable to anything that goes on outside it, and the minute it stops being fun then you might as well have got that job that everybody told you to get, you know. I have a theory myself, people who are in the music industry, as flawed and a fickle as it is, in whatever capacity they're in the music industry, they *must* have a love of music, because there are much easier games to make money in. If you appeal to that in people, if you allow the people you work with to feel a part of what you're doing and invite them in with their ideas, then you will you get the best out of them. If you go into a business relationship with a label with this cynical, "Any day now they're gonna drop us," sort of attitude, then you don't get the best out of them and they don't get the best out of you and it makes life a lot harder all around.

The guy who first signed us, Nick Angel, once we had established that again we were going to get a big record deal, he went to Warner Bros. and said, "I want to set up my publishing company and I can get Elbow, can I have a budget?" and because we were flavor of the month at the time, they gave him his budget and he started his own publishing company. So Nick worked with us because he'd believed in it from day one, and even when he'd lost his job we didn't lose touch. That's the same with everybody, we've had the same band members for twelve years, we've had the same manager we've always had, same with the publishing, you know. Also I don't think it's wise for bands to put all their eggs in one basket, I think anything you can do out of house, you should, so that if the accountants move in at V2 next year and we get dropped, I'm happy that we've still got the same production company going on the side; we've still got the same merchandising going on, we've still got radio support and press support going on from outside V2, in this country at least, you've got to split it up as much as you can so that losing one integral piece doesn't collapse the whole thing.

· · · · · · ·

ARTIST/FILM & TELEVISION RELATED

JOSH ZANDMAN
SongandFilm.com

First concert attended: 10,000 Maniacs

Best concert attended: Coldplay

Top five album recommendations:
1. Coldplay *Rush of Blood to the Head*
2. Radiohead *The Bends*
3. Bruce Springsteen *Tunnel of Love*
4. Def Leppard *Hysteria*
5. Simon and Garfunkel *Greatest Hits*

Best project you were involved with that never made it big: Burlap to Cashmere on Interscope

Recommended Web site: www.SongandFilm.com

Instrument played: Guitar, keyboards

FROM BURLAP TO CASHMERE AND FROM FAITH TO DOUBT: WHEN MANAGERS MANAGE TO TAKE THE MONEY
A CONVERSATION WITH ARTIST JOSH ZANDMAN

Justin Goldberg: I thought it would be interesting to talk to you about how people choose managers, and how your experience might affect the way you would advise a new artist or writer to make a management decision. Your band, Burlap to Cashmere, was signed to Interscope, who managed to turn around three hundred thousand copies of your debut album. Were you signed to your record deal with a manager already in place, or did you find a manager after you signed your record deal?

Josh Zandman: We had a manager who helped put the band together about two years before we were noticed by A&M records. Jim Phalen, who ran the A&R department there at the time, really liked us, and our lawyer worked out a deal for us with A&M. We did have a manager, but he didn't really have much to do with our deal. The band kind of sold itself on the music and the live show.

JG: You have said that your management experiences have left much to be desired—especially with regard to desiring more of the band's revenue. What elements of your story do you think are especially relevant to new artists and writers who might be reading this?

JZ: One element is the personal relationship; in our case our manager was actually partners with his mother and they were a team. But the issues didn't really rise to the surface until one day I received what's called a K-1 form in the mail for taxes, and it's a partnership form. I noticed that on it his salary was way more money than 20 percent, which is what he was designated to receive as a manager. I called the accountant and asked, "What's up with this? It says here that he's getting 30 something percent," and she said that she didn't know. Apparently there were monies being earned in a category described as royalties—despite the fact that we never got royalties—so it was listed differently on the books than it was in reality.

Somehow the way it was manipulated there was an open door for them to claim that there was more income for them to put in their pockets. When I first became aware of this, it began a period where we essentially suspected them of taking the money. They were very offended, and responded with, "We don't steal money." They got really mad at me and this led to me quitting the band, which I managed to do a few times. It was rotten and I couldn't take it. When I came back for the last time, the manager then said to me, "You can come back but only if you give me 30 percent of what you make from this band," which obviously didn't seem appropriate. So if I was to make a thousand dollars that month from the band, I had to give him 30 percent of it to stay in the band.

JG: So he was even going to commission the money that you'd make just from being in the band?

JZ: Right, so after he got his 20 percent, that's when we got paid obviously, then I had to pay him an additional 30 percent. Then I basically I left for good and called them out on their actions and a whole war of sorts broke out between them and the band and they threatened to sue me personally. He sent me papers in the mail saying that I was making up lies and...the whole situation was just a joke.

JG: And so you would have never known had you not seen the K-1 form?

JZ: Yeah, well, when I got the K-1 form, I noticed it was like 30 something percent and they were telling me it was revenue from "other things." My question, which really went unanswered, was always, "What other things? It should always be 20 percent," it just didn't make sense. So when I tried to ask them about it, they became very, very defensive and even called my family to complain about me. But you know, if it wasn't for business, they're nice people. They're fun to hang out with. When it came to business they were very, very poor business people.

JG: I would imagine that the dynamics within a band are affected by such a lack of confidence in its business representation. Was the band ever in full agreement or disagreement about any of these issues, or was that itself also part of the process—trying to get everyone else in the group on the same page?

JZ: It was very difficult in our case because the management company had family ties to one of the band members. Essentially, everyone disagreed on everything. When you're in a band, you should always have one person in the band who has the final business call, the final say and is the only one person who goes to the manager and says, "This is what we have decided as a band," because we had seven people going crazy, making decisions and calling up our manager.

JG: So it sounds like one piece of advice would probably be to be very careful working with family ties to a group.

JZ: In my case, a big yes. I would not work with family again. Definitely not.

JG: So based on your own management experience, what's some advice that you would have for a new artist who maybe signs a new record deal, goes out on tour and doesn't think it's important for them to monitor what the manager is doing?

JZ: Obviously, you have to be careful. If you're a new artist and looking for a manager and the manager offers you a contract right away, don't take it. Recently I had a bad experience with that; this person hadn't even see me live and he offered me a management contract. So right there you know that he wanted me to do the majority of the work and he would primarily be expecting to collect the money. You should always make sure that you get along personally with a prospective manager. You should also research them to see who his or her past or present clients are, have them see you live and base part of your decision on their reaction to the live show. The bottom line is that you need to trust your managers and feel that they are excited about what you're doing. It's all about trust and the experience they have because there are so many managers out there who say, "We're going to do this or that," but in the end they don't do anything.

· · · · · · ·

INTERNAL AFFAIRS:
When Band Members Don't Get Along

All Access Passport

CD-ROM

Keeping a band together is no easy task; the pages of rock and roll history are filled with tales of musicians and songwriters who may have soared to the top of the charts by sharing their talents, but eventually grew to the point of not being able to share a cab. You can start with Lennon and McCartney and end with Oasis; some of the best musical combinations have started or ended up as volatile relationships. One way to minimize potentially difficult situations down the road is adhere to some basics in a written document known as a Band Agreement.

Whether your band is just starting out, or has been together for years, I strongly advise composing and signing a band agreement before recording in a studio, writing material together, or engaging in any type of collaboration as a group to generate either sound recordings or new compositions. It is absolutely critical that you have a written understanding with your creative partners by executing an agreement that allows for clear dealings.

Often musicians get together informally in recording studio settings without any specific idea of how their creative efforts will be treated financially long after they leave the studio. Without a written understanding specifically outlining terms for a musician's compensation on a recording project, recording artists may be taking financial risks with substantial consequences, especially if the recorded material becomes valuable. Seemingly minor creative contributions in the studio by musicians who later successfully claim to have written a percentage of a hit song can represent millions of dollars in publishing revenue.

Because the studio can be a creative environment with its own unique challenges and creative rhythms, the creative roles of producers, engineers, songwriters, musicians and artists often blur; tracing exactly who contributed what to which song can be impossible. Often, once a song becomes successful, musicians claim later that they were involved in the songwriting process but were un-credited and uncompensated—a situation that could be prevented and clarified by a simple document.

Most bands have disputes over songwriting rights and/or recording rights and/or financial responsibilities. It is the exception that everything goes smoothly without requiring attorneys when a lot of money is eventually at stake. *Do Not* make this mistake! Of all the documents in this All Access Series, this is by far the most important for a new band.

The Band Agreement you will find on the enclosed disk contains provisions for "employment" services, which is only one direction for such agreements to take—this usually means that a band leader, or lead writer will actually function as the owner/operator of the organization with terms for compensating band members, and indicates an outline of each other's rights.

This document is provided for your reference only, please amend it to suit your circumstances—and *always* consult an attorney before signing any legal document!

9

FINANCIAL MANAGEMENT
FOR CREATIVE GENIUSES
(and the "budgetarily challenged")

AFFORDING YOUR ROCK AND ROLL LIFESTYLE

One of the reasons I have always loved working with artists and songwriters is that they don't like dealing with and thinking about money.
While most of the world pulses along to the rhythm of 9 to 5 careers and
the worries attendant to that world—office politics, raises, bosses, 401K
plans, punch cards and staff meetings— there are those dreamers among
us who would rather get lost in a melody. The other side of that coin, of
course, is that creative people who make an issue of avoiding financial
management often make critical money mistakes, which, had they been
handled differently, may have allowed them to spend more time ultimately being creative.

AVOIDING THE NIGHTMARE OF THE BIG BOX OF RECEIPTS

When I first started spending money on indie label-related expenses, both
our business plan and list of expenses fit on a single sheet of paper. We
only had two bands on the label, and there wasn't much money to spend
anyway. We agreed on simple terms, based on profit-sharing after expenses were reimbursed. We kept an envelope with some receipts for expens-

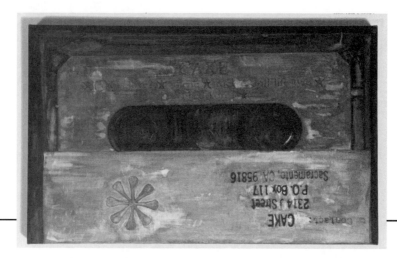

Justin Goldberg, *Cake*, watercolor on canvas, 18½" x 29½"

es in it and figured we'd tally it all up when the money started rolling in. It wasn't long before that envelope turned into a box, and then an even bigger box, and soon the two bands on our roster turned into six, and then three more that were just going to pass through our label for distribution—and each one had different financial obligations. In less than a month, the box transformed into a huge plastic container literally exploding with unmarked receipts. The way we avoided dealing with it, you would have thought it was a box filled with chemical weapons! The thought of halting all business for a week just to enter in all the data was an intimidating thought. It was, to say the least, a paperwork disaster.

Try to avoid my mistake. It's very easy for things to get complicated quickly in the music business, because you never can predict when you might suddenly need to find money in order to make the most of a musical business opportunity. The solution is to create a system for your expenses that is streamlined and easy to maintain so your decisions can be informed and your presentations professional. The very best decision I ever made related to handling money coming in or out (okay, well, mostly out) of my music business ventures was to purchase and learn how to operate QuickBooks on my computer. QuickBooks makes a variety of financial management software products, all designed to organize and simplify the process of keeping track of your money, inventory, customers, checks, taxes—you name it, and there's probably a way to manage it with more accuracy in QuickBooks.

Routine tasks like generating invoices, managing payroll, bills, tracking expenses and monies owed to you are all set up for your computer to customize and "remember" details of your music business. The program leads you through the process of setting up a customized system before you actually begin using the program and entering in data. When I went through this process for the first time and my data was finally entered for the first year of operation, I was able to create—with a few clicks—some very revealing charts, graphs and detailed reports about how I was spending and making money. It was a truly enlightening experience. When you are in some way overseeing the expenses related to an artist's career, especially if you are running a label with a big list of potential artist expenditures, it can be quite empowering to quickly call up the account of that artist and see the exact unrecouped total, or what the spending pattern of a particular artist is when they plead for this or that in a desperate call for more money. Or perhaps it's the other way around, and the artist is doing well enough to consider loosening up additional funds for recording, promotion, or a cash advance. Knowledge is power, especially when you are looking at hard numbers in a chart that clearly identifies where you stand. Other reports, such as a Profit and Loss statement, are important when requesting business (or even personal) loans from a bank, and are easily generated in QuickBooks. (And no, I'm not even getting anything for pimping them like this—it really will just make your life that much easier!)

RECORDING BUDGET

Accurately forecasting what will be spent on recording records is an art form unto itself. You can help the process along by utilizing this pre-formatted Excel chart designed for budgeting recordings. To open this file, simply insert the All Access CD-ROM into your computer's disc drive and open the folder listed as "Excel Chart."

All Access Passport

CD-ROM

BUSINESS MANAGER

BRUCE KOLBRENNER
Kolbrenner, Pagano, & Schroder Inc.

WITH MY MIND ON MY MONEY AND MY MONEY ON MY MIND: THE CFO OF YOUR ENTERPRISE
BRUCE KOLBRENNER, BUSINESS MANAGER, TELLS US MORE

Justin Goldberg: As someone who has worked at record labels such as Elektra and Atlantic overseeing royalty payments, I would imagine you might have some unique insights into how and where monies might have a tendency to hide.

Bruce Kolbrenner: Yes, you might say that.

JG: Let's first discuss what some common misunderstandings are when bands first enter into a deals with a major labels. One theme that has emerged from many of the interviews in this book is that artists should be aware of the fact that they money they receive as an advance is probably the last money they'll see from their label for a long time—if not forever. How true is that?

BK: It is very true. Artists often don't realize that built into that structure are also the expenses incurred by the record label, which are also considered monies that [the artist] receives. In other words, when the record companies pay for a video, for example, the band is receiving that money on the books. If the band is getting shortfall advances for their tour, well, the band is also getting paid there too—but again, they're just not seeing it in their pockets. But the record company is promoting them, and when it comes to promotion, those are monies that are being advanced and will ultimately help them to put money in their pocket. You have to take a longer term view. But yes, in ninety-nine cases out of a hundred, the advances they receive upon signing are the only monies that they're going to see go into their pocket, even if they become a multi-platinum act in their first two records.

JG: Can you explain a little bit about how and why that happens?

BK: It's a timely topic. There has been a great deal happening with this new coalition of artists and how the whole royalty tribunal is trying to recreate the royalty structure, which I doubt will ever happen in a substantial way. It's very easy for the record companies not to pay any further monies once a band has been signed. The reason for that is, if you look how records are made and marketed and how royalties are calculated, you start to see how the math works: if for example, you net one dollar on a record after all is said and done, as an artist's royalty, great. One dollar. And you have to recoup all the costs. Well, let's say you have a record deal, and your first record cost you three hundred thousand. Let's say you spent money on the videos, maybe two videos and it cost you another half a million. That's eight hundred thousand so far. Then let's say you have shortfall advances of another hundred thousand, so now you are at nine hundred thousand dollars worth of expenses. Before you know it, with additional expenses and advances, you're at a million dollars—what's it going to take to recover a million dollars worth of recording costs? Well, it's going to take a million units to do that. You'd have to become a platinum act. But the record company doesn't pay you a million on a million units. They'll hold their reserves back, their returns and their free goods. So what you're talking about is a structure which lends itself to using your own money to pay for further albums while holding back your money so that they can utilize it to pay you for future albums. So more likely than not, unless you get to four or five million records over a period of three to five years, and that's long term, you're not going to be making any more money. That's why the record companies right now are looking to get more advantages by becoming involved with merchandising and touring income, which they have not traditionally been involved with.

JG: There are so many complaints related to unpaid royalties that it can seem that the system was created to avoid paying out the full amounts owed. With all of the auditing that you must hear about or do to track down unpaid royalties, would you go as far as to say that most contract terms related to royalty payments are not honored?

BK: No, I wouldn't say that at all. I think in the publishing area, activity is reported more often than not. I think that the problem we have in publishing is one of human nature, where people don't know how to record certain things in the books within the royalty structure—so in the information being handed down by Business Affairs to royalty departments, or copyright departments and then to the royalty departments, there's a lot of room for human error. In most in my years of dealing in the royalty area, I find that more likely than not, units are simply dropped or reporting licenses don't report. In the artist's royalty area, I think that the overall nature of the one hundred and twenty five page royalty agreement is so convoluted and so complex that it helps create a royalty structure that is bent on not paying. The way I view it, it's not that a record company doesn't want to pay, it's that the nature of the royalty structure doesn't allow them to pay.

JG: So it's set up contractually.

BK: Yes. I am an advocate of the artists, but I'm also an advocate of the record companies, because I do believe that, if not for them, records wouldn't be put out. And the labels do make the investment in these people. So, having seen it for as long as I have, I think that if you are making money and you are a platinum act, you had better audit the label, because more likely than not, you're going to find audit claims. If you are not a platinum act, don't bother. Even if you do find something off, you probably won't recoup your expenses.

JG: What about getting paid from independent labels—is it even harder to collect money and accurate statements from them just because of the nature of independents?

BK: Oh, yeah. I think with the independent labels, you're more likely to find errors than you would anywhere else, because you don't have the professionals that you have at the majors. However, having said that, many of the men and women who are out there aiding the independents with accounting and royalties and doing consulting work—for the most part they're doing it okay, but they're under the constraints to some degree of the ownership. They know what they're doing, but they are just being told how to do it.

JG: What is it that makes one business manager better than another?

BK: Other than the way we look? The way we take meetings. You know, when I was in New York my practice was a significant practice because New York never had business managers, they didn't exist. What did exist were CPAs. It was always a CPA firm, which of course has to be licensed, which does hold you up to a higher authority. It seems to me that there are more non-financial accounting people who are out there, who are in the game as a result of being friends or relatives or whatever, than there were years ago. I think it's important that you look into the financial background that a prospective business manager has. You should have good questions relating to their background; not necessarily who they represent now in terms of hot artists and bands, but from a financial standpoint, what background do they have? I think that's what makes a better business manager than most.

JG: Your firm also handles publishing administration; what would you say to someone who may have some music publishing revenue coming in, who is about to choose between entering into a publishing deal and hiring a business manager to look after the publishing? What are the inherent differences in what you do for a writer versus what a publisher does?

BK: I think the inherent difference is that an outside publisher, which has a large quantity of catalogues to deal with, might not be paying the same attention to the collection process as we would. More boutique publishing situations might be different, but here you are in a better position to have a overview of a client's catalogue. Having said that, there are situations where catalogues just get to be too big to keep in-house at a business management firm and you really have to obtain additional services and consultation.

JG: In terms of actually collecting revenue and having an eye to detail, is this an area where you would be able to make a case that a business manager would more carefully analyze income statements than a traditional publisher?

BK: Oh, absolutely. Without a doubt.

JG: Can you think of anything else that maybe a new artist would need to know about financial management?

BK: Well, I think that there are so many variables relating to business management, relating to new artists, who are usually young people, and they really do not understand what the music business is all about. Another important aspect of a business manager is that they have to be in touch with you in the good times and bad. They have to be in touch with you and teach you to be able to ask certain questions: why are things happening? What will there be for me at the end of the road of my career? What does the future hold? How are things calculated exactly? What should I be wary of when I go out there? I think it's also very important not just not take the advice of management solely, or the record company solely, as it relates to a career. Artists need to have to have a well-rounded team, and in order to do that, they have to be very selective in the process of business management and ask the right questions.

· · · · · · ·

10

CREATIVE CONFIDENTIAL

....

DON'T MAKE BUSINESS, MAKE MUSIC:
EXAMINING THE NATURE OF CREATIVITY IN TODAY'S BUSINESS
WITH CLYDE LIEBERMAN
....

Justin Goldberg: How do you think the creative mind works together with the business mind? What kind of connection is there between the two?

Clyde Lieberman: I think it's really important to post a caveat at the beginning of an interview like this. And that is: if you want to get paid for making music, you are going to have to start compromising immediately. It doesn't matter if you are standing on the street corner singing "The Times They Are a Changin'" for quarters—someone's going to come along and say, "Can't you play 'Maggie's Farm'?" It depends how bad you want that quarter.

There are a couple of things we would all agree with or be able to agree upon. One is, greatness knows no boundaries. I don't think anyone ever told Joni Mitchell how to write songs, nor would anybody dare to do so. But Joni Mitchell was smart enough to hang out with David Crosby, Stephen Stills, Graham Nash, Max Bennett and Jaco Pastorius; to get into Charlie Mingus, to be friends with Neil Young, to hang around with Buffalo Springfield, to know Gordon Lightfoot and know Bob Dylan. These are things she was smart enough to know would help her. And she

ARTISTS & REPERTOIRE

CLYDE LIEBERMAN
Lieberman Creative Services (formerly VP of A&R, MCA Records)

First concert attended: James Brown at Victory Field in Indianapolis

Best concert attended: The Who at Woodstock, 1969

Top five album recommendations:
1. The Beatles *Abbey Road*
2. Buffalo Springfield *Retrospective*
3. Little Feat *Sailing Shoes*
4. Otis Redding *Live in Europe*
5. Eddie Harris *Compared to What*
6. David Bowie *Ziggy Stardust and the Spiders from Mars*

Little known resume entry: I interned for Chick Corea's *Return to Forever* at age nineteen.

Best project you were involved with that never made it big: Time (Four guys who I shopped a deal in 1973. They were absolutely brilliant— beyond the pale. But in classic band form, they imploded from drugs, alcohol and pettiness. It broke my heart!)

Recommended reading: *The New Yorker*, old Pauline Kael film reviews, Susan Sontag (not the novels—only the philosophy)

Recommended film: Anything by Tavernier except *Coup de Torchon*

Instrument played: Guitar

Recent or past signings: The Roots, Ace of Base, Mobb Deep

didn't probably plot that every morning when she left the house—"I think I'll drive by Stephen Stills' house on the way down to the canyon"—but maybe she did. Today, artists are more isolated in home studios, making music frequently for themselves, by themselves, in bands where one person is the leader and the rest of the people are the followers. And making great art, while still in the minds of the artists, is just less likely to happen right now. There are too many forces at work.

Let's face it, one of the greatest artists of our time, who used to be called Prince and is now called The Artist—and there's no argument that he's head and shoulders above 99 percent of the people making records in the last fifteen years—got so frustrated by the music business and the trap he was in, that he almost quit making music altogether, or at least he quit making music for the public. And maybe if it hadn't been for the Internet and digital music delivery and the things that have afforded the possibility for it, he might not have come back. And now he's back signed to a major label and he's trying to cross all the genres again. But as someone working in this business, I try to understand and to define what that frustration is all about: what made John Lennon stop for two years, and why did Joni Mitchell stop making popular music and decide to start making jazz music? All I can imagine is that when you're making popular music, you reach a point where it's something that can eventually be figured out. It didn't just have to be random and it didn't just have to be about a song. It didn't just have to be about an album. There were other ways, there were bigger concepts; bigger fish to fry, for want of a better cliché. I think The Beatles had a similar trajectory. These are, of course, all-time popular artists. Of course, it's ludicrous to try and talk about someone in terms of a Joni Mitchell and those people unless you are willing to find me the Joni Mitchell right now. You could say, "Well, with all the crap that's on the radio, how can anyone find Joni Mitchell?" Listen my friend, in the year that "Clouds" and "Both Sides Now" became hits for the first time, there was *plenty* of crap on the radio. It was called Fabian and Frankie Avalon and the Four Seasons, whom I loved, but in today's terms would probably be considered crap by most people who follow "serious" popular music. Believe me, if Joni Mitchell is around, a new Joni Mitchell, she'll get on the radio. The problem is that the process requires time, and we expect our artists to burst forth from their eggshells and say "quack," or whatever it is that they're going to do, and for it to be brilliant. And it just doesn't work like that.

> Believe me, if Joni Mitchell is around, a new Joni Mitchell, she'll get on the radio. The problem is that the process requires time, and we expect our artists to burst forth from their eggshells and say "quack," or whatever it is that they're going to do, and for it to be brilliant. And it just doesn't work like that.

I think everybody in the business on the creative side is driven by desire—even the people with the biggest egos—driven by a desire to help artists be successful. They may have different definitions of what's successful as to what the artists have, but in their minds and in their hearts, they're making an assumption, which is: you want to be in the rock music business, you want to be in pop music business, you want to be in the hip-hop music business? You probably want to be a celebrity or a star, or you wouldn't be doing this. That's the assumption that has created that rift between the commercial music business and the indie rock music business—that turned into the movement that changed the face of popular music in the late '80s and early '90s. In that gulf, in that gap, a cauldron was formed where it was stirred and stirred and stirred, and all of a sudden, Kurt Cobain's head came up through the miasma and said, "I'm here." And he was talented enough, gifted enough, bright enough, and driven and sharp enough, to make music for the masses that was totally personal. So he was an artist. That's what an artist is.

Right now, today, there are opportunities that didn't exist even five years ago or even three years ago. You can make music in your house. You can post it on the Internet. You can get it heard. There's a way for self-expression now that's better, more complete and more exciting than ever. My feeling about it is that artists should take advantage of all of it. But make music. Don't make business, make music. That's the biggest mistake that I see made. People come into my office and they want to talk about a deal, and I say, "Well, have you got a tape?" They put it on and our exchange might go something like this:

"You know, this tape isn't really very good."

"Yeah, man. But, like, how do I get a deal?"

"You want my advice? My advice is, go home, throw this away and start over. How many songs have you written?"

"Ah man, I've written fifty."

"All right, are these the best?"

"No dude, you should listen to all of them."

I say, "Well, okay, first of all, *you* need to know which songs are your best because I don't have time to listen to fifty songs. I've got time to listen to three or four, maybe. So go home and figure out which are the best, and then throw three of the four away, and write fifty more. And then take the best three or four of those, take the best one of those and then write another fifty. And when you've written two hundred songs, and you have the four you sincerely believe in your heart and soul are the best, *then* call me." Now obviously, I'm going to miss out on a lot of things by saying that to people because they might walk in with the first song they write and it's The Song. But I'm saying from the artist standpoint, from the creative person's standpoint, from the songwriter's standpoint, never be satisfied. And yet you have to have an innate sense of how to edit yourself so you don't just go in a big circle. That's what the great artists have.

. . . .

SONG WRITER

DIANE WARREN

First concert attended: The Beatles

Best concert attended: That one.

Top five album recommendations (not in order):
1. Stevie Wonder *Songs in the Key of Life*
2. The Beatles *Revolver*
3. Prince *Purple Rain*
4. Nirvana *Nevermind*
5. Glen Campbell *Greatest Hits*

Little known resume entry: I worked for Music Express for two weeks—and got fired on my birthday for dropping off tapes of my songs everywhere!

Best projects you were involved with that never made it big: Sue Ann Carwell and Susie Benson

Recommended reading: *The Lovely Bones*, by Alice Sebold (amazing story, amazingly told)

Recommended film: *Citizen Kane* (RKO Radio Pictures, 1941)

Instruments played: Piano, guitar

Upcoming projects: Lots of cool stuff, everything from LeAnn Rimes to Uncle Kracker to Jessica Simpson to Josh Groban to Sara Evans to Meat Loaf to Kelly Clarkson and some artists you've never heard of yet (but you will) and lots more.

COMING TO WORK EVERY DAY AND OTHER MAGICAL TECHNIQUES FOR WRITING MEGAHIT SONGS:
A CHAT WITH DIANE WARREN

Justin Goldberg: I have heard that you prefer to have some degree of lyrical content first before you begin coming up with melodies and playing an instrument when it comes to writing new songs. True?

Diane Warren: True. Yeah, I do.

JG: I have also heard that you consider songwriting to have some logical process to it in the same way that a builder might create a building—in terms of, say, a metaphor of a lyric being like the first foundation of a building and then creating levels to the song section by section.

DW: Yes, it is like building a house, although sometimes building the second floor first works too. It's whatever works for the song.

JG: How does that process usually unfold for you?

DW: I usually have a concept in mind first, but it's hard for me to say exactly what I do—to be honest with you, it's not the kind of cut and dry process where I go from point A to point B. I kind of have an idea of what I want and then I sit at the keyboard to see what happens and where it goes. It's hard for me to say exactly what I do, because it's kind of a magical process for me.

JG: One complaint I hear so often from songwriters is how they get stuck in the middle of writing a song and then guiltily abandon it for a while, until they have a bunch of orphaned little pieces of songs. Do you have any particular method for staying inspired or focused and just not getting stuck in the middle of writing certain songs?

DW: I do get stuck on songs occasionally, but I get through them by just coming into work everyday with the intention of working.

JG: What do you say to those songwriting school academics who might have some particular guidelines or rules about the number of verses or times a chorus is repeated or where a bridge goes? Are there any rules that you follow in your work?

DW: No. There are no rules for me, it's all whatever the song needs. On one song something will work, and on another it doesn't work at all.

JG: What about collaborations?

DW: It's not my thing. I prefer to write by myself. It's much more fulfilling for me to write a song on my own; they've been my most successful songs.

JG: What would you say to someone who might be considering some sort of formal songwriting training? Is that important for a writer to seriously pursue a career as a songwriter?

DW: I would say first, just listen to the radio. Listen to what works. Listen to what's a hit. Listen to what doesn't work too, because that's important also. I guess you can take a course to study song structure, that could maybe be a good thing.

JG: What instruments do you find you write best with?

DW: Mainly piano and guitar. The guitar is much more portable, but the keyboard is really more of a writer's instrument for me.

. . . .

DELUSIONS OF GRANDMA:
Realities of Coping with Success

"Take any twenty-one-year-old red-blooded American kid, give him a giant dose of fame and opportunity, and stand back, cause things are going to get weird."

—*Charlie Sheen (once a twenty-one-year-old kid)*

What!? Does the above subtitle actually suggest somebody would need help with success? "C'mon, get real," you say, "that's the easy part!" But is it really? Having experienced many a wannabe rock star actually turn into one, may I suggest to you that like everything else, all is not what it seems in the realm of musical stardom. If you thought struggling through that long stretch of being unknown and paying your dues was tough when so much seemed to go wrong, try managing life when everything goes *right*—for some people, that's even harder to deal with.

It does sound odd, but it is quite true: success and fame look absolutely fabulous on two dimensional sheets of glossy magazine covers or frozen forever in a music video, but the reality is some artists are better equipped with the social skills and temperament to manage what may be a sudden and drastic shift in work and travel schedules. While a label, publicist, manager or roadie may see to it that you are no longer burdened with some of the more mundane tasks you used to dread, the reason you have these people at hand to help in the first place is because the stakes are higher and the list of responsibilities will quickly be expanding exponentially. With that long list comes an equally long list of items that can go wrong and projects or people who need additional coordination. Few of today's top emerging artists and budding pop stars enjoy the luxuries of leaving business decisions to others while an endless party rages on backstage. It's a job and an experience that some artists do better than others (although all of them are quite sure they're ready for it from their first rehearsal).

From an A&R perspective, where one needs to carefully evaluate factors which may contribute to predicting how well different artists will deal with such pressures, it's an interesting and important equation to evaluate. Sometimes the artists you think lack the background to excel in the public eye actually have what it takes, and vice versa. Some artists recognize early success for what it is—a marvelous but often fleeting window of opportunity to make the most of while the planets are still aligned in your favor. In my view, artists like Beck, Cake and Art Alexakis (from the band Everclear) to name just a few, fit such a description. While other early alternative rock stars were busy being overwhelmed by success (like Adam Duritz of the Counting Crows), or overdosing on drugs and winding up in rehab (like Scott Weiland of Stone Temple Pilots) or overdosing on drugs and tragically disappearing forever (like Shannon Hoon of Blind Melon), these were artists who chose instead to remain primarily concerned with making music and moving their projects forward with no frills hard work.

"...often you have bands that have very promising first albums but disappointing second albums. And a lot of people say in the business, "Well, they had their whole lives to write the first album, but they had only nine months to write the second." On the contrary, I think that when a first album is successful, it's not because they had so much time to write it, it's because there was no mirror. They were doing what they liked, what they felt was the best thing musically that they could do. For the second album, usually, if the first one was successful, there is a mirror that is given to the band saying, "You can't do that. Your fans, the record company, we're waiting for another single like that first one. This is who you are." So suddenly the band goes, "Oh, okay. So that's who I am, okay." And they become self-aware, and then guessing, double guessing...and that's not what the creative process is all about. You have to be doing what really pleases you, because if it doesn't please you, then you have nothing to stand on. Now, somebody might get lucky and say, "Okay, it doesn't please me, but it's a good single therefore it'll sell and I'll get my perks." But, if it doesn't sell, then you didn't please yourself, and you feel like a total loser because you betrayed what you love, and it still didn't sell.

—*Eleven's Natasha Shneider*

BAD ADVICE FROM YOUR ROCK STAR FRIENDS:
Counting Crows and the Little Engine That Could Have

I first experienced the wonderfully emotional and unique sound of San Francisco's Counting Crows at a BMI showcase in 1992. There were maybe twenty or so industry folks gathered for the show at a tiny venue called the I Beam in the band's hometown; it was an impressive performance. Twenty months later they were the hottest musical story to emerge from that town in twenty years and perhaps the biggest new band in the world; their infectiously unstoppable single *Mr. Jones* blared from pop and rock radio stations everywhere as their deeply personal debut album soared through the charts. Lead singer Adam Duritz's dreadlocked visage gazed with sincerity from dozens of magazine covers and told the tale of the band's musical rise—and their uncomfortable new relationship with superstardom. Often when bands become successful at that level, bands that are associated with them in some way also have a moment of recognition, and if they're smart, opportunity. Such was the case of one of my all time favorite signings, Engine.

When Adam Duritz and his band appeared on the cover of *Rolling Stone* magazine, he claimed in the accompanying article that it was one of the "principal disappointments of his life" that he had a record deal and Tom Barnes (his long time buddy and the lead singer of Engine) did not. After reading that article I hopped on a plane to San Francisco to check them out and would soon find that Duritz's sentiments were valid. Engine (who eventually had to change their name to Engine 88) was indeed a band on the brink; they were truly an underground phenomenon with a huge groundswell of local support and rabid fans who looked forward to each hometown show as if it were a major event. I quickly signed them to a publishing deal and began working with them.

But it wasn't long before I would discover a surprisingly disturbing pattern of thinking as we plotted our course toward success. Unlike any other band I had worked with previously who didn't yet have a recording contract in place, their concern was that such a record deal might actually arrive too early and that success in general might progress too quickly and become too mainstream. Having been privy to almost every aspect of the Counting Crows dramatic catapult into what they viewed as the belly of the star-making beast, they were apprehensive about being able to maintain their stability and credibility amidst circumstances similar to their friends' career trajectory. And, happening to be a bunch of extremely genuine guys, there was also concern about being perceived as riding the coattails of the Counting Crows' success; while most bands would kill for the recognition and exposure afforded to them as a result of the *Rolling Stone* article, they were practically mortified at the mention. They wanted their success to be their own. In fact, there was a series of really compelling recordings that featured Adam Duritz's unique vocals alongside Tom's vocals on songs Tom had written for Engine. But, strongly opposed to including the songs on their album, the songs were never heard by the public or even the A&R community. Not that Engine was completely unwilling to accept *some* promotional benefit of having rock stars as close friends, the band did indeed open for the Counting Crows on several occasions. But in general, the band was quite cautious about the connection, when they should have perhaps seized an opportunity that was fleeting. As we considered various strategies for record deals or marketing efforts, the voice of Adam Duritz as the band advisor would in one way or another make its way into our discussions and influence the grand plan. That voice and influence, based on his own extraordinary career up until that point, was quite conservative.

Ultimately Engine released a critically well-received album on revered indie label Caroline Records that did not sell well and three years later the band called it quits and broke up. While it's probably unfair to suggest that Mr. Duritz had a directly negative impact on the band's career decisions, there was always a sense that his level of superstardom was somehow a foe to be wary of. Often those close to very successful artists fail to recognize the various factors contributing to such success or the brief timeline associated with their ability to benefit from the connection. Perhaps if the band were less concerned about maintaining their credibility or being seen as taking advantage of their friends' success, they might have had enough success on their own to sustain the band's career. (Visit www.engine88.com for a listen to what could have been.)

SURVIVING SUPERSTARDOM:
WORDS OF WISDOM FROM THE FRONTLINES WITH RON FAIR

Justin Goldberg: Let's talk about handling success. Is it hard to handle success?

Ron Fair: Yes, I think it is. In our culture, in the United States in particular, we don't have royalty. We have movie stars and athletes and recording stars who are the equivalent of royalty, who get treated as if they are above the average person. When they become successful, they are given things—and the last thing you need when you're a multi-millionaire is to be given a motorcycle or a watch. I think, eventually, what happens is when you are hot—when you're in that position and everybody wants you, everybody wants a part of you, everyone wants to be around you—I think that affects your brain. It's an intoxicating poison. Stardom can be a poison and we've seen many cases of artists who were poisoned by it. And then, there are a few cases where people do wonderful things with their fame or the power that comes from fame—like a Bono or a Wyclef—who become really socially significant in the world. The bottom line is when you throw four million dollars, a five thousand square foot house, a Mercedes, five hit records on the Top Ten, massive television exposure, automatic recognition anywhere you go, unlimited credit cards—you throw all of that at a twenty-two-year-old kid, it is as if several strands of the DNA never had a chance to form. It's like a rapid incubator that just doesn't develop all the strands, and so there are problems.

I think maturity can be a factor. It can come at any age. Discipline, humility, empathy and maturity, all come to people in different ways. There isn't a school for that other than maybe growing up. So many of the people I deal with are really young—in their teens or early twenties—who are just starting to deal with those things for the first time. But we are in the business of selling records, we just we work on the music. But imagine being Eminem. He can't even go to the drugstore without having energy thrown at his head, or some kind of invasion of his space; it really is a peculiar phenomenon. But artists are different. Some are very, very disciplined about their music and want to spend all their time in the studio perfecting it, and others are very laissez-faire about it and just do what they do, and it is what it is. There is no real rule of thumb saying that the person who is in the studio working on a vocal for twelve hours is going to be more successful than the person who came and sang one five minute take and then went out for lunch.

—*Ron Fair, Producer and President of A&M Records*

STAYING CREATIVE IN A WORLD OF BUSINESS

"You have two options. You can stay the same and protect the formula that gave you your initial success. They're going to crucify you for staying the same. If you change, they're going to crucify you for changing, but staying the same is boring. So, of the two options I'd rather be crucified for changing."

—*Joni Mitchell*

On painter Jackson Pollack's tombstone reads the inscription: "Artists are the nerve endings of humanity." Artists look and act much like the rest of us, but they are different. They are both cursed and blessed with seeing what is not there and creating something in reaction to it for others to experience. Indeed, they are special creatures who must be given a certain set of circumstances in which to thrive. Unlike other creative art forms, in this country musical artists are pretty much left to fend for themselves when it comes to surviving financially. As this volume has attested throughout its many interviews, even those lucky enough to receive major label recording contracts or work consistently for those who do are hardly guaranteed to make a living in the long term, let alone be provided with enough resources for essentials like health care or retirement funds. Government grants are virtually nonexistent for musicians in the U.S., and music programs in our schools have either suffered huge financial blows or have disappeared entirely. (Visit www.savethemusic.com for some ways you might be able to help change this.)

Maintaining a focus as an artist becomes, in essence, the process of staying true to a vision that the artist feels compelled to communicate. Artists require appropriate creative circumstances and focus in order to thrive, and it's worth considering what those factors are that contribute to a positive outlook and productive state of mind. Creativity within the music business is not unlike remaining creative within any other undertaking that requires focus and concentration, the main ingredients for inspiration.

Staying true to inspiration is perhaps the only real duty an artist has. Staying true to that same inspiration as part of the music industry then, is the duty of those who support and promote new artists. If you build it from true inspiration, they will come. At least, I will.

HOLLYWOOD CREATIVE DIRECTORY

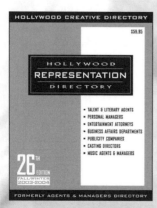

HOLLYWOOD REPRESENTATION DIRECTORY, 26th Edition

- Over 6,500 names of agents and managers
- Over 1,500 talent and literary agencies and management companies coast to coast
- Includes addresses, phone and fax numbers, staff names and titles, and submission policies
- Cross-referenced indices by name and type
- Film and TV Casting Directors and Publicity Companies
- Published every April and October

Single issue	**$59.95**
1-year print subscription	**$99.95**
2-year print subscription	**$189.95**

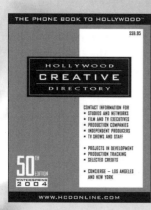

HOLLYWOOD CREATIVE DIRECTORY, 50th Edition

- Over 10,000 film and TV producers, studio and network executives
- Over 2,000 production companies, studios and networks
- Includes addresses, phone and fax numbers, staff names and titles
- Selected credits and studio deals
- Special TV Show section
- Cross-referenced indices by name, type and deal
- Web sites and email addresses
- Published every January, May and September

Single issue	**$59.95**
1-year print subscription	**$99.95**
2-year print subscription	**$189.95**